God Fearing Souls

Revised Edition

Tony Ghepardo

Title ID 5820511

ISBN-10: 1518753663
ISBN-13: 978-1518753664

CONTENTS

PREFACE

Our culture claims to "believe" in science, with or without understanding. Professional scientists are clinically detached from their subject in order to maintain the integrity of testing and not skew results. At the same time, our culture celebrates the heart and emotions. Notice people are more easily manipulated by evoking strong emotions rather than by the powers of reason.

> 4 Maccabees 7:17 (RSVwA) [41] Some perhaps might say, "Not every one has full command of his emotions, because not every one has prudent reason."
>
> (4 Maccabees appears in an appendix to the Greek Bible.) [41]

> 4 Maccabees 7:23 (RSVwA) [41] For only the wise and courageous man is lord of his emotions.

The subject matter of this book concerns the most powerful taboos of our culture. It will not be easy to keep emotions in check, to keep emotions from influencing rational discernment of data, events, and circumstances.

> 4 Maccabees 1:30 (RSVwA) [41] For reason is the guide of the virtues, but over the emotions it is sovereign. Observe now first of all that rational judgment is sovereign over the emotions by virtue of the restraining power of self-control.

1 IN OUR LIFETIME

Introduction

Apocalypse 13:9 (DRA)[31] If any man have an ear, let him hear.

Revelation 13:9 (RSV-C)[40] If any one has an ear, let him hear:

Call me Tony Ghepardo. I have compiled conversations and experiences relevant to my calling to the Roman Catholic seminary in the 1990's. I did not understand "calling" then and cannot explain it still. I can only recount what happened. In Chapter One, I jump from one account to the next. Entries are disjointed and unrelated. Conversations and subjects span three decades. Lack of a unifying thread and some nasty subject matter make Chapter One difficult to read, but it is necessary background information.

To honor the privacy of the people I encountered, I change or withhold their names. I attempt to sanitize my eyewitness accounts by withholding identifying information. I name the seminary staff by their title or station. This is necessary because I am telling you what happened, not hiding behind the designation of a novel. This is my experience, my eyewitness account.

Tony Ghepardo follows his calling in Chapter Two and enters the Pontifical Seminary in Chapter Three. The Church has legitimate proprietary information or secrets that Tony honors by non-disclosure, while exposing the evil and the illegitimate. Proprietary and identifying information is withheld as a matter of integrity. Unfortunately, Tony cannot avoid a paradox of integrity in order to sound the clarion.

Italicized text is used to identify Tony's unspoken thoughts, information, or thoughts inserted at the time of this writing. Cogent Bible verses and other text material inserted after these writings were compiled appear in regular typeface for convenience and legibility. Roman Catholic Bible quotes are taken from the standard Douay-Rheims 1899 translation [31] *and are often compared to other translations.*

Late 1960s

"I was a Methodist before I met your father. I converted to Catholicism before we were married partly because of the physical presence of God in the sanctuary. Recent changes in the Church have ruined the things I liked most about it. They have watered down the prayers until they are the same as Protestant prayers. They have changed everything. There no longer is respect for the sanctuary. People talk in church as if they are in a meeting hall, the same as Protestants. Not to insult Protestants, but their church is a meeting hall. They don't contend Christ is physically present in their church the way Catholics do. The Church is in such a hurry with this ecumenical movement to reunite the churches. The only thing they accomplished was to destroy everything that was good about the Catholic Church."

Early 1970s

JULIE

Tony Ghepardo was a freshman engineering student. His cousin Julie was a student x-ray technician at the university hospital. Tony occasionally caught a ride back home with her on weekends. As Julie drove, Tony took in the snow-covered landscape. Fresh snow gave a pristine hush to the countryside. During this trip, Julie related recent cases she saw in the hospital's emergency room. Julie said men came into the ER with foreign objects inside their bodies. Tony: "Where do they put them?" Julie: "In places where they don't belong, otherwise they wouldn't need to come to the ER." Tony: "What kind of foreign objects?" Julie was too embarrassed to say more. Eventually she stammered, "You wouldn't believe me anyway." Tony: "How does this happen to begin with?" Julie: "It's something homosexuals do. They do it for sex."

On a subsequent drive, Julie was distraught by things she saw at work. She was too embarrassed to elaborate, but Tony was curious and convinced her to tell him. She told of a man who came to the ER. (Details of this case are too graphic and disturbing to recount here.) Tony: "Did it work? That had to be painful!" Julie: "It didn't actually work, not for him at least, and the pain was excruciating!" Tony: "Why did he do it?" Julie: "He was new to homosexuality." Tony: "What does that mean, new to homosexuality?" Julie: "He was young. He must have been socially awkward or simply not successful dating girls.

A group of homosexuals convinced him to try homosexuality, and they took advantage of him. Homosexuals are very mean; even to each other, in fact, especially to each other. They had him do this for their pleasure, not his, and they were amused by the pain and physical harm it caused him. –I was amazed he was still conscious when they brought him in–." Julie continued, "We cannot tell these things to people back home, they won't want to hear it anyway."

Weeks later Tony caught a ride home with Julie again. She was perturbed and remained quiet for a long time. Eventually she said, "There are so many homosexuals in this city you would not believe it. And WHO is homosexual, you would not believe! Doctors, lawyers, public figures, leaders in the community, business men, wealthy men, powerful men, prominent men, politicians, family men that you know their names, people you would not believe are homosexuals; but they are! There are so many of them. And to hear them talk, that is what scares me! They hate us! They hate us in ways that do not make sense. They talk of destroying society simply because they don't like us."

Julie continued, "They hold secret meetings. In these meetings, they discuss their detailed plans to destroy society. They are not planning to destroy this city, but all of society! Their plans are far-reaching. They plan to cause anarchy and destroy this country! They hold clandestine meetings, but they hide in public. They hide in plain sight. Many of them have families: wives and children. You would never suspect they are homosexual, even if I told you who they are." Tony: "How do you know this?" Julie: "They talk about these things in front of me while I'm working in the ER."

Tony: "Why do they talk in front of you?" Julie: "It's like the wealthy talking in front of their servants. What can they do? It's the same with me. I'm just the help. What can I do? So they feel free to talk in front of me as if I'm not there. Their plans are detailed, far-reaching, destructive, and scary as hell! These are powerful and wealthy men, fully capable of acting on their plans and making things happen. These men are respected by the community. Who would believe what I have witnessed without tangible proof?"

Julie told Tony these things without naming names. Clearly, she was afraid of these men. She pointed out no one would believe these things and there was no way to prove them. She insisted Tony agree not to tell anyone. Julie: "There is nothing we can do anyway." Discussing this with other people would accomplish nothing but jeopardize Julie's job and her personal safety. At the end of the ride, Tony got out of the car and put these things out of his mind.

RICH

Tony lived on campus. Eighty-one guys lived on his floor. One day a scrawny, obnoxious student raucously kicked open the door to Tony's room while he was studying. Tony: "Who are you and what do you want?" "I'm Rich T, F'n Q." Tony: "Rich?" The insolent intruder smiled, "Yes, Rich: T, F'n Q." Tony: "I don't get it. What's with the T, F, and Q?" "That's what everybody calls me: Rich the f***ing queer," he grinned. Tony asked, "Everyone really calls you that?" "Yes," Rich grinned. Tony was at a loss, "Are you queer?" Rich smiled, "Oh yes!" Tony: "And you like being called that?" Rich: "I think it's funny." With an edge in his voice Tony said, "I don't think it's funny you barge into my room while I'm studying. You didn't even knock. What do you want?"

"I need dating advice," Rich said. Tony: "What? I can't help you with that." Rich defiantly crossed his arms and said, "I'm not leaving." Tony: "You barge into my room making demands. That alone makes me want you to get out. I don't know you. I know nothing about you. I'm not able to help you. Get out!" Rich shook his head even more defiantly, "I'm not leaving until you help me." Tony: "I can't help you." Rich: "The other guys come to you for advice. You give them good dating advice and you don't know most of them either. I'm not leaving until you help me the way you help the other guys." Tony: "The other guys ask for advice on dating girls. My advice isn't going to work for you. I really can't help you."

Rich: "I need advice. The other guys say your advice is good. I'm not leaving until you help me the way you help the other guys." Rich carried on about wanting equal treatment. Tony: "Equal treatment? I'm not a public institution." Rich: "The guys on the floor come to you for all kinds of advice. I need your advice, and I'm not leaving until you help me." With that, Rich wrapped his arms around the leg of Tony's desk. The most expedient way to get rid of this pest was to dispense advice. Tony: "What's the problem?" Rich: "Nobody likes me because I'm homosexual. I don't want to be homosexual anymore." Tony laughed reflexively, "What are you going to be instead?" Rich: "I'm going to be normal."

Tony: "And how are you going to manage that?" Rich: "I'll see a psychologist. They have something called reprogramming. I'll have a psychologist reprogram me to be normal." Tony: "You're joking." Rich: "No joke. It's a real thing. They can reprogram a homosexual to be normal." Tony was shocked, "People aren't computers. You can't program a human brain the way you program a computer. What makes you think you can?" Rich: "They do it to spies. Cults program people and they can be reprogrammed. Psychologists reprogram homosexuals to be normal. That's what I want!"

Tony: "What they do to spies is irreparable harm. With a cult brainwash victim, the goal is to return them to their original state. You can't be serious. You would subject yourself to such irresponsible brain tinkering on purpose?" Rich: "It's a regular thing they do now. It works. They can make me normal." Tony: "No, you won't be normal, you'll be nothing. You won't be you. You'll be some sort of automaton. You won't be you. You'll be no one. However messed up your life is now, think how much worse it'll be when you find yourself to be a programmed thing." Rich: "But I don't like being homosexual. This is a way out."

Tony: "Suicide is also a way out." Rich: "Are you telling me I should commit suicide? That's mean!" Tony: "No, I'm saying there is no easy way out. Having yourself brainwashed is a crazy idea." Rich: "People don't like me because I'm homosexual. Do you like me?" Tony: "No I don't." Rich: "Because I'm homosexual, right?" Tony: "You barged into my room making demands. You invaded the privacy of my bedroom and interrupted my studies. I didn't like you even before I saw your face. People don't like you because you are obnoxious and aggravating, face it. Don't you know any homosexuals?" Rich: "Sure I do." Tony: "Do they like you?" Rich: "No, they don't like me either." Tony: "You can't tell yourself they hate you because you're homosexual. They can't stand you because you're obnoxious and rude." Rich smirked.

Rich: "Nobody likes me. What can I do?" Tony: "The easy answer is to stop being obnoxious, but that's not realistic. What you need to do is make one new friend and work from there." Rich: "You are my friend!" Tony: "No I'm not. You and I are not friends." Rich: "But you care!" Tony: "Now you insult me. You make me sound like a Democrat." Rich: "But you're trying to help me." Tony: "Only to get rid of you." Rich: "So how do I make a new friend? Everyone who knows me doesn't like me." Tony: "There must be gay bars in this city. Do you know where there are any gay bars?" Rich: "Yes." Tony: "Are you old enough to get in?" Rich: "Yes, I am." *Drinking age was 18 years old at that time.*

Tony: "Go to a gay bar where no one knows you. Behave yourself. Make a new friend. When that falls apart, go back to the same bar and try again. Practice making friends with other homosexuals. Once everyone in that club hates you because you're obnoxious, find a new club and start over. The object is to make a friend that can and will help you." Rich smiled, "That sounds like it will work! Thanks! I knew you could help me. I want you to come with me when I go to a club." Tony: "No!" Rich: "When I make friends I will tell them how you helped me. I will tell them what a good friend you are." Tony: "No. I am not your friend. Leave and don't come back. You got the advice you demanded. You weren't welcome to come into my room to begin with and you still aren't. Go and stay gone. If this doesn't work, I don't have any other ideas for you."

After the weekend, Rich raucously charged through the closed door and into Tony's room again. He was grinning and bragging how he met a guy in a bar and they had sex. Tony: "I don't want to hear it. I already told you I don't want to hear it." Rich's enthusiasm was like an avalanche, "–and I told him how you talked me out of reprogramming, that it is wrong. He says you are a wise man and he wants to meet you. He says you're a friend of gays." Tony: "No! Again, you barge into my room without knocking and interrupt my studies. Don't you have any studying to do?" Rich: "Not really, I'm a photo major." Tony: "Well I have plenty. Right now, I'm working on calculus. I told you don't come back." Rich: "He says you're a wise man and you're a friend of gays." Tony: "What makes him think so?" Rich: "Because you are against reprogramming."

Tony: "I simply know right from wrong. Reprogramming is wrong. I'm an engineering student. Engineers value things that work. In your case, suicide will work. You will stop being homosexual. Clearly, you understand suicide is wrong. Reprogramming is also wrong." Rich: "Why do people think reprogramming is good?" Tony: "Americans believe in psychology. Americans think psychology is a science." Rich: "Psychology is a science." Tony: "Yeah, the science of lame excuses. Instead of recognizing evil as being evil, psychology offers excuses for a wide range of bad behaviors." Rich: "You keep saying Americans, why?" Tony: "In the Soviet Union psychology is used as an excuse to banish political dissidents to Siberia. They understand psychology is bogus."

Rich: "What makes you so sure psychology is not a science?" Tony: "The proper term for psychology is irreligion. Think of it as a formal collection of stereotypes and excuses." Rich: "How can you treat psychology as something trite?" Tony: "Because it IS something trite and because I have a mountain of studying to do before class tomorrow. Psychology is irreligion. Look up the word irreligion. I don't have time for this. Religion is valuable. Religion teaches people the difference between right and wrong. From an engineering standpoint, it works. It infuses moral values, which are useful guides in decision-making in new situations. Look up the word irreligion. Ok now, please leave."

HAPPY HOUR

After class Friday, Charlie knocked on Tony's door. "Let's go Tony, ten cent beers at happy hour." Over beer, Charlie razzed Tony, "I see you've made a new friend." Tony: "Who's that?" Charlie: "Rich." Tony: "That guy. What made him decide to bother me?" Charlie: "Everyone else is sick of him. You're an easy target. You don't lock your door." Tony: "Yeah, well, I do now. I have to live like a woodchuck locked in my burrow because of that guy's defective upbringing." Charlie: "Watching Rich bother you reminded me of something my brother told me recently. He wanted to work out in a gym. He learned he could join the YMCA for cheap. When he went to look the place over, he saw the members were mostly homosexuals, so he didn't join. It was pretty funny how upset he was."

Tony: "I was told the YMCA is a good place. When our soldiers came back from World War II many stayed at the Y until they were situated. I was told the Y is great and it's cheap. They weren't lying to me, they were serious." Charlie: "It used to be what they told you, but homosexuals discovered it and took over, at least the ones where I'm from. Besides being cheap, it's perfect for them; plenty of young, indigent transients to take advantage of." Tony: "But the Y is a Christian organization." Charlie: "They don't care about that. All they care about is: it's cheap, it's convenient, and it's available."

BUSINESS PROFESSOR

A professor in the school of business told his students before class, "A pyramid represents the current distribution of wealth in our society: very few wealthy at the top, more in the middle class, and many poor at the bottom. Society will be transformed in the future. It will be in the shape of an hourglass: many wealthy at the top, almost no middle class, and many poor at the bottom. The middle class will become almost nonexistent. Before this happens, you have to make the jump to the super wealthy, or you'll be pushed down to the very poor." The class asked what economic forces would cause this. The professor admitted, "This change will be driven by politics, not economics." His smile was smug and self-satisfied. The students had many questions. The professor avoided answering them by starting class.

The next time Tony saw Julie he shared the business professor's prognostication. "He's one of them," she said. Tony: "His students said he has a wife and kids." Julie: "A lot of them get married so no one suspects they are homosexual." Tony: "Why would homosexuals want to eliminate the middle class?" Julie: "Their hatred makes no sense to me, but this I understand. It is easy to take advantage of the poor. By expanding the ranks of the poor they have a larger pool of men and boys to prey upon." Tony: "Who is going to expand the ranks of the wealthy?" Julie: "They are. They are going to get rid of heterosexual jobs. Only homosexuals will have jobs."

Tony: "I don't see how that can happen. Jobs aren't divided into homosexual or heterosexual." Julie: "I don't know either, but they are confident they can make it happen. One thing I do know. Homosexuals are big in TV and entertainment, and that involves serious money. Take what that professor said seriously. It's both a threat and a promise. I'm a little surprised he was bragging about it to his class, but that's how confident they are." Tony: "When will this happen?" Julie: "Not right away. They are not in a hurry, but it will happen in our lifetime."

The last time Tony rode home with Julie, she was silent and ashen faced. She drove for twenty minutes before she said, "There are two technicians at work that don't like me. I think they are homosexuals, and it bothers them that I overhear all of the conversations homosexuals have with the doctors about how they are going to destroy this country. What can they do to me at work to hurt me?" Tony: "What do they do?" Julie: "[The manufacturer] is using our hospital to test their new CAT scan machine. It takes multiple X-rays, and a computer uses them to make 3D images. The prototype is in the ER. I am the only one trained to operate it. The company's technicians are there to make adjustments until it works properly." Tony: "They must have to take the covers and shielding off sometimes."

Julie: "Yes, they do. One day they left the covers off and had me run the machine a few times. They said it would be ok." Tony: "Where were they while you were running it with no shielding?" Julie: "They left to get coffee each time. They didn't come back until after I was done." Long silence. Julie: "That was it, wasn't it? That is how they hurt me." Tony: "Where were the doctors when this was happening?" Julie: "They weren't around, they were in a meeting." After a very long silence, Julie asked, "How much radiation do you think I was exposed to?" Tony quietly said, "Too much." They were both silent for the rest of the drive.

Thirty-six years later Julie died of lung cancer, even though longevity is characteristic of both sides of her family. People ask the family if she smoked. (No). No one knows to ask how much X-ray radiation she was exposed to from the

CAT scan prototype in the ER.

Tony used up his savings. He dropped out of school and worked construction jobs. He saved enough money to go back and finish his education.

1980s

COLLEGE

Tony went back to college. Engineering classes had few if any women, three or four tops. Tony filled one of his electives with a gut course, *Sexual Revolution*, where he expected to meet women. On the first day of class, Tony walked into the classroom five minutes early. Eight women were seated in the center of the room. Tony smiled and said, "Good afternoon." They glowered and gave him the cold shoulder. Tony sat on the far side of the room. A minute later, another student came in. He smiled at the women and said good afternoon. They gave him a warm, enthusiastic greeting. He breezed past them, set his books down on the desk next to Tony, smiled, and said to Tony, "My name is Jerry." Jerry turned and breezed out of the room.

The moment Jerry disappeared the women spoke at once. "I like him!" "I think he's sexy!" "I'd like to go to bed with him!" They had plenty more to say, but Tony was busy thinking, *I hate my life.* Tony dressed like an engineering student with a button down, long sleeve shirt and dark trousers. He was six feet tall, medium build, average weight, brown eyes, and wavy dark hair conservatively cut. Jerry was about the same build with straight, sandy colored hair. The women were captivated by Jerry's animal magnetism.

This was when colleges started assigning group projects. Industry needed employees to work together as a team. American management's inability to engender cooperation in the workplace presented a challenge to colleges to produce it for them, according to the instructor. She had several topics for group projects and asked the students to choose a topic. All of the women in the class chose *Sex in Advertising*, so Tony chose that topic too. Jerry was the last student to choose the same topic. The group met after class over coffee to brainstorm and divide the work. The women fawned over Jerry, Jerry ogled Tony, and Tony hated his life.

Midterm, each student delivered an oral presentation on an individual research topic. Tony's presentation was on the Women's Liberation Movement. Tony stood before the class, "Women's Lib was organized by homosexual men in order to undermine the family unit. They intended to fracture society in order to create a place in society for homosexuals." Bedlam erupted! All of the men and women were angry. Everyone objected at once in loud, angry voices. One chump piped up, "Where did you get your research? Playboy? I bet you read Playboy for the articles." This mental giant drew several nervous laughs. A couple more hecklers chimed in with even less inspired gaffes.

The instructor retook control of the class, "I'll end this right now." She turned to Tony and demanded, "Read your bibliography to the class right now." Tony read his bibliography. It contained seven books. The authors were women whose names were well known by their association with the Women's Liberation Movement. One wise guy deadpanned, "No books written by men? I thought you said homosexual men were behind the women's movement?" Tony: "I read two books authored by men. All nine books said the same thing: gays and lesbians do not get along. Gay men brokered a truce with the lesbians. The plan was to undermine the family unit and fracture society in order to make a place in society for homosexuals.

Gay men had the plan, but they needed women in front of the TV cameras for a women's movement. The lesbians agreed. All nine authors agreed on all of these points. The female authors said everyone involved in the movement was homosexual including herself. The male authors differed on only one point. They said everyone involved was homosexual except himself. I did not include the two male authors in my bibliography because their denial undermined their credibility. No information was lost by not including them." Tony continued with his report, "Blacks were brought in to handle logistics because of their experience organizing the Black protests of the 1960s."

The instructor interjected, "When you do a research paper you include all the sources you read whether you draw from them or not. The correct thing to do is to add those two sources to your bibliography if you still have the information." The teacher asked if Tony had any magazine articles and what dates the sources appeared. Tony: "There was nothing useful until the mid-1970s. Articles became more numerous over time. After I had several mainstream women's magazine articles, I found books on the subject. The nine books I found were all published from 1978 to 1980." The professor signaled her approval and motioned for Tony to continue delivering his report. The entire class was flabbergasted.

Material the instructor covered in class one day stated homosexual men have 30 sexual liaisons per month. The class doubted it was possible to meet one new person every day, much less have sex with them too. The women murmured, "Who has that kind of time, even if it were possible?" Tony asked the teacher to clarify, "Does this mean 30 new people or one person 30 times?" Instructor: "No, it means 30 new people."

After class, the *Sex in Advertising* group met at the diner over coffee to work on their group project. Tony's coffee was refilled shortly before the meeting broke up. The women left immediately. Jerry sat across the table fiddling with his empty cup.

Jerry: "Do you mind if I stick around for a while?" Tony: "No. I want to finish my coffee before I leave. It's raining and I'm riding the bike (Honda 350). Besides, I have a couple of questions I'd like to ask you." Jerry: "Why do you want to ask me?" Tony: "Because you're the only person I know who would know the correct answer. What the teacher said in class today, 30 different partners per month. Is that right?" Jerry proudly stated, "For me it's more like 42, but yes, I think 30 is a fair estimate. I normally have sex with between 40 and 45 in a month. Forty-two is a conservative average." Tony: "How many of the 42 are women?" Jerry was mortified, "None of them are women!"

Tony was confused, "You told the women you're divorced. Were you married?" Jerry: "Yes, I was married for three years." Tony: "What happened?" Jerry: "My wife thought she caught me cheating on her and divorced me." Tony: "Were you cheating on her?" Jerry: "No." Tony: "–What made your wife think so?" Jerry: "One day she came home from work early and found me in bed with a man. She filed for divorce the next day. She told her lawyer she caught me cheating." Tony: "–She caught you in bed with a man?" Jerry: "She did." Tony: "And she thought you were cheating on her?" Jerry: "Yes she did." Tony: "But you don't think you were cheating on her?" Jerry: "No, I wasn't."

Tony: "Why do you think being in bed with someone other than your wife isn't cheating?" Jerry: "The things we were doing were not possible for me and my wife to do. It wasn't cheating because it wasn't the same thing." Tony: "So you're bisexual?" Jerry laughed, "There's no such thing as bisexual. Gays don't like women." Tony: "If you don't like women, why did you get married?" Jerry: "I got married because that is what people do. Things weren't going all that well with our marriage." Tony: "Ok." Jerry: "I didn't want to cheat on my wife, so I tried something different. I did not realize I was gay before I was married. If I knew I was gay, I would never have gotten married." Tony was dumbfounded. He drank some more coffee to mask his reaction.

Tony did not do this to be polite. He did it so he could get more information. Tony: "A couple of weeks ago before class, you told me you met a woman at work and she gave you oral sex in the stairwell. If there is no such thing as bisexual, how do you explain that?" Jerry: "Some gays allow women to give them oral sex, some don't. It depends on personal preference, but it doesn't matter." Tony: "Why doesn't it matter?" Jerry: "Women don't count." Tony: "I don't understand." Jerry: "I did not have sex with that woman, she had sex with me. I did not give her sex. I did nothing for her. Women don't count."

> Compare Jerry's statements to those made by President Clinton 18 years later. Refer to entries under Perjury charges, [25] and Denial and subsequent admission. [25] Go to: <http://en.wikipedia.org/wiki/Lewinsky_scandal>. [25]

Tony: "So, the 42 per month is 42 men?" Jerry: "Yes." Tony: "Any women would be added to that number?" Jerry: "Yes." Tony: "Ok, how many women per month?" Jerry thought for a few moments, "Six. That number varies widely from month to month, but I think six is a fair average." Tony drank more coffee while he tried to make sense of this. Tony: "Women don't count. –You don't like women. – So when you have gone too long without sex, you bridge the gap by allowing a woman to give you oral sex?" Jerry beamed, "You do understand. Now, you said you had a second question for me." Tony: "That's right. How do you do it?" Jerry: "Do what?" Tony: "How do you get a woman, a complete stranger, to give you oral sex when you don't even like women?"

Jerry: "That's your second question?" Tony: "Yes." Jerry: "What makes you think I'll tell you the truth?" Tony: "I don't care, lie. How do you get them to do it?" Jerry: "What you're really asking is how can you get them to do it." Tony: "Ok, how?" Jerry: "You simply expect them to." Tony: "Simply expect them to?" Jerry: "Yes." Tony: "Well, –ok then. Thank you." Jerry: "How do you know I didn't just lie?" Tony: "Sex is too important to you for you to be able to lie about it." Jerry looked genuinely surprised. Tony: "I have to go. Thank you for answering my questions. You can see why no one else could have answered them for me." Jerry: "A straight guy could've answered your second question." Tony: "Straight guys like women. I was curious how you do it."

One day a new woman came to class. The other women were jealous because she was pretty. When class started, the new woman went in front to deliver her report. The teacher objected, demanding the new student identify herself. "It's me, Jerry." No one believed her, including the teacher. The new woman opened a handkerchief and started wiping makeup and lipstick off her face. Sure enough, it was Jerry. Everyone was horrified! After Jerry gave his report, he fled the room. The entire class was quiet, disoriented, and completely freaked out. After class, after the women left, one man self-consciously said, "Jerry was a better looking woman than any of the women in class." Two men tentatively agreed.

FINDING WORK 1981

Jobs were scarce when Tony graduated. He was lucky to find work. Tony landed an engineering job in field service working for a military customer. This means short-term assignments in undesirable locations. Most of the tech reps Tony worked with worked in this business for many years. The nature of the work, the far-flung travel, and the inability to establish normal social ties generally turned the old tech reps into drunks, whoremongers, or both.

Bill, one of the younger men at work, told Tony, "They found Noah's Ark." Tony: "Really? Who found it?" Bill: "Officially, it has not been found. In the early 1970s, our satellites saw something deep beneath the ice on [location withheld]. It was a large structure, presumed to be manmade. After a few years, enough ice melted that they were able to determine the object was a wooden structure the exact dimensions the Bible specifies for Noah's Ark." Tony: "How did they see it if it was buried under ice?" Bill: "They were mapping the globe using ground penetrating radar when they saw an anomaly." Tony: "Why haven't they told the public about the Ark?" Bill: "They can't without divulging we have satellites with ground penetrating radar. That is classified. If the discovery of Noah's Ark was made public, what do you think would happen?" Tony: "A team of archaeologists would send an expedition to recover it." Bill: "What religion would send an expedition?" Tony: "Catholics." Bill: "All Christian religions?"

Tony: "Yes, there would be contention." Bill: "Interlopers! What makes you think Noah's Ark is anything other than Jewish? It is located in a part of the world that is Arab Muslim. They don't like Jews or Christians, so how much cooperation do you expect them to give an expedition to recover Noah's Ark? If religious differences aren't contentious enough, consider the politics." Tony: "So, Noah's Ark stays frozen in a glacier?" Bill: "Not forever. Satellites did not see the Ark initially because it was buried under so much ice. Enough ice melted by 1976 to be able to determine the wooden structure was Noah's Ark. As the glacier continues to melt, the entire Ark will be exposed. Locals have known about the Ark for generations. It's only a matter of time before it becomes public knowledge."

Tony: "How do you know all this?" Bill: "I know a guy who knows a guy. I know about the locals because I am familiar with the region. Local guides have been taking wealthy westerners to the Ark for generations. It's in their best interest to keep things just the way they are." Tony: "The glacier is melting?" Bill: "In recent years all glaciers have been melting at an alarming rate. The polar ice caps are melting too. Do you know what this means?" Tony: "No. Is that a problem?" Bill: "Where do you think all that water will go when it melts?" Tony: "The ocean." Bill: "How much will the sea level rise when all that ice melts?" Tony: "I don't know, a few inches?" Bill: "Ice on the polar caps is miles deep!" Tony: "Oh, –ok. How much will the oceans rise?" Bill stipulated the amount in feet.

Tony: "Coastal cities will be flooded!" Bill: "When the polar ice caps melt, a rising sea level and dramatic climate changes are only the beginning." Tony: "What's the cause?" Bill: "You're familiar with weather cycles and climate cycles." Tony: "Vaguely." Bill: "Earth was hot and humid when dinosaurs roamed the earth. After a large asteroid hit, the earth became frozen in an Ice Age. The caveman emerged at the end of the Ice Age. The longest climate cycle is returning the earth to its natural state, a global hot and humid climate. There are several shorter cycles happening at the same time. The shorter cycles confuse the issue. Long-term, the planet is heating back up."

NEWS ITEM

A new and deadly disease slowly leveraged its way into the news. Nothing was known about the disease named AIDS. Bill purchased the book, *And the Band Played On.*[37] He loaned it to Tony saying it was the most definitive book on AIDS. The book tracked North America's outbreak back to patient zero. Tony found the book difficult to read. It was heavy on homosexual lifestyle and light on medical answers. The author told of gay bathhouses (p 196), the CDC's efforts to track the contagion (pp 96, 132), of gay men having 250 sex partners per year (p 83), and political wrangling in Washington DC.

Several men were known to continue frequenting the bathhouses after they were aware they had the new contagion (pp 198, 200). Patient zero was especially pernicious in this regard (pp 247, 251). Authorities in Vancouver, Canada were aware of this man, "the Orange County (California) connection," but decided they had no legal remedy to stop him from willfully spreading the disease (p 262).[37]

Quarantine was discussed in the media. Tony did not understand why AIDS patients were not quarantined. Proponents argued for reason and vigilance. Opponents dismissed quarantine as "medieval" and called for personal privacy and individual's rights. Time has proven quarantine is an effective measure for containing communicable diseases. Quarantine is essential for controlling diseases with no known cure. Since little was known about AIDS, quarantine was the only vigilant recourse to ensure public safety. Our nation's public institutions failed miserably.

> Wisdom 14:22 (DRA) [31] "–they lived in a great war of ignorance, they call so many and so great evils peace."
>
> Wisdom 14:22 (RSV-C) [40] "–they live in great strife due to ignorance, and they call such great evils peace."

REPATRIATION 1987

Tony quit his job in order to return to the States. His first stop was a visit to family and relatives. His uncle told him about the homosexual manifesto. Uncle: "It was published in a homosexual newspaper. I think it was *The Village Voice* in New York City. (Try: Boston's *Gay Community News*, 1987.) YOUR Republican Senator read it into the Congressional Record so it won't become lost, so the public will always be able to access it." *MY Senator? I just got off an international flight. Which Senator is supposed to be mine?* Tony: "Why is this interesting to me?" Uncle: "Didn't Julie tell you what she learned when she worked in the ER?" Tony: "Yes, she did. Was there new information in the manifesto?" Uncle: "Not really." Tony: "Then I don't need to read it. My time is better spent job hunting."

The homosexual manifesto [10] was written into the Congressional Record on July 27, 1987. Here is what Tony did not see:

> 133 Cong. Rec. E3081-02, 1987 WL 950611 (Cong. Rec.) [11]
> Congressional Record-Extension of Remarks
> Proceedings and Debates of the 100th Congress, First Session
> Material in Extension of Remarks was not spoken by a Member on the floor.[11]
>
> HeinOnline -- 133 Cong. Rec. E 3081 1987 [10]

MILITANT WOLVES IN SHEEPISH DRAG, NO LONGER!
HON. WILLIAM E. DANNEMEYER

of California
In the House of Representatives
Monday, July 27, 1987

Mr. DANNEMEYER. Mr. Speaker, since the 1960s and the beginning of the sexual revolution, homosexuals have been striving to change American culture. These "normaphobes" demand that the average American view their aberrant behavior as equal to heterosexuality. They relentlessly seek acceptability and legitimacy. In fact, the homosexual American dream would be to amend the Civil Rights Act of 1964 to include sexual preferences to the list of nondiscriminatory characteristics such as race, creed and color.

But Mr. Speaker, those Americans who believe in the notion of "live and let live," as it applies here, should be aware of the militant nature of the homosexual movement. I commend the following article to the American public so they can read for themselves the extent of homosexual militancy. I commend this article, not because I necessarily believe that these threats would be carried out, but mostly because this published article represents the nefariousness of the homosexual mind.

Fortunately, Americans overwhelmingly view homosexuality in the moral and spiritual abyss in which it exists. I, for one, will never cease to affirm the heterosexual lifestyle as the only lifestyle able to sustain the human race.

The article follows:

[Excerpts of this highly significant article were reprinted in the June 25, 1987, issue of "The Wanderer," America's foremost national Catholic weekly]

AMERICA: IS THIS THE GAY DECLARATION OF WAR?

(By Michael Swift)

This essay is outré, madness, a tragic, cruel fantasy, an eruption of inner rage, on how the oppressed desperately dream of being the oppressor.

We shall sodomize your sons, emblems of your feeble masculinity, of your shallow dreams and vulgar lies. We shall seduce then in your schools, in your dormitories, in your gymnasiums, in your locker rooms, in your sports arenas, in your seminaries, in your youth groups, in your movie theater bathrooms, in your army bunkhouses, in your truck stops, in your all-male clubs, in your houses of Congress, wherever men are with men together. Your sons shall become our minions and do our bidding. They will be recast in our image. They will come to crave and adore us.

Women, you cry for freedom. You say you are no longer satisfied with men; they make you unhappy. We connoisseurs of the masculine face, the masculine physique, shall take your men from you then. We will amuse them; we will instruct them; we will embrace them when they weep. Women, you say you wish to live with each other instead of with men. Then go and be with each other. We shall give your men pleasures they have never known because we are foremost men too and only one man knows how to truly please another man; only one man can understand with depth and feeling the mind and body of another man.

All laws banning homosexual activity will be revoked. Instead legislation shall be passed which engenders love between men.

All homosexuals must stand together as brothers; we must be united artistically, philosophically, socially, politically, and financially. We will triumph only when we present a common face to the vicious heterosexual enemy.

If you dare to cry faggot, fairy, queer at us, we will stab you in your cowardly hearts and defile your dead, puny bodies.

We shall write poems of the love between men; we shall stage plays in which man openly caresses man; we shall make films about the love between heroic men which will replace the cheap, superficial, sentimental, insipid, juvenile, heterosexual infatuations presently dominating your cinema screens. We shall sculpt statues of beautiful young men, of bold athletes which will be placed in your parks, your squares, your plazas. The museums of the world will be filled only with paintings of graceful, naked lads.

Our writers and artists will make love between men fashionable and de rigueur, and we will succeed because we are adept at setting styles. We will eliminate heterosexual liaisons through usage of the devices of wit and ridicule, devices which we are skilled in employing.

We will unmask the powerful homosexuals who masquerade as heterosexuals. You will be shocked and frightened when you find that your presidents and their sons, your industrialists, your senators, your mayors, your generals, your athletes, your film stars, your television personalities, your civic leaders, your priests are not the safe, familiar, bourgeois, heterosexual figures you assumed them to be. We are everywhere; we have infiltrated your ranks. Be careful when you speak of homosexuals because we are always among you; we may be sitting across the desk from you; we may be sleeping in the same bed with you.

There will be no compromises. We are not middle-class weaklings. Highly intelligent, we are the natural aristocrats of the human race, and steely-minded aristocrats never settle for less. Those who oppose us will be exiled.

We shall raise vast, private armies, as Mishima did, to defeat you. We shall conquer the world because warriors inspired by and banded together by homosexual love and honor are invincible as were the ancient Greek soldiers.

The family unit–spawning ground of lies, betrayals, mediocrity, hypocrisy and violence will be abolished. The family unit, which only dampens imagination and curbs free will, must be eliminated. Perfect boys will be conceived and grown in the genetic laboratory. They will be bonded together in communal setting, under the control and instruction of homosexual savants.

All churches who condemn us will be closed. Our only gods are handsome young men. We adhere to a cult of beauty, moral and esthetic. All that is ugly and vulgar and banal will be annihilated. Since we are alienated from middle-class heterosexual conventions, we are free to live our lives according to the dictates of the pure imagination. For us too much is not enough.

The exquisite society to emerge will be governed by an elite comprised of gay poets. One of the major requirements for a position of power in the new society of homoeroticism will be indulgence in the Greek passion. Any man contaminated with heterosexual lust will be automatically barred from a position of influence. All males who insist on remaining stupidly heterosexual will be tried in homosexual courts of justice and will become invisible men.

We shall rewrite history filled and debased with your heterosexual lies and distortions. We shall portray the homosexuality of the great leaders and thinkers who have shaped the world. We will demonstrate that homosexuality and intelligence and imagination are inextricably linked, and that homosexuality is a requirement for true nobility, true beauty in a man.

We shall be victorious because we are fueled with the ferocious bitterness of the oppressed who have been forced to play seemingly bit parts in your dumb, heterosexual shows throughout the ages. We too are capable of firing guns and manning the barricades of the ultimate revolution.

Tremble, hetero swine, when we appear before you without our masks.

HeinOnline -- 133 Cong. Rec. E 3081 1987 [10]

133 Cong. Rec. E3081-02, 1987 WL 950611 (Cong. Rec.) [11]
END OF DOCUMENT

After writing most of this book, Tony went to the County Public Library in search of this document in the Congressional Record. The research librarian was stymied by the fact the library had the entire bound collection of the Congressional Record except for three volumes that were missing from the 1980s, including 1987. The librarian called the main library in Philadelphia and found their collection was also missing the 1987 volume.

Tony went to the legal library in the County Building. They did not have the Congressional Record containing the homosexual manifesto in print. The librarian in the County Building printed a copy off their computer (Westlaw ® [11]). That copy had a disclaimer at the bottom: (© 2012 Thomson Reuters. No Claim to Orig. US Gov. Works.).

A second research librarian at the County Public Library assured Tony she could secure a photocopy of the Congressional Record from the collection in the state Capitol. It took more than a week to secure said copy. The copy appeared to be photocopied from the Congressional Record, but had the notation: (HeinOnline -- 133Cong. Rec. E 3081 1987) [10] *at the bottom of each page. This copy confirmed the accuracy of the Westlaw ®* [11] *copy.*

The County Public Library still had all of the index volumes of the Congressional Record. Tony counted one hundred line items in the Congressional Record Index for the One Hundredth Congress (1987) listed under the heading HOMOSEXUALITY. The above article was listed in the index as: America-Is This the Gay Declaration of War?, 21195 [27JY]. Under the subheading DECISIONS was one line item: Constitutional Right to Homosexual Activity: Supreme Court, 28707 [210C]. (The court ruled against the plaintiffs.) Most of the remaining ninety-eight line items contained the word AIDS or otherwise referenced that disease. Tony wondered if other states had the same problem of the Congressional Record of 1987 gone missing from their libraries.

The research librarian stated public online access to the full Congressional Record starts with the 101st Congress (1988) and covers everything since.

Tony quit his job in order to return to the States. This landed him in California. Tony found a job while thousands of engineers were being laid off. (Democrat controlled House and Senate.) If someone talked to Tony, it meant they were not born in California. Several people Tony met said, "This really is Sodom and Gomorrah; San Diego and LA." Tony found native Californians had no opinion on any subject except cigarette smoking. In California, smoking is the only thing they call evil and is the only behavior they censure. Tony did not enjoy California. He worked, he went home, and he read his Bible. [18] Tony owned his Bible for eight years. Only now was he diligent to read it. Tony profited on California real estate when he moved away.

1991

Tony never owned a television. He promised himself he would buy a TV the next time there was a disaster in California. *I want to watch.* It was raining when Tony drove out of California. By the time he reached the Midwest, there were news reports of mudslides in California. Tony bought a used TV to watch the mudslides. Tony did not enjoy watching nature smite California as much as he expected. After a couple of weeks, he saw enough Californian tragedy. The economy was still in the tank. TV news showed several thousand unemployed men and women in Chicago standing in line in foul winter weather to interview for 450 minimum wage jobs working in a new downtown hotel.

Tony found a job as a factory supervisor. One of the hourly workers told the manager second shift needed another worker and his cousin was available. The manager agreed, "Call your cousin and tell him to come in Thursday for an interview." The cousin did not make it there until the following Tuesday. The manager hired him. The new hire worked for Tony. He was Mexican and spoke no English. His cousin was going to train him on the machine. Tony asked to see the new man's ID. Both men were afraid. The English-speaking cousin refused. Tony: "Look, I know it's fake ID. I want to see why my boss doesn't know it. I just want to see it."

The new man's driver's license and Social Security card looked real. Tony asked how they got such good-looking IDs. They had a guy. Right. Tony asked how the cousin got here from Mexico so quickly. Denials. Tony: "He rode in with you. Your excuse that he had car trouble doesn't fly. I'm curious is all. I'm not trying to make trouble." Worker: "My cousin should have been here by Thursday. He crossed the border four times. They caught him the first three times and sent him back to Mexico each time. That's why it took him six days to get here." The new man hitchhiked from the Mexican border to his cousin's place in Chicago.

Tony asked the manager his method of hiring. Manager: "I take referrals from the people already working for me. If I run an ad in the paper, I will get 500 or more applications to fill one position. If I don't hire a Black, I will be sued for discrimination. Even if I hire a Black, I will probably be sued anyway. When you ask the Mexicans to do something, what happens?" Tony: "They do it." Manager: "If I hire a black guy, what is the first thing he's going to say when you ask him to do something?" Tony: "I don't know." Manager: "Sure you do. He's going to say you're discriminating against him because he's black. Haven't you worked with Blacks before?"

Tony: "Sure. Recently in California, a black guy on my crew used that line on me. I pointed out everyone else was working. I invited him to join us. In the 1960s, I worked with a black man. I was 11 years old; he was 18. He worked very hard." Manager: "Things certainly have changed. I hire referrals. I don't have to advertise and I don't need a lawyer." Tony thought of the thousands of unemployed citizens he saw on the news. *What is wrong with this picture?* One thing is for sure, Latinos know how to cooperate, to work together for the common good.

The company was bought up by venture capital. It was purchased for the sales list and assets. The plant was closed. Tony was unemployed. Eventually he and his girlfriend broke up. Tony assessed the situation: the economy, American society, life. Tony finished reading his Bible. [18] Tony applied to go to the seminary. He applied locally, but was turned away. Tony moved north, to a small town in the sticks where he could live off his savings.

2 LEVERAGED BY TECHNOLOGY

1992

Tony Ghepardo moved to a small town in another state. The locals had a slight Canadian accent. They ended many of their declarative sentences with the question, "Eh?" Local industries included agriculture and wood products. This far north, the sun and soil mostly grew trees for pulp, not lumber. Women and children harvest brush from white cedars in the fall and winter. It is hard work in cold weather to produce tons of brush for very little pay. Family men work jobs that pay six dollars an hour.

Many farms had stacks and rows of abandoned, rusted cages. Tony's neighbor said the cages were used for raising furbearing animals. It was a way for farmers to generate income in the winter. Neighbor: "Mostly we raised mink in this area, but some people raised other animals such as chinchillas. There are a couple of people still raising animals. They sell a few furs, but mostly they raise animals to sell to pet stores." Tony: "Why did everyone stop?" Neighbor: "Remember a few years ago a handful of crazies in New York City threw paint on women wearing expensive fur coats?" Tony: "Yes."

Neighbor: "Almost immediately the market for fur dried up: not just expensive furs, all furs. Raccoons used to bring as much as thirty-eight dollars a pelt. Now you are lucky to get two-fifty. No one bothers to hunt raccoons anymore. Coons have overpopulated the woods. Overpopulation causes disease outbreaks, especially mange and rabies. A mangy pelt cannot be used, and rabies is dangerous for everything living in the area. You can see there is very little economic opportunity here. There is nothing to replace the lost income from furs, and the wild raccoon population runs unchecked, all because of a handful of wackos in New York City."

It was disconcerting to see how empty the church was on Sunday. Tony went to different Masses, but the result was the same, the church was mostly empty. Tony asked why so few people were in church compared to how many lived in the area. Parishioners were reluctant to respond, but eventually an older gentleman confided the current priest paid too much attention to young children. Parishioner: "He had this problem at the last two parishes too. Rather than fix the problem, the bishop sweeps it under the rug by moving him to another parish. People stop going to church when they have a bad priest, and this is our third bad priest in a row. I can remember when the church was full on Sunday, but that was a long time ago. We are supposed to get a new priest soon. We'll see what they send us this time."

Father Nick

The new priest arrived early in the summer, fresh out of the seminary: Father Nick. His public speaking skills were impressive. His sermons were engaging! Tony's travels allowed him to witness the sermons of countless priests. Perhaps suffer the sermons of countless priests is more accurate. The new priest was truly gifted. Not since Tony was a child had he heard such inspiring sermons. Reverend Fulton J. Sheen was the last Catholic priest Tony could remember that was notably talented at delivering sermons.

By the fourth Sunday after Father Nick's arrival, it became a challenge to find a place to sit ten minutes before Mass started. In subsequent weeks, Tony went to different Masses to see which one was not overcrowded. The 5:15 p.m. on Saturday was packed. Plus, people were standing across the back and partway down the side aisles ten minutes before Mass. The only Mass you could still find a seat ten minutes before Mass was at seven o'clock Sunday morning.

After Mass, Tony commented to fellow parishioners on the striking surge in attendance. Tony: "I didn't realize so many people lived here. Is everyone who lives in the area Catholic?" Parishioner One: "No. Word has gotten out we have a good priest again. People I haven't seen in church in years have come back." Parishioner Two: "Not all of these people are from our town. People in surrounding areas heard we have a good priest and they make the drive rather than go to their own church." Parishioner Three: "People are finding out we have a priest that can actually preach, and he's good at it. One family I met after Mass last Sunday was from three parishes away." Parishioner One: "Even Indians from the reservation are coming back to church. I haven't seen them in our church in years. That's the difference a good priest makes!"

Singing in Catholic churches falls into two categories. One, the parish has a choir. The congregation is silent. They listen to the choir sing. Two, there is no choir. One parishioner leads the congregation in song: good luck getting participation from the congregation. The new priest was "an old-time priest" in spite of his youth. People literally flocked to church. The celebration of the Mass was truly a celebration, not a spectator gathering. The full-throated sound of joyous song filled the church! There was a small choir, but everyone sang. It was remarkable! How could the presence of a new priest instantly cause full participation in singing hymns?

One Sunday after Mass, Tony thanked a member of the choir for doing an outstanding job. She appreciated the recognition. After she left, another woman complained, "The choir sings the same few, simple songs. They don't spend enough time practicing. They don't try to extend their talent with new material. That's why I quit the choir, I got bored." She prompted Tony for comment. Tony: "I haven't heard singing like this in church since I was a kid. I wondered what was different. Here, the entire congregation is singing their hearts out. It's impressive! I wondered, why here and nowhere else? I believe you have the answer. The choir sings songs that are familiar and don't require extensive talent."

Woman: "But I was bored with the choir. It wasn't challenging." Tony: "That's why the congregation is able to sing with such joy and enthusiasm, it's not a challenge. It's a celebration and it sounds great!" Woman: "As a choir they're only mediocre at best." Tony: "Ok." An older gentleman standing nearby signaled his agreement, "Make a joyous noise–." The woman was frustrated, "But you thanked that woman for doing an outstanding job. The choir's singing talent is not outstanding." Tony: "The choir led the congregation in joyous song. They did an outstanding job of that today. I'm not a musical person. That's why I like this choir." Woman: "But I was bored singing with this choir." Tony: "I can see how that could happen." The woman left. The older gent smiled and nodded, "It certainly was beautiful."

Debbie

Tony purchased a "fixer upper" farm. The farm produced a negative cash flow, but it kept Tony busy. Tony lived off his savings. Debbie and Tony had been coworkers in California. They exchanged Christmas cards since he left California. Recently, she started writing letters. Debbie was tall and statuesque, with brown eyes, long black hair, and a warm smile. She was interested to see Tony's farm during her vacation. Tony: "Great. I look forward to your visit." When the time came, Tony met her at the airport. Turns out Debbie's boyfriend broke up with her. She was no longer "just friends" with Tony; she was suddenly amorous. Over the course of a week, Debbie demonstrated her cooking skills and her interest in home canning.

Debbie proved herself an invaluable addition to the farmstead. Tony explained he could not make a living farming. Unless he found a job, he would eventually have to sell the farm. Tony: "I applied to the local pulp mill. Due to recent upgrades to the plant, they need a manager with an engineering background. I sent my resume and got no response. There was a job fair at the plant three weeks ago. The HR lady gave me the brush-off and didn't even pretend to look at my resume."

Debbie: "Why?" Tony: "My east coast accent makes it obvious I'm an outsider. I mentioned this to a couple from church. The husband asked if I knew anyone at the mill. Since I don't, he said they will never consider hiring me."

Debbie said, "There must be something you can do. Try to meet people who work at the mill. Try networking." Tony: "In a small town like this, it'll be more like stalking. The people here are incredibly clannish. My neighbor's family moved here 20 years ago. They are still "the new folks." If I get a job at the pulp mill, I can live like a king. I don't need much of a job to make a go of it here, but finding anything is going to be tough." Debbie: "Why did you move here to begin with?" Tony answered, "To watch Rome burn from a safe distance. Nero was more cultured than I am. He played the violin while Rome burned. –Our society is circling the drain and the public doesn't even know it."

Tony and Debbie went to Sunday Mass. After Mass, Debbie asked why Tony did not go to communion. Tony: "After spending the week breaking the Sixth Commandment, I can't go to communion without going to confession first." Debbie was disappointed, "I thought that was why, but it's ok since we are in love." Tony: "We aren't married. That makes it adultery." Debbie explained her view that love makes intimacy beautiful and therefore it is not a sin. Tony: "I didn't make the rules, God did." Debbie: "You mean the Ten Commandments?" Tony: "Right."

Debbie said the week they spent together was wonderful. In her mind, it was somehow exempt from "thou shall not." She was certain God "was flexible." Tony: "I don't think so. The Ten Commandments are written in stone." Debbie was embarrassed and self-conscious, "Then why bother going to church?" Tony: "That would be the Third Commandment." Debbie's California boyfriend was gone and the scheduled plant closing meant so was her job. The company would transfer her to a plant in another state. Debbie's visit ended on a sad note. She took the new job offer. Tony went to confession the following Saturday. The priest was unusually quizzical and chatty.

Calling

After Mass, Father Nick always stood by the main entrance to greet the congregation. During Lent, Tony got the impression Father Nick wanted to speak to him. Rather than avoid the greeting line as usual, Tony shook hands and introduced himself. The priest had something to tell Tony but was self-conscious. What could he possibly have to say that requires privacy? This made Tony skittish. *I get it. I've heard stories about such priests. No, that can't be right either. He heard my confession after Debbie left. My accent makes it too easy to match the face to the confession. This is a good priest. What could he possibly want to discuss in private?* Tony avoided the greeting line the next two Sundays.

After Mass, Tony visited with another parishioner. When their discussion ended, Father Nick approached and commended Tony on his Lenten devotion. Tony: "Thank you. Father, it has been decades since I've seen the entire congregation sing." Father Nick was pleased as well. Tony: "And everyone goes to communion. I've never seen that before. I think that's great." The priest looked sad, "It's not as good as you think." Tony: "Why not, Father?" Father Nick: "If you saw how few people come to confession, you'd see the problem. What do people think? "Well, I didn't kill anyone this week, I'm good." I'd be happier with everyone going to communion if more people came to confession first."

Once the last of the hangers-on were out of earshot, Father Nick got down to business, "Have you ever thought about becoming a priest?" *Didn't see that coming!* Tony: "Yes, actually, I did. Before moving here I applied and was turned down." Father Nick: "What reason did they give for turning you down?" Tony: "They said because I had been an engineer I was too logical. They said I wouldn't make a good priest because I am too logical." Priest: "I used to be an engineer! We do not have a problem with logic here. I think you would make a fine priest." He invited Tony to make an appointment at the office during the week so they could discuss this further in private.

Tony met with Father Nick, who asked questions to learn how Tony came to the decision to go to the seminary. He asked Tony to recount his experience with the people who rejected his first application, and asked why Tony did not reapply when he moved to this diocese. Tony: "They told me to accept the fact I was rejected and move on with my life. They specifically told me to not go around applying and reapplying until I was accepted." Father Nick asked where the turning point was in those interviews, and things started to get negative.

Tony: "Everything was positive and upbeat until they asked if I was still dating. I told them I broke up with my girlfriend a couple of months earlier. They said they were concerned that two months was not enough time. The two of us could easily get back together." Father Nick: "Did they refer to that as a reason your application was rejected?" Tony: "No, the only reason given was that I was an engineer and I was too logical for the job." Father Nick: "Well, we like logical here!" Tony asked, "What about not going around applying and reapplying?" Father Nick: "You didn't reapply, I asked you." Father Nick talked about the seminary he attended. He recommended it for its superior academics.

Tony commented on Father Nick's engaging sermons and asked if his alma mater routinely produces such talented speakers. Father Nick: "You're familiar with football players videotaping themselves and studying the tapes to improve their performance? Well, that is what I did. I taped myself giving sermons and studied the replays. The other students laughed at me." Tony: "They watched while you practiced and laughed?" Father Nick: "No, they thought I was crazy to spend my free time working." Father Nick asked to meet again in a week to discuss further Tony's interest. At that meeting, Tony told Father Nick he was ready to proceed.

Jury Duty

Tony received a summons for jury duty. This was his first experience with jury selection. The prosecuting attorney questioned Tony first. He asked if Tony had any close relatives in law enforcement. Tony: "Yes." This raised questions of how many relatives and their relation to Tony. The judge asked Tony a few questions and was satisfied Tony could be impartial. The defense attorney asked Tony how much education he had. Tony: "An MBA in operations management and a Bachelor's in electrical engineering." Defense Attorney: "What type of work did you do at your most recent place of employment?" Tony: "Supervisor." Defense Attorney: "Before that?" Tony: "Manager." Defense Attorney: "Before that?" Tony: "Test engineer."

Defense Attorney: "Have you ever been found guilty of a crime?" Tony: "No." Defense Attorney: "Have you ever been a victim of a crime?" Tony: "Yes." Questioning revealed Tony was mugged once and his house was robbed once. Defense Attorney: "What was the outcome (of each crime)?" The mugger did not get the gas station's cash. Tony worked with the sheriff who caught the kid three days later. Tony did not press charges because the kid was underage. Tony could not be bothered taking the kid to family court. The kid's weapon was not recovered. Years later, Tony's house was robbed. Tony worked with local law enforcement. Two weeks later the police caught the man, who spent ten months in jail. Tony recovered his watch, but not his camera.

The defense attorney used one of his votes to send Tony home. Tony did not understand why he was summoned and not allowed to serve. A nice lady Tony's age, who worked in the courtroom, confided to Tony that defense attorneys do not like engineers because they are logical and examine the facts. Likewise, they do not like managers because they are decision makers, and are adverse to jurors with higher education in general. Tony did not need an explanation for relatives in law enforcement, that he was the target of two crimes, and that he worked with law enforcement to catch the perpetrators. As Tony left the courtroom, he passed the nearly completed jury. Basically, it was made up of housewives over the age of fifty. The defense attorney looked pleased.

Religious Instruction

Part of the process of applying to the seminary includes service to the church community. Fall religious instruction classes would start soon. The second grade and seventh grade still needed an instructor. Tony was given the opportunity to volunteer to teach one of those classes. He chose the seventh grade because, "They are old enough to reason with." The other instructors were mothers from the parish. One mother said, "You obviously don't have children of your own." Tony: "Why is that?" She sounded foreboding, "You think it's possible for seventh graders to be reasonable."

Class was held one evening per week. Tony wore a jacket, white shirt, and tie. The first class went off without a hitch. The students were very well behaved. At the start of the second class, the students asked Tony what is his name. Tony: "My name is Tony." "No, who are you? You aren't from around here. My parents want to know who you are." "Yeah, mine too. Our teachers write their name on the board the first day of class, you didn't do that." Tony: "Oh, you're right. I'm sorry." Tony printed his name on the green chalkboard. "My parents want to know where you work." Tony: "I bought a farm, two square forties–." "We know that. How do you make the payments?"

Tony: "I don't have a job. I paid cash." The class gasped! "How did you do that?" Tony: "I bought property in California when I worked there. I made a substantial profit on real estate when I left." The class was fascinated with California and bristled with questions. Tony: "Forget California. I hated it. I was happy to leave. The best thing about California was profit taking on their real estate." "Why did you move here?" Tony: "This was the only place I could afford to pay cash to buy land without using all of my savings." "My mother said you are applying to the priesthood, is that right?" Tony: "Yes, I am."

By the third class, other instructors were opening the door and peeking into the classroom. "I'm sorry. I wanted to see what was going on in here. It's so quiet. I thought maybe you canceled class or something." How can an instructor be productive in a classroom of bedlam? On the first day of class, five minutes into the session, Tony closed the door to shut out the noise from the other classrooms.

Before the start of the fourth class, four instructors gathered to meet Tony. They were baffled by the fact his class was so well behaved. Tony: "I have been a supervisor and a manager. I conduct class the same as I would conduct a meeting. It seems to work." The mothers agreed it was working, but why? One of them pointed out Tony was overdressed. "You don't have to wear a jacket and tie you know. We don't wear formal business attire." Tony: "I'm comfortable dressing this way for class." As the women left to go to their own classrooms, Tony could not help but notice the way they were dressed: baggy sweatshirts with writing and pictures on them. Two of the instructors wore sweatpants.

Tony encouraged the students to ask questions, but they were reticent. At the start of the fifth class the dam burst. There was a flood of questions. There would be no lecture until their questions were answered. The smart girl wanted Tony to explain eternity. Tony drew an engineering representation of three-dimensional space on the chalkboard. This confused the entire class. Tony: "Ok, how would you draw a representation of this book on my desk? The book is three-dimensional, the chalkboard is only two-dimensional." No response. Tony drew his version on the board. Peals of laughter filled the classroom. Tony: "This is called a schematic drawing. Engineers use drawings like this to convey ideas."

"It looks funny!" More laughter. Tony: "The drawing is not made to look pretty. It is made to communicate ideas. Ok, compare the lower left-hand corner of the book I drew on the board with this. These three lines are the X, Y, and Z-axis. This represents three-dimensional space. Now, I add a fourth axis and label it "t."" The smart girl interjected, "That stands for time!" Tony: "Yes, that's right. Time is the fourth dimension. Time is a component of matter. Therefore, time only exists inside the universe. Once you are outside of the universe, there is no matter and therefore, there is no time. That is what we call eternity, the absence of time." The class was animated!

"Draw the universe on the board." Tony drew a figure 8 lying on its side. He drew a thin disk bisecting the lobes. Tony: "Ok, this is my version of the universe. It is a cut-and-paste that consists of one widely held theory, one lesser theory, and one disputed theory. I combined the three to make a closed universe model." "Why did you combine theories?" Tony: "Each theory has problems. No one theory is accepted as the correct answer. My model is a closed universe. The advantage is; I am able to draw it. So, this is where we are, in the positive universe represented with the (+) and this is the antimatter (-) universe. The two are separated by this disk, which is a strong magnetic field."

"Where are we located?" Tony: "Right here. This would be relatively close to the surface, and not far from the end. You can't tell from looking at my drawing, but this represents 84% of the universe is newer than where we are located." A boy's voice: "That means 16% of the universe is older." Tony: "Older?" "Eighty-four percent plus sixteen percent. Sixteen percent of the universe is older than earth." Tony: "Yes, right. I would say our solar system rather than earth, yes." "Does the Bible say anything about life on other planets?" "Is earth the only planet where there is life?" A number of questions were asked simultaneously. Tony: "The Bible does not discuss life on other planets. The Bible addresses life on earth." *Ecclesiasticus (Sirach) Chapter 17*

"How do you know this?" Tony: "I've read the Bible from cover to cover." "According to the Bible, is it possible there is life on other planets?" Tony: "You're familiar with the quote: "Be fruitful and multiply, and fill the earth?"" Yes, they were. Tony: "If the world was not created to be a void, how can we expect the rest of the entire universe WAS created to be a void? Maybe someday we can continue the go forth and multiply directive beyond the confines of our planet." "Why doesn't the Bible address life on other planets or space travel?"

Tony: "Much of the Bible was written 3,000 years ago, the rest was written almost 2,000 years ago." "What good is it to us today?" Tony: "After reading the Bible, I saw human nature has not changed in 3,000 years. Our ability to be lazy and greedy has not changed. Our ability to make war has become much greater because our technology for war is much greater. I do not see where we have made great technological advances to increase our ability for making peace, loving God, or for loving our neighbor as ourselves. The Bible is even more important today than it was in the past."

"Why?" Tony: "Because today our sins are leveraged by technology. Today the same sin will cause much more damage to many more people." "Some people say the Bible is just a storybook, like a fairytale. What do you say to that?" Tony: "I say no. That is not the case. Different parts of the Bible were written by different people, so it contains different styles of writing. The original transcripts of the Bible were written in four languages: Hebrew, Aramaic, Latin, and Greek. I wondered about the historic accuracy of the Bible too. In college, one of my professors had been a General in the Egyptian army. He was exiled to the United States after Mubarak took over in Egypt. After class, I told him my religion uses the Bible.

The General said he was familiar with the Bible. I asked him if the recorded history of Egypt told of similar events as those in the Bible. The General said, "Those events did occur, but you have to understand, we used the conventional weapons of the time. It was standard practice for the victor in war to take possession of the land, the cattle, and the people they fought. Women, children, everything became their property. They were the spoils of war. We beat them fair and square. We followed the standard rules of warfare of the time. We used the conventional weapons of the time." Then my professor became emotional and said, "BUT THEY CHEATED! THEY HAD GOD ON THEIR SIDE!""

The class had a strong reaction to the General's testimony. They were teaming with questions about the General. Tony: "I can't answer those questions. I didn't think to ask him those things." A boy raised his hand, "What were you thinking?" Tony: "I thought: I want to cheat too. I want God on my side. I wondered why the Egyptians did not start worshiping the God of Israel. My professor's statement shows they knew God was with the Israelites. Instead, they've remained enemies for thousands of years." "Did you ask him?" Tony: "No." "Why not?" Tony: "He was a foreboding man in an emotional state. I already got more information than I expected. Leaving well enough alone seemed like a good idea."

A student asked Tony to explain the Trinity. Tony: "St. Patrick has as good an explanation as I've heard." "We're familiar with that. We want to hear what you have to say." Tony: "We have to accept it on faith. It remains a mystery." The room filled with muttering and grumbling. "Mystery! For years, religious instructors answered all of our questions with, "It's a mystery." You answered our other questions, why won't you answer this one?" Tony: "I have no answer for this one. It really is a mystery. That is what religion is, mystery and faith. There is no science or history to help me answer that question." The tension in the classroom abated. "How come you answered our other questions and none of our other instructors did?" Tony: "How many of your instructors were engineers?" Silence.

Tony: "Your instructors weren't holding back. They explained everything the best they could." "We didn't understand half of what you said. Couldn't you give us simpler explanations?" Tony: "No, I can't. You asked very difficult questions. The concepts are difficult to understand, and I am finding out they are even more difficult to explain. I answered them the only way I know how." "What good does it do us if we don't understand your answer?" Tony: "It shows you there is an answer. You do not understand it today, but someday maybe you will. If nothing else, it demonstrates the importance for learning. No matter how old you are, no matter how many books you read, there's still more to learn." The class was ready to proceed with the scheduled lesson.

Another night a student asked, "What is heaven like?" Tony quoted the Bible, "Eye has not seen, ear has not heard–." Several students cut him off, "Never mind that, tell us what heaven is really like." Tony: "We have no eyewitness accounts to tell us what heaven is like. The only information I have is what's in the Bible." The students grumbled and started to get ornery. Tony: "Look, I'm not trying to avoid the question. I don't know what you want." A boy's dour voice asked, "Is heaven going to be like church?" Tony: "Well, God is present in church in the form of the consecrated host. God is present in heaven in person, in all his radiant glory. In that way, heaven is like church only much better."

Another sour voice asked, "Is it going to be like going to church on Sunday?" Tony: "Yes it will. We go to Sunday Mass to hear the Word of God. In heaven, we will be in the presence of God. At Mass, we sing praise to God. In heaven, we will join the choir of Angels in singing praise to God." "How can you know that?" Tony: "In the Old Testament King David praised God with music and song. David had his soldiers play musical instruments and sing praise to the Lord. This was exceedingly pleasing to the Lord, so count on singing in heaven." The students were cantankerous and continued complaining.

Tony: "Look, I'm not trying to dodge your questions. I don't know what you want. Obviously, you have something specific in mind. Ask me what you really want to know so I can answer it." The smart girl's voice was sour and had a sharp edge as she asked, "Is there going to be a sermon in heaven?" Tony laughed. The class was confused. "Why is that funny?" "I've heard sermons that seemed like they lasted forever," Tony laughed. "Well, is there?" "Yeah, is there?" Tony: "I can give you my personal guarantee there will be no sermons in heaven." "How can you promise that?" Tony asked, "Why does the priest give a sermon?" The students exchanged blank looks.

Tony: "The sermon explains the readings of the day. The sermon is to help teach us the way to heaven, to help us find our way, to teach us about God so we can be united with God." The students were baffled. This was news to them. Tony: "Once we are in heaven we will no longer need to be shown the way to heaven since we are there. We will not need to be taught about God, or how to be united with God, since we will be in God's loving presence. We will be enveloped in God's Divine peace. We will join the Angelic choir and sing everlasting praise to the Lord." This seemed to allay the class' darkest fears concerning heaven.

The class feared there would be sermons in heaven, but voiced no concerns over the torment of burning in the eternal fires of hell. Since they are oblivious to the profound joy of being in the holy presence of God, how can they understand the anguish of being overwhelmed by the infinite doom, despair, and emptiness that pervades hell due to the absence of God?

Tony recalled anecdotes concerning hell discussed by coworkers where he used to work. "I have to be good so I don't go to hell. All of the evil people will be there. All of my enemies will be there. Our boss will probably be there. Most of my relatives will probably be there. I have to be good so I don't go to hell." Another coworker agreed, "Hell will be like going to the in-laws for the holidays, minus the food and alcohol, except hell lasts forever."

Second semester, the class got to the chapter on birth control. The seventh graders were well versed in statistics and they knew the percentage of efficacy of each type of birth control. Tony: "The Church forbids the use of all types of artificial birth control." "Does that mean there is a natural form of birth control?" Tony: "There is something called the rhythm method." The class broke into a cacophony of discussion that concluded with two voices saying the rhythm method does not work. An overwhelming majority of the class was saying, "My mother uses the pill." One girl said her mother could not use the pill, so she was using a diaphragm with spermicide. Tony was aghast, "If your mothers knew you were talking about what they use for birth control in public they would be embarrassed to death. I can't believe you're telling your classmates and religious instruction teacher." The class fell silent. Their faces turned red. Embarrassment appeared to be an unfamiliar emotion for them.

The lecture delved into the material. The class insisted the pill was the best form of birth control since it was the most effective. Tony: "I'm supposed to teach religious instructions. To begin with, the Sixth Commandment is "Thou shall not commit adultery." Since you have no intention of committing that sin you have no need of birth control." "What about when we get married?" "Yeah, what about then?" "We get married. We have a couple of kids and can't afford to have any more, what then? That's when we'll need birth control." Tony: "You've decided to solve a problem with a sin. That seems inappropriate in a religious instruction class." Students responded, "Let's get real." "Yeah." "Yeah, real."

> Ecclesiasticus 27:1 (DRA) [31] Through poverty many have sinned: and he that seeketh to be enriched, turneth away his eye.
>
> Sirach 27:1 (RSV-C) [40] Many have committed sin for a trifle, and whoever seeks to get rich will avert his eyes.

Tony: "Ok, the class thinks the pill is best. Someone explain "best."" The smart boy raised his hand and gave the pill's percentage of efficacy. Tony: "Round that down to the nearest integer and explain what that means." "If 100 girls are taking the pill, only one will get pregnant." Tony: "Are you sure that's all it means?" "What else can it mean?" Tony: "What happens after a husband and wife have sex 100 times during their marriage?" The class was baffled. Tony: "In your example there are 100 girls. Your statistics indicate only one will get pregnant. The original question was, "What is a married couple supposed to do?" Any thoughts?" The same boy answered, "Use more than one form of birth control at the same time. The synergetic effect will make it virtually impossible to get pregnant."

Tony: "Virtually impossible?" "Yes, almost impossible. It won't be zero, but it will be a very small number." Tony: "The statistical probability of pregnancy is the only criteria you're using to decide what is best?" The class was confused by the question. A girl in the back asked, "What else is there?" Tony: "I want you all to ask your mother to give you the little paper that comes with birth control pills. Read it. That paper is a list of the side effects caused by the pill. It is a very long list that includes blindness, blood clots, and several conditions that can cause serious complications including death. My friend in college got married. His wife lost her eyesight after taking the pill. She stopped taking it but she is still legally blind. What little she can see she describes as shadows."

"My mother doesn't take the pill." "I'm not going to ask my mother that." "Me neither." Tony: "All drugs have side effects, but the pill is in a class of its own. The pill is incredibly dangerous. If you do not know what the side effects are, you do not have enough information to make a rational decision. Valid scientific inquiry requires a thorough investigation. It sounds like you are just listening to the commercials and not investigating anything. The pill is unconscionably harmful to the woman taking it and can cause horrendous birth defects if she stops taking it and gets pregnant." "Which form of birth control do you suggest?" Tony: "The book says the rhythm method is acceptable. I suggest the rhythm method." "You said the pill has the most dangerous side effects. What method has zero side effects?"

Tony: "Anything that uses chemicals or pharmaceuticals is going to have side effects. Barrier methods have fewer side effects, but not zero." "Condoms have side effects?" Tony: "Latex allergies are not common, but an allergic reaction can be life-threatening." "But condoms are only 84% effective." Tony: "The only safe birth control method is the rhythm method." "The rhythm method isn't effective." Tony: "The Bible tells us to avoid sin for two reasons. First, sin is displeasing to God. Second, sin is harmful to us. Artificial birth control is a sin. You would have a better understanding of the first reason if you read the Old Testament. You would have a better understanding of the second reason if you read the side effects of the birth control method you are investigating."

When class ended, the students still thought the pill was a necessary part of modern life. Since their mothers were taking the pill, they had no doubt the pill was safe. This was confirmed in the next class. The subject was abortion. Tony covered the class material. The students were absolutely silent. Tony foolishly thought this was a good sign, that the students were paying rapt attention. When Tony finished covering the material, the smart boy said, "You have to have abortion." Tony: "What makes you think you need abortion?" "You have to have abortion for when your birth control fails." Tony was crestfallen. It was like trying to push a chain uphill.

Jeremias 4:22 (DRA) [31] For my foolish people have not known me: they are foolish and senseless children: they are wise to do evil, but to do good they have no knowledge.

Tony: "Help me understand the logic. You commit the sin of birth control for economic reasons. That sin fails, so you commit a bigger sin of killing your baby before it is born. Have I got that right?" "What else are you supposed to do?" Tony: "I'm covering the material in the book but it isn't getting the message across. Let me draw from other people's experience. When abortions were first legalized, a woman went to the doctor in my town for an abortion. The doctor refused to perform the abortion. She demanded he do it. She said it was her right to have an abortion. The doctor explained it was his right not to kill her baby. She said the law gave her the right to have an abortion. He said the law did not force him to perform one.

As a doctor, he took an oath to do no harm. Performing an abortion violated that oath. She asked what she could do since he refused. He told her to wait until the baby is born and then drown it in a pail of water. The woman was horrified!" And so was the class! "What did she say to the doctor?" Tony: "She got in the doctor's face, but the doctor asked her what was the difference if he killed her baby or if she did. Having him kill the baby with surgical equipment made it easy for her. Giving birth to the baby and then drowning it in a bucket of water was not so easy for her. Either way, the baby would be killed." "What did the woman do?" Tony: "She stormed out of the doctor's office."

Tony: "I have traveled quite a bit. I have met a lot of people. Over time, I met five women who had abortions. Four of the women were guilt ridden and messed up." "What about the fifth one?" Tony: "She was scary. I would not want to meet her in a dark alley. Who knows if she was like that before the abortion? The other four women said essentially the same thing: "No one told me it was going to be like that. Everyone said it was nothing. I felt my baby alive inside me. After the abortion, it was dead. I killed it! It was so awful! I felt so terrible! No one told me it was going to be like that. Even though it happened years ago, I still feel awful, and it's still hard to talk about." Three of the four women were sterile after their abortion."

The class responded, "That's why abortions were made legal, so that wouldn't happen." "Why did a legal abortion leave those women sterile?" Tony: "The women didn't know why. I asked if there were complications or unusual factors. There were not. They should not have been sterile, and yet they were sterile after the abortion." A boy's voice said, "Something's going on." Tony: "I agree. It is suspicious. The point is they were told it is ok to have an abortion. What they found out is; abortion is a sin. It is displeasing to God and is harmful to everyone involved."

The smart boy asked, "What do we do when our birth control fails?" Tony: "Solving one sin by committing another sin doesn't work. Two wrongs do not make a right. Why does everybody think of abortion? What about putting your baby up for adoption?" The students were adamant adoption would cause feelings of guilt and remorse that would haunt them for the rest of their lives. Tony: "The women I talked to had worse feelings of guilt and remorse for having an abortion and killing their baby. Two of them said they wished they had the baby and gave it up for adoption. They knew that would have its baggage and take its toll, but they were certain it would be far less than the awful nightmare they were living after having an abortion."

> Isaias 49:15 (DRA) [31] Can a woman forget her infant, so as not to have pity on the son of her womb? and if she should forget, yet will not I forget thee.
>
> Isaiah 49:15 (KJV) [32] "Can a woman forget her sucking child, that she should have no compassion on the son of her womb?" yea, they may forget, yet will I not forget you.

> Wisdom 12:5-6 (DRA) [31] 5 And those merciless murderers of their own children, and eaters of men's bowels, and devourers of blood from the midst of thy consecration, 6 And those parents sacrificing with their own hands helpless souls, it was thy will to destroy by the hands of our parents,
>
> Wisdom 12:5-6 (RSVwA) [43] 5 their merciless slaughter of children, and their sacrificial feasting on human flesh and blood. These initiates from the midst of a heathen cult, 6 these parents who murder helpless lives, thou didst will to destroy by the hands of our fathers,

One evening Tony gave the class a respite from his lecture by showing two VHS tapes. One tape chronicled miracles of the Eucharist. One Eucharist was nearly two centuries old and had no signs of deterioration, even though it was exposed to the ambient atmosphere (not sealed in a vacuum). Another Eucharist had small amounts of tissue around the edge. Testing confirmed the tissue was human male heart muscle. The consecrated wine tested to be human male blood, type O, with no Rh factor. It was still liquid and unspoiled, even though it was a century old and exposed to the atmosphere. One of the students asked why this does not happen every time the wafers and wine are consecrated.

Tony: "I think it's for our own good. Eating something that tastes like bread and wine works for me. Can you imagine eating raw heart muscle and drinking blood?" The class agreed that would be unpleasant. One student said, "Human heart muscle and human blood." The same student asked, "Why haven't we heard about these miracles before? Why doesn't the Church tell us about this?" Tony: "The Church believes miracles do not lead people to have faith. Only if you have faith first will you appreciate the miracle." "Why did you show us this tape instead of something else?" Tony: "My main concern was to treat the class by showing you two tapes. This one was the most interesting to me. I hoped you would like it too." The class considered the other tape a complete snooze.

Birth control and abortion were rough patches, but the rest of the year ran smoothly, or so Tony thought. There were only two classes left. Near the end of class the smart boy said, "Tony, you're a scientist, you know there really is no

God." That took the air out of Tony's lungs! Once Tony could breathe again he said, "I used science to explain the questions you had about God and religion. Obviously, I failed." "It's not you Tony. Everybody knows there's no such thing as God." "We know you have a job to do." "We understand. You're just doing your job." Tony was speechless. It was time for class to end. The students looked to Tony to see if it was ok to leave. Tony nodded, "Good night, see you next week."

Tony sat at the teacher's desk in the empty classroom. He reviewed his time with the seventh grade religious instruction class. Do they really think of God the same way they think of Santa Claus? The "just doing your job" comment was an unhappy indication. There was one more class before the school year ended. Tony realized he learned more from the students than they learned from him.

During the winter, Tony put on weight. His sports jacket was too tight. Tony wore a sweater instead. He still wore the white shirt and tie underneath. That one change compromised control of the classroom. The students were noisy that night. Over the course of the evening, three other instructors opened the door to peek in to see what was going on. Tony went back to the jacket and tie, but the students never fully returned to their original behavior. For the rest of the year Tony's class was less formal. Not the total bedlam the other instructors faced, but not the well-behaved class he enjoyed the first semester.

Tony gained insight into the morality of his generation and that of their children. The last night of class, everyone gathered for refreshments in the gymnasium of the public school where classes were held. A banner across the back wall read: "Excellence is not taking drugs." Tony asked a couple of the mothers what they thought of the banner. They agreed it was a positive thing. Tony: "I remember when excellence was something you had to strive for and work hard to achieve. Now, excellence is the absence of taking drugs. I think that's sad." The two women were taken aback. "I never thought of it that way." "You're right, it is sad."

Apollo 13

Tony worked with Roy when he was in field service. Now Tony worked on his fixer upper farm and Roy was retired. Roy called, "Have you seen Apollo 13? It is in theaters now. You have to see it on the big screen, you won't be disappointed." Tony and Roy visited by phone a few times a year. The next time they talked Roy asked, "Did you see Apollo 13?" Tony: "It was very good, almost like a documentary. I was glad to see the movie mentioned the House and Senate passed a resolution to ask the American people to pray for the safe return of the astronauts." Roy: "It was a miracle those men returned to earth at all, much less unharmed. The public has no idea." Roy was not known to be a religious man.

Tony: "It looked like the movie did a good job recounting actual events." Roy growled, "Not according to the people I know." Tony: "Where did the movie break from reality?" Roy: "In the movie, mission control decided rather than turn the craft around where it was they would slingshot off the moon. That discussion never happened. The term "sling shot" did not exist at that time. Turning around in mid-traverse is never an option, and there wasn't enough fuel to make the standard slow-down on lunar approach." Tony asked, "What about aero braking?"

Roy: "In 1970 only one man thought aero braking was possible, the man who came up with the theory. NASA was never willing to spend the money to test his theory. No one believed it would work except that one man. After the explosion onboard Apollo 13, he argued now was the time to test his theory. There was no downside. The men and the mission were already lost. With three of our best pilots on board, aero braking would succeed if it were ever going to. The rebuttal was; the astronauts could not make it back to earth alive even if the maneuver succeeds. He argued the mission could perform this one experiment rather than be a total loss. There was a flurry of activity in Houston to prepare the astronauts for the unscheduled aero braking maneuver.

Aero braking was validated when Apollo 13 reappeared from behind the moon. The craft was traveling much faster than anyone anticipated. Today we call that "slingshot." With Apollo 13 headed back to earth at a higher than expected velocity, Houston went hard at it to reassess the situation. In the movie, they said there was enough oxygen to bring the crew back alive. There wasn't." Tony: "What about the carbon dioxide mechanism they assembled with duct tape?" Roy: "That was a filter, not a converter. It captured CO2; it did not convert it back to oxygen. The crew only had enough oxygen to get back to earth's atmosphere. Their oxygen should have been depleted by the time they entered the radio blackout zone during reentry.

Remember they shut down the computer to save power? The computer cold soaked for three days before they powered it back up, and you know the problems you get with cold soaking. Engineers on the ground considered three possibilities when the astronauts powered the computer back up.

1) Most likely: it would display garbage, in which case the astronauts were dead. They could not hope to navigate the keyhole in the sky simply by looking out the port.
2) Less likely: the screen would be blank and all the programming lost; again, no joy.
3) The least likely possibility: the computer would come back up exactly where it left off. You know enough about computers to know how unlikely that is.

The movie did not mention the navigation gyros. Those gyros cold soaked for three days. They required preheat. The movie claimed they gave the nav system two minutes of preheat, but there was not enough battery power for any preheat. When aero braking worked and the astronauts were headed back to earth, NASA engineers began running experiments starting cold soaked nav gyros with no preheat. The lab ran the experiment 21 times. All trials failed. The closest they came was two broken gimbals in two of the trials. The rest of the trials had four or more broken gimbals. The nav system won't work if any gimbals are broken.

The astronauts started the nav system 30 seconds early. That's all the extra power they could give the nav, an extra 30 seconds to spin up to speed from a frozen stand still. I count three miracles: the oxygen, the computer, and the navigation gyros. God answered our nation's prayers that day. It was the hand of God that brought those men back alive." Tony: "I think that was the last time our nation officially and publicly prayed to God for help."

On April 18, 1970, President Richard Nixon addressed a crowd in Houston about Apollo 13's return. He read a wire he received from Pope Paul, "To the President of the United States, For the safe return of three astronauts, we express profound gratitude to God, to men of science, and to all of those who contributed to make this possible.–." ABC News Video. [02]

Joyous Families Fly with Nixon to Three Astronauts [21]
Honolulu, April 18 (UPI).

–A brilliant rainbow arched today as America's three astronauts from Apollo 13 embraced their loved ones.
New York Times, Sunday, April 19, 1970. [21]

Nixon, in Hawaii, Joins Astronauts and Honors Them [34]

—The Medal of Freedom citations that were presented to the mission operations team read in part: "The men and women of the Apollo mission operations team performed a miracle, transforming potential tragedy into one of the most dramatic rescues of all time.–
New York Times, Sunday, April 19, 1970. [34]

Text of President's Welcome and Lovell's Response at Honolulu [03]

Captain Lovell: "–well, I think the secret was the fact that we have in America something that has always been part of us and that's teamwork.–"
New York Times, Sunday, April 19, 1970. [03]

Special Rites Set for a Day of Gratitude [04]
by the Associated Press.

Churches and synagogues across America planned special services today, the national day of prayer and thanksgiving for the safe return of the Apollo 13 astronauts. [04]

President Nixon proclaimed a special day, urging all Americans and "all the peoples of the world to join with me in offering another prayer, one of deep thanks for the safe return of the crew of Apollo 13." [04]

In New York, Governor Rockefeller proclaimed this day as a "day of prayer and thanksgiving in New York State" for the astronauts return.
New York Times, Sunday, April 19, 1970. [04]

Canon Law

During the school year, Father Nick was transferred to the Vatican for two years. The parish was incensed at losing Father Nick! Parishioner: "The bishop gave us bad priests for so many years. Finally, the bishop sends us a good priest, and he doesn't let us keep him for a full year." Father Nick was resigned to follow orders, but was unhappy he had to leave. He told Tony he enjoyed being a parish priest, but he was being sent to the Vatican to study Canon Law for two years. He would return to work in the Chancellor's office to handle annulments. Father Nick: "I didn't become a priest to handle annulments." Father Nick got the paperwork for Tony to fill out to attend his alma mater.

Father Nick helped Tony with the process of applying. Seminarians have a spiritual director and a formation director. Father Nick gave Tony his recommendations for each. Before leaving, Father Nick assured Tony, "The man replacing me is a classmate and a friend. We graduated together. I told him about you. You will be in good hands. He will help you with whatever you need to be accepted. You will be able to start school in the fall." Father Nick gave Tony contact information to reach him in the Vatican. Father Nick: "Call any time, for any reason. When you are in school, you may feel like just talking to someone. It will be good to hear from you. Don't worry about the time difference, just call."

Father Gary

The replacement priest was Father Gary. Tony introduced himself to the new priest after Mass. The priest gave him a blank look. Two Sundays later Tony introduced himself again. Father Gary gave him an annoyed look. Three weeks after that Tony greeted Father Gary after Mass. This time the priest voiced his annoyance, "What is it you want?" Tony: "Father Nick told me to introduce myself, you would be expecting me." Father Gary was aware who Tony was and had no interest in the duty he had been volunteered for. Father Gary thought for several long moments. He devised an amenable way to handle this unwelcome chore.

Father Gary: "Come to the 5:15 Mass on Saturday from now on. We can have dinner together at the restaurant afterwards. We can take turns picking up the check. This way we both eat a good meal at least once a week and we can discuss your formation for the priesthood. This will take care of everything without adding to my schedule." Tony did not have an income. He was living off his savings. Tony was opposed to spending money on restaurant food, but he agreed. They carpooled in Father Gary's car. After the meal, Tony ordered scotch. The priest did not want to order a drink, and he did not seem to be familiar with scotch. Tony: "My treat Father, let's have a Highland single malt." Subsequent dinners included scotch.

Father Gary grew up in this part of the state. Tony expected the parish would readily accept him. Not so. Tony focused on his own rapport with the priest who was going to sponsor him. As the weeks passed, Sunday attendance dwindled. After only a couple of months, you could show up late for Mass and find a good seat. Father Gary was uninspiring. Going to dinner with him was awkward. Conversations with Father Gary over several weeks revealed the priest disdained dealing with the women of the parish. This is odd, since the parish runs on the volunteer efforts of the dedicated women. It was obvious he was no friend to Father Nick. For starters, he and his friends snickered at Father Nick for working so hard.

Father Gary gave parishioners the impression he could not be bothered. This quickly killed the enthusiasm of volunteer workers. Father Gary came to the parish around the same time Tony's religious instruction class explained to Tony there really is no God. Tony would have discussed that with Father Nick if he was available, but Father Nick was in transit. He was visiting friends and family before going to the Vatican. Father Gary was still giving Tony the brush off at that point.

Vocation Director

Early summer, Tony had an interview with the diocesan vocation director. It was a long drive to the appointment. The vocation director interviewed Tony in a manner similar to a human resource interview, except he also asked questions about Tony's dating history. Tony said he broke up with his last girlfriend two years ago. The director smiled at Tony the way people smile at a drunk. The director appeared to think Tony was lying, and he was pleased.

The director apparently believed Tony told three or four lies, and he approved. Tony was angry. What was worse, the answers this priest decided were lies meant he thought Tony was homosexual. This made Tony even angrier! Tony tried to maintain. He saw provocation used in interviews before. He concluded the interview was a disaster and he would not be going to the seminary. *What makes this priest think I'm a homo? What makes him think I lied? He is a priest, why does he approve of liars? None of this makes sense.* And nothing did make sense. Tony passed the interview. Weeks later, he made the long drive back to meet the bishop.

Diocesan Meeting

Later still, there was a meeting of all the seminarians of the diocese. Tony felt as uncomfortable at the meeting as a cat in a room full of dogs. *What is going on?* Seminarians gathered in a large room. They were scattered across the room in clusters of two to five men engaged in conversation. One seminarian ran up to Tony. He was talking a mile a minute. He learned Tony was accepted to the Pontifical College. Excited Seminarian: "I go there too! This is my second year!" Tony was not comfortable with the people that filled this room to begin with. Now this guy runs up to him and is oppressively friendly. The man wanted to move Tony away from the crowd for a private conversation. *No way!* Tony gave him the brush-off, "I'll see you at school. We can talk then." This made the seminarian even more manic and more insistent, which repulsed Tony even more. Excited Seminarian: "I have to talk to you now!" Tony: "I'll see you soon enough when we start school. We can talk then." The meeting was about to start.

Preparation

Tony had plenty to do before moving to the seminary. He had to sell his farm and his machinery, divest possessions he would no longer need, place into storage things he would need later, and pack the things he would need at school. Father Gary discussed Tony's progress at dinner Saturday. Father Gary: "It's a daunting task. You have so much to do in a short amount of time. After you wrap things up here you'll be moving." Tony assured the priest he was up to the task and would be ready to start school on time. Tony said, "No delays, no excuses. I'll be there on time Father." Father Gary: "This will be our last dinner together. You don't have enough time as it is." The priest was relieved to be rid of his unwanted chore. He did appear to enjoy scotch.

3 GEHENNA NOT HADES

Moving Day

Tony loaded his pickup truck the afternoon before disembarking for the seminary. After a short night's sleep, he started the long drive at O-dark-hundred. When he reached his destination, he found a self-storage facility near the seminary and unloaded the bulk of his vehicle's cargo into a storage unit. He arrived on campus mid-afternoon. A couple dozen students were milling around. Tony was given a room key and two upperclassmen helped him move his things to his dorm room on the second-floor. It was a good location at the start of the corridor and close to the chapel.

With so much help, the move-in process was quick. Tony left the boxes piled in his room and moved his truck to the far parking lot. This was Tony's first chance to relax after several hectic weeks. He wandered around campus to see what it looked like and get his bearings. The depression era brick architecture was stately, the campus idyllic. Students continued arriving. As the population density increased, the hair on the back of Tony's neck stood on end. *What is going on? These are seminarians. This is a school for priests. What is going on?*

Tony tried to think of all the times the hair on the back of his neck warned him of danger. There was the time a biker showed Tony his watchdog. The man kicked open the side door of his garage. A napping timber wolf rose to its feet and turned to face Tony. *No timber wolves here.* Tony remembered the time he responded to a roommate wanted ad in the newspaper. He did not know the man was homosexual, but the hair on the back of his neck did. *That cannot be right! That can't be right!* As Tony walked around campus, his stomach chimed in with harbingers of doom. *No! That can't be!*

At dinner, a large group of students sat at four adjacent tables and talked about the football game they played that afternoon. The game itself was a joke and the score immaterial. Their conversation relived the excitement of both teams ganging up on one of the players and pulling his pants off. They hooted how embarrassed the women were when they saw this. Tony: "What women?" Three men spoke at once, "The families that brought their sons here today stayed and watched the football game." "Mothers and sisters mostly."

The young men at these four tables laughed as they ruminated the moment they pulled the guy's pants off. Tony asked for clarification, "He did still have his underwear on, yes?" All four tables roared with laughter! One of the men explained, "No! That's why the women were so embarrassed." They laughed even harder! At another table, a bewildered young man sat alone, cowering and embarrassed. Tony sat alone too until late arriving students filled the cafeteria. The food was delicious, unbelievably so since it was served cafeteria style.

There was an orientation meeting for transfer students after dinner. Tony was one of five transfer students. Tony was in his late 30's, the other four students were late 20's or 30-ish. They immediately designated Tony "the old man." "They say after 40, memory is the second thing to go. Ha-ha-ha. Is that right? Ha-ha-ha. Well Tony, tell us, is that true?" "Yeah, that sounds about right," Tony answered reluctantly. "So what's the first thing to go?" The other four grinned with mischievous anticipation. Tony paused, –then slowly said, "I don't know, –I forget." The four were baffled, –then laughed heartily. That was not the response they anticipated.

Orientation

The next day there were more orientation meetings. Large numbers of students gathered ahead of time. A group of students were discussing [name withheld] seminary in [city withheld] Wisconsin. "That place has been having trouble for years, but this time they went too far." "I heard two students were having sex in a common area, right out in the open." "Yes, I heard the same thing." "Were they at least on campus?" "Yes, but can you imagine? The Rector had no choice but to expel them." "It's hard to imagine someone being that blatant." "That would never happen here. The Vice Rector would see to that."

The group acknowledged Tony's presence. One of the men introduced himself and stated where he was from. Tony reciprocated. The man asked Tony, "Doesn't your diocese send most of their candidates to that seminary?" Another asked, "Why did your diocese send you here? Wisconsin is a lot closer to your diocese." Tony: "My parish priest graduated from here. He highly recommended it. At a diocese meeting, some men were talking about the seminary you were discussing. They said there was a recent homosexual scandal. I came here, where it will be safe." The men in the group exchanged confused looks.

The next morning the Vice Rector sought out Tony. "Tony, when you filled out your admissions form you left the contact information blank." Tony: "Yes Father." Vice Rector: "Tony, we need contact information for next of kin in case of an emergency." The Vice Rector requested Tony's parents address and phone number. Tony was reluctant to accede. Vice Rector: "Tony, all employers require this. The Church is your employer now." Tony resisted, but soon exhausted all polite reason. Tony: "I don't want anyone bothering my parents Father." Vice Rector: "No one is going to bother your parents Tony. We are not going to contact your parents. We just need their contact information." *Right.* Tony eventually caved in and gave the information to the Vice Rector. *After all, he IS a priest.*

The day was expended in orientation meetings. The transfer students ate dinner together. Tony had been an engineer and a manager. Leo was ex-Navy, David was a businessman, Greg was well dressed and charismatic, and the fifth man was morbidly obese. These five men would be in classes together for the next five years. Leo started to strike up a conversation with Tony. David complained he forgot to bring a bathrobe. David: "I can't get to the store. It's too late to go shopping anyway." Tony offered, "I have an extra bathrobe you can have." David: "Why do you have two bathrobes?" Tony: "I was in a hurry when I packed. I grabbed everything and threw it in boxes. You can have the extra one."

David talked about the things he needed to shop for. Of the five students, only Tony had a vehicle. Tony: "When I first went to college I didn't have a car. I remember what it was like trying to beg rides. Make a list and I'll take you shopping." David: "You don't have to do that, just give me your car keys." Tony: "It's a pickup truck and I don't loan it out. I'll drive you." A couple of the men murmured and giggled. They presumed normal behavior dictated Tony should just fork over his keys. Eventually one of them said so. Tony was unapologetic, "My truck is only insured for me to drive. If you need a ride, I'll drive you." David said he would be ready at ten the next morning to go shopping and, "We'll be back in time for lunch."

Saturday

Two men going to the store: let's go, start motor, and drive off. It is that simple. Tony is not just punctual; he has the annoying habit of being a few minutes early. David was not ready. David really was not ready. After ten or fifteen minutes of rushing around his room, David was ready to leave. After locking the door, he remembered something and went back in to retrieve it. After two more false starts, he locked the door and the trip to the mall was finally under way. David made a shopping list but needed twice as much as was on the list.

Tony was patient. He was careful not to rush David least he forget something and need to go back. After shopping in two or three stores, David had everything he needed except a fingernail file. He picked up something that looked like sandpaper. Tony: "You don't want that thing. Get a real file. They usually keep the good ones in back of the pharmacy counter." Tony asked the girl behind the counter for a Diamond Deb ®. The store had no such thing. Tony: "I have an extra one. Turns out, they last forever. I'll give you my old file when we get back to campus."

David took his things to his room while Tony got the old fingernail file and brought it to David. David was impressed with a real file compared to a sandpaper board. David: "I've never seen anything like this. Where did you learn about a file like this?" Tony: "I dated a girl that was a beautician. She cut hair and did nails." David was instantly and outrageously furious! *Now what?* Tony excused himself, "I have things to do." *Talk about ingrate. Some people have a curious way of saying thank you, but this is a new one: mental episode. I have to be nice to the other students.* The Vice Rector had warned the new students, "How you get along with your fellow seminarians indicates how you will relate to the public at large." *It is not going to be easy to get along with people this temperamental.*

At lunch, Leo struck up a conversation with Tony. "I served in the Navy. What did you do before you came here?" Tony: "Right out of college, I was in field service. I worked for a military customer. More recently, I was a test engineer and a manager." Leo was interested in Tony's military related employment. Tony: "That was during the Reagan administration. We were proud to serve on the Gipper's watch." Leo glumly admitted, "I served under President Clinton. Our service was without honor." The two talked military, but Tony wished to discuss more recent endeavors. Tony: "Later, I worked in test engineering. I wrote test specifications and ran tests. What did you do?"

Leo told of his duties aboard ship. He had a leadership position in maintenance. Tony: "Why did you leave?" Leo: "I served aboard the Tarawa. We were tasked to bring relief aid to Haiti. Our amphibious vehicles were loaded with food. Our orders were to drive the vehicles a quarter mile in from the beach without stopping. Under no circumstance whatsoever were we to stop. There were two separate factions. One group crowded at the water's edge. They stood all along the beach. The crowd must have been 20 or 30 feet across. The other group was located a quarter mile inland. It turns out we weren't there to bring aid to Haiti, we were there to bring aid to one faction."

Leo choked with emotion and could not speak for several moments. "Before we reached shore the crowd along the beach ran into the water. The driver stopped. He was ordered to keep driving and not to stop until he was a quarter mile inland. He objected. People were trying to climb into our vehicle. There was a densely packed crowd in front of us. People would be killed if the vehicle moved forward. The order was repeated to drive without stopping. People were screaming as our vehicle ran over them. I will never get those sounds out of my head. Not just the screams but the other sounds too!" Tony: "Why didn't the people get out of the way?" Leo: "They couldn't because of the crowd. The other vehicles also ran over people as they drove through the crowd."

Tony: "Couldn't you go around?" Leo: "The crowd lined the beach as far as the eye can see in both directions. There was no going around." Tony: "Couldn't one vehicle follow behind the other?" Leo: "No! The crowd knew we would be told not to stop. They knew the food was for the other faction. These people were desperate. They tried to stop our vehicles with their bodies while others tried to swarm the vehicle. They were starving. They were emaciated. They were dying." Leo's emotion switched to anger, "It was just like Tiananmen Square, except it was us doing it, not the Chinese. Remember when the Chinese ran over college students with tanks? As thick as the crowd was, our vehicle must have ran over dozens of people. The other vehicles did the same."

Tony: "How many vehicles were there?" Leo: "Haven't you ever watched war movies? When a naval vessel launches amphibious vehicles, they don't launch one or two. There was a ship full of relief supplies. We deployed with all due haste." Leo's mood grew darker, "You never saw this on television. Americans saw Chinese tanks running over Chinese students. Americans never saw this. American TV cameras were there when we delivered the aid. All you saw back home was happy faces where the amphibious vehicles stopped and food was thrown over the side, into the crowd. They never showed our vehicles driving through the crowd on the beach. I don't believe anything I see on TV, and I never will again. You don't seem surprised Tony. You don't believe me, do you?"

Tony: "I believe you. The locals' decision to stop the vehicles with their bodies explains why they did not move out of the way. If you stopped your vehicle, the crowd would have swarmed it. I can imagine the sounds you heard, the ones worse than the screams. When you are an old man, you will still hear those sounds in your nightmares. Allow me to offer my condolences, and to thank you for your service to our country." Leo: "That's something I've never heard before." Tony: "What?" Leo: "Thank you for your service to our country." Tony: "I hope it's not the last time you hear it." Leo: "What about television? Do you believe what you see on TV?"

Tony: "No I don't. TV news lost all credibility with me when they booted Walter Cronkite off the air. The lame excuse the network gave was he was too old, the network wanted a younger face to match a younger demographic. Their excuse did not pass the smell test. They replaced a popular journalist; a true professional of unimpeachable integrity, with a "cub reporter who earned his stripes," a copyreader touted for his "in your face" interviewing style. That marks the beginning of tabloid "reporting" masquerading as professional news journalism. It scares me how people can listen to boldfaced lies and believe them simply because they saw it on TV." Leo: "What do you think is going on?"

Tony: "I don't know. Pro-socialism and anti-religion have been media trends. Politically Correct is a more recent development. I don't see what these things add up to." Leo: "I think the government forced them not to show what happened on the beach." Tony: "Maybe, but the media maligns the government and the military on a regular basis. I find it curious they didn't jump on this opportunity with both feet." Leo: "You're right. The media has dumped on the military since Vietnam. That's why I think the government stopped them from showing what happened on the beach in Haiti."

Opening Prayer

During orientation, there were plenty of meetings. Each opened with a prayer. The faculty selected a seminarian to deliver the opening prayer. Tony knew people who could pray extemporaneously before a gathering and do it well. Those people are Baptists or members of a Bible church. Tony did not know any Catholics so gifted. The four days of orientation did nothing to alter that notion. Prayers delivered by new students were long, rambling, and at times incoherent. A few students used this opportunity as their own personal soapbox, which was exquisitely painful to listen to.

Vice Rector: "We want you to deliver the opening prayer for this meeting Tony. Be ready, you have 20 minutes to prepare." Tony was graciously willing to forgo the honor, but the Jesuit insisted, "We want to hear from each of our new students. This gives us a chance to gauge their prayer life." Making small talk, the Vice Rector asked, "Do you speak Latin Tony?" Tony: "Yes Father, I speak fluent Latin. I know two words." Both priests had confused expressions until Tony said, "*Per diem*, –says it all." The Jesuit smiled, "Those words will be useless to you now that you are here Tony."

Tony stood before the assembly, made the sign of the cross, and prayed, "Teach us O Lord: goodness, discipline, and knowledge. Holy Spirit, bless us with your wisdom, your grace and your love. Bless this meeting and its participants, that we may be productive and our labors pleasing to the Father. Amen." When Tony finished he noticed people were just getting comfortable, preparing themselves to fall into a waking coma while sitting upright. He spotted several disappointed frowns when the prayer ended, which signaled the meeting was about to begin. Others showed various degrees of surprise.

After the meeting, the Vice Rector thanked Tony for delivering the opening prayer. Somewhere behind Tony, a student groused, "You were just trying to make the rest of us look bad by delivering such a short prayer." The Jesuit murmured his appreciation of the invocation of the Holy Spirit. Vice Rector: "Tony was concise, covered all the bases, and got right to the point. You cannot ask for more than that." The Vice Rector spoke words of approval but his voice sounded dubious. Another student said, "Less is more, thank you Tony. We can only hope others will follow your good example."

Matthew 6:7 (DRA) [31] And when you are praying, speak not much, as the heathens. For they think that in their much speaking they may be heard.

Cigars

The entire campus: the faculty, theology students, and pre-theology/liberal arts students assembled for Sunday Mass in the church. The campus church was large, cavernous, and classic. Its pipe organ was portable, a custom design built on wheels.

The seminarians gathered for a banquet Sunday evening. Everyone was seated at long tables. Waiters served Delmonico steak *au jus* with mushrooms and baked potato. Tony bought cigars to smoke after dinner. He learned the Friar appreciated a fine cigar and offered him one. The Friar was an affable man. Tony chose him for his spiritual director on Father Nick's advice. Tony and three other students went outside to smoke after the meal. The Friar wished to save his cigar for another time. "It would be inappropriate for me to leave the banquet to smoke."

Word circulated Tony smoked decent cigars. The rumor mill was fast and efficient. The next day, cigar smokers gravitated to Tony. A small group gathered in someone's room. There was conversation and banter. Someone mentioned cigars. The room's owner designated his room the smoking room. Tony fetched five cigars. One non-smoker fled the room after the first cigar was lit. With five men puffing on cigars, visibility was reduced to ten feet. One smoker left, then returned with a fan. He placed it in front of the open window. Smoke and conversation continued until mealtime. The group adjourned to the cafeteria for dinner, leaving the fan running so the room would be habitable again.

After class on Tuesday, the Friar motioned Tony aside. He told Tony smoking in the dorms was a problem. Friar: "Other students complained about the smoke." The Friar suggested if Tony must smoke, he should take it outside. *Fine.* The Friar asked if Tony realized there was a pub in the basement of the dorms. No, he did not. Friar: "It's a place to go to unwind at the end of the day. You can buy soft drinks and there is always free popcorn. You can socialize over popcorn as an alternative to cigars." Tony liked greasy, salty, buttered popcorn. He checked out the pub that evening.

Art, one of the pub's two bartenders, and some stale popcorn were on duty. Art: "It's always dead on Monday, everyone's doing laundry. Since today was the first day of class this week, it is just like a Monday. Come back any other night." Tony: "The Friar told me about the pub. He said you have soft drinks and popcorn, but I see you have beer too." Art: "There's a two beer limit. The bartender cannot serve anyone more than two beers and is supposed to report anyone trying to drink more." It was easy to detect when the pub was open. The smell of fresh popcorn popped in coconut oil wafted up the stairwell to the dorm, and Tony's room was directly across from the stairwell. Tony did not schedule study breaks. If he smelled popcorn and he was bored: study break.

Day Two of Classes

Tony woke during the night. He donned bathrobe and clogs and walked down the corridor to the bathroom. On the way, he saw someone come out of a dorm room two thirds of the way down the hall on the right side. The man quietly pulled the door shut, walked to the end of the hall, and started to unlock the last door on the left. It was David. Tony waved his hand side to side so David could see it in the unlit corridor. David stood in front of the windows at the end of the hall. David leaned forward, squinted, and scowled angrily. He unlocked the door, stepped inside, and forcefully slammed the door shut. BLAM! *I've seen temperamental before. This is not it. This is mental. Mental plus temper, with extra portions.* Tony looked up at the twelve-hour clock near the bathroom entrance: 03:00 hours.

In class that morning the morbidly obese man looked daggers at Tony every chance he got. *Now what?* At lunch, the other four transfer students were sitting at a table together. At orientation meetings, the Vice Rector made a big deal out of making people feel welcome and sitting together in the refectory. He warned seminarians against walking past a partially filled table to sit at a table by themselves. Getting along with all types of people is an important quality for priests to have. Anyone showing insult by not joining the people at a partially filled table raises questions about their formation. There is to be no discrimination of any sort.

The other four transfer students sat at the next table to fill, so Tony brought his tray to their table. The morbidly obese man and David both hissed, "We're having a private conversation here. Go sit at another table." The Vice Rector was seated at an adjacent table and ignored the commotion completely. Tony sat at a table by himself. He watched the obese man and David angrily carry on.

After lunch, Tony went to class. Throughout class, the morbidly obese man and David glared at Tony with anger and malice. By the end of class, Tony suspected the room David exited at three a.m. belonged to the morbidly obese man. Seminarians gathered for Evening Prayer in the theology dorm chapel. After prayer, they went to dinner. The cafeteria served the most incredible food! Tony sat at a table where two other seminarians were already seated. Everyone exchanged cordial greetings but there was no conversation. Tony faced the table where David and the obese man sat. The two were telling an emotional tale frequently interrupted by angrily glaring at Tony.

Soon the entire table was upset. Everyone at the table took turns glancing at Tony with disapproval. The story told at that table soon transferred to another table and another. Upperclassmen Tony had not met were glaring at him from across the room. Tony felt awful. A room full of seminarians suddenly hated him. *Why? Now I appreciate what those pot smokers in college were talking about when they said, "I'm confused."* Tony's attempts to lip-read failed. People were talking and eating. *I should have started lip-reading David and his buddy when I first sat down. Too late now.* Tony noticed not all of the tables were privy to the gossip.

Vice Rector

Thursday morning the Vice Rector happened to see Tony in the corridor after breakfast. He asked Tony how things were going and if he came to look at the campus before applying to go here. Tony: "No." Vice Rector: "Why not?" Tony: "I saw no reason to make such a long drive to look at a bunch of buildings. This is a Pontifical seminary, that's all I needed to know." In short order the Vice Rector asked Tony how he was getting along with David. Tony: "I should expect I get along with him quite well." The priest considered this for a moment, –then asked, "You said "should expect." What is the actual situation?" Tony: "David had an emotional episode. I don't understand why." Vice Rector: "What did you do wrong?" *What did I do wrong? WHAT DID I DO WRONG?*

Tony: "David needed a bathrobe. I had two; I gave him one. He needed a ride to the mall. I gave him a ride. He needed a fingernail file and couldn't find a decent one at the mall. I had two, I gave him one." Vice Rector: "Why didn't you just give him the keys and let him drive himself?" Tony: "I don't give my own mother the keys to my truck, so I'm certainly not going to hand them out to strangers." Vice Rector: "These are not strangers Tony. These are your fellow seminarians." The Vice Rector's voice was laden with accusation, "Why did you give him a ride in the first place?" Tony: "He needed a ride. When I first went to college, I didn't have a car. I remember what it was like begging rides. I gave David a ride to the store. It's called charity. It could also be considered to be compassion."

Vice Rector: "If you wanted to be compassionate you would have given him the keys to drive himself." Tony: "Compassion was the free fingernail file. Handing out the keys to my vehicle would be irresponsible." Vice Rector: "Why do you feel it would be irresponsible?" Tony: "I don't have collision and I have $1,000 deductible. These students are indigent. If any little thing goes wrong, they can't pay for it and my insurance only covers me. It would be irresponsible for me to hand my keys to anyone, knowing they have no insurance coverage." The Vice Rector was aghast. He never heard of such coverage. Vice Rector: "Why would you buy coverage like that?" Tony: "I don't pay for insurance I don't need Father."

Vice Rector: "You mentioned David got emotional. How did that happen?" Tony: "David couldn't find a decent fingernail file. When we got back, I gave him my old one. Instead of saying thank you, he got unconscionably angry." Vice Rector: "There must have been more to it than that. What was the conversation just before he became angry?" Tony: "He asked where I learned about such a file. I told him I dated a woman that was a beautician. She showed me." Vice Rector: "I think he misunderstood your intentions." Tony: "Intentions? Like what?" Vice Rector: "What do you think happened?" Tony: "I have no idea. Some people have a funny way of saying thank you, but this guy was bizarre. I have no life experience to draw from to help me understand his actions. Do you have any insights Father?"

Vice Rector: "He probably had thoughts of dating. You dashed his hopes when you told him you dated a woman." Tony could not have been more shocked if he stuck his finger in a light socket! Vice Rector: "Tony, what do you think? Does this explain what you saw?" Tony reviewed events with a new perspective. Tony: "A 200 pound man acting like a jilted twelve-year-old girl? I guess so." The priest got starchy, "Don't tell me you've never had a man try to pick you up before." Tony drew a blank. Vice Rector: "You probably didn't recognize it, just as you didn't recognize it this time," he said, his voice both accusing and condescending.

The Vice Rector thought for a moment, "There must have been gays where you worked. How is it you don't recognize when they are interested in you?" Tony: "There weren't any where I worked Father." Vice Rector: "That can't be right. EEOC makes sure there are." Tony: "I did contract work for the government. It was illegal for them to be where I worked." The Vice Rector huffed in disbelief, "They could be there and you would never know it." Tony: "Father, I have no experience with adult men acting like a school girl, and I certainly don't expect sexual advances from men, especially in a seminary. Besides, priests are supposed to be celibate."

"Seminarians do not take their vow of celibacy until they are ordained," the testy priest sniped. Tony: "Wait a minute. Are you saying I can bring a girl to my room to squawk the springs and that's not a problem?" Now the Vice Rector's voice was properly authoritative and righteous, "That would definitely be a problem in your formation." With an accusing edge in his voice the priest demanded, "What were you doing in the corridor two nights ago?" Tony: "I had to use the toilet." The Vice Rector demanded, "What were you doing up at three a.m.?" Tony: "I had to take a leak, it happens. Middle-aged men wake up in the middle of the night with an urgent need to urinate. You are my age. You don't need me to explain this to you."

The Vice Rector considered, –then continued, "What did you see as you walked down the corridor?" Tony: "I saw someone come out of a room on the right side. He walked to the end of the hall and unlocked the last door on the left." Vice Rector: "What did you do?" Tony: "I waved." The priest menacingly demanded, "Why did you wave?" Tony: "It was David's room. I waved to David." The priest's voice was vehement and accusing, "Why did you wave to David?" Tony: "Part of our formation is to be congenial, if not cordial. David is in most of my classes." Vice Rector: "You felt you just HAD to wave to him?" Tony: "It was more of a reflex actually." The Vice Rector obsessed at great length over Tony's hand waving.

Tony retorted, "You and I both know who Emily Post is. Certainly I don't have to explain the concept of civility to you." The Vice Rector pondered for a moment before pursuing a different line of questioning. "You saw David come out of a room on the right hand side, walk down the corridor, and unlock his door on the left hand side." Tony: "Yes." Vice Rector: "Whose room did he come out of?" Tony: "I have no idea. It was two thirds of the way down the hall." Vice Rector: "What did you feel he was doing coming out of someone's room at three a.m.?" Tony: "I didn't think about it. I had an urgent need to use the toilet." Vice Rector: "What do you feel now?"

Tony: "I'm not curious." Vice Rector: "He was probably studying with a friend, wouldn't you agree?" Tony: "No. Not possible." Vice Rector: "How can you be sure?" Tony: "After the first day of classes? We haven't been assigned enough work to require studying." The Vice Rector took umbrage. He accused Tony of making light of the academic workload. He asserted the other students were perhaps more diligent in their studies than Tony. Tony was unmoved. Vice Rector: "Just because you are not yet challenged academically does not mean things come so easily for other students as they do for you." Tony: "Ok." Vice Rector: "Ok? What is that supposed to mean?" Tony: "Ok means ok. Is there anything else I can help you with Father?" The priest did not look satisfied but said, "No, that's all."

> Luke 12:3 (DRA) [31] For whatsoever things you have spoken in darkness, shall be published in the light: and that which you have spoken in the ear in the chambers, shall be preached on the housetops.

> Luke 12:3 (KJV) [32] Therefore whatsoever ye have spoken in darkness shall be heard in the light; and that which ye have spoken in the ear in closets shall be proclaimed upon the housetops.

The Friar

Lunch on Thursday was another episode of *The Twilight Zone* (Black & white TV series.). Students Tony did not know were randomly glaring at him in the cafeteria. It was most disquieting. Tony choked down his lunch and went to his next class. Tony was the first to arrive. The instructor was the Friar. Tony's other instructors were priests. When David, the obese man, and Greg arrived for class they rushed up to the Friar. The Friar's visage looked empathetic. After class, the Friar invited Tony to have a discussion with him if he was not rushing off to another class. Tony: "Sure, I have time."

The Friar asked Tony why he was in the hallway at three a.m. Wednesday morning. Tony: "I needed to use the toilet." The Friar said this was suspicious activity. Tony: "I'm a middle aged man. You know as well as I do, middle-aged men wake up in the middle of the night with an urgent need to urinate." Friar: "You have a sink in your room. From now on, piss in the sink, then you won't get yourself in trouble." The Friar unceremoniously gathered his things from the desk and abruptly left. Tony was flabbergasted as he stood alone in the empty classroom.

> Ecclesiasticus 4:26 (DRA) [31] Accept no person against thy own person, nor against thy soul a lie.

> Sirach 4:22 (RSVwA) [43] Do not show partiality, to your own harm, or deference, to your downfall.

Tony went back to his room. He had time to kill before Evening Prayer. *From now on piss in the sink, then you won't get yourself in trouble. What is that? I have to live like a slob so I don't disrupt the nocturnal traffic around here? Queers have the right-of-way? Obviously they do. I sold my farm and machinery on short notice. I sold at a sacrifice. I gave away most of my stuff. The objective was to work for God. In the war between good and evil, I signed up for boot camp for the forces of good. This is a Pontifical seminary. This is supposed to be a holy place filled with holy men. Instead, I find myself inside the gates of hell (Gehenna, not Hades).*

Hell

Tony recalled the nun who taught first grade. One day she read from an old European book that the Church declared contraband. Tony remembered the description of Satan: "–celebrate the sabbat with an orgy. –food, – wine. –have sex the rest of the night. —Satan's large, scale covered phallus–. –anal sex is his favorite kind." At the time, Tony guessed what "phallus" meant. Remembering that now, he considered how scales lie in one direction. The Bible does not describe hell or demons the way the nun's prohibited book did. Her book described demons as profoundly huge and having great strength: overwhelmingly large and powerful. Humans are pitiful in comparison. Demons regard humans with tremendous loathing. They are extremely jealous that humans have a corporeal body and they do not. They detest humans and begrudge their very existence. Demons will spend eternity tormenting humans in hell.

Today Tony remembered that long forgotten day of disquietude and embarrassment. People are able to dismiss the eternal flames of hell: fire that burns forever without consuming. Not possible, cannot be, therefore; does not exist. Since it cannot exist here on earth, it cannot exist in the dimension beyond the veil of death. Sure. The nun's foreboding book seemed most cogent today. Since it exists here in the Pontifical seminary, surely it exists in hell. *("–have sex the rest of the night. –anal sex is his favorite kind.").*

I am not going to be able to endure five years of this place. I want to get in my truck and drive away right now. Problem is; no one is going to believe what I have witnessed here. I looked, I saw, and still I refused to believe what I was seeing. What was David doing in another man's room until three a.m.? Duh. The priests' job is to censure sexual activity in the seminary. Instead, the clergy here sanctions homosexual activity!

How long has this been going on? How extensive is it? So many students in the cafeteria today were angry because two homosexuals were afraid they were found out. Some students were left out of the loop. Coming here was a monumental mistake! I hate when I do that! If I leave now, it will be a complete waste, and a very expensive one. The Bible says to do what is right and do not calculate the cost. What can I do? What should I do? Tony was overwhelmed! *The Catholic*

Church was not like this when I was a kid. This problem has happened during my lifetime. I need to learn what is going on here. I have got to know.

It was time for Evening Prayer. The liberal arts college students (pre-theology), theology students, faculty, and staff celebrated Sunday Mass in the campus church. The theology community gathered weekdays in the theology dorm chapel for midday Mass and Evening Prayer. After weekday Mass, the entire theology community went *en masse* to lunch in the cafeteria. Not everyone gathered in the cafeteria for dinner after Evening Prayer, most notably the faculty and staff. When Tony was in the cafeteria, it was obvious he was a pariah.

Leo

Leo sat with Tony at dinner. Leo usually hung out with Greg, David, and the obese man, but somehow he was an outcast. Leo was chatty and full of questions. He asked what the Friar talked about after class. *None of your business! Someone is on a fact-finding mission.* Tony: "I used the bathroom at three a.m. one night this week. That seemed to cause two people serious emotional problems." Leo: "I know what you mean. Did you know what that was all about?" Tony: "No, but I figured it out after everyone started glaring at me." Leo: "What did the Friar have to say about this?" Tony: "He told me to piss in the sink so I don't get myself in trouble. I have to live like a pig so I don't disturb the nefarious nocturnal activities of homosexuals, otherwise I'm in trouble."

Leo feigned agreement, "That doesn't seem right." It was not difficult to limit this conversation to only one man. *When these same words come back to me, I will be able to track the homosexual grapevine.* It did not take long. The next day before class the Friar whined to Tony about being characterized as a pig for having suggested pissing in the sink. The Friar did not see a problem with using the sink for a urinal. Friar: "All you have to do is run the cold water so it doesn't smell. To save on energy costs, just use cold water." *Why is Leo outcast from the rest of the homosexuals?*

Greg

Between classes Friday, Greg struck up a conversation with Tony. Greg always shunned Tony. Suddenly he's Tony's friend. Greg started bitching about queers, using the word "queers" and complaining. Tony decided to play along. *He pretends to be straight. I will test that pretense.* Greg was being clever to trick Tony into saying something incendiary that he could use against Tony. Tony decided to accommodate him. Tony bitched vociferously about queers. Greg's face flushed, and then turned purple. Tony ended with, "Queers should all go back to hell where they came from." Greg went into a catatonic frenzy! He decided Tony cursed gays, damned them to hell. Tony corrected him, "I noted they are originally from hell.

I'm saying they should go back where they came from."

Fuel

Tony always got up early. At that time of day, he was the only soul alive in the dorm. The shower floors were cold and dry. The water had to run a long time before it was hot. After getting ready, he prayed Morning Prayer in his room since the chapel was locked. Then he read until the cafeteria opened. Tony loved breakfast. When he got to the cafeteria, the first pancakes were just coming off the griddle. Along the side wall was a colossal stainless steel toasting machine. Slices of four types of bread, croissants, Danish, or bagels could be loaded onto a chain drive feed, towed into the heater, and dragged out perfectly browned. The chain-feed and a myriad of heating elements were energized before Tony arrived for breakfast and continued running until lunch.

Such a spectacular and egregious waste of kilowatt-hours! Such profligate opulence! Next to this magnificent appliance was a tray piled high with crisp bacon. Tony started to feed his aggravation with pancakes, pure maple syrup, and copious amounts of bacon. Next to the bacon were sausages the size of a fountain pen. Tony prudently limited himself to only two. This meant nothing since he ate a pile of bacon.

After breakfast Saturday, the Vice Rector made it his business to bump into Tony. Vice Rector: "Tony, I do not want to hear you ever again say homosexuals are fuel for the fires of hell!" Tony marveled at the eloquence. *Fuel for the fires of hell! How clever is that? Much better than what I said to Greg. How adroit. Fuel for the fires of hell!*

> Jude 1:7 (DRA) [31] As Sodom and Gomorrah, and the neighbouring cities, in like manner, having given themselves to fornication, and going after other flesh, were made an example, suffering the punishment of eternal fire.
>
> Jude 1:7 (D-C) [18] Just as Sodom and Gomorrah, and the neighboring cities which like them committed sins of immorally and practised unnatural vice, have been made an example, undergoing the punishment of eternal fire.

Vice Rector: "What do you have against homosexuals?" Tony: "They're not supposed to be here Father." Vice Rector: "They have as much right to be here as you do Tony." Tony: "Homosexuals cannot be ordained priests. They are not supposed to be here." Vice Rector: "The pope said homosexuals can be ordained." Tony smiled. He smiled that cloying, aggravating smile one has when talking to a drunk. The priest was crestfallen, "Really Tony, the pope did say homosexuals can be ordained." Tony: "I know that's not true Father. I have read the Bible. Certainly, the pope has read the Bible. He's the pope. You can't read the Bible from cover to cover and condone ordaining homosexuals." In a very small voice the Vice Rector said, "It's true Tony. He really did say it's ok to ordain homosexuals." Tony: "Yeah, right."

> Osee 4:14 (DRA) [31] I will not visit upon your daughters when they shall commit fornication, and upon your spouses when they shall commit adultery: because themselves conversed with harlots, and offered sacrifice with the effeminate, and the people that doth not understand shall be beaten.
>
> Hosea 4:14 (RSV) [20] I will not punish your daughters when they play the harlot, nor your brides when they commit adultery; for the men themselves go aside with harlots, and sacrifice with cult prostitutes, and a people without understanding shall come to ruin.

> Malachias 2:1, 9 (DRA) [31] 1 And now, O ye priests, this commandment is to you. 9 Therefore have I also made you contemptible, and base before all people, as you have not kept my ways, and have accepted persons in the law.
>
> Malachi 2:1, 9 (RSV-C) [40] 1 "And now, O priests, this command is for you. 9 and so I make you despised and abased before all the people, inasmuch as you have not kept my ways but **have shown partiality in your instruction."** [f]
> [f] Or *law*
> (Bold type added by author.)

> 3 Kings 15:12 (DRA) [31] And he took away the effeminate out of the land, and he removed all the filth of the idols, which his fathers had made.
>
> 1 Kings 15:12 (KJV) [32] And he took away the sodomites out of the land, and removed all the idols that his fathers had made.

Prayer and Contemplation

Tony tried to go to the chapel to pray, but it was locked. Ditto the church. *No off-hours access, no personal prayer in sight of the sanctuary. What kind of seminary is this?* Tony prayed in his room. After he prayed, he considered his situation. He sold his assets and gave away most of his chattels to come here. As much as he hated being here, leaving without knowing the full story was wrong. For his own self, Tony had to know. What about his calling? Why was he here to begin with? How did he ignore or underestimate the warnings? What did God want of him? He knew homosexuals infiltrated the church. He did not know so many had. He never suspected they had already taken over. Tony prayed more.

By Sunday night, Tony decided he would stay as long as he could in order to learn what had happened, what was happening. He knew there was an infiltration problem before he came here. He did not know it was so pervasive. Was it too late to fix the problem? It seemed so, but was there ANY chance? For his own mind and his own soul, Tony needed to know. He had to gather intel. Only then could he accurately assess the situation. Homosexuals were excommunicated from the Church when Tony was a kid. Now they can be ordained priests? Really? We believe God has changed? Tony prayed still more. He decided he must stay and gather intel. *Two spies were sent to the city of Jericho (Josue 2:1).*

Refectory

Monday Tony started sitting in the back of the chapel for efficient egress. After midday Mass, Tony kept a lively pace down the corridor to the cafeteria. He was first in line for lunch. He exchanged pleasantries with the servers and sat at the first table with his back to the serving line. This guaranteed he would not accidentally make eye contact with anyone moving from the serving line to the tables.

During orientation the Vice Rector stressed tables in the refectory were to fill one at a time. Vice Rector: "You do not insult someone by passing their partially filled table and starting a new one. To do so is a formation problem. You are jeopardizing your ability to become a priest by doing so."

Student after student walked past the first table. When everyone was seated for lunch, Tony sat alone at the first table. Even the priests and faculty walked past and sat elsewhere. On the second day of Tony-is-first-in-line-for-lunch, the results were the same. On day three, two priests were a few people back in line from Tony. They commented to Tony about his eagerness to eat lunch. Again, Tony sat alone at the first table. The Jesuit was Tony's formation director. He was the most vocal about Tony's predilection to be first in line. The Jesuit was an elderly man. He was always several people back in line. He made quips and wisecracks to Tony and asked about his fascination with lunch as they wended their way down the lunch line.

Getting to lunch first became a contest of strategy, logistics, and even sprinting down the corridor. This is why the Jesuit was not able to get as close to Tony in line as he wanted. Wednesday of the second week of Tony-is-first-in-line-for-lunch, the Jesuit sat at table one with Tony. His conversation was stilted. The Jesuit heaped consoling reassurances on Tony. The Jesuit was concerned Tony's feelings were hurt. Tony assured his formation director he was fine. The Jesuit saw this was true and was frightened, "What's going on?" Tony: "I'm eating lunch." The Jesuit said something was fishy. He had no idea what, and that bothered him. The Jesuit tried to interrogate Tony.

Tony spoke of how delicious the food was. Tony: "This is not just amazing for institutional food. This is incredible compared to most restaurants. I bet it rates a four-star Michelin rating." Jesuit: "At first I thought you had a problem with gluttony or some kind of food fixation, but that's not it at all. Food is not even a consideration. What is going on here?"

The next day the Jesuit again sat at table one with Tony. Two upperclassmen joined him. The students offered no real conversation with a faculty member at the table. There were some stilted attempts at small talk. The Jesuit was not able to interrogate Tony in the presence of other students.

The Jesuit joined Tony a third day in a row. For the first time, table one was filled. Upperclassmen sat down with the Jesuit and Tony before a second table was approached, just as the Vice Rector decreed during orientation. At the end of the meal, Tony said to the Jesuit, "You've succeeded. You can go back to eating with the faculty. I think we can take the training wheels off now." The Jesuit smiled. This is Friday of week 2 of Tony-is-first-in-line-for-lunch, trial number 10.

On Monday, table one filled up almost immediately after Tony sat down. Tony observed. Attempts at small talk were painfully awkward. By the end of the meal, one of the upperclassmen stated the Jesuit told him to see to it table one was filled before starting a second table. *This is Monday of week four of school. It is the beginning of week three of Tony-is-first-in-line-for-lunch, trial number 11.*

The student with the candor to explain he was ordered to sit at Tony's table, Brian, continued to follow orders. For the next four days, the seminarians sitting at Tony's table were upperclassmen. They established a comfortable level of banter. Toward the end of the meal on Friday, someone's conversation was left hanging with a statement, "–a guy on this side and a guy on that side." Tony quipped, "I don't know who those other two guys are, but the guy in the middle looks like Willie Nelson." At a table of eight men, only Tony, Brian, and one other man laughed. The other five men looked at each other with blank expressions. One of them asked, "What's so funny?" Tony: "I was just being silly. I wasn't really following the conversation." "Why did those guys laugh?" Tony: "They were laughing at me."

Morning Prayer

Tony was exiting the cafeteria when he met the Vice Rector going to breakfast Saturday. It was uncommon to see the Vice Rector this time of the day. Tony: "Good morning Father." Vice Rector: "Good morning Tony. You are up early.

Have trouble sleeping?" Tony: "No Father, I always have breakfast this time of the day. Father, I am amazed at the fine cuisine we have here at the seminary. I've never seen cafeteria food that's on an equal par with the food they serve on cruise ships." Vice Rector: "Refectory. This is a refectory Tony, not a cafeteria. I have never been on a cruise ship, so I am not familiar with cruise ship cuisine." Tony: "I'm surprised to see institutional food of this caliber Father. How is it the seminary maintains such a menu?"

Vice Rector: "Well Tony, I think it is important for student morale. Academic pressures, along with the difficulties and rigors of seminary life; I feel good food is a small comfort we can offer our seminarians. I feel it is important." The Vice Rector scrutinized Tony. "You have been awake. You did not just get up." Tony: "That's right Father." Vice Rector: "Why are you up so early?" Tony: "I always wake up at six o'clock Father." Vice Rector: "Why? Do you set an alarm?" Tony: "I don't use an alarm. I wake up at six because it's time to get up." Vice Rector: "What do you do that time of the day?" Tony: "I use the shower. There is no line that time of the day." Vice Rector: "I imagine not." Tony: "I get ready, pray Morning Prayer, and read until the refectory opens for breakfast." Vice Rector: "How can you pray Morning Prayer? The chapel is supposed to be locked that time of the day."

Tony: "It is locked Father, I checked. I pray in my room." Vice Rector: "You are not required to pray Morning Prayer you know." Tony: "Father, God is especially delighted with predawn prayer. The Old Testament instructs us to seek wisdom, that she is easily found early in the morning. We should gather for Morning Prayer in the chapel the same as we do for Evening Prayer. Why don't we Father?" A dark look enveloped the Vice Rector's face, "Most of the seminarians who have an eight o'clock class can barely make it to class on time. The closest they come to eating breakfast is to grab a bagel as they pass the refectory and eat it on their way to class. They certainly do not shower before class when their first class is at eight o'clock."

Tony: "They need discipline Father. Four years of Morning Prayer, breakfast, and proper preparation for the day will give them the discipline they will need after they are ordained. It's a priest's duty to pray the Office of Readings every morning. If they aren't disciplined to pray Morning Prayer now, there can be no reasonable expectation they will ever pray the Office of Readings Father." "The Office of Readings does not have to be said before dawn," the Vice Rector snapped, "you can catch up later in the day if you have to." Tony: "With no discipline, there is no preparation and no wisdom. We should pray Morning Prayer as a community Father."

The Vice Rector's face showed impatience and anger, "When we have our next monthly meeting for the entire theologate, why don't you address the assembly from the podium and make the suggestion that we all gather for predawn prayer on a daily basis?" The Vice Rector had a slight grin of self-satisfaction. Yes, he was ever so clever! Tony: "Father, we really should gather for Morning Prayer the same as we do for Evening Prayer." The Vice Rector suddenly looked harried, "I am too busy first thing in the morning to be able to hold Morning Prayer every day in the chapel." Tony: "You don't have to be there yourself Father." Vice Rector: "I am busy, I have to go!"

Wisdom 6:15 (DRA) [31] He that awaketh early to seek her, shall not labour: for he shall find her sitting at his door.

Wisdom 7:28 (DRA) [31] For God loveth none but him that dwelleth with wisdom.

Exodus 29:38-39 (DRA) [31] 38 –sacrifice –every day continually. 39 One lamb in the morning and another in the evening.

Jeremias 26:5 (DRA) [31] To give ear to the words of my servants the prophets, whom I sent to you rising up early: and sending, and you have not hearkened:

Psalms 5:4 (DRA) [31] For to thee will I pray: O Lord, in the morning thou shalt hear my voice.

Wisdom 6:18 (DRA) [31] For the beginning of her is the most true desire of discipline.

Wisdom 6:17 (RSVwA) [43] The beginning of wisdom is the most sincere desire for instruction, and concern for instruction is love of her,

Parents Weekend

After four weeks of classes, it was "parents and family weekend." Parents and siblings came to visit their seminarian. In the refectory, a large number of parents and family members glared at Tony with expressions of profound anger and disapproval. Tony estimated that at least half of the theology students had been glaring at him in the lunchroom over the past three weeks. The parents and siblings of those same students did likewise during parent's weekend. Tony was mortified! Tony thought he understood why the students glared at him, but he was baffled that parents and siblings did too. *What is going on?* The Jesuit was the only faculty member who ate lunch in the refectory during parent's weekend.

Foreign Students

The handpicked upperclassman was no longer under the Jesuit's orders to sit at table one. On Monday, Tony found himself seated with foreign students. There were five seminarians from China and two from Uganda. For three days, they sat with Tony at lunch and not one word was spoken. The Chinese students reminded Tony of geese on watch. They swiveled their heads in both directions almost constantly. The Chinese students appeared apoplectic, the Ugandans somewhat cataleptic. Suffice it to say they were on heightened alert. None of these men were taller than five feet six. The majority of men in the room would present as physically imposing by comparison. Tony noticed a calm within himself simply by sitting at the same table with these men. Doubtless, these were holy men.

Thursday one of the Chinese students, John, started talking to Tony with the comfort and ease of old friends. It was small talk at first. Tony asked if they were Taiwanese. No, all five were from the mainland. John: "Why are you not afraid of these people?" Tony: "I think they are afraid of me." John: "Why are they afraid of you?" Tony: "I don't know. I'm not sure." After more small talk John asked, "Are all Americans homosexual?" If it were possible to laugh and cry at the same time, Tony would have.

Tony: "I've never seen this many homosexuals in my life, much less all gathered in one place. The Church used to screen them out. They were not allowed to be seminarians. Obviously, homosexuals have infiltrated the Church. It looks like they have taken control of this facility. Apparently, they are using the mechanisms that once filtered out homosexuals to now filter out straight men." An involuntary shiver wracked John's body. John was the only Chinese seminarian who spoke because his English was the best.

On Friday, John asked Tony why some people get sex change operations. Tony admitted he had no idea. John: "They must be crazy. Having such surgery is crazy." Tony agreed completely.

4 EXECUTIVE ORDER 12968

The Pope's Visit

The topic of conversation in the refectory and between classes this week was the pope's upcoming visit to the States. When the theology community first heard of the pope's visit, everyone assumed he would also "visit us since this is a Pontifical seminary." As the time for his trip neared, it was learned he would not visit the Pontifical College Jeroboam. This news was monumentally disappointing. The administration paid for hotel accommodations and chartered buses to take seminarians to New York City to see the pope during his visit to the United States.

As Tony was leaving the refectory, Juan, an upperclassman asked, "Did you sign up for the bus trip to see the pope?" Tony: "No." Juan: "No! Why not?" Tony: "I don't see myself taking a long bus trip." Juan: was incredulous! "Not even to see the pope?" Tony: "It's an awfully long trip." Juan: "I see, many boring hours on a bus, only to arrive in Sin City. I get it." Tony: "Only to turn around and spend many more boring hours on a bus to go to Blase's." Juan was startled, "You think this place is hell? Why?" Tony: "You know what goes on here." Juan looked confused. *(From the nun's contraband book: "–celebrate the sabbat with an orgy. –food, –have sex the rest of the night–.").*

Tony's classmates obsessed for days over the pope's upcoming visit. They complained, "The pope is snubbing us. He should visit us since this is a Pontifical seminary." Tony's four classmates were worked up over how insulting it was for the pope not to visit the Pontifical Jeroboam. David: "I heard it has been five years since the last time the nuncio was here. His office is in Washington DC. He used to come out here for at least one week every year. He stopped coming here five years ago." The four complained about the nuncio "snubbing us."

David: "Tony, why do you think the nuncio stopped coming to see us?" Tony: "What is his job?" David: "He's the pope's eyes and ears. His job is to make an inspection and report directly to the pope." Tony: "He probably wants to establish culpable deniability." David: "And get in trouble for not doing his job?" Tony: "He will get in some trouble for not doing his job. He will get in a lot more trouble if he comes here and fails to report the problems he finds." David: "There's nothing wrong here for him to find." Tony: "If he thought there was nothing wrong, he'd still be making his visits."

Dinner

Tony was careful to position himself in the back of the chapel for optimum egress after Evening Prayer the same as he did for midday Mass. He did not manage his placement in line for dinner. It took a while for the theology community to realize this. Initially, students became competitive with Tony. Their daily attempts to get to lunch before Tony always failed. Numbers of seminarians kibitzed to occupy all the seats in the rear of the chapel for Mass and for Evening Prayer. Eventually they succeeded at filling the rear half of the chapel for Evening Prayer before Tony arrived. Upon exiting, the crowd kept Tony hemmed in. Their successful efforts after Evening Prayer did not bother Tony, which bothered them.

One afternoon after Evening Prayer, two large upperclassmen, Juan and Brian, physically restrained Tony in the corridor outside the chapel. Each grabbed one of Tony's upper arms and held him until everyone, both clergy and students, passed by and disappeared down the corridor. The three then proceeded to the refectory. They were the last three in line for dinner. Tony: "I admit this was a pretty good goof. Too bad you guys are stuck at the end of the line with me."

There was no line for breakfast, certainly not when Tony was there. Tony made sure he was first in line for lunch after Mass, regardless of everyone's efforts to thwart him. The community assumed Tony wanted to be at the head of the line at dinner. It took weeks before they realized he could not care less, although he was not especially fond of growing old standing in line. The disparity caused confusion, and for a while, confusion was good.

Latin Mass

Tony's turn to serve on the altar in the chapel fell on a feast day. The Vice Rector said Mass in Latin. He barreled through the prayers without pausing for a response. Tony was halfway through the Latin response before the priest stopped in midsentence. He looked down at Tony in amazement. After Tony finished, the priest continued. For the balance of the service, the priest properly paused for the response. After Mass, the other servers were impressed Tony correctly responded in Latin, since they could not. The priest asked, "Tony, why didn't you tell me you knew the responses in Latin?" Tony: "I wasn't sure I remembered all of them." Vice Rector: "When did you learn Latin responses?" Tony: "When I was an altar boy." Vice Rector: "You couldn't have. They changed from Latin to English back in–."

Tony: "Nineteen sixty-five, that's right. I was an altar boy for two years before they changed to English." Vice Rector: "When I signed you up for classes you said you don't speak Latin." Tony: "I don't." The Vice Rector was incredulous. He told Tony his Latin was flawless. Tony: "I don't speak Latin Father. When I was an altar boy, we learned the prayers by imitating sounds. That's all I'm able to do, make the right sounds in the correct order." Vice Rector: "That is all language is." Tony: "I don't understand one word." Vice Rector: "You know the prayers in English, so you know what the Latin translates to." Tony: "I've never consciously made the correlation. When I pray in English, I have understanding. When I pray in Latin, I am repeating sounds I memorized years ago."

Politics

Tony always was a loner, and he was not in a hurry to make friends at the Pontifical Jeroboam. Since he had no close associates to converse with, eavesdropping on conversations around him was spontaneous. Seminarians talked politics between classes, in the refectory, walking through the corridors, wherever. The students doing the talking were Democrats. Tony wondered why they were unhappy with the President. One day the instructor was late for class. Tony's classmates were having a lively discussion. Greg was defending the President. David objected, "He's one of us! He should be doing more for us! What has he done for us so far?"

Greg started listing accomplishments, but David protested, "He should be doing so much more for the gay community than he has. What good is it to have one of our own in the White House if he can't get anything done for us?" "Give him time," Greg reasoned. David: "Give him time? His first term is over next year and look at the polls. He's not going to get reelected!" Tony butted in, "How do you guys know the President is homosexual?" All four of Tony's classmates methodically exchanged blank looks with each of the others. When the process was complete, all four men laughed hysterically!

> President Clinton signed Executive Order 12968 [13] on August 2, 199512, which subjects the U.S. government's security clearance process to EEOC standards [PART 3 – ACCESS ELIGIBILITY STANDARDS, Sec. 3.1. Standards. c)]. [13]
>
> (*Homosexuals can now get security clearances and access classified information*).

Love

The insidious smell of popcorn popping in coconut oil wafted up the stairwell from the pub. Tony's dorm room door directly faced the stairwell door. Fresh popcorn was not popped at the same time each night, but Tony was the first to smell it when it was. Art was the assistant to Jack, the seminarian who managed the pub. Art would pop a batch of corn to eat while he opened the pub. Art and Tony were the only ones in the pub early. Art told Tony, "This place doesn't get busy until around ten. You should come down later, you'll meet more people." Tony: "I'm asleep by ten. I'm only here for the popcorn."

As the school year progressed, a few other patrons sporadically came to the pub early. One evening David came to the pub. He asked Art for a basket of pretzel bits. David: "I don't like popcorn very much." Tony: "I didn't know they had baskets of pretzels." David: "Art puts them out later, when the place fills up." Art interjected, "Tony is asleep by the time we get busy here." David smiled, "You should stay up past your bedtime and meet some of the other students Tony. We have a good time, you should join us."

The next time David saw Tony in the pub he was boisterous. David: "Last night I only got three hours of sleep, and I feel great." David carried on at length. He often repeated how great he felt, "–even though I only got three hours of sleep." David slyly winked, "Remember nights when you got no sleep and you felt great the next day Tony? Remember what you were doing those nights instead of sleeping? Remember what those nights were like before you came here? You won't be able to have nights like that now that you are here, not unless you go to a hotel. A tightwad like you would probably go to a motel," he jeered. David kept repeating a cliché that begs the response, "It must be love," but Tony did not respond. Only Art, Tony, and David were in the pub. David turned it off when more patrons arrived.

One subsequent night in the pub, David bragged to Tony about being in love. He told how happy he was with his love life and laughed at Tony. "You don't have a love life Tony. You can't bring girls in without being seen, and you can't leave campus without raising suspicion." David bragged he could be with his lover every day, "–and I don't have to pay for a hotel room like you would if you were dating a woman." David bragged he could go to his lover's place, and vice versa, without cost or travel time, "There is no commute. It's so convenient." Tony tried to deny David the satisfaction of showing a visceral reaction to his antagonism. Tony's efforts frustrated David.

Gays Bashing

The refectory was never busy on Saturday for dinner. Tony was surprised his four classmates joined him for dinner since there were plenty of empty tables. With an edge in his voice, David asked, "Mind if we join you?" Tony: "Fine." After everyone was seated, the obese man snarled at Tony and demanded, "What is your problem? What is your beef with us?" Tony turned to Leo, "Do you and I have a problem?" "Not at all," Leo smiled. Tony: "David and I don't have a problem. I gave him help when he needed it, yes?" David was embarrassed, "Yes, you were quite generous."

Tony: "Greg played a goof on me. I'm sure he was disappointed to learn I am a man completely devoid of humor." "Or something," Greg snarled. "Ok, what is your beef with me," the obese man demanded? *This is rich. What interaction have I had with this man?* Tony: "Oh, I don't know. One day, for no reason, you started making faces at me." Tony made his best imitation of obese man's angry glare. Leo stifled a snicker. The other three men clenched their jaws. Tony: "Within two days you had over three dozen seminarians angrily glaring at me without provocation." David shamefacedly admitted, "He's right you know."

Tony: "So, you sat here tonight to clear the air. Great. My name is Tony." Silence. Tony: "My name is Tony. Now it's your turn to talk." A malevolent smirk filled the obese man's face, "I know your type. You beat up gays when you were in high school, probably grade school too!" Tony: "No." Obese Man: "Don't lie! I know you did! Don't deny it!" Tony: "Afraid not." Obese Man: "LIAR! I know you did! You're the type of guy who beats up gays!" Tony: "I'm from a small town. They didn't have queers where I come from." Greg chuckled, "What makes you think so? Gays are everywhere."

Tony considered this. Tony: "You're right, there was one. He was the town queer." The other four men laughed! Greg: "If he was the only gay in town, why did he stay? Why didn't he move?" Tony considered, "–Yeah, you're right, that does seem unlikely." The other four laughed again. The obese man told Tony all about his unhappy childhood at great length, and his unhappy adulthood, and somehow Tony was complicit. Obese Man: "And why do you insist on using the word queer instead of gay?" David spoke, "Tony is ten years older than we are. That's the only word people his age use." Since everyone was finished eating, it was time to leave. With a parting shot, the obese man said, "And you smoke smelly cigars too."

Core Board October

Seminarians meet with their core board once a month. Tony's five-member core board included the Jesuit (Tony's priestly formation director. None of Father Nick's recommendations for PFD were available to Tony), the Vice Rector, a Nun, and two civilians (lay people), a man and a woman. The purpose of core board is to determine if the seminarian has a valid calling, the nature and strength of his calling, and his fitness to fulfill it. Divulging details about core board is wrong. Making this process public would help someone who is unfit to game the system.

Allowing men who are unfit to be priests to pass through one of the seminary's finer filters in the formation process would be immoral and irresponsible. It would be destructive to the Church, and subsequently have a deleterious effect on society. Placing someone in a position of trust and moral leadership who is immoral and untrustworthy is certain disaster. For hundreds of years, the Roman Catholic Church has responsibly scrutinized their seminarians to prevent such a travesty from happening.

Tony's first core board brought the term "Spanish Inquisition" to mind. The Vice Rector machine-gunned Tony with personal and probing questions. TV personalities who use an "in your face," "up your nose," confrontational interviewing style pale in comparison. At several junctures, at least three of the other core board members were aghast at the vehemence of the Vice Rector's attack. At one point the Jesuit was unable to contain himself and burst, "It has been years since I've seen an authentic calling from the Old Testament! It certainly is good to see!" Tony was surprised the Jesuit reached this conclusion so soon, and even more surprised that he said so. The Jesuit decided Tony's calling was based on Jeremiah.

The Vice Rector pulled out Tony's resume and started asking biting questions about job changes. Tony answered his questions matter-of-factly. The Vice Rector looked disappointed. Then he asked Tony why he quit the California aircraft factory to be unemployed, and smiled with smug malevolence. Tony: "My boss asked me to put together some financial metrics to measure his accomplishments. That project gave me access to a wide range of financial information. I discovered a group of managers were embezzling one hundred thousand dollars a week from the company."

The Vice Rector accusingly said, "You're a whistleblower!" A couple of the other core board members looked askance at the Vice Rector, who continued hammering at Tony. The Jesuit asked Tony in a calm voice, "Did you report this immediately after you discovered it?" Tony: "No, I was new to the job. I did not want to have to look for another job so soon." Jesuit: "What was the moral thing to do in that situation?" Tony: "Immediately report what I found." Jesuit: "What did you do?" Tony: "I did nothing. I tried to sit on it." The Jesuit's questioning was calm and devoid of emotion. Jesuit: "Why did you do nothing if the right thing to do was to report?"

Tony: "With so much money involved, it wasn't safe to disrupt their criminal activity." Jesuit: "Why didn't you report this to the boss of the managers involved?" Tony: "I didn't investigate who was involved. I was in danger simply by knowing someone was stealing one hundred thousand dollars a week. If I reported this to a manager and he was involved, I would have to worry about being shot instead of just being fired." Jesuit: "How high up do you think this went?"

Tony: "I quit the company once I learned the vice president of our division was involved." At this point, there was full participation from the board members. Jesuit: "What makes you think there would have been gun play?"

Tony: "There was a brisk drug trade inside the factory. At least two managers were involved. I fired a lazy man for his bad attendance. Turns out, he was their bagman. Union gunmen followed me home after work two nights later." Jesuit: "How can you be sure they had a gun?" Tony: "The next day at work, both of my crews were laughing at me. One of my foremen, O'Brian, sauntered up to me smirking. I was angry and demanded, "Everyone on both crews knew gunmen were going to follow me to my house and nobody warned me! Why is that funny?" O'Brian was confounded, "You approached their car knowing they were armed?"

The foreman admitted not everyone on the crew knew. He was amazed I guessed which two men were left out of the loop. O'Brian asked me what happened. I told him I watched the car tailing me. There were only two men, which meant the driver and one gun. "I pulled over, got out of the car, and stomped back toward their car. When I got halfway there, I saw there was a little guy in the back seat. I hate when that happens! Two guns, not one! The foremen said, "You're not afraid of one gun but you're afraid of two?" "Aw, come on O'Brien, even I'm not that good." He asked if I owned any guns, then ran off to warn his union buddies."

The lady core board member asked, "How many guns do you own?" Tony: "At that time I had several. I tried to sell all of my guns before coming here, but I still have my bird gun. There is no decent bird hunting anymore, no one was interested in it." Lady Member: "What is a bird gun?" Tony: "It's the 12-gauge shotgun I use to hunt pheasants." The male lay core board member asked, "You weren't afraid to approach their car, knowing they had a gun?" Tony: "I got scared when I was halfway to their car and saw there was a second gunman." Lay Man: "I hate when that happens. That's you being scared?" Tony: "It was unlikely they would shoot me in bumper-to-bumper traffic."

Vice Rector: "You thought the odds of that changed after seeing the second gunman?" Tony: "Yeah, two guns presented a different dynamic." Vice Rector: "Why were you able to take this in stride?" Tony: "This wasn't the first time I worked in a union environment." Vice Rector: "You think unions are violent?" Tony: "The construction unions certainly are. I've worked with three different construction unions. All three were violent. I was a card-carrying member when I operated a magnet crane in a scrap yard. My coworkers wanted to knife me because I worked too hard." Vice Rector: "Did you slow down?" Tony: "No. I worked at my pace. They disapproved." Vice Rector: "You fired the drug dealer and did not suffer reprisal?" Tony: "I didn't get shot if that's what you mean."

Jesuit: "What did you do about the managers embezzling from the company?" Tony: "I reported them to corporate after I left the company." Vice Rector: "Do you have some kind of personality problem? Are you unable to deal with authority?" Tony: "I hate it when the bad guy gets away. You could call that a personality problem, but I was not hunting these guys. They kept crossing my path. Jobs were hard to come by. I did not want to look for another job. I tried to ignore them, but their guilt and their fear kept driving them under my feet." The Jesuit's voice filled with curiosity, "What brought you to finally take action?"

Tony described [unique sequence] (*not to be shared with the public: must not compromise the integrity of core board*). Tony did not understand why the Vice Rector's face turned pale. With a dour expression the Vice Rector said, "There was a student who had a problem with you the first week of class. What happened there?" Tony: "Same thing; the guy was guilt ridden from being caught doing something he wasn't supposed to. I was completely oblivious. He made a nuisance of himself to me. He was like a piece of chewing gum stuck to the bottom of my shoe." Vice Rector: "What action did you take?" Tony: "None."

Vice Rector: "When did you first realize someone had a problem with you?" Tony: "On Wednesday this guy is glaring at me with an angry expression. I didn't know him, and had no idea what his problem was. I was bewildered by his behavior and subsequently the behavior of others." The Vice Rector admonished Tony for not knowing the obese man's name. Tony: "In a community as small as ours, how is it possible he knows my name and I don't know his? This guy is in at least half of my classes." "Maybe you could be more sociable," the Vice Rector wryly suggested. *Uh-huh.*

Jesuit: "Does this sort of thing happen repeatedly?" Tony: "What sort of thing?" Jesuit: "You witness wrongdoing at work?" Tony: "There is no shortage of evil in the world Father. I see bad things all the time." Vice Rector: "Do you report everything you see?" Tony: "Of course not. That's not possible." Vice Rector: "How do you choose what you report?" Tony: "I don't choose. I only report the wrongdoing that attaches itself to me." Jesuit: "Does that happen very often?" Tony: "It happens often enough I have a name for it." Jesuit: "What do you call it?" Tony: "I call it, "the catch, and the fix."" All five members snickered. The Jesuit asked Tony to explain. Tony: ""The catch:" some guilty guy doesn't just cross my path; he wraps himself around my legs like a lonesome cat seeking attention. This is what I call "the catch.""

Simply by being in the wrong place at the wrong time, I witness wrongdoing." "Or right place at the right time," the Jesuit murmured. Tony: "I don't want to jeopardize my job, so I try to ignore the problem, but the more I ignore it, the more [unique sequence] happens. The more I ignore the problem, the more the bad guys stick to my shoe and the more [unique sequence] happens. Finally, [unique sequence] starts adversely affecting my health. I have no relief until I do the right thing. This is what I call "the fix."" "[The Jesuit's question?]" "[Tony's answer.]" The Jesuit was excited, "This is how God works! This is how the hand of God guides us to do his will! No wonder [the Jesuit's excited remark]! I can see how you would!"

Vice Rector: "Did you file a police report?" Tony: "No, I went to the union hall with some of my information. I sent a copy of my files to corporate headquarters after I left the company. I tried to handle it internally." Vice Rector: "What was the result?" Tony: "Nothing happened." Vice Rector: "Why not?" Tony: "The union's men said the union was implicated in criminal wrongdoing for years by the evidence I had. They were not interested. Corporate could not be bothered. They sent my files back to the ombudsman at the plant. The ombudsman had no interest in doing her job. I wasted my postage." Vice Rector: "Why didn't you go to the civil authorities?"

Tony: "My friend and mentor at work counseled against going to the authorities. I would put myself in jeopardy and accomplish nothing. He said the authorities would never take action against such a large employer, and I would never find a lawyer willing to take on the union. I could have bought shares in the company and filed a shareholder's lawsuit, but I decided not to." Jesuit: "Why not?" Tony: "The fox has its den; the wolf has its lair. California is where evil resides. I did not belong there; I was not like them. The thing for me to do was leave." Jesuit: "You said there was drug trafficking inside the factory. Did you report that?" Tony: "No. I discussed it with one of my foremen. I said at least one manager had to be involved with the drug trade inside our building. He said there were two.

I asked who they were and he panicked. He said, "I can't tell you! If I do, we will lose you as a boss, and we've just gotten you broken in. I know you, that good Catholic upbringing of yours is going to get you in trouble. You always have to do the right thing. If I tell you which managers are involved, you won't be able to help yourself, you'll report them, and that will get you killed! I'm sorry, but I can't tell you. It's for your own good." The FBI periodically monitored the plant, or at least they used to. My foreman strenuously insisted I leave that to the FBI. His counsel was sound. I took his advice. In a way, my experience in California ultimately brought me here."

The Vice Rector asked Tony [a personal question]. Tony answered, "The bird of bad news." The core board members exchanged confused looks. The Vice Rector asked Tony to elaborate. Tony: "The bird of bad news is from Italian folk lore. Legend is: if you are downwind of a screech owl's hoot during the full moon, a family member will die within the month, hence, the bird of bad news." Vice Rector: "Do you believe this works?" Tony: "No." Vice Rector: "Do any of your relatives believe?" Tony: "No, it's just a story from the old country. It's folklore." Vice Rector: "No it's not, it's superstition!" Tony: "Many cultures have their own version of "A little birdie told me." This one is more foreboding than most."

> Job 12:7 (DRA)[31] But ask now the beasts, and they shall teach thee: and the birds of the air, and they shall tell thee.

> Ecclesiastes 10:20 (DRA)[31] –because even the birds of the air will carry thy voice, and he that hath wings will tell what thou hast said.

As Tony explained the bird of bad news, the member's faces showed approval, except for the Vice Rector's. His blanched face betrayed fear. Vice Rector: "Exactly how does this pertain to you?" Tony: "I bear witness to wrongdoing. The bad guys get angry with me for ratting them out." Vice Rector: "So! You're a tattletale!" Tony: "No, I bear witness against evil. There's a difference."

Ecclesiasticus 4:33 (DRA)[31] Strive for justice for thy soul, and even unto death fight for justice, and God will overthrow thy enemies for thee.

Mr. Stevens

Tony's core board meeting was Tuesday evening. Tony's discussion at core board included the words "ratted out." The Vice Rector admonished Tony at core board for not knowing the obese man's name. The next day Tony's classmates made an unusual effort to sit with him at dinner. They asked him questions and made sly comments that highlighted the fact they were privy to the contents of his core board. The other four transfer students were delighted to use the obese man's name again and again and again without prompting. Obese Man was quite proud of the many odious ways he could refer to himself by name.

The obese man was quite inventive with witty wordplay, combining ethnocentric aspersions with perversions. He creatively linked Tony's Italian ancestry to his own perverse predilections by parsing his own last name. The obese man explained his adroit invective in protracted detail, insinuating Tony's ancestry was related to his unsavory penchant. During their dinner conversation, Tony used the words "ratted out." The other four students exchanged knowing smirks. Obese Man coyly asked his pals, "Where have we heard that before?"

Proverbs 18:8 (DRA)[31] The words of the double tongued are as if they were harmless: and they reach even to the inner parts of the bowels. Fear casteth down the slothful: and the souls of the effeminate shall be hungry.

Proverbs 18:8 (RSV)[20] The words of a whisper are like delicious morsels; they go down into the inner parts of the body.

Proverbs 18:8 (WYC)[29] The words of a double-tongued man be as simple; and they come unto the inner things of the womb. Dread casteth down a slow man; forsooth the souls of men turned into women's condition shall have hunger. (A gossip's words be tasty; and they go down into the innermost parts. Fear casteth down the lazy; and those who be timid shall have hunger.)

On the website, <Biblegateway.com>,[31] thirty English translations are available for Proverbs 18:8. Only the DRA[31] and WYC[29] translations contain the second half of this passage.

Priestly Formation Director

Wednesday night Tony was scheduled to meet with his formation director (PFD) for the first time. The Jesuit was happy to see Tony. He repeated his joy at seeing a genuine calling from the Old Testament, especially one from Jeremiah. Tony thought it was inappropriate for the Jesuit to decide so soon his calling was genuine, much less share those thoughts with Tony.

Jesuit: "I was surprised how intense the questioning got at your core board. Usually the first core board is a simple introduction and background information. The depth and intensity with which you were questioned usually takes place the junior year. Since you are a transfer student, I would have expected that line of questioning not to take place for another three years. A couple of gems you were hit with are reserved for seniors, just before they are ready to graduate. I do not understand why you were given such an intense interview on your first core board. I hope this doesn't scare you off."

Tony: "If I'm not supposed to be here, I want to know that now, not later Father. I find it reassuring you and the Vice Rector have concluded my calling is genuine." Jesuit: "Where do you get the idea the Vice Rector has reached such a conclusion?" Tony: "His facial expressions gave him away Father." Jesuit: "That doesn't square with what he had to say to me." *No doubt.* The Jesuit outlined the format and purpose of formation meetings. He made small talk. He asked Tony a couple of questions about his fascination with being first in line for lunch. Tony explained (*cover story*) he was an early riser and ate breakfast early, so by lunchtime he was famished.

The Jesuit said the Vice Rector mentioned Tony had a problem with another student during the first week of school and asked Tony to elaborate. Tony: "I woke up in the middle of the night to use the toilet. On my way to the bathroom, I saw David and waved. The next day Mr. Stevens (the obese man) was glaring at me." Jesuit: "What did the Vice Rector say about this?" Tony: "He was upset that I was in the corridor at three a.m. He said David was probably studying with a friend."

The Jesuit noted guests appeared uncomfortable around Tony in the refectory during parent's weekend and asked Tony what he did to cause this. "It's most unusual for parents to have a negative reaction to a particular seminarian. This is a serious cause for concern." Tony: "It appears to be related to my seeing David in the hall at three a.m." The Jesuit stated that was not logical. "Why would that make parents uncomfortable around you?" Tony: "If the parents know their son is homosexual, they would see me as a threat the same as their son does."

The Jesuit scoffed at the idea. He grilled Tony until Tony estimated half of the students are homosexuals. The Jesuit chuckled, "You are paranoid Tony. There is no homosexual activity here. You should take a picture the next time you see homosexual activity in the showers so you'll have proof." The Jesuit chuckled some more. *Such a comedian should work the Catskills. The showers are private stalls, similar to toilet stalls.* Tony: "I don't own a camera Father." Jesuit: "You can buy something cheap like an Instamatic ® –." The priest appeared to be proud of how clever and amusing he was.

The Jesuit asked Tony about his prayer habits, to recount the circumstances that led up to his coming to the seminary, and who his mentor is. Tony: "Father Nick. He graduated from here two years ago." Jesuit: "I remember Father Nick. Did you see the campus before choosing the Pontifical Jeroboam?" Tony: "No. It was a long drive for no reason. Father Nick's recommendation was all I needed." Jesuit: "When do you meet with your counselor?" Tony: "I don't meet with a counselor." Jesuit: "All seminarians meet with a counselor once a month, it's a part of their formation. I want you to make an appointment and see a counselor before our next meeting. You and I will continue to meet here in my office the first Wednesday of the month at seven p.m."

Counselor? That doesn't sound right. He sends me to the counselor, but it appears I went voluntarily. The counselor decides I'm homophobic, which is the excuse they use to ship me off to Siberia (bad formation, reason for expulsion). What can I do but play along?

Steers

The next day the four classmates joined Tony at dinner. "Texas? I heard they only have two things in Texas: steers and queers, and I don't see no horns," David exclaimed! The four classmates laughed! Greg murmured, "Any." Greg asked, "Where do you come from?" David answered, "Texas." All four chimed in, "There's only two things in Texas: steers and queers, and I don't see any horns!" All four laughed again! The four looked at Tony for a reaction. Tony was confused. "What do you think Tony?" They heckled Tony until he admitted, "I don't get it."

All four indicated David was from Texas. "And I don't see any horns," David grinned. The four pressed Tony for his reaction. Tony: "I've never been to Texas." They continued to press Tony for a reaction. Tony: "Even the Germans make fun of Texans. In Germany, their imitations were hilarious! I laughed so hard I cried. I don't know what else to tell you." David hated it. Greg growled, "What about what David said?" Tony: "Is he really from Texas?" They all agreed he was. Tony: "Well then, I'll have to take his word for it because I've never been to Texas." All four hated it!

Leo hung back so he could walk back to the dorm with Tony. He quizzed Tony on what the Germans had to say about Texans. Tony: "It wasn't so much what they said, but the fact they said it. The concept of people living half way around the world accurately imitating a Texas drawl killed me, especially after drinking three or four liters of German beer." Leo: "How were they able to do it?" Tony: "They were making fun of American tourists. They said Americans treat Europe like it is their own full-scale Disney attraction, and they hate it. They had plenty of caustic and painfully accurate observations of American tourists. What they had to say about American's fixation with toilet paper was absolutely brutal."

Pedophiles

Tony's four classmates conversed as they journeyed through each day. Tony's proximity to them as he attended the same classes gave him witness to their discussions. A recent item in the news sparked much lively and heated discussion among the four classmates. A Roman Catholic priest was accused of child molestation. Soon enough, other victims came forward, and the topic *de jour* was of a pedophile priest. TV's talking heads speculated the accusers would sue the priest or even the Catholic Church. The classmates discussed this topic on a daily basis at length and *ad nauseam*. Their early discussions speculated on the avarice of greedy and litigious victims.

Their deliberations migrated to pedophiles. The more they dwelled on the subject, the more disdain, disgust, and hatred they conveyed. After hearing their expressed view of pedophiles several times over, Tony butted into their conversation, "How come you guys don't like pedophiles?" David snapped, "Pedophiles are perverts! They're disgusting!" "Pedophiles are homosexuals just like you guys," Tony purported. David: "No they're NOT! They're perverts! They're sick and twisted!" "Male priest, altar boy, that's homosexual," Tony asserted.

Greg vehemently objected, "We are consenting adults! We are normal! Haven't you ever heard of the concept of consenting adults? We are normal. Pedophiles are perverts! They have sex with children, they're sick! They're nothing like us!" "It's still homosexual activity," Tony maintained. Mr. Stevens: "Pedophiles are perverts! They are nothing like us!" *What?*

The four classmates discussed their hatred and loathing of pedophile priests for weeks. In a subsequent discussion Mr. Stevens said, "They are making things bad for us. I wish there was something that could be done about it. They should never have been made priests. They have no business being priests." *Yeah, right? No irony here.*

Tony's Vocation Director

After Evening Prayer, Tony's classmates were animated. As they were walking down the corridor, they had a lively exchange, sharing some fresh gossip, and they were delighted. In the refectory, Greg called Tony over to their table. David and Mr. Stevens could barely contain themselves. David blurted, "We understand your vocation director is coming to see you next week. What did you do? Why is he making a special trip to see you?" Mr. Stevens grinned malevolently, "You must be in big trouble for your vocation director to make such a long drive. Why didn't he just call you? If he wants to see you in person, it must be bad news. Especially so soon! You have barely been here two months! Do you think he's going to revoke your diocese's sponsorship?"

Tony: "What makes you think my vocation director is coming to see me? I haven't heard anything." Leo arrived after Tony and sat at a different table. Mr. Stevens and David took turns heckling Tony. Greg mostly smiled and smirked. Tony: "How do you guys know my diocese is sending someone here when I don't?" No one offered an answer. All three grinned and leered. These three men and Tony were from four different states. There was no obvious explanation for their knowledge of Tony's pending visit. The three relentlessly taunted and badgered Tony. His lack of reaction disappointed them. Finally, Greg said to Tony, "This is a serious matter. Why aren't you concerned?"

Tony: "My conscience is clear. I haven't been having sex with other seminarians." David and Greg were incensed! Mr. Stevens immediately stood up, grabbed his tray, and stormed off. He had only eaten half of his meal. When he got to the exit he paused, then found another table so he could finish eating. David and Greg continued to eat. A minute later, they exchanged glances, nodded, and slowly stood up. They took their trays to another table. Tony had the table to himself. He enjoyed the rest of his meal in peace. He celebrated by getting a second dessert.

Before class the next day, Leo said to Tony, "I saw what those guys were doing to you at dinner. I didn't sit with you guys because I didn't want to be a part of it. What did you say that made them get up from the table?" Tony: "I told them "up your nose."" Leo: "You said more than that judging from the way (Mr. Stevens) left the table. You must have been so insulted when he did that." "Please," Tony deadpanned. Leo: "That must have hurt your feelings." Tony: "He was gone. Good riddance." Leo looked disappointed, "So what did you say to those guys exactly?" Tony: "I said: up your nose with a rubber hose and twice as far with a chocolate bar." Leo: "I doubt you said anything like that." Tony: "Fine. Ask them, see what they say."

Halloween in the Pub

The smell of fresh popcorn beckoned Tony to the pub Saturday in the middle of the afternoon. *What?* Tony went down the two flights of stairs to investigate. The pub was busy! Twenty percent of the patrons were wearing costumes. A small framed, dark haired, smiling man rushed up to Tony. He thrust his hand out to shake hands and introduced himself. "I'm Javier. It's good to finally meet you Tony. I've had trouble finding you. I'm sorry it has taken so long for us to meet." The man was small in stature, but Tony found his manic introduction off-putting. Tony: "Why have you been looking for me?" Javier: "I'm having girlfriend problems, I need advice. There's no one else I can go to." Tony: "What makes you think you can trust my advice?"

Javier: "I know your friend Jake. He's from your diocese. He used to go here." Tony: "I don't know anyone named Jake." Javier smiled, "Jake knows you. He met you at the seminarian meeting in your diocese. He wanted to talk to you, but you blew him off." Tony: "That was Jake?" Javier: "Now you remember?" Tony: "Yes." Javier: "Why didn't you talk to Jake when he saw you?" Tony: "I was in a room full of people that made my skin crawl. At the time I didn't know why they gave me the heebie-jeebies." Javier roared with laughter! "But you do now!" Tony: "Oh yeah." Javier: "So why wouldn't you talk to Jake?" Tony: "I was in a room full of strange characters. My skin was crawling. Some guy comes running up to me. He's all over me, and he immediately wants to get me alone for a private conversation. It was incredibly off-putting."

Javier was stunned, "What were you thinking when I came running up to you just now?" Tony: "The same thing I thought when Jake did it. I wished I had pepper spray." Javier was aghast! "You can't tell I'm normal? You don't trust me?" Tony: "After my third day here I stopped trusting gravity. When I was in college the pot smokers would say, "Hey man, I'm confused." I did not understand then, but I do now. I'm con-FUSED!" Javier laughed excessively, as a man emotionally distressed. He was laughing at Tony, he was laughing with Tony, and he was laughing at himself. Javier: "Con-FUSED! There's an understatement!"

Tony looked around the pub. "Why is the pub busy Saturday afternoon? And why are people wearing costumes?" Javier: "Halloween. Where have you been?" Tony: "Halloween is not until Tuesday." Javier: "Gays are big on Halloween. They will be celebrating all weekend. One night after class just doesn't cut it." Javier wanted to discuss his girlfriend situation. Tony: "What year are you in the seminary?" "Javier: Junior year." Tony: "A seminarian with a girlfriend. Yeah, I can see how that would be a problem. Tell me about her."

Javier: "I met her in the parish where I did my internship last summer. She is so nice. I love her. I love her a lot. She's beautiful, she works hard, and she is so smart! She doesn't want me to be a priest. She asked me to stay with her instead of going back to school." Tony: "Do you want to be a priest and have a girlfriend on the sly?" Javier hemmed and hawed. Tony: "Javier, you have to choose. You have to decide which one." Javier told Tony they were very much in love. They had to be secretive because he is a seminarian. She hated that. She wanted him to quit the seminary so they could be together.

Tony: "You can't be a priest and have a woman on the side. You know better than that, right?" Javier told Tony how wonderful she is, and how very much in love they are. Javier painted a beautiful portrait of love and romance, except for the part about Javier being a seminarian. Tony: "Why did you leave her and return to the seminary if you love her so much?" Javier: "I have always wanted to be a priest. I still want to be a priest."

Tony saw a student dressed as a Star Trek character. Tony: "I always liked Star Trek." Javier: "What do you think about his costume?" Tony: "I actually like that one." Javier: "He's a grown man dressed like a TV character. Don't you think that's kind of creepy?" Tony: "I think almost everyone in this room is creepy. Seeing a familiar face wearing a Starfleet uniform is comforting. Maybe someday we will discover a planet that actually has intelligent life. Beam me up Scotty, no intelligent life down here." Javier: "You haven't finished your first beer. You can't be drunk." Tony: "I'm sober. I realize my intelligent life fantasy is never going to happen. When I saw the Commander over there, reality was suspended for a couple of seconds." Javier: "I never liked that show and I still don't." Tony: "I don't like the one we're watching in Sensurround® right now."

Javier: "Jake is ex-military. He was a student here last year. He reported homosexual activity to the administration. The priests told him there is no homosexual activity here at the Pontifical Jeroboam. They sent him to see a counselor. There are two counselors: an old man and a woman. He went to the old man. The old man diagnosed him as homophobic. All the priests and the counselor told Jake he was imagining things. Jake described pranks the other students played on him. He reported the pranksters to the administration.

Several witnesses came forward and testified these things never happened. Other witnesses testified the people supposedly involved were somewhere else, and witnesses who saw Jake at the time these things allegedly happened stated no such thing ever occurred. Pretty soon, Jake started to doubt himself. "Why would all these priests lie? Why would so many seminarians bear false witness?" Jake started drinking. He intended to return this fall, but at the last minute, he quit. Right now, he is staying with his sister. All he does is drink. He's a total wreck. Jake is in no condition to hold a job, much less find one. He's lucky his sister is willing to put him up at her place."

Tony: "My formation director told me to make an appointment with a counselor before our next session. He said all seminarians meet with a counselor once a month." Javier: "That's bull! If your PFD sent you to see a counselor, it means he thinks you have a problem. Don't do it! Seeing a counselor is voluntary." Tony: "Looks like my PFD volunteered me. I'm sure I'll have a problem with my formation if I don't play along." Javier: "At least don't go to the old man. We already know for sure he cannot be trusted. If you're going to go, sign up with the woman." Tony: "I'm sure she's paid to do the same job the old man does." Javier: "What do you think their job is?" Tony: "Protect the homosexuals and get rid of the straights."

Javier chuckled, "You and Jake are so much alike. Neither one of you trusts gays. You must have been in the military. The military doesn't trust gays, isn't that right?" Tony: "On my first job out of college I worked with the military as a civilian contractor. The military is vigilant about security. Yes, homosexuals are a security risk." Javier: "That's ridiculous. I have friends here that are gay and I trust them. Why does the military have a problem trusting gays?" Tony: "Our military's history is older than our country. Their security measures are based on long experience. When I first started working with the military I thought some of their practices were curious, but over time I saw their security measures were necessary."

Javier: "What kind of work did you do for the military?" Tony: "I fixed electronic equipment." Javier: "Come on, you must have done more than that." Tony: "I'm an electrical engineer. I did a tech's job. I repaired circuit boards. If that wasn't boring enough, our duties were station-keeping." Javier: "What is station-keeping?" Tony: "That's what firemen do. They have to be body present at the fire station in case there's a fire." Javier: "That seems like a waste, paying men to stand around doing nothing." Tony: "It's the same for firemen. Would you feel better if firemen were fighting fires eight hours a day every day? The world is better off if firemen are playing cards in the firehouse instead of "earning their pay" fighting five alarm fires every day, trust me."

Javier asked Tony what the deal was with his being in such a hurry to get to the refectory after Mass. Tony: "(*cover story*) I'm from New York State. New Yorkers hate standing in line." Javier: "Everybody talks about it. They think there is something wrong with you. Maybe that's why your formation director is sending you to see a counselor." Tony: "Take a number? I don't think so." Javier: "You realize being first in line every day isn't normal." Tony: "Look around this room right now and tell me all about being normal."

Javier laughed. He told Tony about friends he made at the seminary. He talked about hanging out with these guys and offered to introduce Tony to some of them. Tony: "When Jake told you about the pranks these people pulled, did you believe him?" Javier: "At first I believed him, but then he started doubting himself." Tony: "Wonder if he was right? Wonder if those people really did pull pranks on him and their buddies lied about it?" Javier: "You're starting to sound as paranoid as Jake." Tony: "You said Jake reported homosexual activity to the administration. The administration told Jake there is no homosexual activity. Was Jake wrong?" Javier: "I haven't seen any gay activity."

Javier remembered Tony gave him the brush off a week earlier. "I came out of my room. I was locking my door when I saw you. I waved and said, "Wait up," but you ignored me. What was that about?" Tony: "Whose room is next to yours on the east side?" Javier: "Which side is east?" Tony: "The east end of the corridor has windows. My room is at the west end." Javier named the man living next door. It was Mr. Stevens.

Tony: "Before the second day of class I woke up in the middle of the night to use the toilet. I was in the hall when I saw a man come out of one room, walk down the hall, and go into his own room." Javier: "Who did you see?" Tony: "David." Javier: "How do you know it was David?" Tony: "He unlocked the last door on the left and entered the room." Javier: "Did he see you?" Tony: "Yes, I waved to him." Javier: "Oh no! You shouldn't have done that!" Tony: "Ya think?" Javier: "What room did he come out of?" Tony: "The location was about where your room is; two thirds of the way down the hall on the right. The next day Mr. Stevens was looking daggers at me, so was David. I didn't know why those men were angry at me." Javier blanched, "The day you saw me lock my door you thought it was my room?" Tony: "Either yours or the one next to it, yes." Javier: "That's why when I asked you to wait for me, you took off?" Tony: "Yes, that's why."

Javier was rattled. "What time did David come out of that room?" Tony: "Three o'clock in the morning." Javier: "Did you report it to the Vice Rector?" Tony: "No, but somebody did. The next day the Vice Rector interrogated me for being in the corridor at three a.m. After he finished grilling me, he said David must have been studying with a friend. That morning was going to be the second day of class." Javier: "That guy doesn't waste his time studying." Tony: "The Vice Rector was cross with me for walking down the hall to use the toilet in the middle of the night. When I had a class with the Friar, he told me to piss in the sink so I don't get myself in trouble." Javier: "Did he really tell you to piss in the sink?" Tony: "His words exactly: "Piss in the sink so you don't get yourself in trouble.""

Javier's eyes widened, "Maybe Jake was right. The guy next door to me has people coming in and out of his room all the time. I wondered what was going on. How did you figure it out?" Tony: "I didn't. If those two clowns behaved themselves, I would have been none the wiser. Instead, they acted like nasty little children. Within three days, they had half the student population glaring at me, and the Vice Rector and the Friar were no better. I didn't have to figure it out, it got dumped on me." Javier: "Half of all the students?" Tony: "Easy, at least half." Javier: "Oh no! Jake was right! You should have talked to Jake when he saw you." Tony: "I see that now. He would have warned me off. I wish I talked to him."

Javier: "No, I mean he might still be here now if you talked to him." Tony: "No, I would have known better than to come here in the first place." Javier: "You and Jake don't trust gays. That's funny. I get along with them just fine. In fact, I've made friends with some of them." Tony: "The guy who lives next to you, David, and two other guys talk about getting someone thrown out. They kibitz and plan. After two weeks of scheming, they took their lies to the Rector. Their lies were inadequate reasons to give this seminarian the boot. The Rector explained why their testimony was insufficient. Currently, they are working on their third iteration to get rid of him." Javier: "Who is it they're trying to get thrown out?" Tony: "Some seminarian with a girlfriend."

The blood drained from Javier's face, "They were talking about me! The guy next door to me was there when I told my friend about my girlfriend! What else did they say?" Tony: "They described a problem this guy had drinking alcohol. They were brainstorming, trying to use that to concoct a scheme to get this seminarian expelled. I sat at the table next to them. I got sick of listening to them carry on. I told them maybe he is allergic to alcohol." Javier: "What did they say to that?" Tony: "They got excited. They decided maybe he cannot be ordained if he's not able to drink wine." Javier: "That fat guy wasn't there when I was drinking. I was drinking with someone else.

I had been fasting. I did not eat food for two days, and then my friend came to visit and brought a sweet alcoholic drink. It had a strange taste and high alcohol content." Tony: "I'm guessing he is homosexual and is not really your friend." Javier: "This guy is my friend. I trust him. It's you and Jake who don't trust gays." Tony: "Did your friend know you had been fasting?" Javier: "Yes, he did." Tony: "Blonde hair, blue eyes, intelligent, from Minnesota?" Javier: "Yes, that's him." Tony: "He's one of the four guys trying to get a seminarian expelled. By now, they have gone to the Rector to find out if an alcohol allergy is enough to get someone expelled. I think they take turns going to the Rector instead of the same one going back each time."

Javier: "It doesn't matter. I'm not allergic to alcohol." Tony: "You can't trust that guy. He is not your friend." Javier: "Earlier you mentioned the Friar. Why do you call him a friar?" Tony: "First of all, he's a Franciscan. Second, he looks like Friar Tuck. The robe, he's portly, even his haircut looks like Friar Tuck's." Javier wore Tony out with a detailed and pedantic explanation of why the man was actually a brother and not a friar. After hearing the full explanation, Tony concluded Franciscan Brothers work in the community and Franciscan Friars live in a monastery. *We will continue to call him the Friar.*

Talking politics, Javier called himself a Democrat. Tony: "You're Catholic, how can you be a Democrat?" Javier did not understand why the two should be mutually exclusive. Tony: "During the 1930s the public developed a strong aversion to the American Communist Party. At some point, the Democrats welcomed the Communists into their party with open arms. Communists are atheists. In the 1980s the Democrats welcomed homosexuals with open arms." Javier: "What's wrong with that?" Tony: "Why would God-fearing souls vote for godless and perverse leaders?" Javier: "Democrats include more than those two groups." Tony: "I'm talking about the politicians, not the voters. Right now, the party is split into two factions.

The party's history explains the two groups of politicians. The ones that call themselves liberals are a blend of faux European socialists and communists. No one uses it, but I prefer the term Marxists. Their voters include the unions and the New Deal folks. Homosexuals are a more recent political force. The homosexual manifesto [10] was published in a gay newspaper and was later read into the Congressional Record in 1987. Homosexuals promised to destroy this country." Javier: "Have you read this manifesto?" Tony: "No, it was described to me." Javier laughed it off. He recounted the popular view of Senator Joe McCarthy in the 1950s and scoffed, "–and what makes you think Democrats are either Marxists or homosexuals?"

For an opposing view of Senator Joseph McCarthy go to: <http://www.senatormccarthy.com/>. [23]

Tony: "The House and Senate are both controlled by Democrats. The President is Democrat, but he cannot pass his pet legislation. Democrats can do whatever they want without the Republicans, yet Clinton's legislation languishes. The President has started issuing Executive Orders [13] to push his pet projects through. The party is clearly split in two. I contend there are Marxist politicians who actually believe large central government is good (for them), and there are homosexual politicians who want to destroy society. Their conflicting goals explain the deadlock." Javier: "I agree the party is split in two, but I disagree with your description of the split." Tony: "Ok. When you can describe the two groups, tell me, because I'm curious to know."

Javier stated Social Security is a popular program. He challenged Tony to find fault with it. Tony: "Ok, the first beneficiaries of Social Security are the depression era generation. They have always worked hard and saved their money. They have no need of Social Security. Go to any casino on the fifteenth and thirtieth of the month and watch busloads of retirees cash their Social Security checks and play until the money is gone. That's some investment of public funds." Javier chuckled and shrugged it off as a small percentage of the total number of retirees.

Tony: "I had a next door neighbor who was ninety-two years old. His wife of fifty-seven years died. He was alone. He met a widow. They ended up moving in together. The grandchildren on both sides went crazy. "Grandma and grandpa are shacking up!" My neighbor said, "We were old and ready to die. Why should we get married? But the grandchildren were driving us nuts, so we gave in and got married. We were collecting two Social Security checks. When we got married we had to give up one of our checks, but we did it to appease our grandchildren." My neighbor smiled, "We've been married for eleven years now." Social Security pays a substantial cash incentive for older couples to live in sin, and you don't see a problem with that?"

Javier: "I didn't know that." Tony: "Nobody does. When the government is giving away free money, no one asks questions. That's the problem." Javier: "Well, they should only have one check. They were gaming the system. Their grandchildren kept them honest." Tony: "The system is designed to induce immoral behaviors, including fraud. People hide assets or transfer assets to their children to maximize government benefits. I'm not suggesting there are minor flaws in the design of the system. I'm saying the system is evil by design." Javier challenged Tony, "To what end?" Tony: "Haven't you ever read the works of Niccolò Machiavelli?[27] At the very least, the Democrats are using public money to buy votes.

Machiavelli[27] warns against flagrant largess of public funds because it will inevitably cause the destruction of the Republic. Social Security is a fiscal time bomb." Javier vehemently disagreed, "The Germans invented the Social Security type retirement. They aren't making plans to self-destruct." *Is our system identical to theirs? Not likely. Karl Marx is German but is buried in England. His ideas made him a pariah on the continent.* Javier: "All other industrialized nations have a much greater degree of socialism than the United States. The U.S. needs to catch up with the times." Javier liked the Democratic Party because it is similar to his favorite political party back home. He challenged Tony to produce facts and numbers to prove his point.

Tony: "Forbes magazine's November 14, 1988 issue features an article titled: *Consuming Our Children?.*[08] It has all the facts and numbers you could want. The article describes in detail how government largess is robbing the grandchildren's future to pay for Social Security and Medicare. No one wants to admit it's a government run Ponzi scheme." Javier: "You pay into Social Security and Medicare your whole life. It's insurance, it's your money." Tony: "That's how they advertise it, but that's clearly not true. You want numbers, read the article. Learn about intergenerational theft on a massive scale. Learn how retirees are robbing their grandchildren's future."

Javier changed the subject. "I was listening to music. One of the songs contained the line, "The New York Times said God is dead." What was that about? Did that really happen?" Tony: "Yes, the New York Times had an article that contained the words "God is dead" in the title during the 1960s." Javier: "Why did they do that?" Tony: "I was a kid. I didn't read the article, I don't know. The sad thing is Christians in this country are not zealous for God. The forces of evil are zealous and ambitious to oppose God. There is no longer a war between good and evil. The good guys stopped holding up their end of the flight."

"God is Dead" Debate Widens, [09] *New York Times* January 9, 1966, E7.

"God is Dead" Doctrine Losing Ground to "Theology of Hope," [14] *New York Times* March 24, 1968, 1, 75.

"God is Dead" Theme Assailed by the Pope, [33] *New York Times* January 7, 1970, 3.

April 8, 1966: *Time* magazine's cover story was, "Is God Dead?" [12]. The article featured some of the ideas (God is dead) of Dr. William Hamilton, who was a tenured professor of church history at Colgate-Rochester Divinity School when the article was published.

"God is dead," [28] Nietzsche, Friedrich. *The Gay Science*, section 125, tr. Walter Kaufmann.

Noises

The pub was full well beyond safe occupant capacity when Tony left. The refectory was deserted. After dinner, Tony returned to his room. He read, prayed, and went to bed the same as he did every night. On this night, sleep did not come soon enough. Tony could hear the commotion in the next room, followed by the hushed voices of two men. Tony lay in bed trying to sleep. The whispering finally stopped. Tony drifted off to sleep but was awakened by new sounds. He was confused. He listened to the unusual noises. *What?* It was a human voice, although it sounded like a pigeon cooing. Tony was not curious why a man sounded like a pigeon cooing. He pulled the pillow over his head to muffle the noise.

The entire campus went to Sunday Mass in the campus church. After Mass, the refectory was filled to capacity with students only. The complete lack of faculty and staff was atypical. The crowd was exuberant and conversant. The term "gay" always seemed a misnomer to Tony, but on this day, in the refectory, it was accurate. There were a few men who looked either bored or isolated. If there were any straight men to be found on campus, these were promising candidates. Tony was exiting the refectory when he passed Javier going in. Javier: "You should've waited for me. We could've eaten together." Tony: "I wondered why I didn't see you." Javier: "The place is packed. Will I be able to find a seat?" Tony: "I just left an opening at table three."

5 MAD DOG

Trouble Sleeping

Javier stopped by Tony's room after lunch. "Could you believe how obnoxious it was in the refectory today? Do you think we act that way after we spend time with our girlfriend?" Tony: "If you mean raucous, loud, and excessively happy, I'm sure we do." Javier: "We certainly aren't that obnoxious." Tony: "We must be cloying to anyone who hasn't had a recent date when we act that way." Javier: "I doubt you and I act like that." Tony: "All the administrators were careful to not be there today." Javier: "I noticed. You look tired. Have trouble sleeping?" Tony: "Yeah. The guy who lives next door to you was with the guy next door to me starting yesterday afternoon. My neighbor is quite; your neighbor, not so much."

Javier laughed, "I'm starting to really hate that guy. He always has people in his room and he's always so noisy. He talks loud and he makes loud noises. Last night was the first decent sleep I've had in weeks. Have you talked to him yet?" Tony: "All four of my classmates graced my dinner table with their presence so he could clear the air." Javier: "What did he say?" Tony: "He said I'm the type of guy that beats up gays. He decided I beat up gays when I was in grade school and high school." Javier: "Did you?" Tony: "No. To begin with, there weren't any where I lived." Javier: "What was high school like for you?" Tony: "I was four feet eleven when I started high school. In gym class they used me for the football." Javier chuckled, "Did you tell that to my neighbor?" Tony: "No way. I wouldn't give him the satisfaction."

Javier: "We should have breakfast together so we don't have to eat alone. What time do you go to breakfast?" Tony: "I'm there when they first open. I'm done eating by the time six or eight people show up." Javier: "That's too early for me. I go to breakfast ten minutes before class starts." Tony: "I'm *persona non grata* with this crowd. Anyone who regularly eats with me will end up becoming a target." Javier: "I laughed at you before, but now I'm not so sure. I mentioned your name to a few of my friends, asking if they knew anything about you. They didn't seem to know much about you, but they don't like you." Tony: "Maybe I'm not a nice person." Javier: "No, they all hate you because you did something to my neighbor. What did you do to him?"

Tony: "Nothing. I saw David come out of a room at three in the morning. The next day, your neighbor was glaring at me all day long." Javier: "You told me you couldn't be sure which room David came out of." Tony: "That's right. I had no way of knowing it was his room until he started acting weird." Javier: "These people are angry with you for getting him in trouble." Tony: "He made his own trouble without my help." Javier: "Did you tell the Vice Rector what you saw?" Tony: "No. I didn't realize I saw anything, but somebody went to the Vice Rector. The Vice Rector got in my face the next day because I was in the hall and saw David. It was the Vice Rector who decided David was studying with a friend. Your neighbor's guilty behavior is what gave him away." Javier: "After listening to what these guys say about you I realize they have some serious anger issues which have nothing to do with you."

Tony: "These people are special that's for sure. Are you aware the Vice Rector has one of his trusted lieutenants in charge of communications?" Javier: "What do you mean, in charge of communications?" Tony: "They have the capability to monitor the mail and the telephones." Javier: "You can't be serious. It's a federal offense to open the mail. Are you saying they open our mail?" Tony: "They have the means in place. Do they open our letters? I have not witnessed that. How can I? They certainly keep track of the amount of mail we get and where it comes from." Javier: "And you think they monitor our phone calls?" Tony: "I believe they do, yes." Javier: "What makes you think so?"

Tony: "I overheard the Vice Rector's discussion with the man in the mailroom. There was a particular student the Vice Rector was interested in, and the sort of information he was looking for indicated this man was tasked with spy detail." Javier: "What about the telephones?" Tony: "I don't have anything solid yet. It's easy to eavesdrop on telephone calls. If they are closely monitoring the mail, they certainly monitor our phones. Why do you think they forbid seminarians to have cell phones?" Javier: "I don't believe that. I think you're worried over nothing." Tony: "I came to a Pontifical seminary to ensure I would be surrounded by holy men. These are not holy men." Javier: "Are you saying the priests here are not holy men too?"

Tony: "Yes I am. So far, I have only found two holy priests here. Students and clergy are angry with me because I witnessed the nocturnal hall traffic. How can they be holy men if they condone homosexual activity in a seminary?" Javier: "What about the Rector?" Tony: "(*Cover story*) I don't know yet. I don't see very much of him." Javier: "Why don't you go to his office? Tell him what's going on." Tony: "I expect he knows exactly what's going on. I need a better understanding of what goes on here before I knock on his door." Javier: "What do you think is going on?" Tony: "It looks like homosexuals have taken over this facility. They maintain the appearance of a seminary, but it's just a bunch of homos using the Church's resources as their own." Javier: "How can you say such a thing?" Tony: "Because that is exactly what I see."

That evening the refectory was deserted. Tony and two other seminarians showed up for the evening meal. Each sat alone at separate tables. Tony returned to his room after dinner. He studied until the noise coming from next door became too annoying. Mr. Stevens was still visiting next door. His voice was loud and intelligible. The man who lived there was soft spoken. It was possible to tune him out. Tony was caught up with his studies, so he went to the pub.

The pub was deserted except for Art. Tony started eating stale popcorn. Art made a fresh batch for his only customer. Art: "Can I get you a soda?" Tony: "No thanks." Art: "How about a beer?" Tony: "No thanks." Art: "Let me guess, you're here for the popcorn." Tony: "That's it." Art: "The pub doesn't make any money off of you, that's for sure."

When Tony returned to his room there was still noise coming from next door. Tony's prayers were not efficacious under these conditions. Tony went to bed at the usual time. Lying in bed, he heard more animal noises: long, low, grunting sounds. The same noise a cow makes when the veterinarian does a pregnancy check. When the grunting sounds stopped, one man was whispering and Mr. Stevens was speaking normally. Tony pulled his pillow over his head, but could not shut out the corpulent man's voice. *(Tony's first grade teacher's book: "–rest of the night having sex. –is his favorite kind.").*

Reelected

David raced into the classroom, his eyes distended in panic! "Did you guys hear? One of our people told me if they can't get Limbaugh's TV show off the air President Clinton will never get reelected!" A lively discussion ensued among Tony's classmates. Greg was skeptical and questioned David's source. David: "He's a reliable source. He's one of us. He's an insider." Greg looked over and saw Tony was interested in the conversation. Greg motioned to the others and the discussion became hushed. The only snippet of conversation audible to Tony after that was "–working on it. They have to make it happen soon, otherwise Clinton won't get reelected." The instructor was late for class, so their conversation did not interrupt class.

Shrink Lady November

The Shrink Lady, an attractive woman with blonde hair, blue eyes, and fair complexion welcomed Tony into her office. After pleasantries she asked, "What can I help you with? What seems to be the problem?" Tony: "I don't have a problem." Shrink Lady: "Then why are you here?" Tony: "I was told everyone has to see a counselor." The Shrink Lady looked confused, "No, students only come to me when they have a problem they want help with." Tony: "My formation director told me everyone has to see a counselor at least once a month. He told me to see a counselor before our next meeting." This threw the Shrink Lady off balance. She gathered her thoughts and asked, "Do you know why he sent you here?" Tony: "Yes. I used the toilet at three o'clock in the morning. Apparently that's a problem."

Shrink Lady: "It's not uncommon for a man your age to use the toilet in the middle of the night." Tony: "I know." Shrink Lady: "There must be a reason your formation director thinks this is a problem." Tony: "I expect the Vice Rector told him to send me here. The Vice Rector interrogated me. He was unhappy I walked down the hall at three a.m. to use the toilet. My spiritual director told me to piss in the sink so I don't get myself in trouble." The Shrink Lady recoiled, "Someone actually told you to piss in the sink?" Tony: "Yes, so I don't get myself in trouble." Shrink Lady: "That's disgusting! Are you serious?" Tony: "I'm quoting him verbatim." The Shrink Lady looked confused. "I don't understand why you would be in trouble for going to the toilet in the middle of the night?" Tony: "Neither do I." The Shrink Lady considered this.

Shrink Lady: "Did anything unusual happen while you were in the hall?" Tony: "Not really. As I walked down the hall I saw one of my classmates going into his room and I waived." Shrink Lady: "That's not a problem." Tony: "Shouldn't be." Shrink Lady: "So why is there a problem?" Tony: "The next day some guy who is in most of my classes started glaring at me. The guy I waived to also glared at me. At lunch they talked to people around them in an angry and animated fashion, and those people glared at me." Shrink Lady: "And how did this make you feel?" Tony: "Confused, really confused." Shrink Lady: "And how did you feel about these people glaring at you?" Tony: "I felt like I was surrounded by five year old children who weigh 200 pounds each. It was creepy. For a few moments it made my skin crawl."

Shrink Lady: "It sounds to me like they have a problem." Tony: "I thought so." Shrink Lady: "You must be leaving something out. What happened before you waived to your classmate in the hall?" Tony: "The hall was empty. He came out of one room, walked to the end of the hall and fumbled with his keys to unlock his door. He looked up and saw me at the far end of the hall. I waived. He leaned forward, squinted, grimaced, and then disappeared into his room." Shrink Lady: "Were the hall lights turned on?" Tony: "No." Shrink Lady: "Why didn't you turn them on when you went into the hall?"

Tony: "Apart from not knowing where the light switch is, I could see where I was going. There was no reason to turn on the lights." Shrink Lady: "Why did he fumble with his keys?" Tony: "His eyesight isn't very good and it was dark." Shrink Lady: "How could you see he leaned forward, squinted, and grimaced if it was dark?" Tony: "He stood in front of the windows at the end of the hall. I have better than normal vision and pretty good night vision." Shrink Lady: "Normally people start to lose their vision by the time they are your age." Tony: "It hasn't happened yet. I eat plenty of carrots, apparently that helps."

Shrink Lady: "What did you think when you saw your classmate come out of one room and go into another at three o'clock in the morning?" Tony: "I didn't think. I waived. It was a reflex once I realized who it was." Shrink Lady: "What did you feel?" Tony: "I felt an urgent need to use the toilet. The next thing I felt was the urge to go back to sleep." Shrink Lady: "The next day what did you feel about seeing that man in the hall?" Tony: "I forgot about it. It was a non-event. If those two comported themselves as adults, it would have been forgotten." Shrink Lady: "With a group of seminarians glaring at you in disapproval, did it occur to you your formation would be in jeopardy?" Tony: "Yes it did." Shrink Lady: "What did you do about it?" Tony: "Nothing."

Shrink Lady: "Nothing? Something like that could jeopardize your becoming a priest. You must have done something." Tony: "I'm an adult. I comported myself as such. Since I did nothing wrong there was no need for corrective action. I saw a lot of adult men acting like children. It was disconcerting. It was creepy. I didn't understand what was going on." Shrink Lady: "This must have made you think about what went on in the hall the night before." Tony: "I was busy being baffled by everyone's bizarre behavior. Before I could make sense of things, the Vice Rector got in my face. He ended up telling me two guys were probably having a study session." Shrink Lady: "Until three a.m.?" Tony: "After the first day of class." Shrink Lady: "Did you believe him?" Tony: "Not!"

Shrink Lady: "What did you think?" Tony: "I didn't have to think, it was obvious." Shrink Lady: "You jumped to a conclusion. What did you conclude?" Tony: "Lawyers use the phrase, *Res ipsa loquitur*. That means it is obvious to all and no argument is needed to explain it to the court." Shrink Lady: "Nothing is obvious to me. What is supposed to be obvious?" Tony: "Two men in their 30s acting like angry, nasty children. The Vice Rector decides they were studying together until three o'clock in the morning after the first day of class. Explain to me the part I don't understand." Shrink Lady: "What are you accusing the Vice Rector of?"

Tony: "I am accusing him of jumping to a conclusion in the same manner you just accused me. Look, I was half-asleep. I didn't see the obvious. Now I'm wide-awake. The Vice Rector drew me a picture in case I wasn't bright enough to figure things out myself. I'm embarrassed I didn't catch on sooner. Let's move on." Shrink Lady: "Do you have anything else you would like to discuss?" Tony: "No." Shrink Lady: "Nothing else important has happened?" Tony: "No." Shrink Lady: "How do you feel about being told you have to piss in the sink in your room rather than walk down the hall to the bathroom?" Tony: "Disgusted." Shrink Lady: "What do you feel that is all about?" Tony: "Apparently my use of the corridor after ten p.m. is disruptive to the nocturnal habits of the indigenous wildlife."

The Shrink Lady pointed out Tony's answers were terse and guarded. "You don't trust me. I am here to help you. I can't help you unless you give me your full cooperation." She intimated Tony had "trust issues." Tony: "You're not here on my behalf. You work in the service of the administration." Shrink Lady: "As your counselor, I am here to help you. I work on your behalf. The fact that you don't trust me demonstrates you have issues." Tony: "First of all, I don't have a problem, so there's nothing to fix. I didn't come here of my own volition, I was sent." Shrink Lady: "You were sent here by your formation director. Clearly, he feels you have a problem in formation." Tony: "Ostensibly. The real reason I'm here is the administration had him send me here."

Shrink Lady: "Sounds like paranoia right there–." The Shrink Lady laid out a scenario for Tony, which clearly landed him in paranoia territory. Tony: "That would be true if I were paying for your time, but I'm not. The administration pays your wage. Your duty of agency is to the administration, not to me." Shrink Lady: "See, this is a perfect example." Tony: "Rather than embarrass yourself, go to the file cabinet and pull my file. Really, right now, we have time. –Ok, look at my transcripts. I earned an MBA. The course, business law, describes your position right now. Your duties of agency are to the people who pay your wage. Explain to me the part I don't understand."

The Shrink Lady was stymied. After fidgeting and expressing more than one personal tick she asked, "Why did you choose me as your counselor?" Tony: "There are only two counselors, I chose you." Shrink Lady: "Why did you choose me? Did you know the other counselor is a man?" Tony: "Yes, I did. I also know he expelled a young man from my diocese by labeling him homophobic." Shrink Lady: "He does not have the authority to expel anyone." Tony: "No, his job is to hang the homophobic label on political dissidents so they can be shipped off to Siberia. He doesn't do the shipping, he just labels the package." Shrink Lady: "Siberia? Who said anything about Siberia?" Tony: "In the Soviet Union psychology was used to dispose of political dissidents."

The Shrink Lady did not seem to have knowledge of the Cold War or the former Soviet Union. Tony: "Are you familiar with Project Blue Book?" She was not. Tony: "Project Blue Book was closed in 1969. For roughly 25 years, the U.S. government threw a blanket over credible reports of UFOs by publicly discrediting anyone reporting UFO sightings. The government destroyed people's credibility and careers by making them appear to be mentally unsound." Shrink Lady: "Sounds like paranoia." Tony: "If you were the target you'd call it psychological warfare."

Shrink Lady: "Everyone knows there is no such thing as UFOs." Tony: "That's the spirit! Not only was the project effective, its effect is enduring." Shrink Lady: "There really are no UFOs. Do you believe in UFOs?" Tony: "I know the government ran Project Blue Book for two decades. They had a reason to start and they had a reason to stop. My point is; governments use psychology as a weapon. The Soviet approach was swift and inexpensive: declare them crazy and ship them off to Siberia." Shrink Lady: "And you think my job is to ship you off to Siberia." Tony: "*Res ipsa loquitur*." Shrink Lady: "It's not!" Tony deadpanned, "Please."

Shrink Lady: "You avoided the other counselor because you felt he misdiagnosed the seminarian from your diocese, is that correct?" Tony: "Psychology has no legitimacy. That man cannot diagnose nor misdiagnose." Shrink Lady: "Psychology is a science!" Tony: "Psychology is irreligion." Shrink Lady: "What do you mean by irreligion?" Tony: "Look it up. Basically, irreligion means it is garbage. In the 1930s, a woman's magazine had a personality questionnaire, one of those "rate your mate" things women's magazines are so fond of. Someone decided the thing actually worked, and it became a treasured psychological tool for human resource departments for decades. Today we call it the Minnesota Multiphasic Personality Inventory. Are you familiar with it?"

Shrink Lady: "Yes. It has been used for over half a century." Tony: "Human resource personnel use psychology. By their own rating, they are only 25% effective when hiring. They change interviewing tactics to the latest flavor of the month to improve, but still they remain at a 25% success rate. Companies can double their hiring success rate by flipping a coin instead of using their current HR process. It's the same with therapy. Those receiving therapy take twice as long to recover than those in the control group." Shrink Lady: "What do you suggest?" Tony: "Go to a bar, spill your guts to the bartender, and get smelly, stinking, falling-down drunk. Your money buys you a splitting headache and you forget your troubles."

Shrink Lady: "Do you believe psychology is useless?" Tony: "It depends on the application. The FBI uses psychology as a blunt instrument. It works great for them. The military uses it as a weapon. They get results. Our courts use it and shame on them for allowing such garbage in the courtroom." Shrink Lady: "You've done it again. You avoided answering my question. Why did you pick me over the other counselor?" Tony: "He proved himself to be a shill. You are an unknown." Shrink Lady: "What made you choose me?" Tony: "Two counselors, he's out, who's left? No offense, but you win by default." Shrink Lady: "Does the fact that I'm a woman have any bearing on your decision?"

Tony paused, then answered, "You don't have to fish for compliments. Before I came to the seminary you would have been someone I'd ask on a date." Shrink Lady: "Why is that?" Tony: "You're good looking, intelligent, and professional." Shrink Lady: "What makes you feel I am professional?" Tony: "Your poise, your demeanor, even the way you dress." Shrink Lady: "The way I dress?" Tony: "Yes, you wear Scottish wools; classic patterns in traditional business colors." Shrink Lady: "What does this remind you of?" Tony: "It reminds me of when I worked in a professional business setting. It also reminds me of when I was in Scotland." Shrink Lady: "What else does it remind you of?"

Tony slowly shook his head no, but he searched his memory anyway. Tony: "Wait a minute, our grade school uniforms. The boys wore dark pants with a blue shirt and tie and the girls wore a blue tartan skirt. I never realized it before. They started training us to wear proper business attire at age five." The timing of the Shrink Lady's disappointment suggested she was hoping for an excuse to hang some sort of sex fantasy on grade school uniforms. Shrink Lady: "Do you feel any sexual tension with only the two of us here in my office?" Tony: "As I said before, you comport yourself in a professional manner. I too am professional." Shrink Lady: "Maybe I'm just not attracted to you. How do you feel about that?" Tony: "That makes things easier."

The Shrink Lady was startled, "Easier! Easier how?" Tony: "If you invite me back to your place after work, I have to resist the temptation." Shrink Lady: "Doing that would cost me my job!" Tony: "And we're back to your being professional." The Shrink Lady fished and wheedled until she got Tony to say, "Some men handle rejection by saying, "She must be a lesbian." In high school that's funny. By the time a man is in college it's just immature." The Shrink Lady was eager to examine this further, "How do you feel about lesbians?" Tony: "I don't know any. I don't have a basis to form an opinion." Shrink Lady: "You have a negative opinion of gay men, otherwise you would not have been sent to see me." *Did she just jump to a conclusion?* Shrink Lady: "What do you have against gay men?" Tony: "They don't belong here."

Shrink Lady: "Let's operate on the premise that you have a negative opinion of gay men, at least to the extent you feel they don't belong in the seminary." Tony: "Ok." Shrink Lady: "How do you feel about lesbians in comparison?" Tony: "I'm ashamed to admit I don't have negative feelings about lesbians." Startled! Shrink Lady: "Why should you be ashamed of that?" Tony: "The sin is the same. The taboo should be the same, but it's not. Logically, my feelings should be the same, but they aren't." Shrink Lady: "Why do you feel that is?" Tony: "How would I know if a woman is a lesbian? Women who are not attracted to me are not all lesbians. Conversely, if a lesbian is attracted to me, how would I know she is a lesbian? What's a lesbian going to do that is different from a regular woman?"

Shrink Lady: "So you're ambivalent?" Tony: "I guess." The Shrink Lady was delighted! "How does that compare to gay men?" Tony: "We already agreed to color them negative." She verbally pounded Tony until he admitted, "They have the ability to be physically threatening in an invasive manner." Shrink Lady: "This is a seminary. No one is going to physically attack you. They would be sent home if they did. Are you afraid someone will attack you?" Tony: "I lock my door before I go to sleep at night, does that count?" Shrink Lady: "No, everyone locks their door at night, that's normal."

Prostate Cancer

Tony sat at his desk studying. There was a knock on the door. Javier: "Hi Tony, I'm just coming back from dinner. I wanted to see how you are doing. I'm not interrupting am I?" Tony: "No, I'm glad to see you." Javier: "It's so convenient to visit on my way back from dinner." Tony: "Good. I want you to feel free to drop in. So, what's going on?" Javier: "Nothing special, how about you?" Tony: "All week my classmates have been carrying on about celibacy and what a joke it is. They think gay priests can have all the sex they want and no one will suspect. There was a news item concerning prostate cancer. Men who are sexually inactive are at especially high risk of getting prostate cancer."

Javier: "Yes, I heard that." Tony: "So did my illustrious classmates. They laughed because straight priests are either caught having liaisons with women or die of prostate cancer. They made a special point to tell me on several occasions they are in no danger of ever having prostate cancer and I can plan on having it for sure." Javier: "Tell them you'll never get AIDS." Tony: "I can't be bothered. A fire burns as long as you throw on more wood. If I say nothing the conversation burns itself out."

Vocation Director's Visit

Tony's vocation director called. The priest made small talk before saying he was driving down the next day. Vocation Director: "I have meetings to go to, but I'd like to visit over lunch on Friday. Can we meet in the refectory at noon?" Tony: "Thank you Father. Yes, I'll see you Friday." Three days later at lunch, the conversation was superficial. The two men had only met once before. The vocation director asked how Tony liked the school, how things were going, and how was he doing academically? Tony politely and prudently lied, saying the school was fine and things were going well. It was true he was doing well in his classes. The priest gave Tony a Byzantine icon as a gift from the diocese with no explanation. Tony knew nothing about icons and neither did the vocation director.

After Evening Prayer, Tony's classmates paced him going down the corridor to the refectory. They sat with him at dinner. David and Mr. Stevens were keen to heckle Tony. David: "Was that your vocation director you had lunch with today?" Mr. Stevens: "We saw you having lunch with the vocation director from your diocese. He was here two days before he saw you. You must be in big trouble." David: "What did he want?" Mr. Stevens: "Did you feel bad, knowing he was here on campus and wouldn't make time to see you until today?" Eventually even Greg got sick of listening to them and asked Tony what happened.

Tony: "He had business on campus. Today at lunch he gave me a Byzantine icon and tried to make conversation." The four classmates did not know what a Byzantine icon was either. Greg: "What business did he have here?" Tony: "I have no idea." Mr. Stevens stated, "With all the trouble you've been in, he must have been called here because of you. I'll bet he was told to pull you out." David pelted Tony with similar ideas. Mr. Stevens continued heckling Tony until Greg stopped him. They were disappointed Tony was not upset. *I wish to deny them the satisfaction.*

Pavers

There was a chill in the air on this sunny Saturday morning. All the seminarians were assembled in the courtyard. There was plenty of sand and pavers strategically placed. The Vice Rector managed with military precision. This project was no different. His trusted lieutenants divided the crowd among them. Each lieutenant instructed and oversaw his team. Within minutes, everyone was busy and productive.

While the seminarians worked, the Rector and Vice Rector were immersed in serious discussion. The Rector noted the importance of holding a public activity once every quarter "–so the Board can see we are active in the public's eye." The next scheduled activity was a prayer vigil outside an abortion clinic. The two priests sounded like lawyers as they discussed plans, logistics, and manpower to be deployed outside the clinic. The Rector discussed the school's finances, fundraisers, donors, and patrons. He reviewed their concerted efforts to maintain revenues in the face of the shrinking economy: how they stimulate donor and patron enthusiasm for continued support, and how they increased fundraisers to offset waning support.

Rector: "–and we need to give more attention to bequests. That is important too. –major source of funding going forward. –We should never overlook any source of revenue–." The Rector's analysis of macroeconomic and demographic factors was insightful. With the contracting economy, the next generation would be unable to replace current donors, as their earnings would be far less. Nor could they replace current patrons, as their savings and asset accumulation would be insufficient to match the current level of patronage. Bequests from the present generation are the last large source of potential funding. Rector: "We must start now to cultivate future bequests–." The $123 million currently in the Jeroboam's coffers will be necessary to fund operations when the next generation is unable to maintain the current level of support.

When the Rector asked how progress was coming with their problem, both priests glanced sideways at Tony. The Vice Rector said it was going to take a while. They finished their conversation in hushed tones before the Rector left.

The bulk of the pavers were finished within two hours. Only five laborers remained. Tony finished his work and took the opportunity to converse with the Vice Rector. Tony: "I have never heard a priest warn his parish how the Democratic Party's agenda is against our religion." Vice Rector: "What makes you think it is?" Tony: "Welfare for example. Supplying someone with a free livelihood for the rest of their life kills their spirit. This is easy to see in wild animals. You feed a feral animal and soon it can no longer take care of itself. That's called "learned dependency." Somehow, we deny seeing the same deleterious effect in humans. The Old Testament warns against this."

Vice Rector: "It is charity. It is the same thing the Church does: charitable works. In the New Testament is says to feed the hungry." Tony: "It says feed the hungry Father, it doesn't say feed them for the rest of their life. One time I was starving. I had nothing to eat for two weeks. I went to sign up for welfare. The woman told me to go to a soup kitchen if I needed food. "Soup kitchen? What is welfare for?" She said, "Welfare is not a charity. If you need food, go to a charity. Find the nearest soup kitchen." I asked her, "If welfare is not a charity, what is it?" Her jaw dropped, she thought for a few moments, and then she closed her mouth and went on break in the back room." Vice Rector: "So what do you think? If it is not charity, what is it?"

> Ecclesiastes 3:22 (DRA) [31] And I have found that nothing is better than for a man to rejoice in his work, and that this is his portion. For who shall bring him to know the things that shall be after him?

2 Thessalonians 3:10 (DRA) [31] For also when we were with you, this we declared to you: that, if any man will not work, neither let him eat.

Ecclesiasticus 12:4 (DRA) [31] Give to the merciful and uphold not the sinner: God will repay vengeance to the ungodly and to sinners, and keep them against the day of vengeance.

Sirach 12:4 (RSVwA) [43] Give to the godly man, but do not help the sinner.

Tony: "It is government corruption Father. It is one political party buying votes with public money. The government has gone into competition with the charities, and it is unfair competition." Vice Rector: "Is it even possible to be in competition for performing good works?" Tony: "Yes it is Father. It is predatory behavior. Here is an example. In Upper Peninsula Michigan, the Catholic Church had two re-employment centers. Both centers were full service and provided reasonable access. They offered donated clothing for job interviews, resume writing and job-hunting assistance, and each had a food pantry. When times were tough and the centers ran out of funds, the government gave them money to keep them going.

Today there is only one re-employment center in the Upper Peninsula. It is located in Escanaba. It is a government unemployment office. A charitable organization offers donated clothing for interviews at a nearby location. There is also a nearby food pantry. The unemployment office is the standard government fare: unemployment compensation, resume writing assistance, and job search assistance. People at the ends of the peninsula have a 150-mile drive to get there. Both Catholic centers closed years ago.

This is an example of the government competing with charities. The Catholic Church delivers 97 cents of every dollar of charitable donations to the needy. Jewish charities deliver 98 cents of every dollar. Welfare only delivers 23 cents on the dollar. Like the woman at the welfare office said, welfare is not a charity." The Vice Rector laughed, "I don't see how the government's involvement in charity is against the Church's teachings. What you described is the separation of church and state. The government cannot give taxpayer's money to the Church." Tony: "Giving money to the Church's relief efforts was the most cost efficient means for the government to deliver help to the needy during hard times Father."

Tony's figures are from the 1980s. Government investment in computers since then hopefully has improved the 77 cents on a dollar handling cost. Tony assumes the government's cost of administering welfare is similar to the cost of administering Social Security. How many people invest their IRA's with brokers whose brokerage fee is 77 cents on the dollar? Social Security is insurance? Where is the proper accounting that attests to that? MY social security? MY money? Indeed! They took your money. It is gone. You trusted them. You messed up.

Welfare and Government Entitlements

> Ezechiel 13:19 (DRA) [31] And they violated me among my people, for a handful of barley, and a piece of bread, to kill souls which should not die, and to save souls alive which should not live, telling lies to my people that believe lies.

> Jeremias 17:5 (DRA) [31] Thus saith the Lord: Cursed be the man that trusteth in man, and maketh flesh his arm, and whose heart departeth from the Lord.

Tony: "My economics professor in grad school was the economic advisor to President Carter. He said when something is free you get less of it and in lower quality. He used public schools versus private schools as an example. You can send your child to public school for free, or you can spend thousands of dollars a year to send your child to private school. Most people send their children to public school. The result is less education. Less education of lower quality is provided for society as a whole. This is due to unfair competition by the government in education."

The Vice Rector became annoyed, "You are jumping to a baseless conclusion. You assume all public education is inferior without proof. You have no proof. Besides, I do not recall a strong economy during the Carter administration." Tony: "I asked the professor about that since he was the President's advisor. He laughed. He said, "These men campaign for over a year. They win the biggest popularity contest on earth, making them the most powerful man on the planet as a result. Anyone's ego will lose perspective after all that. They think they don't have to listen to anyone's advice, and they're right. They don't have to. I gave the President sound economic advice. That doesn't mean he used it. He had his own ideas."

Of course the public school system doesn't compare to private schools. No one is going to pay money to send their child to an inferior school. I went to a Catholic school, K through 8. The parish's collection partially funded the school. Students had fund-raising activities to help cover costs. The priests and nuns were the teachers and administrators. As fewer and fewer nuns were available, lay teachers were hired. The operation of our school was a fraction of the cost per student compared to the local public school." Vice Rector: "Your school did not charge tuition?" Tony: "No, the parish funded the school. There was no tuition." Vice Rector: "Your school did not have the resources the public school had, did it?"

Tony: "True. The public school used their buses to transport our students along with their own. The public school had a gymnasium, a swimming pool, sports fields, and overall better capital plant. They had newer books, newer facilities, well-paid union teachers, and many highly paid union administrators. Our eighth grade graduating class was 36 students. We joined the public school to form a class of 128 high school students. During our junior year, we took the statewide scholarship exam. Fourteen students won scholarships. Twelve of those were Catholic school students." Vice Rector: "Where did the public school students place in the scoring?" Tony: "Two public school girls had the top two scores." Vice Rector: "Where did you place?"

Tony: "I had the third highest score. One third of the parochial students won state scholarships. Our lower paid teachers were more dedicated and garnered superior results with fewer resources and older books." Vice Rector: "Sounds like there was creaming." Tony: "You could jump to the baseless conclusion that Catholics are just smarter Father." The Vice Rector frowned, "How did the Catholic school deal with disruptive students? How were students with behavioral problems handled?" Tony: "Discipline was part of the curriculum. Teachers took repeatedly disruptive students to the principal. Subsequent instances brought the student and parents to the principal. Further instances involved the priest and parents. The next step was expulsion."

Vice Rector: "Problem students were sent over to the public school? That is called creaming. How many students were expelled from your class over the course of eight years?" Tony: "Five." Vice Rector: "Is it possible there were more than five?" Tony: "Yes, it is. Once they disappear it's easy to forget them." Vice Rector: "How many of your parochial school classmates dropped out of high school?" Tony: "One that I know of." Vice Rector: "There could have been more?" Tony: "Yes, there could have been others." Vice Rector: "If you add expelled students back into the eighth grade graduating class you have 41 or more students?" Tony: "Ok." Vice Rector: "Instead of a third of the parochial students winning scholarships, the real number is closer to one quarter, don't you agree?"

Tony: "Ok, one quarter versus two percent. Clearly, the parochial school did a much better job with less funding and fewer resources than the state run school." Vice Rector: "Do I understand the public school provided taxpayer support to the parochial school in the form of providing busing? Was that even legal?" Tony: "There was opposition to the cooperative arrangement, but wisdom prevailed. The two schools were in close proximity of each other. The marginal cost of this cooperation was small. I don't know if taxpayers ate that cost or if the parochial school paid to offset it." Vice Rector: "How did elected officials justify using public assets to benefit a private school?"

Tony: "Real estate taxes financed the public school and its buses. Catholic families paid real estate taxes that funded the public school, yet their church community paid for their children's education. Catholic school students represented a tax savings. Basically, they paid for education twice." The Vice Rector retorted, "The public school lost matching funds from the state and federal government for every student attending parochial school. Operation of the parochial school cost the public school an overall loss of funding. How does that save taxpayers money?" Tony: "The government's matching fund is precisely what gives the government an unfair advantage when it competes against the free market. It perverts economic logic. It creates a disingenuous predatory economy.

Santa Clause does not live in Washington DC or the state capitol. Those funds are also taxpayer's money. After the Catholic school closed, the same buses transported the same students, only now the buses dropped all students off at the same school. The voters and the elected officials in our town had the wisdom to do the right thing. Supporting the parochial school's efforts was beneficial to the entire community." Vice Rector: "How can you know that?" Tony: "Four years after the Catholic school closed, the number of scholarships won by high school students dwindled and then stopped altogether. Pregnancy rates climbed until they became the highest per capita in the state. No student from that high school has won a state scholarship in years."

Vice Rector: "Some other cause you are not taking into account could explain these results." Tony: "No Father. There were no demographic changes, and scholarship testing was statewide and standardized." Vice Rector: "Why did the Catholic school close?" Tony: "We had fewer and fewer nuns, which meant an increasing number of lay teachers. Taxes and inflation were on the rise. With rising taxes and rising costs, parents and parishioners lost the ability and the will to support their school. Catholic families lost heart. Their taxes supported the public school and they had to support their own school as well. Parishioner support waned. The bishop was all too happy to close the school. Our parish eventually stopped objecting. Our parish did not know the real value of our school until years after it closed.

In recent years, a small Bible church opened a one-room schoolhouse in an obscure rural location. Word circulated about the students' superior scholastic performance. The school accepts students who are not part of their faith community. Parents drive their child to and from school in order to give their child a superior education and avoid the drug trafficking at the public school. It's too bad Catholic parishioners did not understand the true value of their school. The experience of the people in my hometown demonstrates the value of a dedicated, faith-based school."

The Vice Rector retorted, "Parental participation is also a big factor in a student's overall performance." Tony: "Yes it is Father. Public school teachers I know used to enjoy teaching. In recent years, they complain some students are unmanageable and violent. When parents are brought in to help discipline the student, the parents become defensive of their child and antagonistic toward the teacher. Instead of helping solve the student's behavioral problems, the parents enable their child's bad behavior. The parents bully the teacher with threats of suing the teacher and the school.

In the rural parish where I lived before coming to the seminary, I taught seventh grade religious instruction one night per week. The students were candid. The smart boy told me during class, "Tony, everyone knows there really is no God." The smart girl summarized, "You are only doing your job." I was mortified. These seventh graders showed me the most important reason for a faith community to have a faith-based school." The Vice Rector said he was late for a meeting and walked away.

Money Talks

Javier stopped by Tony's room after dinner. "How are you getting along with your classmates?" Tony: "Peachy, how else?" Javier: "What have they been up to?" Tony: "One of our classes got these guys going on money and the papacy. Mr. Stevens thinks most of the money going into the Church comes from the United States." Javier: "I believe that's true." Tony: "He thinks that gives American bishops plenty of leverage on the pope, so much leverage they can make demands of the pope." Javier: "I'm sure the pope is aware of where the Church's resources come from, but I doubt he kowtows to American bishops. The United States is a significant source of funding, but it has always been a mission country." Tony: "What do you mean, mission country?"

Javier: "The United States has always used more priests than it produces. Of all the priests you have ever known, what nationality is the most prevalent?" Tony: "Irish. It seems like more priests are Irish than anything else." Javier: "That's right. Ireland produces more priests than any other country. Ireland exports priests. The United States has always been a mission country. It has never produced enough of its own priests for its churches. It has always relied on foreign born priests." Tony: "Mr. Stevens is fascinated with the wealth of the Vatican. He is convinced American bishops can steer the pope in the direction of their choosing based on the cash flow they command." Javier: "What makes him think so?"

Tony: "In one of our classes we received some handouts on marriage annulment. One of the Kennedys applied for an annulment. His wife refused to agree to it. She is trying to fight it, but she is not being included in the proceedings." Javier hung his head, "This pope recently liberalized annulments, but he didn't make them that liberal. Both husband and wife have to sign off on an annulment. Kennedy's bishop is doing that, not the pope." Tony: "My classmates were happy to review scandals involving the pope and money." Javier was sad, "Scandals involving the Vatican's bank are common in Italy in recent years. I don't understand why your classmates are happy about this." Tony checked the time. "I've got core board. We'll have to continue our conversation another time."

Core Board November

Tony's second core board proved anticlimactic. Members more equally shared the questioning. The Vice Rector's rabid dominance was not in evidence. The nature of the questioning and the material itself under scrutiny fascinated Tony. The Jesuit revisited Tony's employment at the factory with the drug dealer and the embezzling managers. Jesuit: "You must have told your family about your experiences at the factory. How do you explain the outcome?" Tony: "My family doesn't doubt my eyewitness accounts. Other people don't believe me." Jesuit: "Why do you think other people don't believe you?"

Tony: "Maybe the events and certainly the results are unlikely. After I fired the drug dealer, I sought the counsel of a stalwart coworker who served in the military. I asked him to brief me so I could survive the week. He said there had been five drug-related shooting deaths so far that year in the parking lot where I park. I was number six. He already counted me among the dead." Jesuit: "Drug related? You!" Tony: "I fired a drug dealer. Retaliation would come from drug people, *ergo*, drug-related." Jesuit: "Weren't you afraid?"

Tony: "Yes I was, and I sought the counsel of a trustworthy military man. His advice was invaluable. I prayed to God not to let the bad guys win. My survival would give hope to the workers. My being shot would paralyze my crew with fear. I prayed a lot." Jesuit: "What about the embezzling managers?" Tony: "I prayed three times as much. The insidious nature of men in legitimate positions of authority using their authority for criminal activity turns the battle between good and evil on its head. I didn't pray for my safety, I asked God to not let the bad guys win." Jesuit: "What do you think they would have done to you?"

Tony: "Knowledgeable people I trusted warned me someone would put drugs in my locked desk and then report me before I had a chance to discover the planted drugs. They saw this happen before." Jesuit: "You were more afraid of the managers than you were of two gunmen?" Tony: "Much more. Greater evil was resident in those socially respected men holding legitimate positions of authority. The law and the public would presume their testimony to be reliable. They only needed to refer to me as a disgruntled ex-employee and I would have zero credibility. Conversely, it would be an uphill battle to convince a jury of their guilt." Jesuit: "God answered your prayers?"

Tony: "Yes, he blessed me with good counsel and critical timing. When I went to the soldier for advice, he was packing his desk and personal effects. He said, "You fired three union hourly and the union didn't come after you. This one is different. He sold their drugs. How do you do it? I only fired one hourly worker and union stooges threaten my wife and kids. They drive back and forth in front of my house while I'm at work and my wife is home by herself." The soldier recounted an anonymous (union) phone call: "I saw your little girl waiting for the bus this morning wearing her pretty pink backpack. Click." Then the soldier briefed me on what I needed to know to stay alive.

Soldier: "I want to stand up to the union, but–. –my wife and kids! What can I do? I resigned my position here. We're moving. If you came to my office five minutes later you would have missed me, I would have been gone. I'm a soldier and I can't even protect my family from these bums." His eyes welled up, "I'm not a pussy. I served in the first Gulf War. I fought overseas to protect my country, and I come home to this! I can't even protect my family from union scum in my own country! Unions–. I have the utmost respect for you. How do you stand up to the union and I can't?" I told him I don't have a wife and small children for those evil cowards to threaten. If I did, I would have to do the same thing he is doing. Months later, the Vice President of our division tipped his hand of his involvement in the embezzlement scheme."

Jesuit: "What happened?" Tony: "I resigned my position on Wednesday. The following Monday six managers transferred, one manager resigned, and one was fired. I prayed to God to not let the bad guys win." Jesuit: "Do you feel God's presence in your daily life?" Tony: "No." Jesuit: "Do you ever feel God's presence?" Tony: "Yes. When I'm surrounded by evil, I pray to God for help. I feel his presence then." Jesuit: "When things are going well do you feel God's presence?" Tony: "No. It's too easy to think things are going well due to my own efforts, because I'm cool, or because I'm just that good. When I'm outnumbered and outgunned by evil, reality sets in."

> Deuteronomy 8:17 (DRA) [31] Lest thou shouldst say in thy heart: My own might, and the strength of my own hand have achieved all these things for me.

Jesuit: "Your educational background shows you've taken two courses in statistics. What odds would you place on having reached the same results without praying?" Tony answered reflexively, "A snowball's chance in hell." Tony paused in awkward self-consciousness, "I can put a number on that if you'd like." Tony's irreverent remark was inappropriate. The members tried to keep from smirking. Jesuit: "You do see why people who don't know you find it hard to believe your account of events?" Tony: "Not until just now. They have never engaged in the war between good and evil. I'm describing things outside of their field of experience." Jesuit: "Have you ever told people how hard you prayed during these trials, these confrontations?" Tony: "No. I never thought to." Jesuit: "Maybe you should."

Core Board Redux

The next day Tony's classmates made the predictable effort to grace his table with their illustrious presence. They questioned Tony about places he used to work. Their questions jumped ahead of the information Tony gave them. Mr. Stevens was especially skilled in this regard. Tony mentioned six managers transferred and Mr. Stevens asked about the manager who resigned. Mr. Stevens butted in before Tony mentioned a manager who resigned. Tony kept the conversation flowing, "Five managers transferred to different buildings, the other transferred to our sister plant in Columbus, Ohio."

All four of Tony's classmates were gripped with fear! David: "You have put us all in danger!" Tony was confused, "How are you guys in danger?" David: "We are in Columbus, Ohio." Tony: "So?" All four were terrified and started babbling. Tony was baffled by their baseless fears. Most of the silliness came from Mr. Stevens and David. Greg was the most intelligent of the bunch, but he was afraid. Leo was ex-military, but he too was afraid. "Please," Tony deadpanned, "be serious." Mr. Stevens started in on Tony, "You think it's funny you put us in danger, don't you?" He carried on at great length.

Tony did not understand their fears. Tony: "I dealt with those people years ago. I took sufficient precautions at the time. It's over." David: "One of those men is here in this city. He could end up bumping into you on the street." Tony: "How does that put you guys in harm's way?" Mr. Stevens: "He could follow you back here." They convinced themselves they were in jeopardy. The more they obsessed, the more they were convinced the entire seminary was in danger.

Tony laughed, "Be serious." Mr. Stevens got himself so worked up spittle started collecting at the left corner of his mouth. It looked like he was starting to foam at the mouth. *Mad dog! Mad dog!* Tony turned to Leo, "Explain to this man he's worried over nothing. Look at my face. Do I look worried? Even if I had cause for concern, which I don't, you guys certainly don't." Leo: "I'll see what I can do." Tony turned to Greg, "Please, talk some sense to your friend."

> Wisdom 17:10 (DRA) [31] For whereas wickedness is fearful, it beareth witness of its condemnation: for a troubled conscience always forecasteth grievous things.

Formation Director November

Tony went to his November meeting with his PFD. The Jesuit and Tony had a productive discussion on prayer. The priest shared his suggested reading list with Tony. Then the Jesuit asked, "Did you meet with a counselor?" Tony: "Yes, last week Father." Jesuit: "What did you discuss?" Tony: "She thought I was there voluntarily, but I assured her I was enjoined by my formation director to be there." The Jesuit flushed, "Did you establish a rapport with her?" Tony: "Yes, I did."

The priest looked confused. Jesuit: "I doubt she would agree. She feels you do not trust her. In fact, she said you think the practice of psychology is irreligion." Tony: "Correct and correct." Jesuit: "Do you know what irreligion is?" Tony: "Yes I do Father." Jesuit: "Stating you think her field of expertise is garbage is what you call establishing a rapport?" Tony: "I established an understanding, a rapport. I didn't say it was a warm, fuzzy one." Jesuit: "Do you plan to see her next month?" Tony: "It's a waste of time." Jesuit: "I want you to see her every month." Tony: "If I am forced to see her every month, I will." Jesuit: "Yes, I want you to continue seeing her."

The Nun

After leaving the meeting with his formation director, Tony wended his way down dimly lit halls to return to the dorm. Before he reached the main corridor, the nun who sat on his core board stepped out from the shadows. She was waiting for Tony. Her face clearly showed she was troubled. When she spoke, her voice trembled. She immediately confided, "No one here at the Pontifical Jeroboam likes me. No one talks to me. I don't understand it. These are all priests and seminarians. They are not even civil to me. They are nasty and rude for no reason. I don't understand it. Can you tell me what's going on?" Her voice quavered so much it gave Tony a sick feeling in his stomach.

The nun was so distraught! Her face and her voice told of the great anguish she suffered from being ostracized and isolated. Nun: "I don't understand why no one likes me. Can you tell me what's going on?" Tony did not know what to say. This woman just filleted her heart open to him and exposed the raw nerve endings. It was as profound as it was sad. Nun: "Is it me? Is there something wrong with me? Is that why no one likes me?" Her voice was laden with distress.

If I tell her it is because they are homosexuals, will that answer her question and assuage her tortured soul? Will she believe me? She is on my core board. Mishandling this could get me the boot immediately. Her coming to me is highly improper. Is she here at the Vice Rector's direction? It is not possible to fake the limbic reactions she is displaying. Her voice sounds like her soul is deeply tormented. Five years in this place will make me every bit the basket case she is, or worse. The only student I know is Javier, and he is doomed. Saying the wrong thing to this nun can spell instant disaster for me.

Tony was unsure how to proceed. He wanted to help the nun. Tony: "I haven't made friends with anyone since I've been here. You're right, everyone is very standoffish." Nun: "They're not just standoffish, they're nasty and mean. These are priests and seminarians. What's going on?" As much as Tony wanted to help the nun, he decided he could not. The fact she had a stakeout and ambushed him was disconcerting. Tony: "Sister, it's not you, and it's not your imagination. There are some seriously miserable people here." Nun: "But these are priests and seminarians!" Tony: "Sister, I want you to feel free to talk to me anytime. Please join me at lunch in the refectory some time. I always sit at the first table at lunch."

Nun: "Yes, I've noticed. Why don't the other students sit with you? You seem friendly and sociable." Tony: "Like you said Sister, they're not civil to me either." Nun: "Aren't you afraid there's something wrong with you?" Tony: "No Sister. I have traveled quite a bit. Everywhere I went I was well received until I moved to California. I got exactly this same reception in California." Nun: "Why did people in California snub you?" Tony: "The easy answer is: they don't like people from the east coast, they don't like Italians, and they don't like engineers. The real answer is: California is filled with godless people." Nun: "Are you saying the priests and seminarians at the Pontifical Jeroboam are godless?"

Tony: "I haven't figured out what's going on here Sister. I haven't been here very long. Whatever it is, you and I are outsiders. You and I need to figure out what group these people are members of. Until we do, don't even for a moment think there's something wrong with you, because there's not. In the meantime, feel free to join me at lunch." The nun gained some reassurance from Tony. The wild look in her eyes faded. Nun: "Well, since I'm on your core board it would be improper for me to visit with you. I hoped you could answer a couple of questions for me." Tony: "I'm sorry I was unable to help." "No," she said thoughtfully, "you've answered at least one question for me. I appreciate your help."

Tony: "Why did you come to me Sister?" Nun: "I was impressed by you in core board, just as the Jesuit undoubtedly is. You're not like the other seminarians I have for core board. I hoped you would know how you are different from the others." Tony: "Check with me again Sister. I'll tell you what I learn."

The nun never did check back with Tony. At subsequent core boards, the nun was pensive. Tony was confident her clandestine conversation was genuine.

6 THEY THAT CONSENT

Mexican Restaurant

Javier stopped by Tony's room after dinner. He was seething! Javier: "I need to talk! We can't talk here. They can listen through the walls if they want. We can't go off campus either." Tony: "Why can't we go off campus?" Javier: "We don't have a car. Even if we did, we don't have money." Tony: "I have a truck, and I have money. Let's go someplace and have a beer." Javier: "I can't ask you to spend your money when I don't have any." Tony: "Look, I could use a cold beer to wash the bad taste of this place out of my mouth. You're the only friend I have here, and I don't drink alone." Javier: "Why don't you drink alone? Are you a recovering alcoholic?" Tony: "No, thank you very much. I want to drink beer and bitch about queers. I can't do that by myself. Are you going to help me or not?" Javier smiled brightly!

Javier accompanied Tony to his pickup in the far lot. The starter groaned as it slowly cranked the reluctant motor. Javier: "What's wrong with your truck?" Tony: "Neglect. I parked it here during orientation and haven't seen it since. Letting it sit for over two months nearly killed the battery. Good thing we decided to get off campus. This will recharge the battery." As Tony drove, Javier noted, "Your headlights are dim. What's wrong with them?" Tony: "The battery is that low. Running the motor will fix it." After a short drive, they found a Mexican restaurant. The place was deserted. They sat at a table and ordered beer. The waitress brought chips and hot salsa. Javier recently got a letter from his girlfriend. He was upset by the letter, but even more upset by the antics of his fellow seminarians.

Javier: "I talked to one of my friends about my girlfriend's letter. Two hours later the Vice Rector was in my face! That lousy queer ran right to the Vice Rector! I had a different conversation with another friend on a different subject. Within a half hour, the Vice Rector was in my face again! These stinking queers are in a hurry to get me kicked out! I thought these guys were my friends. Now I find out it's them against us! They want all straight guys kicked out of here. Last night one of the guys I thought was my friend spent the night with that fat slob next door. They were making noise, talking and laughing, and making strange sounds all night long. I didn't get any sleep. He was one of the guys who went to the Vice Rector to tattletale on me. How would he like it if I told on him?"

Tony: "You do understand reporting homosexual activity to the Vice Rector won't work, right? The Vice Rector supports homosexuality above all else. Incidentally, the Vice Rector is on my core board." Javier: "How unlucky for you." Tony: "I'm not convinced his being on my core board is a random event. Anyway, subject matter discussed at my first core board Tuesday evening was the subject of conversation among my classmates the next day." Javier: "How many of them are gay?" Tony: "All four." Javier: "Do you know this for sure?" Tony: "With absolute certainty." Javier: "Are you sure they haven't heard these things from someone else you talked to?" Tony: "Absolutely, I don't talk to anyone, so there is no confusion. The Vice Rector is sharing the content of my core board with the queers."

Javier: "Core board is supposed to be strictly confidential! How can you be sure it's the Vice Rector?" Tony: "Three of the members have limited access to the students, they're not likely suspects, and there's no way the Jesuit is doing it." Javier: "That's a very serious accusation to make. Can you prove it?" Tony: "Of course not." Javier: "You should go to the Rector with this!" Tony: "The day they had us installing pavers in the courtyard I overheard a conversation between the Rector and Vice Rector. They were discussing me. The Vice Rector said it was a problem and it was going to take time. I am their problem because I witnessed hall traffic at three a.m. For that, the Rector and Vice Rector want me gone.

You and I came here to be priests. We thought this was still a seminary. Turns out homosexuals have taken control of the facility and turned it into Club Queer. It's like being trapped in the *Twilight Zone*." In his best Rod Serling voice, Tony said, "Javier and Tony, two theology students, thought they were entering the Pontifical seminary, but instead were entering: the *Twilight Zone*." It was wasted on Javier. He had no idea what the *Twilight Zone* is. Javier had more than a year to go before he would be ordained. He was still optimistic he could make it.

Javier: "You have over four years to go Tony. Do you think you can do it?" Tony: "I know I can't. I don't want to work with these perverts anyway. I certainly don't care to live with them. Even if I wanted to stay, they won't let me." Javier: "If you've already made up your mind, why don't you leave now?" Tony: "(*Cover story*) It's almost winter. This is the wrong time of the year to look for a job. I want to hold out until spring at least. I'd feel better if I could finish the year." Javier: "Do you think they'll let you?" Tony: "Not on purpose. It looks like they focus everyone's attention on one target at a time. I think they'll continue to concentrate on you." Javier laughed, "I agree. After they get rid of me, they will come after you next. What will you do when they come after you?" Tony: "I don't know. I don't think there's anything I can do. They isolate their target."

Javier: "What does that accomplish?" Tony: "Look what it did to Jake. Look what it is doing to you. It's very effective." Javier: "What possible reason would the Vice Rector have for doing these things?" Tony: "Head games." Javier: "You think that's what they did to Jake?" Tony: "That's what they did to Jake." Javier: "You think this is the same thing?" Tony: "Yes, this is the same thing." Javier: "What makes you so sure?" Tony: "The Vice Rector uses military tactics. This is textbook psychological warfare." Javier: "If we know what they're doing, we will be able to stop it, right?" Tony: "Wrong. It's only a matter of time. The weak and untrained fold quickly, the strong and trained last only a little bit longer. The Vice Rector uses it because it works."

Javier: "I thought you and Jake were both paranoid, but now I'm not so sure. Why didn't I see what they were doing to Jake?" Tony: "They isolate their target so there are no credible witnesses to actual events. They isolated Jake. You were never able to witness the events they staged." Javier felt guilty, "I should have been a better friend to Jake. I'm sorry I doubted him." Tony: "The Vice Rector runs a well oiled machine. He knows what he is doing and he is confident of the outcome. There is nothing you or I can do to stop him." Javier was optimistic, "I majored in theology, but minored in psychology. Their head games won't work on us. If the two of us stick together, they won't be able to break us the way they did Jake." Tony: "Yes they will." Javier: "No. All we have to do is stick together."

Tony: "Tuesday night I had my second core board. The next day my classmates showed off the fact that they were fully briefed on what I said at core board the night before." Javier was instantly angry! He had plenty to say on the subject and railed at length. Tony: "I know core board is supposed to be confidential. Yes, I think the Vice Rector is briefing my classmates on my core board but I am unable to confirm that and I certainly cannot prove it. It's the same thing that happened after my first core board." Javier: "It happened twice?" Tony: "Yes, after each core board. This time Mr. Stevens demonstrated detailed knowledge of what I said at core board." Javier's temper spiked! "Doesn't it make you mad that fat slob can parrot your core board conversation back to you?" Tony: "Of course it does." Javier: "Why would the Vice Rector reveal your core board to your classmates?"

Tony: "Who knows?" Javier: "You should tell the Rector what's going on!" Tony: "How did that work for Jake? If I accuse the Vice Rector without evidence, where does that leave me? When the Rector interrogates my classmates, what sort of testimony can I expect from them?" Javier was quiet for some time. "This is the same thing they did to Jake," Javier said slowly, "they're messing with you at the same time they're messing with me. This can't be good. What do you think it means?" Tony: "It means the Vice Rector is highly confident of his methods. It means he's in a hurry to get rid of us both." Javier was lost in thought. Once Javier returned to the conversation he said, "Jake was right all along. I'm sorry I doubted him." Javier talked about the letter from his girlfriend. Tony ordered another round.

Javier asked Tony what was new with him. Tony: "The nun on my core board ambushed me. She was a mess." Javier: "What do you mean she ambushed you?" Tony: "She surreptitiously waited for me to come out of the Jesuit's office so she could talk to me in private." Javier: "What did she want to talk about that required a clandestine meeting?" Tony: "She was in the deepest funk I've ever seen. No one here likes her. No one talks to her. Everyone is mean and nasty to her and she doesn't know why. She asked me what's wrong with her." Javier: "What did you tell her?" Tony: "I assured her there's nothing wrong with her." Javier: "You can't tell her what the problem is! She is on your core board! It's a trap!" Tony: "This woman was in agony. Her soul was wrung out like a wet dishrag."

Javier: "She could've been acting!" Tony: "It's not possible to fake the limbic reactions she displayed. She was in torment. I wanted to help her." Javier: "You can't take the chance!" Tony: "I didn't. I told her people in California treated me the same way. I assured her it's them and not her." Javier: "She had to ask what was wrong with Californians. What did you tell her?" Tony: "I told her Californians are godless people." Javier: "Why did you tell her anything?" Tony: "She asked for help and she seriously needed it." Javier: "No! No! You said too much! You would have her infer the people here are godless? What did she say to that?" Tony: "Twice she said the behavior of the people here doesn't make sense since they are all priests and seminarians and are supposed to be holy men. After I shared my California experience with her, she said it one more time."

Javier: "I don't know Tony. If she is not on the level, it could work against you. Why did she come to you?" Tony: "She said I'm not like the others. She asked me if I knew how I was different from the rest." Javier: "You didn't tell her!" Tony: "No, I didn't. If I told her this place is rife with homosexuals she might not believe it." Javier: "Implying these people are godless isn't much better." Tony: "Yes it is. It's more to the point, and it's something she will be able to come to terms with a lot sooner." Javier: "I hope you're right Tony."

Javier drained his glass, "What about the Jesuit? He sent you to a counselor. Do you think he's gay?" Tony: "No." Javier: "What makes you think so? He's cooperating with them." Tony: "He has the knowledge of a priest and he does the business of the Church."

Javier: "What about the Vice Rector?" Tony: "He has no knowledge of the Old Testament. He has demonstrated that time and again in core board. When I reference something in the Old Testament, he turns to the Jesuit for confirmation. He does the business of homosexuals and not the business of the Church." Javier: "Do you think he at least believes in God?" Tony: "He believes in something. At core board he showed fear every time the others showed approval." Javier: "He's a practiced bureaucrat. His fears could have nothing to do with faith." Tony: "I'm not sure whether he believes in God or not, but he is reticent to bet against Him."

Javier: "What makes you think the Jesuit and the Vice Rector are so different? Why do you think the Jesuit sent you to a counselor?" Tony: "I think the Vice Rector told him to." Javier: "Why would the Jesuit cooperate with homosexuals to the detriment of the Church?" Tony: "He's an old man. It's probably a case of go along to get along." Javier: "Jesuits are the Church's version of the Marines. If you are suggesting he is too old to fight, I disagree. I say that's not possible, he's a Jesuit!" Tony: "Maybe he doesn't know what's going on, the same as the nun. He's just following orders; nothing more, nothing less." Javier agreed that was likely.

Byzantine Priest

The five transfer students were the only members of a rhetoric class. The instructor is a Byzantine priest. During class discussion the instructor asked, "Why are we able to scientifically quantify our world, yet we are unable to do the same with God?" Tony offered his closed universe model, the one he presented to the seventh grade religious instruction class. The priest was curious what possible connection a model of a closed universe could have with religious instruction or his language class. He encouraged Tony to go to the chalkboard and quickly explain. Tony drew a sideways figure 8 bisected by a thin disk and quickly described his model. Byzantine: "How does it relate to this course?" Tony: "Math and physics are the languages of science. They describe matter and energy, so those two languages can only describe what is inside this three-dimensional figure 8.

Because they can only be used to describe physical existence, they are unable to be applied outside of this figure." Priest: "What is the significance of a closed universe model?" Tony: "It's a convenient contrivance. It simplifies the description and hopefully facilitates understanding. If nothing else, it gives me the ability to make a schematic drawing. To answer your question, math and physics can only describe what is inside this figure. Things outside, such as God, heaven, and hell, cannot be described by math or physics. Language is the only thing we have to describe God, spirituality, and all that is outside of our physical universe." The instructor looked on with interest. Mr. Stevens taunted, "God is everywhere. God is also inside your figure 8. Explain that!" The instructor frowned.

Tony: "Examining consubstantial matter under a microscope has its challenges. However, in Italy there is a communion host on display that is a century old. During the Mass when it was consecrated, the edge turned into flesh. Neither the flesh nor the wafer has deteriorated in a century, even though it is exposed to ambient atmosphere. Examination under a microscope shows the flesh is heart muscle from a human male." The other four students spoke at once, asking the priest if this was true. He smiled and nodded to affirm. Turning to face Tony, Mr. Stevens irritably demanded, "Why have we never heard about this?" Tony: "How hard have you looked? The Church does not advertise miracles to convince people to believe. Faith is not based on miracles."

During another class, the instructor selected different types of poetry for demonstration purposes. One short piece did not seem to be a poem. (Taken from a poster created by Cassandre A.m. Adolphe Jean-marie Mouron in 1935).

Dubo
Dubon
Dubonnet

The instructor smiled and asked, "Where does this poem place you on the planet?" The students exchanged blank expressions. Priest: "Where are you standing?" Tony was inspired, "On the platform in a subway station in Paris." The priest smiled, “Are you sure you’re on the platform?” Tony sounded doubtful, but said yes.

The priest smiled, “I am on a train coming into the station, looking out the window at the platform of a Paris subway station.” Tony: “Oh yeah, right. The growth of the word demonstrates the motion of the train.” The other four students were incensed! Mr. Stevens: “How are we supposed to get Paris subway station from that little bit? Those aren’t even words!” Mr. Stevens turned to Tony and indignantly demanded, “How did you know that?” Tony: “Because I was there. I remembered where I saw the Dubonnet poster.” The other students complained, “What is Dubonnet?” Instructor: “Tony, can you tell them?” Tony: “Dubonnet is an aperitif, an alcoholic drink served before the meal.” The priest agreed. Tony’s classmates were not endeared to Tony to begin with. Attending this class together did nothing to improve the situation.

Tony managed to produce one assignment to his classmates’ approval. It was a written assignment:

Chanting the Liturgy of the Hours

Evening prayer at the seminary was my first encounter with the Liturgy of the Hours. The vivid, compelling language of the Psalms was enhanced by the simple, clear tones chanted by eighty-five voices. The antiphonal method of chant softened the Psalms and highlighted the Psalm-prayers and antiphons. Like any new skill, the first few times my mind was preoccupied with technique, rather than content. By the end of the second week, I was unconsciously matching my voice to the one group voice while studying the contents and the message of the Psalm being chanted.

The conversations, praise, and lamentations chanted to God inevitably touched upon personal experiences in daily life. Public praise to God was familiar enough in the Mass. Community lamentation to God was a new experience; both startling and reassuring. It expanded the range of human emotions that are okay to present to God.

Participation in the one group voice blurred the mental boundary between myself and the whole. My awareness spread out like water to the far reaches of the chapel. Chanting the Psalms enlarged my sense of the whole. These shifts in perspective made possible new vistas of thought and emotion relative to God, to the group, and to the entirety of mankind. Alternately and at once, I was alone and was part of a large group, a nebula before God in prayer. The chant focused my mind on the Psalm and unfocused background self-consciousness; my thoughts were clear of all but God’s word.

Piano Bar

After dinner, Javier stopped by Tony's room. "This is Karl. He is Eastern European. He's even more freaked out by gays than you are." Karl was similar to Javier in stature and build, compact with dark features. Javier: "We should get together and exchange notes someplace where we can't be overheard." Tony: "Let's go to a bar and have a few drinks." Javier and Karl both had no money and did not want to mooch. Tony: "Look, I want something good to drink. I drink single malt scotch and I don't want to drink alone. Do you guys think you can choke down at least one scotch?" It took some convincing before they agreed they would like to try a scotch.

Tony: "Good. Let's eat dinner early tomorrow, leave the refectory separately, and meet in the far parking lot." Javier: "Karl doesn't know where your truck is parked." Tony: "Head for the access road, Javier and I will pick you up on our way out."

The next evening Tony went to dinner. His meal was half eaten before Javier and Karl joined him. Javier apologized for being late. Tony: "This is better this way. Everyone saw me come in alone. You two were spaced far enough apart so it's not certain you were together. If we each leave the table when we finish eating, no one will think we were together." Karl was in full agreement. Javier scoffed at the idea, "Sounds paranoid to me." Tony: "It's not paranoia if they really are out to get you. You know they really are after you, right?" Karl smiled in agreement. Javier started a conversation. Karl was content to listen. Tony finished his dessert and excused himself. Tony: "Take your time. I am going back to my room to get my jacket. Later."

Tony retrieved his jacket and sauntered across the parking lots. He checked under the hood and checked tire pressure. When he saw Javier, he started the truck. Javier got in and Tony drove down the access road. He stopped to pick up Karl. Javier got out so Karl could sit in the middle. No way was Karl sitting in the middle. The two were at an impasse. Tony: "Can't you see Karl doesn't want to sit next to me? He doesn't know me, he only knows you. You have to sit in the middle." Javier: "I don't want to sit in the middle. I want to sit next to the door." Tony: "Javier, you have to sit in the middle. Get in or I'll leave without you." Javier got in. Karl smiled. Javier pouted because he had to sit in the middle.

Tony: "Karl doesn't know me. Can't you see he's scared?" Javier: "I told him we're friends. I told him you're ok." Tony: "You've been fooled before. I don't blame him for being careful." Karl smiled again. Javier: "Where are we going?" Tony: "I found a piano bar in the newspaper that plays jazz. Let's go there unless you have a better idea." Javier: "I feel funny going to a piano bar with guys. That's the type of place I'd take a date." Tony: "We have to go to an upscale place if we hope to be served a decent scotch. In a piano bar, we can talk above the music. Anyway, there are three of us. Piano bar it is."

The place was deserted. It was too early for anyone but the piano player to be there. Tony ordered three McCallum ® neat with water back. Javier and Karl agreed this was a treat. The three discussed the miserable situation at the seminary. Karl: "If the homosexuals see us together they'll know we are straight and target us. The only way a straight guy can survive here is to remain isolated. That way, they can't be sure we are straight." Tony agreed, "That makes sense. There is a man in my classes who hangs out with the queers, yet he's an outcast. It took me weeks to figure out what the deal was. The rest of them are sexually active. He's an outcast because he's not having sex with them." Karl smiled, "All the homosexuals know who you are Tony." Tony: "I know. I'm their primary target once they finish with Javier."

Javier noted this was the first time he saw Karl relax all year. Tony: "That's why we came here, to relax and get our blood pressure down." Karl: "You have high blood pressure?" Tony: "Not until I came to the seminary and started living in a five story queer's nest." Upon questioning, Tony likened the theology dorm to a beehive. Karl nodded. Javier scoffed.

Karl: "I apologize Tony, but if I'm seen with you too much on campus they'll target me too. I prefer to meet with you and Javier in private and limit the number of times we eat together." Javier: "Karl and I live near each other. We can be seen eating together more often without raising suspicion, no offense." Tony agreed, "Extra precautions make sense. We need to protect Karl. Of the three of us, he's the only one they have not targeted." Javier: "No offense to you Tony." Karl: "No disrespect Tony." Tony: "I know. I agree. We have to take every precaution to protect Karl. I will not be allowed to graduate. We all know that. I want to be careful not to put my stink on anyone else. We all have to be careful."

Karl felt bad. He was compelled to explain why he is vulnerable. He came from Eastern Europe. His sponsors pay for his schooling only. He has no stipend for living expenses. His parents are poor and unable to send money. He is half a world away from anyone he knows. Karl: "The only people I know here at school are you two, and being seen too much with you guys will get me kicked out. You know I would like to hang out with you guys. You also know why I can't." Javier: "I know." Tony: "We understand." Karl: "I am so sorry."

Tony: "We are too." Karl: "How about you Tony? Who is your sponsor? What kind of support do you have?" Tony: "I come from a rural diocese. They pay for me to go here. They paid for the four volume set of *The Liturgy of the Hours* [42] for me." Karl: "That's expensive. I have a used copy of the single volume in paperback. I had to buy it myself." Javier also had the single volume edition. Tony: "My vocation director visited recently. We had lunch in the refectory. He gave me a small icon, compliments of the diocese. I don't even know what an icon is." Karl: "The Byzantine Church uses icons. An icon is considered to be a window into heaven. We have a Byzantine priest here. Talk to him, he will explain icons to you. It is much more than a statue or painting and requires special treatment."

Tony: "The vocation director just handed it to me as if it were a religious souvenir." Javier: "Why did your vocation director drive all the way here to see you? Are you in trouble?" Tony: "My classmates started heckling me, telling me my vocation director was coming to see me and I must be in big trouble. They heckled me for days before the director called to tell me he would be down the following day." Javier: "I'll bet my next door neighbor was doing most of the heckling." Tony: "Ding, ding, ding! We have a winner." Karl: "What did he want? Were you in trouble?" Tony: "He was probably called here to receive instruction because he messed up. I am the second straight candidate he sent here in two years. He decided I was a queer when he interviewed me." Javier: "What made him think that?"

Tony: "A holy priest lined me up to come here, but he was transferred to the Vatican. His replacement was stuck completing the process. The vocation director must have thought the replacement was my mentor instead of a reluctant proxy. When I answered the director's questions about dating and girlfriends I told him the truth, but he thought I was lying. At the end of the interview, I knew he thought I was a homo. At the time, I did not know why he thought so. Now I know. The replacement priest must be a homo." Javier: "Didn't that tip you off something was wrong?" Karl: "That should have scared you off immediately!" Tony: "My mentor, Father Nick, is obviously a holy man. I was moving forward on his recommendation. I was looking forward to working with him.

The day I got here, the hair on the back of my neck stood on end. Still, I would not let myself know what was wrong. After three hours, I could no longer deny the obvious. I felt incredibly stupid. There were a number of times I should have been alerted to the problem. I realized homosexuals were infiltrating the ranks of priests. I did not realize they had already taken control." Javier laughed, "You remember Jake. Jake met Tony at a meeting before school started. Jake was excited and in a hurry to explain things to Tony. He wanted to talk to Tony alone, away from the gays. Tony was afraid to talk to him in private. Jake never got to warn him." Javier and Karl could not stop laughing! Tears streamed down Karl's face from laughing so hard. Tony ordered another round.

Javier and Karl tried to apologize, but they could not stop laughing. When they finally did stop, they felt terrible for having laughed so hard. Tony: "Our nerves have been through a meat grinder, and it's not over. There was a lot of nervous tension being cut loose in those laughs. We are all in the same boat." "And the boat is sinking," added Javier. All three men nodded agreement. Karl: "Do you have any support beyond what you've mentioned?" Tony: "The diocese must have given my name and address to groups or clubs. One month I received a nice card from an elderly lady. She added a short note expressing support and thanking me for my service to the Church. She put a $5 bill inside the card.

The next month I received a card from a different lady. She sent similar expressions of moral support and gratitude. She put a $10 bill in the card. Once a month I receive a card signed by little children, I'd guess second graders. I know very few people in the diocese. I'm surprised how uplifting it is to receive cards like these from strangers." Karl: "Did you have encouragement from your family to join the priesthood? Are there any inspiring stories you can share with us?" Tony:

"Relatives I expected to congratulate me held their breath when I told them. Their reactions made no sense then, but they do now. There was something my confirmation sponsor told me that I thought was pretty good. He is an engineer. When someone at work busts on him and asks him to explain his view of the Bible he tells them:

> As an engineer, I design electro/mechanical machines for the company to manufacture. My assignment is not complete until I write the manufacturer's manual for the operation and maintenance of the machine.
>
> I specify the parameters required for the proper function and operation of the machine. The power requirement is: 120 V, 60 Hz AC +/- 5%. Fairly clean power, but not prohibitively so. The humidity should be between 40% and 85%. You don't want electronics to short out due to condensation, and you don't want seals to dry out and crack due to extreme arid conditions. The ambient temperature should be between 50°F and 80°F. If the temperature strays outside that range, the machine will still operate, but not as efficiently and with degraded quality. The machine needs to be reasonably level for optimum efficiency. I specify a preventive maintenance schedule that includes periodic cleaning and lubrication of specified locations. If you operate the machine inside these specifications, you can expect maximum productivity and a long service life. If you operate the machine outside of these parameters, the warranty is void, and you can expect problems including but not limited to; loss of productivity, degraded quality, shortened service life, machine malfunction, or system failure. Operating outside of specified parameters can cause electrical shock hazard and/or fire hazard.
>
> I look at the Bible as the Maker's manual. Operate inside these specifications and you will have trouble-free operation and a long service life. Operate outside these parameters, and you are on your own. The Maker's warranty is null and void and you can expect problems.

Karl: "What did his coworkers think about that?" Tony: "They started out messing with him. They didn't have any snappy remarks after he finished." Karl: "Do you hear from your family?" Tony: "Not much. I moved away from where my folks live years ago. I call them a few times a year." Karl: "Your situation is not much different than ours." Tony: "The cards I receive from strangers in the diocese are starting to look like a big deal. I feel like a thief receiving cash from old ladies when I know I am not going to be able to become a priest. I sold my house, so I have savings and I own a vehicle. That's a big advantage over you guys' situation." Javier: "You can get in your truck, drive away tomorrow, and live a normal life again. We have no place to go and no way to get there."

Tony: "If you guys need help with anything, say so." Javier: "We can't take your money. You said you feel bad for taking money those ladies send you. That is how we would feel if we take your money. We feel bad you have to pay for the drinks." Tony: "You wouldn't let me drink alone would you? Given our situation, we need to do this more often." Karl: "Have you spoken to the priest that is your real mentor since you've been here?" Tony: "Yes, after I was here for a few weeks I called Father Nick. He was happy I called. He asked, "How are they treating you?" I told him, "The full treatment." "Uht-oh, that doesn't sound good." I told him it looks like I won't be working with him after all. I felt bad deserting him, especially now that I know what he's up against."

Karl: "Did he know about the queers?" Tony: "He was oblivious. He did admit he thought thirty percent of the students were homosexual." Karl: "How many did you tell him there are?" Tony: "Twice that and I'm not done counting." Karl: "Why do you think the homosexuals didn't stop him from graduating?" Javier: "I'll bet he doesn't use the word "queers" all the time the way Tony does. You realize they prefer the word gay, don't you?" Tony: "I know." Javier: "Why do you insist on using the word queer?" Tony: "It makes the job of sorting them out a lot easier." Javier: "It makes them angry with you!" Tony: "Like I said. To answer Karl's question, I expect Father Nick was much more congenial and diplomatic than I am." Karl snickered.

Javier griped, "I've made friends here, but the ones who are gay have turned out to be backstabbers." Tony: "Father Nick probably comported himself the way Karl suggested. He must have kept to himself and allowed everyone to ignore him." Karl: "Will you call him again?" Tony: "No. We both felt bad this is not going to work. I felt guilty for deserting him. He is a holy man fighting the good fight. He could use some help."

Javier asked Karl and Tony about their dating experience before entering the seminary. His own experience was ongoing. This part of the conversation lasted through two more rounds of drinks. The end of the discussion reminded Tony of a conversation he had with Roy. Tony: "I used to work with Roy. He is retired now and lives on his boat on Puget Sound. He called last year and read an ad from the personals: "Single white female, 5'6", twenty-one, blonde, blue eyes. I am Republican, I hate Bill Clinton, and I vote."" Javier: "She's too young for you Tony." Tony: "I know, but as soon as Roy read it I said, "Honey, I love you!" Roy laughed. He said he felt the same way.

Roy called her. He said he just had to tell her how much he loved her ad. He apologized for bothering her. She said she understood. She got hundreds of phone calls in response to her ad. Men her age are smitten with her based on the ad. Older men called to tell her how much they appreciated her and to wish her the best. I asked Roy if it was my imagination or was she the only Republican woman in the country. Roy said, "She got hundreds of phone calls, so we're not the only ones that feel that way."" Javier: "It's not too late Tony. You can join a Republican club and meet single women your age after you leave the seminary."

Tony: "That's a good idea. What about you Javier? Has your girlfriend written recently?" Javier: "Yes, she has." Tony: "You asked for my advice before Halloween. Do you still want it?" Javier: "Yes, what do you think?" Tony: "I think the students concocting lies will get you thrown out. If you quit the seminary and return to your girlfriend, you will be happy together. If you get expelled first, your girlfriend will feel like she is plan B and will leave you." Javier: "No. We love each other. She won't leave me." Karl: "Javier, no woman wants to be second best. Take her letters at face value." Tony: "You know the lies won't stop until they get you expelled. If you don't quit first, you will lose your calling and your girlfriend. If you quit and return to her, she will love you even more."

Karl: "Why are you still here Tony? You already know you will be leaving at the end of the year, if not sooner." Tony: "At my first core board, the Jesuit decided I have a genuine calling from the Old Testament, from Jeremiah. He was delighted. With further questioning, I told the core board about "the catch and the fix."" Both men scoffed. Javier: "What is that supposed to mean?" Tony: "I am minding my own business and some anonymous bad guy not only crosses my path, but tangles himself around my legs like a lonesome cat. Once is not enough. The bad guy makes a total nuisance of himself, like chewing gum stuck to the bottom of my shoe." Javier: "Just like the guy who lives next to me!"

Tony: "Exactly. That is what I call "the catch." Unable to avoid the reprobate, I catch him in his wrongdoing with no effort on my part." Javier: "What about "the fix?"" Tony: "I am plagued by [unusual sequence] until my health suffers. My only remedy is to "fix" the situation." Karl and Javier were both excited! Javier: "What did the core board members think about "the catch and the fix?"" Tony: "The Jesuit, the Nun, and the two lay people loved it. The Vice Rector's face turned pale with fear." Javier blurted, "You're God's cleaner! The Vice Rector knows you were sent here to clean up this mess! Your calling is God's cleaner!" Karl asked Tony, "Do you think so? Have you prayed on this?"

Tony: "When I was first here I prayed normally. My prayers quickly deteriorated into lamentations. One night I was overwhelmed. I asked God why He sent me here. He knew I would not be able to deal with this. Certainly, He must want this cleaned up. He must have someone he can count on, a standup guy willing and able to do the dirty jobs. He must have someone with the skills needed for the job. He must have at least one standup guy He can count on. I sat and I pondered what particular skills would be needed to get the job done." Javier could not contain himself, "It was you! He sent you! What do you think? What do you think?"

Tony: "When I made an accounting of the arcane skill set needed, my heart sank into my shoes." Javier: "He sent you!" Karl: "He sent you!" Javier: "What do you think?" Tony: "I didn't smile." Karl and Javier laughed and laughed! Javier: "That fatso that lives next to me, he's "the catch" and the Vice Rector knows it! What are you going to do? What can you do?" Tony: "Bear witness to what goes on here. I'm going to get an eye-full before I leave." Karl: "You need evidence. No one will believe you if you don't have hard evidence." Javier amused himself by repeating, "God's cleaner," at random intervals. Tony: "I think a cleaner is a contract killer. That is not what I do. I catch, I fix."

Javier scoffed at Tony and Karl's aversion to homosexual seminarians. He believed gays could have valid callings to the priesthood in spite of what he saw at the Jeroboam. Tony: "They aren't supposed to be here." Karl agreed, "All of this is the pope's fault. He has not come right out and made a statement forbidding it." Javier objected, "The pope allows gay ordination." Karl rebutted, "Not officially. I searched through the records we have in the library. I found nothing that states homosexuals can be ordained." Tony: "After two thousand years of prohibiting it, a precedent has been set." Javier: "You must have missed it Karl, because it's ok. They only have to be celibate, same as us."

Tony: "Yeah, like that can happen. The covenant with Moses instructed the Israelites to kill homosexuals, male and female." Javier: "That same covenant allowed divorce. Do you think we should be able to divorce?" Karl: "Jesus forbids Christians to divorce." Javier: "Was Moses really instructed to kill gays?" Tony: "Yes." (*Leviticus 20:13*). Javier said condescendingly, "They were also instructed to stone adulterers to death. Does that mean we should kill people for sexual misconduct today?" Tony: "God's covenant with us doesn't require nor allow it. It's clear in the Old Testament that homosexuals are not allowed in the sanctuary, and certainly are not acceptable to God to be ordained priests."

Karl emphatically nodded agreement. Javier scoffed at them both, "It's ok now because the pope said it is. You guys have a medieval attitude. These are modern times." Tony: "Under God's covenant with Moses, homosexuals and adulterers were killed. Today, our Civil Code gives homosexuals protected and or preferential legal status and gives adulterers the option to kill their unborn babies, have taxpayers provide for them, or sue the father for support. Yes, these are modern times indeed."

> Romans 1:27, 32 (DRA) [31] 27 And, in like manner, the men also, leaving the natural use of the women, have burned in their lusts one towards another, men with men working that which is filthy, and receiving in themselves the recompense which was due to their error. 32 Who, having known the justice of God, did not understand that they who do such things, are worthy of death; **and not only they that do them, but they also that consent to them that do them.**
> (Bold type added by author.)

> Romans 1:27, 32 (RSV) [20] 27 and the men likewise gave up natural relations with women and were consumed with passion for one another, men committing shameless acts with men and receiving in their own persons the due penalty for their error. 32 Though they know God's decree that those who do such things deserve to die, they not only do them **but approve those who practice them.**
> (Bold type added by author.)

> 3 Kings 22:47 (DRA) [31] And the remnant also of the effeminate, who

remained in the days of Asa his father, he took out of the land.

Javier was curious why Tony compares the Pontifical Jeroboam to hell *(Gehenna)*. Tony told of when his first grade teacher read from an old European book. Karl and Javier were shocked! They both knew what the book was and said the Church forbids that book. Tony: "The nun told us the book was contraband." Javier: "Then why do you refer to it?" Tony: "It also told of black masses." Javier: "What is a black mass?" Karl said angrily, "It's a satanic ritual that desecrates whatever holy objects it can." Javier was horrified! "Why did the nun tell first graders these things?" Tony: "She warned us of great evils the Church doesn't talk about." Karl: "Do you really think it's that bad here Tony?"

Tony: "I have a bad feeling. I have to know for sure." Javier scoffed. He doubted it was anything like that. Karl doubted the situation was rosy.

> Acts 20:28-29 (DRA) [31] 28 Take heed to yourselves, and to the whole flock, wherein the Holy Ghost hath placed you bishops, to rule the church of God, which he hath purchased with his own blood. 29 I know that, after my departure, ravening wolves will enter in among you, not sparing the flock.

Javier: "Tony is negative about TV too. Why do you hate it when they say, "pushing the envelope" on TV?" Tony: "When they say that, they are bragging about pushing back the limits the FCC placed on indecency over the airwaves. These are the same people who foisted PC onto the public, "and they care,"" Tony said as he poked his index finger into his mouth to feign a gag response. Karl was curious, "Why does the term "pushing the envelope" bother you?" Tony: ""Pushing the envelope" is an engineering description of what test pilots do with an airframe during flight test." Javier laughed, "It bothers you gays stole an engineering term." Tony: "Usurped and perverted, yes. What is it they are doing? Sinning faster than the speed of sound?"

Javier and Karl laughed. Tony: "Really. TV's talking heads brag about encroaching on the FCC with ever-increasing indecency and vulgarity. That's not an accomplishment and it's not funny." Javier: "What does the speed of sound have to do with anything?" Tony: "High performance aircraft break the sound barrier. "Pushing the envelope" describes testing the airframe at its design limits. TV's talking heads use of this term implies their exploits of airwave depravity are as exhilarating and heroic as the flight test prowess of Chuck Yeager. Not! Major General Yeager is an honorable man who served his country with distinction. The talking heads are not in the same universe, much less the same league. The debauchery of TV despoils our nation and defiles all who watch it."

Javier: "What other problems do you have with TV?" Tony: "After debauchery? TV has hypnotized the public to desire "new and unproved."" Javier: "You mean new and improved." Tony: "The marketing mantra is "new and improved," you're right, but the reality of many products is new and unproved. Americans have been conditioned to crave the new and the novel. Detergent soaps have a history of being touted as "new and improved." The brainwash conditioning for "new and improved" is frightfully pandemic. Marketers tap into a group of people they call tastemakers, people with an emotional and mental need to be the first to have a new product. This behavior has been generalized so Americans react negatively to the old and the traditional."

Javier: "Why is that a problem?" Tony: "When something works, it gets used. That is how the old ways became established as the old ways. The established ways became tradition because they worked, because they survived the test of time. Blindly and reflexively throwing away things proven over time in favor of something unproven, new, and novel is irresponsible, imprudent, and completely devoid of wisdom. AIDS patients are not quarantined, for example, even though there is no cure or treatment." Javier: "Quarantine is medieval." Tony: "My point exactly. Established wisdom is dismissed without the scrutiny of logic or reason by using the sound bite "medieval" as a derisive insult.

1 Thessalonians 5:21 (DRA) [31] But prove all things; hold fast that which is good.

1 Thessalonians 5:21 (RSV-C) [40] but test everything; hold fast what is good,

TV portrays the corruption and incompetence of managers and businessmen and the harm they can do to society. I don't recall scientists and technicians receiving equal scrutiny on television." Karl: "Why do you think that is important?" Tony: "If science is going to work as advertised, there must be strict adherence to the rules. It is no longer science if there is incompetence or cheating. For example, Salk, Sabin, and a third doctor were doing research to find an efficacious polio vaccine. The third doctor went to Africa, where he could work on his vaccine unfettered by ethical oversight. He cheated the scientific method and basic safety protocols in order to accelerate his research and perform it on the cheap.

The region where his test subjects lived was shown on a map in *The Lancet*, the British medical journal. Some twenty years later that same area is where the AIDS outbreak started. I'll bet no American can name the third doctor." Javier and Karl both knew the doctor's name. Javier: "Why do you think there has been no news coverage of this in the U.S.?" Tony: "I think the American media wants to replace God with science. Exposing this catastrophe demonstrates that science is simply a tool that is only as good or as evil as those who employ it. I think that's why Americans will never know the third doctor's name."

Proverbs 16:3 (DRA) [31] Lay open thy works to the Lord: and thy thoughts shall be directed.

Tony: "Another problem I have with TV is crowding." Karl: "What is crowding?" Tony: "Time is a limited resource. If I watch two hours of TV after dinner every night, that's 14 hours a week I'm not doing something else, such as reading, exercising, studying, socializing, meditating, praying, relaxing, or anything else. The fourteen hours wasted in front of the television has crowded out other activities." Javier: "Watching TV is relaxing." Tony: "It's less relaxing than you think. When I bought my first TV, I was startled at how tense watching TV made me. TV is not as innocuous as people believe." Karl: "Did you know there's a TV lounge in the dorm, one floor below us?" Javier chuckled. Tony: "Are you kidding?" Karl and Javier assured Tony it was true.

It was time to return to campus.

When they got back to campus, Karl asked to get out on the access road. This saved him some walking but also saved him time. He was in the dorm a good five minutes before Tony and Javier. Karl had a good understanding of security measures. Javier, on the other hand, saw no reason not to tag along with Tony.

7 REFUSE TO OBEY

Stand

Mass at the Pontifical Jeroboam was a little bit different. The seminarians stood during the consecration rather than kneel. The majority of students were proud of this fact. One day Mr. Stevens had an urgent message for his cohorts before class. "Did you hear? The pope sent a communication directly to the administration! He ordered we immediately discontinue the practice of standing during the consecration. He said we have no special privileges just because this is a Pontifical seminary. We have to kneel during the consecration the same as the rest of the world." After the four men complained about the pope's mandate David asked, "What do you think Tony?"

Tony: "I was confused why we were standing to begin with. Kneeling is much more reverent. I'm embarrassed the pope had to specifically issue instructions to us on how to comport ourselves during Mass." Greg talked between his teeth in a low voice to his cohorts, "Ignore him, what does he know? He's a killjoy anyhow."

All seminarians discussed this for the next two days. Three days after the theology students were unofficially aware; the Vice Rector officially announced the pope's mandate before midday Mass in the chapel. When it was time for the consecration, everyone remained standing. The pope's order was ignored again the following day.

The pope made a phone call to the Vice Rector. (The Rector recently started a month long vacation to spend two weeks in China and one week in the Vatican.) The pope was adamant. He was not amused. The Pontifical Jeroboam finally followed instructions. Greg griped, "There has to be a snitch. It has to be one of the students." All four classmates looked accusingly at Tony. Tony: "Don't look at me. I don't know how to contact the pope."

Spiritual Advisor

The Friar was a compassionate, empathetic man who performed his job duties with diligence and perhaps zeal. During the first week of class, he scheduled Tony to meet with him the beginning of the second week. Their first session was awkward. The Friar was self-conscious and embarrassed that Tony recoiled at the Friar's good idea of having Tony urinate in the sink in his room. Friar: "I don't see why using the sink is a problem. All you have to do is turn on the cold water to make sure it doesn't smell. You have to protect yourself. You saw what a stir it caused when you were in the corridor in the middle of the night. You don't want to go through that again." Tony: "I prefer to use the toilet. I don't see what the problem is. I wore clogs and a bathrobe over my pajamas (gym clothes repurposed as sleep wear)."

The Friar flashed with anger, "Your presence in the corridor at that time of the night is disturbing to the other students!" Tony: "I was careful to be quiet so I wouldn't wake anyone." Friar: "For your own good, don't use the corridor late at night! There's no reason you can't use the sink!" Ok, after that business was out of the way, the Friar performed his job well and with gusto. His sessions always had plenty of instruction and information, usually printed materials for handout, and were always interesting. He thanked Tony once again for the cigar. Tony had three sessions with his spiritual advisor before his first session with his formation director or his first core board. This illustrates the industry and dedication of the Friar. He had an open door policy and encouraged students to stop by his office to discuss class, spiritual matters, any questions whatsoever, or just to say hi.

The Friar addressed his class: "It's December already. Where does the time go? There is a parish on the south side of the city that has requested our help. The pastor is close to retirement and has asked us to send some seminarians to help out. When he was first ordained, he was assigned to that parish. There were not enough parishioners to keep the doors open. The bishop sent him there with instructions to close the church within a year. Instead, he discovered bingo. Monday night bingo was so successful he expanded into Tuesday night as well. With the proceeds, he runs the best soup kitchen in the city. Indigents and homeless people from the north side take a bus to eat in his soup kitchen. The food is that good.

Over the years, there have been many write-ups in the newspaper praising the quality of food served in his soup kitchen. With so much notoriety and favorable press, the bishop has not been able to force his hand to close the parish." Tony: "It's unusual for a priest to spend his entire life in one parish." Friar: "Yes it is. With so much press coverage, the bishop has left him alone completely. That priest used bingo to finance his life's work of running not just a soup kitchen, but the best soup kitchen in the metropolitan area. His assignment however, was to close an empty church. He needs the church in order to run the soup kitchen. The problem is the church is still empty. *That priest is using the Church's assets as his own.*

Catholics do a lot of things well, but evangelism is not one of them.

Shamefully, the Catholic Church does almost no evangelism inside this country. Overseas missions emanating from America are many. They are strong, prolific, and abundantly fruitful; which makes it all the more embarrassing we do almost nothing inside our own country. The pastor invited us to his parish to help evangelize the surrounding neighborhood. I want to use the students in my class for this assignment. Be sure to tell your formation director you are participating in this and keep him apprised. One of the seminary's vans will take the five of you down this Sunday for ten o'clock Mass and to meet with the pastor.

Our van will pick you up and bring you back here in time for lunch. You will leave here from the refectory at eight o'clock. I am not sure exactly what he is going to have you do. I feel guilty we did not get back to him sooner. He has been asking us to send seminarians to help him for quite some time now. Remember that you are there representing the Jeroboam. As far as anyone who sees you is concerned, you ARE the Pontifical Jeroboam. Comport yourself accordingly and perform your job in a manner we can all be proud of."

Tony's classmates had much trepidation over being volunteered for an unknown assignment. David sniped about the lazy priest who does not honor his vow of obedience to the bishop his entire life. "I don't want to be this guy's slave labor. What do you think Tony?" Tony: "I signed on to do God's work. There is going to be a lot of this over the next five years. Think of it as a hazing and you'll be mentally prepared for whatever they throw at us." "Sounds like slave labor to me," complained Mr. Stevens. Tony: "Indentured servitude is more accurate." David: "What's the difference?" Tony: "There is no difference to us. We are enjoined to work without pay." David: "You're no help."

South Side

Tony was always an early riser. Sunday he ate a big breakfast. He was on his second cup of coffee when Leo showed up for breakfast. At five minutes to eight, Leo and Tony followed the driver out of the refectory. They passed David and Greg running in to grab something to eat in the van. The driver gave up waiting for Mr. Stevens and started to drive off when David spotted him coming out the side door of the residential hall. David: "Stop! Stop! There he is!" The driver objected, "I was told to leave precisely at eight o'clock. It is now ten after eight. I've waited too long already." David and his two cohorts made such a vociferous protest the driver relented.

Mr. Stevens stopped running when he saw the driver stop to wait for him. The driver reflexively started to drive off once again. The three cohorts strenuously objected! Once Mr. Stevens was inside the van, he complained to the driver for attempting to leave without him. The driver hotly retorted, "I was told to drive off at eight o'clock! It is now twelve minutes after eight!" Many grumpy faces. David choked down the bagel he grabbed from the refectory. Greg managed to fill his travel cup with hot coffee. His three cohorts were jealous. It took an hour to get to the south side parish, plenty of time for Mr. Stevens to wake up and start carping.

When the van arrived at the south side church, a man was there to meet them and give them a tour of the church and a rundown of available activities and resources, but omitted the bingo operation due to the seminarians' late arrival. Parishioners gave the seminarians a warm welcome and thanked them for coming to help. The church architecture was classic, built of massive stone with a tall bell tower. The interior was huge. It could easily seat a thousand. Greg: "More like 1,200." The ten o'clock Mass was the only Sunday Mass, and only three or four dozen parishioners and five seminarians were there to celebrate with the parish's young assistant priest.

After Mass, the assistant priest ushered the seminarians from the church to the old priest's office. David commented on the young priest's mannerisms in a hushed voice to Greg, "Could he be any more obvious?" The two snickered nervously. Mr. Stevens giggled. Leo had a sour face for his cohorts. *Swishy may not be the correct term. Light in the loafers maybe?* After introductions, the south side pastor excused the assistant priest and addressed the seminarians. Old Priest: "The surrounding neighborhood is full of Catholics who have not been to Mass in years. I know, because they come to church Monday and Tuesday nights for bingo, but they do not come to Mass on Sunday. I want you to go into the neighborhood knocking on doors asking people to come to church on Sunday.

Write down their name, address, and phone number. Tell them we will have someone from the parish contact them and give them a ride to church on Sunday. I want you to start Saturday if possible. Dress appropriately for the weather. You will be going door to door. Eat an early lunch. I expect you to be here by one o'clock. You will canvass the neighborhood all afternoon and return to my office by five so we can review results. Leave the addresses you collect with me so the parish can follow up by contacting those people. Any questions?" Mr. Stevens: "Where will we eat dinner?" Old Priest: "There won't be anyone here to serve food. You will return to the seminary and eat a late dinner. Arrangements will be made to accommodate you on your end."

Mr. Stevens was in a dark mood during the ride back to campus. "They have the best soup kitchen in the city. They feed bums from as far as 50 miles away, but they won't feed us." David was also in a dark mood, but thankfully, he was quiet. Mr. Stevens muttered and bellyached enough for everyone. As the van neared campus, Leo asked Tony, "Were you surprised they aren't going to feed us?" Tony: "Not really. Soup kitchens don't serve three meals a day, do they? Besides, we have excellent food waiting for us on campus."

Mr. Stevens barked, "They will hold leftovers from dinner for us!" Tony: "We should finish by five-thirty, putting us back on campus before seven." Mr. Stevens: "The refectory will be closed by then!" Tony: "A couple of kitchen staffers will get stuck staying late to feed us. The food will still be warm." Mr. Stevens: "Ok Mister First-in-line-for-lunch, how are you going to like being an hour late for dinner?" Tony: "I'll live." Greg: "The staff will be waiting for us to finish so they can clean up. They will stand there watching us. We will be hurried. We won't be able to enjoy our meal." David: "Yeah, what do you think about that Tony?" Tony: "Sounds right. We will be hungry. We will eat fast. We will be in the mood to accommodate the staff."

Monday

The next day the five seminarians had class with the Friar. He asked the seminarians about their assignment on the south side, and then tried to brainstorm. The four morose malefactor students drew a blank. They were unable to appear cheerful, and the Friar insisted it was essential for their formation that they do. Tony had experience canvassing door to door. He suggested carrying two pens, a pocket sized notebook, photo ID to reassure residents, and sufficient cold weather clothing. Tony: "Dress to be outdoors all afternoon." Greg objected, "We will be inside people's homes most of the time."

Tony: "Good luck with that. Glass half-full thinking is adorable but counterproductive. You can't stay warm by thinking warm thoughts. Wearing a hat and gloves is not going to be good enough. We need to wear an extra heavy hat and cold weather gloves, something capable of keeping us warm all afternoon. We cannot plan to stay inside someone's house to defrost. Another thing, it is improper to ask to use their bathroom. We will be in a residential neighborhood, so there will be no other option. We need to plan ahead." David challenged, "How do you plan for that?" Tony: "My plan is to avoid coffee at lunch, and to use the rectory restroom just before we start canvassing." David, Mr. Stevens, and Greg scoffed.

David giggled at something Mr. Stevens muttered. The Friar thanked Tony for his input. The Friar concurred it was important to dress warmly, "The weather is forecast to turn much colder by the time you go canvassing Saturday. It is important to make sure you have something warm to wear. I have made arrangements with the refectory staff. The five of you will be able to eat lunch at eleven-thirty Saturday. The van leaves at noon to take you to the south side. The staff will make arrangements for you to eat when you return. The parish is looking forward to your help. Do a good job and make us all proud. Remember, you represent the Pontifical Jeroboam. Everything you do reflects on us all."

He Is Up To Something

Tuesday during lunch, the Vice Rector and the Old Testament Instructor stood on the edge of the refectory eyeing Tony. The Vice Rector faced Tony, the Old Testament Instructor stood on profile. Tony was only able to lip read the Vice Rector, who was agitated. Vice Rector: "I know he is up to something but I can't figure out what." The Old Testament Instructor nodded agreement and turned to glare at Tony. The conversation continued for some time. The Vice Rector said the students were nervous, wondering what Tony is up to. As Tony ate, he casually studied the room. Sure enough, the students he confirmed were homosexual were visibly anxious. This was yet another opportunity to sort out more of the students.

The next day at lunch Tony noticed everyone in the lunchroom was agitated. The homosexuals were glaring at Tony. The straight seminarians were stressed and bewildered because of the homosexual's disturbing level of anxiety. After lunch, Tony had an appointment with the Shrink Lady. He noticed she was not in the lunchroom, which was odd. She always ate lunch in the refectory when Tony had a one o'clock appointment.

In addition to observing student behavior in the lunchroom, Tony noted the social interaction between himself and the food servers. During the first week of classes, all of the servers were friendly and conversant. By the time Tony started placing himself first in the lunch line, he noted some servers were no longer responsive. One of the servers made it a point to stop being polite. After three weeks of class, only two servers would exchange greetings with Tony, the woman and one man. Over time, Tony noted all but the same two servers were friendly with homosexuals and ignored everyone else. Tony helped himself to a second dessert and a cup of coffee to kill time before his meeting.

Shrink Lady December

Tony went to his appointment. The office was empty. The Shrink Lady was always prompt, always prepared, and always in her office before her appointments, but not today. Tony sat in an empty office for five minutes before she rushed in. She was talking fast and saying three different things at once. By the time she was seated she started repeating herself. Tony: "How much coffee did you have?" Shrink Lady: "Why do you ask?" Tony: "You probably should cut back on the caffeine." She was insulted. She comported herself and started speaking at a normal rate, but she was still incoherent. Tony: "Let me guess, the administration jumped on you with both feet. They don't know what I am up to in the lunchroom and they are angry with you because you can't explain it. That's why you're so wound up."

The Shrink Lady smiled, "Are you up to something in the lunchroom Tony?" *She is so foxy when she is in attack mode.* Tony: "I've made it my business to be first in line for lunch every weekday. You have seen this yourself. In fact, you made two or three witty remarks one day." Shrink Lady: "You thought my barbs were witty?" Tony: "Absolutely. Everyone else's wisecracks were strictly low rent." Shrink Lady: "What makes you think the administration is concerned?" Tony: "Yesterday the Vice Rector and the Old Testament Instructor stood by the east wall of the refectory talking about me. The Vice Rector said he knew I was up to something but he didn't know what."

The Shrink Lady smiled, "You know what that sounds like don't you?" Tony: "Delusional and paranoid. Yeah, I thought of that myself. I might believe it too except for the fact that I can lip read." Her eyes widened. She was horrified! She dashed to the file cabinet. Tony: "It's not in there. There is no way you could have known. I used to work in a high noise environment, plus one of my coworkers was deaf. We learned to lip read each other. The conversation I was telling you about, I only caught half of it. The Vice Rector was facing me. He is easy to lip read, especially when he is upset. The Old Testament Instructor was on profile. I'm not able to read lips on profile." Shrink Lady: "I don't think anyone else can either. You have been evasive and uncooperative so far. Now you are going to gloat?"

Tony: "No, I'm going to explain to you what I was doing." Shrink Lady: "Why would you do that?" Tony: "The entire student body is upset. It's time for me to stop." Shrink Lady: "Sounds delusional." Tony: "Usually I can hear the student's conversations, I don't have to lip read." Shrink Lady: "So what is it you have been doing Tony?" Tony: "I've been running a behavioral experiment. I don't have the expense of white mice and I don't have to clean their cages." Smiling, she taunted, "What are you using for a control group? Valid experimentation requires a control group." Tony: "You know the problems with human psychological testing. I have been conducting an open frame experiment. I took a course in undergrad: *Methods of Social Measurement and Testing.* It's in my transcripts."

Her face turned pale, then gray. Tony: "Further testing will not yield new results. I've learned all I'm going to." Shrink Lady: "What were you testing for?" Tony: "I set up an experiment to sort out the homosexuals from the straights." She smiled, "How can you be sure your methodology is appropriate?" Tony: "What I call diligence you call OCD. You know I am most diligent and if you look at my transcripts, you'll see I aced that course. I designed the experiment to screen the students. I did not intend to apply it to the faculty, but it sorted the faculty out as well. (*Baiting and bluster*)." Shrink Lady: "A good design works on all subjects." She was no longer smiling. "What were your results?"

Tony: "Without a calculator, I can't give you exact numbers, but I have confirmed over half of the students are homosexual." Shrink Lady: "That can't be right." Tony: "Using convergence theory, I estimate the final number will go as high as 82% homosexual. I still have unknowns." Shrink Lady: "You said half are homosexuals and there are unknowns. How many do you think are straight?" Tony: "The remainders are straight." Shrink Lady: "You can't give me a number?" Tony: "It's not like I have written a formal report. If you really want a number, hand me a calculator." Alarmed! Shrink Lady: "Do you intend to write a formal report?" Tony: "You mean for publication? I don't see the point." Shrink Lady: "Why did you run a test to begin with?" Tony: "I have to know. On a basic and primal level, for my own soul, I have got to know."

Shrink Lady: "And how did the Vice Rector fair in the testing?" Tony: "It's testing when you only discuss numbers. It's gossip when you name names. The test was only designed to sort the straights from the homosexuals. The test did have an unforeseen consequence. It proved the Vice Rector is a liar." Shrink Lady: "How did it do that?" Tony: "Quite effectively. During orientation, he made a big, hairy deal out of filling one table at a time in the refectory. He specified consequences for those not following this procedure. I sat at the first table. The first seven weekdays the entire student body and the entire faculty walked past my table. So much for his empathy speech and not hurting people's feelings." Shrink Lady: "Were your feelings hurt?"

"Please," Tony deadpanned, "be serious. If you had been in the refectory for lunch the last two days, you would have seen every seminarian in there had their stomach tied in a square knot. I am guessing the Vice Rector solved the problem by dumping it all on you, winding you up three full cranks too many, and sending you in here to get answers. That would explain why you were incoherent when you first got here." She looked down at the floor, "I appreciate your candor. Why have you offered to tell me these things today?" Tony: "So the students can relax and enjoy lunch." Shrink Lady: "How will they know?" Tony: "Please. They will know. The homosexual grapevine is hardwired and extensive. They'll know." Shrink Lady: "What about the straight students?"

Tony: "When they see the homosexuals relax, they will relax." Shrink Lady: "The straight students must have their own grapevine." Tony: "Ok." Shrink Lady: "How will the homosexual grapevine know to relax?" Tony: "I'll stop being first in line. It won't take forever to figure it out." Shrink Lady: "If they can figure it out, it was not necessary to tell me. You told me to get me off the hook with the Vice Rector, didn't you?" Tony: "You're welcome. You'll report to him after our session, yes?" Shrink Lady: "I have another appointment after yours." Tony: "He will expect you to report to him before you leave for the day." Shrink Lady: "What else would you like to talk about? We still have plenty of time." Tony: "Did you eat lunch today?" Shrink Lady: "No," she answered in a small voice. Tony: "The Vice Rector spent your entire lunch period screaming at you?"

"I was late for our appointment," she answered, her voice still small. Tony: "His tirade ran into overtime? Wow. If we stop now, you'll still have time to eat. If you hurry, the refectory will still be serving." Shrink Lady: "That's not necessary." Tony: "Yes it is. Besides, you earned your paycheck for the week. Your blood sugar is low, you really need to eat." The Shrink Lady wanted to be stalwart and professional. She tried to continue the session. "You'll be in no shape to meet with the Vice Rector if you don't eat," Tony said as he got up to leave. The Shrink Lady looked at her watch. She could in fact still eat a hot meal. Tony's next appointment was set for the first week in February, after Christmas vacation and the retreat. The Shrink Lady thanked Tony and hurried off.

Thursday

The next day Tony sat in the back of the chapel as usual. Again, he was first in the lunch line. Tony sat at table one as usual. Within seconds, the table filled. Upperclassmen that Tony knew were homosexuals were vying to sit with him. Everyone introduced themselves and everyone was conversant. The tension and anxiety that filled the lunchroom for the past two days was gone. *These people are psychic. It's not possible the Vice Rector shared the Shrink Lady's report on Tony's session with the homosexual seminarians. The only explanation is these people are psychic.* From this day on, tables generally filled as the Vice Rector described during orientation. Tony stopped racing to be first in line for lunch.

PC

Tony asked the Byzantine priest, an accomplished linguist, "What translation of the Bible do you read Father?" The priest smiled, "I read the Bible in the original script." Yeah. Tony: "What translation do you recommend for me?" Priest: "The RSV translation is the most accurate modern translation." Students were told during orientation to purchase the New Revised Standard Version (NRSV) of the Bible for scholastic use at the seminary. Tony: "I don't like the NRSV translation that we were told to buy." The priest agreed, "I don't feel comfortable with the inclusive language incorporated into the NRSV." Tony: "You call it inclusive language, as if it were something legitimate. I have always considered that to be a precursor to Politically Correct, which is something devised by homosexuals." The priest was repulsed by Tony's loose talk.

Tony: "I know it sounds fat-mouthed Father, but in undergrad I wrote a paper on the Women's Liberation Movement. Women's Lib was engineered by homosexual men. They brokered cooperation with lesbians since they needed women in front of the TV cameras for a women's movement. They enlisted Blacks for their logistics experience gained during the Black protests of the 1960s." The priest was further incensed at such an offhand and outrageous contention. The priest demanded Tony substantiate his claims. Tony: "Father, I read nine books before I wrote that paper." Priest: "Do you still have the paper?" Tony: "No Father, I threw it away. I didn't see a reason to keep it." The priest sounded cross, "Can you name the authors?"

Tony named two authors and mispronounced the name of a third. The priest corrected the name. Tony: "Yes Father, that's it. I don't remember the other authors. However, it should be easy to research in the library. Those books were published in 1978, 1979, and 1980. I wrote the paper in 1980, late in the year." The priest was interested, "Please continue." Tony: "Ok. Women's Lib was engineered by homosexual men who recruited homosexual women. NOW, the National Organization for Women, was started by some of those same women." The priest arched his brow, "Are you saying NOW was formed by homosexual women?" Tony answered the priest, "Yes."

Today, more than three decades later, Tony is unable to locate the original nine books he used for the 1980 research paper to confirm that assertion. He asked the research librarian what happened to these books. She explained old inventory is replaced with new. Searching library inventory by subject, keyword: women's lib, the search jumps to feminist. Tony's experience with the library's missing 1987 Congressional Record (Refer to Chapter 1) convinced him not to waste more time than he already had looking for these nine books. Tony also struck out with a computer search of the Library of Congress inventory. The three authors whose names Tony recalled published a book once every three years. Each author's bio shows an anomalous gap that corresponds to the 1978-1980 timeframe.

Tony: "The charter membership of NOW included notable women associated with the Women's Lib movement. Politically Correct was the brainchild of NOW. When Politically Correct was first foisted on the public, it was homosexuals saying you cannot call homosexuals "queers." The public ignored them, so they changed tactics. PC said you can't use the N-word. This heightened Black sensitivity and Black awareness. Blacks got on board with PC, which gave PC traction. After that, PC reintroduced the imperative to use the word "gay" instead of "queer." To keep the momentum going they periodically hype another word they decide is a slur. But exactly who are they? The practice has devolved from the ridiculous to the sublime." Priest: "What possible motive do you see?"

Tony: "Initially I thought it was just to have the public stop using the word "queer." Inclusive language has the appearance of being separate from PC." Priest: "They are separate." Tony: "They were introduced separately. Inclusive language is reputed to have originated in academia by feminists. I am not aware of a specific college or institution, or specific authors responsible for the inception of inclusive language. PC originated from NOW, also a group of feminists. I am not convinced the two are at arm's length. I suspect inclusive language and PC share the same headwaters. Once the public acquiesced to inclusive language, there was a green light to rewrite existing literature and the Bible, ostensibly to remove gender bias. By folding PC into the mix, rewriting history also became feasible. Apparently, homosexuals have a motive to rewrite history.

Who is going to proofread behind the people rewriting the Bible, rewriting literature, and rewriting history? You are a linguist Father. Read the parts of the Old Testament where it discusses homosexuals. See what you think." The Byzantine was skeptical, yet his interest was piqued. Priest: "I will investigate this myself. I have felt very uncomfortable with the inclusive language translation of the Bible." The priest gave Tony a scholarly description of how most of the languages he works with use the masculine term in a manner similar to English. The French assign a gender to inanimate objects. He named languages and described how they lose accuracy when subjected to inclusive language. The texture, intricacies, and nuances of the Hebrew language suffer the most. Tony: "The destruction of our language has been exported?" Priest: "Inclusive language is now global, so is PC."

Tony: "Father, I believe this attack on language also gives cover to an effort to erase God and morality from society." Priest: "Do you have specific examples of history being rewritten?" Tony: "History? No. Morality? Yes. I saw a movie on late night TV in 1979, *Bedazzled*, a British movie written by Peter Cook and Dudley Moore. Peter Cook played the devil. Dudley Moore played the character who sold his soul to the devil for the price of seven wishes. Moore was tempted with the seven deadly sins. It was the sort of movie I would show to a high school religious instruction class. It was thoughtful, intelligent, and well done. It was a brilliant morality play. At the end of the movie, Moore got his soul back.

Dudley Moore worked in a hamburger joint, the Tasty Burger. I remember the Tasty Freeze my parents took us kids to in the early 1960s. Tasty Freeze had a walk up window where you could order a burger, fries, soda, and vanilla or chocolate soft ice cream. I thought the Tasty Burger in the movie was a satire of America's Tasty Freeze. At the end of the movie, the devil storms out of the Tasty Burger screaming he is going to win the next contest for souls with God. The devil ranted, "There'll be a television in every room, a Tasty Burger on every corner, and I'll get them all! God will not get a single soul!" How prophetic for a movie made in 1967: a television in every room, a Tasty Burger on every corner.

I rented *Bedazzled* from Blockbuster® in 1991. It was the same as the version I saw twelve years earlier. During Thanksgiving break, I called Blockbuster® stores to rent the original *Bedazzled* again. I finally found a copy, but it had been adulterated. It was no longer an intelligent morality play. It was now owned by Fox Studios. Everything that was clever and moral had been voiced-over. It was not just dumbed-down; it was destroyed. It was not worth watching. Plus, it had been updated. Tasty Burger was changed to Wimpy Burger ®, a contemporary burger chain in Britain. Clever morality lessons were replaced with inane and senseless voice-overs. At the end, the prophetic "–a television in every room, a Tasty Burger on every corner–" line was gone.

Fox Studios also produced a remake of *Bedazzled*, a contemporary version with fresh faces, but it is as vapid and inane as the corrupted original version. Inclusive language and PC gives the homosexual community an excuse to rewrite history and redact morality as easily as Peter Cook's and Dudley Moore's brilliant morality play was despoiled." The Byzantine priest had a serious look on his face. He was deep in thought. He thanked Tony for his insights.

Brian

Javier and Karl planned to meet in Tony's room after dinner Friday. They showed up with a third man. "This is Brian, he's a senior. He's a friend, you can trust him," Javier told Tony. Tony smiled and shook hands with Brian. Tony: "I know Brian is straight, and I know he's trustworthy." Brian's jaw dropped, and then he slyly grinned, "How can you be sure? What makes you so sure I'm straight?" Tony: "Remember when you sat at my table at the beginning of the semester?" Brian: "Yes, the Jesuit told me to sit at your table. He told two of us to sit with you at lunch. What was it you were doing? No one could figure out what you were up to." Tony: "I was running an open frame experiment." Brian: "What were you testing?"

Tony: "I was trying to identify who is straight and who is homosexual." Brian laughed. Javier was keenly interested, "What were your results?" Tony: "I determined 62% of the theology students are homosexual before I had to stop the experiment." Javier: "You didn't finish?" Tony: "No." Javier: "There could be more?" Tony: "I expect the final numbers to exceed three quarters of the student population." Brian scoffed, "Yeah, right. You could tell that by being the first one in the lunch line." Tony: "By being the first one in the lunch line every Monday through Friday week after week, yes. I had to be first in line every day in order to get valid results. I also sat facing away from the point of entry to avoid unintended bias. I was running an open frame experiment."

Brian: "What is an open frame experiment?" Tony: "In a lab you have fixed conditions and you run the experiment against a control group. With social testing, it is not always possible to have a control group. It's called open frame testing. Basically, it is testing in the wild, on the fly." Brian: "That doesn't sound very scientific." Tony chuckled, "Ask Javier, he's the psychology expert. Tell Brian the validity of open frame testing." Javier nodded, "He's right, we use it all the time. Open frame testing is the best we can do sometimes. In this case, that was Tony's only option." Brian was serious and interested, "What did you learn about me?"

Tony: "I forget the conversation, but one of the men said, "I don't know about those other two guys," and I interjected, "but the guy in the middle looks like Willie Nelson." Brian and Tony chuckled. Javier and Karl exchanged confused looks. Javier: "I don't get it." Tony: "It's a joke. (An American joke) .A hooker has two new tattoos, one on the inside of each thigh, Elvis Presley and Johnny Cash. She showed her new tattoos to a customer, but he did not recognize the musicians. This infuriated the hooker. She spots a drunk sitting in the alley. She runs up to the drunk, pulls up her skirt, and tells the drunk her tattoos are of her favorite musicians. She demands he name the musicians. The drunk answers, "I don't know who those other two guys are lady, but the guy in the middle looks like Willie Nelson.""

Brian and Tony chuckled again. Javier and Karl still looked confused. Tony: "Willie Nelson is a musician with a large, unkempt beard." Brian was concerned, "Only three of us at the table laughed when you said the one in the middle looks like Willie Nelson. That was enough for you to know for certain I am straight? How can you be sure?" Tony: "That indicated you two guys might be straight." Brian: "That's no guarantee I'm straight." Tony: "No, not by itself. However, mornings I passed you in the hall after taking a shower. You always held your left fist at belt level. You smiled and said good morning, but your fist was at belt level.

After we laughed about the guy in the middle looking like Willie Nelson, there was no more fist. When you passed me after that, you smiled a wide, friendly smile, said good morning, and genuinely meant it." Brian objected, "I never made a fist." Tony: "Yes you did. Your forearm was held against your side, your fist was somewhat surreptitious, but you made a fist." Brian was concerned, "If it only took you two conversations to know I'm straight it would be that easy for the gays to figure it out. I graduate at the end of the year. I don't need to have them figure out I'm straight. They could stop me from graduating." Tony: "I have an arcane skill set and I'm older than the other students. Your only concern is the Vice Rector."

Brian told the others about his diocese. "Very few people live there. Everyone farms, and each farm is huge. Your next-door neighbor lives a mile and a half or more down the road. Our church is small, but our parish covers a vast expanse. People living at the far ends of the parish drive over three hours to get to church. There has been a priest shortage in our diocese my entire life. That started me thinking about becoming a priest at an early age. Our parish priest is the only priest for four parishes. He flies a small plane, a single engine high wing with tricycle gear. He needs the plane to get from parish to parish because they are so far apart.

This Sunday he says Mass in our parish. During Mass, he consecrates enough hosts to last our parish four weeks. Wednesday he flies to the next parish where he blesses enough hosts during Sunday Mass to last a month. Third week, third parish, fourth week, fourth parish, and then he returns to our parish. The three weeks our parish is without a priest, the congregation gathers on Sunday to pray the Liturgy of the Hours, and the Eucharistic ministers give communion afterwards." Javier: "How can the congregation go without Mass on Sunday?" Brian: "They don't have a choice. There is no priest. It's not so bad. They still keep holy the Sabbath by coming together as a community to celebrate the Liturgy of the Word, which does not require a priest, rather than the Liturgy of the Eucharist, which does.

Since the priest stockpiles consecrated hosts, they don't have to go without the sacrament of the Eucharist. What they do go without is the sacrament of reconciliation. They only have the opportunity to go to confession once a month. That limitation brings more people to the confessional more often than what I have seen in other places. Anointing of the Sick is always a long shot. When you are dying, there is only a one in four chance the priest is somewhere in the parish. It can take nearly seven hours to drive from one corner of the parish to the other, so even if he is in the parish, it's unlikely he will be able to reach you. This is another reason we have long lines at the confessional when the priest is in town." Tony: "You must have a young priest if he flies his own plane."

Brian: "No, he's not. His eyesight is a concern. We are afraid he will be grounded after his next physical. We think he has been pushing himself because of the need. I can't get back there soon enough to relieve him." Tony: "Do you have a pilot's license?" Brian: "No. I'm sure there'll be a lot of pressure for me to get one once I go back as a priest." Javier: "There must be other parishes in your diocese with similar circumstances." Brian: "I'm sure there are." Javier: "What happens when a priest taking care of three or four parishes dies and there's no replacement?" Brian: "Then the people have no priest." Karl: "There are places in Africa and South America with thousands of people and only one priest. The priest does what he can, but mostly the people go without the sacraments. That's why we're here, to make the sacraments available."

Tony: "What was going on with our seminarians standing during the consecration?" Brian and Javier strenuously denounced the practice. Karl nodded agreement. Javier: "By doing something different than the common practice, there's a question if the consecration was even valid." Tony: "The pope contacted this place twice before the Vice Rector demanded compliance with the pope's order." Javier: "He called three times." Tony: "The pope's first order was ignored for three days before the Vice Rector made the announcement, and then no one followed it." Brian: "What did you do Tony?" Tony: "I knelt, but the guys on either side of me grabbed me by my arms and pulled me back up." Brian: "You didn't try again?" Tony: "No, I didn't want to cause a commotion during Mass."

Javier: "Almost everyone stood even after the Vice Rector made the second announcement, which is why the pope called him a third time. Remember how angry he was the next day? That's why. The pope called him twice in two days." Tony: "How did the pope know his orders were ignored?" Javier: "Someone here called him. That's the only explanation." Tony: "Good." All four men agreed it was good. Brian: "Underclassmen wouldn't realize this was a problem." Javier concurred. Tony: "I don't think a student could get the pope to take his phone call. A priest or board member would be more likely." Brian: "No board members or visiting priests were here at that time." Tony: "Whoever it was waited until the Rector was gone and the Vice Rector was here by himself."

Javier: "Why is that important?" Tony: "Maybe he knows the Vice Rector is the brains of this operation and wanted to put a spotlight on him for the pope. The only way to establish his guilt unambiguously is to make the report when the Rector is out of town. Better still, the Rector will fly from China to the Vatican next week." Javier: "Internal politics? That makes sense. The Rector is going to the Vatican to meet with the pope to discuss his next assignment. This is the Rector's last year of his eight-year appointment. The office of rector has an eight-year term limit to prevent a rector from establishing a corrupt influence. The Vice Rector has been here for sixteen years. There is no term limit on the office of vice rector, but there should be. If somebody wants his job, this could be a way to create an opening."

Tony: "The Vice Rector has been here long enough to build his own fiefdom inside the seminary's bureaucracy." Brian chuckled, "Do you guys think there is that much cloak and dagger involved?" The other three all said yes. Brian: "One of the seminarians could be reporting to his bishop and he could be calling the pope." The others agreed that was also possible. Karl: "Tony, what did you think about the seminarians standing during the consecration?" Tony: "It seemed profoundly disrespectful. Now I see it was blasphemy." Brian panned, "Blasphemy is a bit extreme, don't you think?" Tony: "I'll have to check my dictionary to make sure I understand the meaning of the word blasphemy. Standing certainly was disrespectful at the most critical part of the Mass."

> blasphemy n., 1 profane or contemptuous speech, writing, or action concerning God or anything held as divine 2 any remark or action held to be irreverent or disrespectful [01]

Karl: "I'll check my dictionary too. What did you think when the Vice Rector and the seminarians repeatedly disobeyed the pope's orders?" Tony: "They identified themselves as a bunch of reprobates and infidels with that move. I also thought it was ironic." Brian: "Ironic?" Tony: "Yes, ironic. My four classmates carried on at length that the pope disrespected us by not coming to visit the Pontifical Jeroboam when he was in the United States last October. They whined about it for over a week. Then they ignore the pope's direct orders? Such chutzpah! From day one, the administration had us standing during the consecration six days a week. It didn't feel right to me, but this is a seminary, this is where seminarians are trained by priests to become priests. Now that you guys have explained it to me, I see it was much more than just disrespectful."

1 Kings 15:23 (DRA)[31] Because it is like the sin of witchcraft, to rebel: and like the crime of idolatry, to refuse to obey. Forasmuch therefore as thou hast rejected the word of the Lord, the Lord hath also rejected thee from being king.

1 Samuel 15:23 (KJV) [32] For rebellion is as the sin of witchcraft, and stubbornness is as iniquity and idolatry. Because thou hast rejected the word of the Lord, he hath also rejected thee from being king."

2 Machabees 4:12-14 (DRA)[31] 12 For he had the boldness to set up, under the very castle, a place of exercise, and to put all the choicest youths in brothel houses. 13 Now this was not the beginning, but an increase, and progress of heathenish and foreign manners, through the abominable and unheard of wickedness of Jason, that impious wretch and no priest. 14 Insomuch that the priests were not now occupied about the offices of the altar, but despising the temple and neglecting the sacrifices, hastened to be partakers of the games, and of the unlawful allowance thereof, and of the exercise of the discus.

Brian asked Tony, "You don't think the Vice Rector is doing a very good job, do you?" Tony: "Absolutely not! Whoever placed three calls to the pope thinks likewise." Karl asked Tony, "What have you discussed with the Vice Rector?" Tony: "When we laid pavers last fall, I talked to the Vice Rector. I asked him why the Catholic Church doesn't denounce the Democrat's Marxist policies. I used welfare as an example. He answered with the rhetoric of a registered Democrat." Tony's friends agreed with the Vice Rector's position that government largess is charity. *WHAT?*

Government Entitlements
(Entitlement: that which you are not entitled to.)

Psalms 117:9 (DRA)[31] It is good to trust in the Lord, rather than to trust in princes.

Psalms 145:2-3 (DRA) [31] 2 Praise the Lord, O my soul, in my life I will praise the Lord: I will sing to my God as long as I shall be. Put not your trust in princes: 3 in the children of men, in whom there is no salvation.

Politicians selling the public on the idea of welfare said, "It is for the children. It is to feed and care for the children." Federal welfare: A single woman with a child goes on welfare. If a man joins her household, she loses her welfare income and medical benefits. If she remains single and has additional children, her income increases for each additional child. The government clearly pays her a direct cash incentive to remain single and to have more children. (Federal welfare was foisted onto the state governments in 1996).

> Ecclesiastes 10:19 (DRA) [31] For laughter they make bread, and wine that the living may feast: and all things obey money.

> Ecclesiasticus 27:1 (DRA) [31] Through poverty many have sinned: and he that seeketh to be enriched, turneth away his eye.

The purpose (job) of the social institutions of government and religion is to bolster society and therefore the family unit. Using taxpayer's money to destroy the family is opposite of society's best interest. Proponents of this evil ("government charity") blame its shortcomings on fraud and individual abuse (welfare cheats, people who game the system), deflecting attention from its obvious and fatal design flaws. The writings of Machiavelli [27] warn such excessive largess will cause the loss of the Republic.

> Wisdom 3:16-17 (DRA) [31] 16 But the children of adulterers shall not come to perfection, and the seed of the unlawful bed shall be rooted out. 17 And if they live long, they shall be nothing regarded, and their last old age shall be without honour.

> Deuteronomy 23:2 (DRA) [31] [Same as Deuteronomy 23:2 (DRV) [19] below but without the footnote.]
>
> Deuteronomy 23:2 (DRV) [19] A mamzer, that is to say, one born of a prostitute, shall not enter into the church of the Lord, until the tenth generation.
> Chap. 23. Ver. 1 (&2). *Into the church.* That is, into the assembly or congregation of Israel, so as to have the privilege of an Israelite, or to be capable of any place or office among the people of God.
>
> Deuteronomy 23:2 (KJV) [32] "A bastard shall not enter into the congregation of the Lord; even to his tenth generation shall he not enter into the congregation of the Lord.

Marxists defend government programs, "–will work, it just needs fine tuning." Seven decades of fine-tuning did not change the fundamentals: 23 cents of every dollar goes to the needy, 77 cents of every dollar sticks to the barrel (cost of administering the program). That is one corrupt charity! Notice: welfare "cheats" are "stealing" from the 23 cents. Who assumes the 77 cents is an honest cost of business when administration of Jewish charities costs 2 cents and Catholic charities costs 3 cents of every dollar to do a much better job?

Before entitlements sprang up like grass, proponents complained traditional charities preached religion. The public was asked to support government "charity" so the needy would not have to listen to religious preaching. Their example: needy people use the services of the Salvation Army but complain they have to listen to sermons concerning God. The public swallowed this malarkey. Other entitlements follow the same pattern: the public is sold happy sounding lies about a fatally flawed premise.

> Galatians 6:10 (DRA)[31] Therefore, whilst we have time, let us work good to all men, but especially to those who are of the household of the faith.

> Ezechiel 22:27 (DRA)[31] Her princes in the midst of her, are like wolves ravening the prey to shed blood, and to destroy souls, and to run after gains through covetousness.

> Ecclesiasticus 12:5-7 (DRA)[31] 5 Give to the good, and receive not a sinner. 6 Do good to the humble, and give not to the ungodly: hold back thy bread, and give it not to him, least thereby he overmaster thee. 7 For thou shalt receive twice as much evil for all the good thou shalt have done to him: for the Highest also hateth sinners, and will repay vengeance to the ungodly.

People need jobs, not the opportunity to sell their soul for government freebies. Entitlements are evil by design and not merely flawed. This becomes clear when you see the U.S. Federal government has quietly used the tax code to export our industrial base, which will inevitably bankrupt the government and the economy. For decades, the government has been paying American businesses with tax incentives to "move manufacturing jobs offshore" (To give away our industrial base, our lifeblood, our economy). This is not about helping people. This is about debasing souls and destroying our country. The design and intent is evil and most heinous. Who has not read Machiavelli?[27] Who has not read the Bible?[19]

In 1973, Julie told Tony that one day, only homosexuals would have jobs and straights would not have jobs. The government has methodically and willfully given away our industrial base and our manufacturing jobs through the tax code ever since.

Proverbs 22:9 (DRA) [31] He that is inclined to mercy shall be blessed: for of his bread he hath given to the poor. **He that maketh presents shall purchase victory and honor: but he carrieth away the souls of the receivers.**
(Bold type added by author.)

Isaias 28:15 (DRA) [31] For you have said: We have entered into a league with death, and we have made a covenant with hell. When the overflowing scourge shall pass through, it shall not come upon us: for we have placed our hope in lies, and by falsehood we are protected.

For a second opinion, refer to Star Parker, [30] author of Uncle Sam's Plantation at:
<http://townhall.com/columnists/starparker/2009/02/09/back_on_uncle_sams_plantation/page/full/>. [30]

How does society benefit by giving homosexuals extra-normal treatment like EEOC's Title VII and other "equal treatment" sanctions in the face of homosexuals' stated anti-social, anarchist aspirations? [10]

Sirach 4:22 (RSV-C) [40] Do not show partiality, to your own harm, or deference, to your downfall.

Sirach 12:4 (RSV-C) [40] Give to the godly man, but do not help the sinner.

Tony shared the conversation he had with the Vice Rector on parochial schools. That was a different matter. All three objected! "He's a priest! How can he say that?"

Tony shared his conversation with the Vice Rector concerning Morning Prayer. Brian was taken aback, "I've been here four years. I never thought about Morning Prayer, much less about the fact we weren't doing it." Tony: "Yeah, and when we pray Evening Prayer we always skip the hymn. We always pray the abbreviated version."

Guests of the Jeroboam, such as visiting clergy, alumnus, board members, patrons, and donors are often invited to join the seminarians in Evening Prayer. Joining eighty or more voices chanting (Gregorian chant) the Psalms and Canticles is both inspirational and magnificent. Tony guesses none of the VIPs ever asked to be invited to the more important and slightly longer pre-dawn Morning Prayer. If they did, they would have learned the seminarians at the Jeroboam do not gather for Morning Prayer.

Karl agreed with Tony wholeheartedly. Karl: "I'm new here, it's not my place to say, but I think it's wrong that we don't gather for Morning Prayer. Tony is right about the Office of Readings. If these guys have never prayed Morning Prayer, it's unlikely they're going to pray the Office of Readings after they leave here." Brian and Javier grudgingly agreed, but both admitted they enjoyed sleeping late. Javier hinted there was no reason to request the Vice Rector include Morning Prayer in the schedule. Tony: "With the discipline of Morning Prayer there would be fewer study sessions that end at three o'clock in the morning."

Ecclesiasticus 33:29 (DRA) [31] For idleness hath taught much evil.

Brian: "What's he talking about? What happens at three a.m.?" Javier: "I'll explain it to him later Tony. Right now, we have to get going." Tony: "I'm happy to finally visit with you Brian. I want you guys to stop back any time. I'm always glad to have you visit.

Everyone left, but five minutes later Karl returned. Karl: "I apologize for bothering you Tony." Tony: "Not at all, come in." Karl: "You know who called the pope, don't you?" Tony: "I have a candidate in mind, but I can't be absolutely certain." Karl: "How did you figure it out?" Tony: "I didn't deduce anything, I got lucky. When two seminarians picked me up by my arms during the consecration of the second defiance of the pope, I saw movement in the corridor. It was a priest, who ran up the hall to the open doors of the chapel. He looked inside and became infuriated! He turned and ran back. I am guessing he went straight to his office and placed the call."

Proverbs 27:19 (DRA) [31] As the faces of them that look therein, shine in the water, so the hearts of men are laid open to the wise.

Karl: "Which priest?" Tony: "Does it matter?" Karl: "It will help me if I know which priests are trustworthy." Tony: "Oh, right. I don't know his name." Karl: "Get your directory. Show me his picture." Tony found the priest's picture in the directory. Karl smiled broadly, "I chose him to be my confessor!" Tony: "You chose well." Karl beamed! He was relieved to have confirmation this was a proper priest. Karl: "I won't tell anyone about this. You said nothing earlier because Javier trusts too many people. Thank you for telling me." Tony: "I'm glad I told you."

That moment was the happiest Tony would ever see Karl.

8 LA CASA

South Side 2

Late Saturday morning Tony prepared for an afternoon of canvassing. He put on thermal underwear, pulled wool socks over a pair of cotton socks, and stuck a pocket notebook, pen, and mechanical pencil in his shirt pocket. He put a plastic zip bag in his left jacket pocket, two handkerchiefs in his right jacket pocket and one in his hip pocket. He piled his heavy sweater, heavy stocking hat, and his heaviest gloves on top of his ski jacket, folded the jacket in half to contain everything, put it under his arm, and headed to the refectory. It was twenty-five after eleven when he walked into the refectory and set his jacket on a table. One of the staff objected, "You're early." Tony: "I know. I'll wait." The man relaxed and continued working. Tony visited the toasting machine. He made two pieces of toast and cut a thick slab of cheddar from one of the two cheese blocks.

Tony shuffled the toast and cheese together, placed them in the plastic zip bag, and stowed it in his left jacket pocket. Staff: "We're open." Tony: "Thank you." Not all of the food was ready, but it was a good start. Tony put food on his tray and ate. After finishing, he returned to the serving line for seconds. Everything was ready and piping hot. Tony made selections that would see him through a cold afternoon including a piece of apple pie. A small glass of milk was the only drink he allowed himself. Three of his classmates trailed into the refectory as he sat down. When they joined him David said, "I'm surprised we got here when you did. You're usually early for everything." Leo pointed to the clothes on the adjacent table, "That's a good idea. I wish I brought mine."

There wasn't much chitchat. Everyone was wolfing down their food. By the time Mr. Stevens arrived, the others were halfway through their meal. Shortly, Tony looked at his watch, "It's five minutes to twelve." Mr. Stevens snarled, "So? We've still got five minutes." Leo's eyes widened, "I have to go back to my room to get my coat!" David and Greg panicked! The next 30 seconds was reminiscent of the *Keystone Cops* as everyone disappeared from view. Mr. Stevens was bitching he hardly had anything to eat. Tony finished eating his pie before he put on his cold weather gear and headed to the van.

Tony was comfortable in the third row seat before three of his classmates piled into the second row seat. Everyone impatiently waited for Mr. Stevens. The driver started to drive off when David spotted Mr. Stevens coming out of the dorm. David: "There he is!" The driver was seething, "I was told to leave precisely at twelve o'clock. I was told specifically to not wait even one second." But he waited. Mr. Stevens climbed into the front passenger seat and started complaining vociferously when Greg told him, "Not today! No one wants to hear it!" Mr. Stevens: "But I've had almost nothing to eat and we won't get back until late!" David growled, "Whose fault is that?" Greg had his travel cup of coffee. "I should have grabbed something more to eat when I went back for coffee." Mr. Stevens carried on like a wounded bear. And he carried on at great length.

Finally, Tony said, "I have a slab of cheddar cheese between two slices of toast if you're interested." Silence. Tony brandished the plastic bag for all to see. Mr. Stevens sniped, insulted, and complained. Leo: "What did you bring that for?" Tony: "I planned to eat it after we finish canvassing. This was the only thing I could think of that would travel well." David was incredulous, "And you're willing to give it to him? Why?" Tony: "He almost has to shut up while he eats. I'm willing to give up my cheese sandwich for two minutes of peace." Mr. Stevens carried on some more. Tony brandished the cheese and toast again. Tony: "Last chance." Mr. Stevens nodded to David. David said thanks, took the bag, and passed it to Mr. Stevens, who muttered and complained while he ate.

The south side pastor told the seminarians which streets he wanted canvassed. He said the people living in this neighborhood came from Appalachia. "These people are the salt of the earth. They will be able to see right through you. There is no hiding what you're made of from them." He said this as a stern warning. The priest instructed Tony and Leo to work together, Greg and David, and Mr. Stevens was to work alone. Then he deployed the seminarians. When Tony excused himself to the restroom, Mr. Stevens tittered and muttered. Upon Tony's return, the others asked him if he had an extra pen. Leo had a wooden pencil stub. The others had nothing to write with. Tony loaned Greg his mechanical pencil.

Greg: "Why did you bring a pencil?" Tony: "The pencil will still write after the pen freezes." Mr. Stevens: "Give me your pen. You can share Leo's pencil." Tony: "The pen will be useless to you guys. The winter gear I'm wearing may keep the pen from freezing." Mr. Stevens tried to bum Leo's pencil, "You can share Tony's pen." Leo: "No." Mr. Stevens: "Why not?" Leo: "When his pen freezes we'll have nothing to write with. Ask the priest for a pencil." While David went to ask the priest for pencils for himself and Mr. Stevens, Tony shared pages from his notebook with the other two teams. Once outside Greg said, "I checked out this parish. This priest has $8 million in Church real estate tied up for his personal bingo/soup kitchen operation." All five seminarians disapproved. *Tax-free bingo operation, free use of paid-for assets, his own personal charity: what's not to love?*

There had been a sharp change in the weather overnight. It turned bitterly cold, overcast, and windy. Leo: "I don't see how to divide this between two guys, do you?" Tony: "Not really." Leo: "I'll do it for a while and then we can switch off." Tony: "Sounds good." Leo started knocking on doors. Someone answered the door at the third house. Leo spoke three or four words and the homeowner slammed the door in his face! A few houses later, it was the same thing plus some angry words. Several houses later, there was a tirade of virulent shouting at Leo by the homeowner before he slammed the door shut! With the wind blowing so hard, Tony heard the venomous voices but the words were unintelligible. Leo and Tony were aghast! Leo: "Wow! What was that?" Tony: "Ouch! Looks like it's going to be a long afternoon." Leo agreed. Both men were grateful for the doors that went unanswered.

Leo: "Hey, do you mind if we switch off for a while? I'll knock on doors and you deal with the homeowners." Tony: "Ok." Leo: "You've canvassed neighborhoods before?" Tony: "A long time ago." Leo: "Ever see anything like this?" Tony: "Never." Tony spoke to the people who answered their door. Some did not open the door; they just said they did not want any. Some said they were not Catholic. A nice lady invited the seminarians inside and offered to make coffee. Tony: "No thank you." Leo nudged Tony with his elbow. Tony turned to Leo, "If we drink coffee before three o'clock we're going to have problems later." Leo: "Oh, yeah." The nice lady gave her information so the parish could give her a ride to church. She asked for a phone number from the seminarians to make sure there would be follow up. Leo readily agreed. Tony told Leo, "I'll give her my number," as he continued taking her information.

Before the seminarians left, the nice lady insisted, "Here, you boys at least take a cookie with you." When the two were outside Leo said, "Do you mind dealing with the people? They seem to get along better with you." Tony: "Ok, but no more giving out our phone number. We don't want them calling us. They're supposed to call the parish." Leo: "Those first few houses, what was that?" Tony: "I don't know, distemper?" Leo: "No, I'm serious. Why do you think the first few people were so angry?" Tony: "I don't know. Maybe they had a hangover." Leo: "I feel bad you're doing all the work." Tony: "Forget it. I'll take point. After two or three homeowners bark at me, we'll switch off again." There was only so much door-knocking Leo could do before his hands froze. Leo: "I'm sorry. I'm sticking you with all the work." Tony: "Forget it. You don't have heavy enough gloves. I'm worried you're not going to make it until five o'clock."

Leo: "Don't say no to coffee if we get another offer. I could use some hot coffee." Tony looked at his watch, "Yeah, ok. It's close to three anyway. We may not have access to a toilet until we get back to the rectory was my concern." Leo: "I knew that's what you meant before. You're wondering how I stood night watch aboard ship but can't go door to door, aren't you? I didn't bring my foul weather gear to the seminary. I didn't think I'd need it." Tony: "Yeah, there are some things I wish I still had with me too." Leo and Tony were offered coffee and cookies by another nice lady and another after that. They got a second name and address for the parish as well. Leo: "More people were willing to give us coffee and cookies than were willing to go to church." Tony: "Yeah. Prospects offer hospitality to buy off their guilt for saying no. A good salesman never accepts hospitality so he can close the sale." Leo: "But we're not salesmen." *That's for sure.*

After a bone-chilling afternoon of canvassing, the seminarians returned to the old priest's office. Tony and Leo entered the office last, at exactly five o'clock. The old priest asked for their results. Tony handed him a page from his pocket notebook with two sets of names, addresses, and phone numbers. The old priest angrily inquired, "How do you think you did today? What is your assessment?" "Only two names is a poor showing Father," Tony said with embarrassment. Old Priest: "What will you do the next time to get better results?"

Tony: "I don't know. It's not as if we made mistakes. I will give this some serious thought when I warm up. Right now I'm too cold to think." Old Priest: "You'll try harder next time?" Tony: "Yes Father, we will. Father, one of the women asked for the parish phone number and I don't know it. Do you have business cards for us?" Old Priest: "That's a good idea." The priest reached across his desk to retrieve business cards and handed one to each seminarian. The priest dismissed them with, "I'll see you next Saturday."

The ride back to the seminary was absolutely silent. *Thank you Lord.*

In class Monday, the Friar faced three students with watery sniffles and one with a gagging cough. Friar: "You guys didn't wear warm enough clothes Saturday, did you?" He tried to brainstorm to improve productivity, but no one had new ideas to offer. The Friar was very disappointed with the group's failure to prepare and their subsequent poor performance. He repeated the recommendations from their earlier brainstorming and underscored their importance. Greg, David, and Mr. Stevens were sick by Wednesday. Leo's cough improved. The Friar canceled Saturday's canvass. With exams and Christmas vacation coming up, the next trip to the south side was delayed until January.

Canvass Review

The next time Tony met with his spiritual advisor, the Friar reviewed the evangelizing mission. Friar: "I understand you and Leo were the only ones dressed to work outdoors." Tony: "Pretty much." Friar: "You and Leo got the only two phone numbers." Tony: "Leo and I collected two phone numbers, that's right." Friar: "No one else got any phone numbers." Tony: "Really?" Friar: "How is it you didn't know?" Tony: "We got to the office last and no one was bragging later." Friar: "What did the priest have to say before and after your canvass?" Tony: "Before we got started, he told us the people in the neighborhood were from Appalachia. With too much levity in his voice, he said these people would see right through us and would know what we were made of."

Friar: "What do you think he meant by that?" Tony: "I have no idea." Friar: "What kind of first impression do you think you made on him?" Tony: "He looked at me askance." Friar: "Where do you think that came from?" Tony: "Who knows, my regional accent maybe?" Friar: "What happened at the end of the day?" Tony: "Leo and I entered the office at precisely five o'clock. I gave the priest the two addresses we collected. He was angry with our overall poor performance." Friar: "The others told me you gave (Mr. Stevens) a cheese sandwich. Why did you make a sandwich for him?" Tony: "I made it for myself, to eat after canvassing. He didn't eat lunch, so I caved in and gave him my sandwich."

Friar: "You shared your extra supplies with the others." Tony: "I was properly outfitted for myself. I did not bring extra to share. Three out of five men had no pencil and no paper." Friar: "Why do you say pencil?" Tony: "By the end of the day ink would freeze. A pen would stop writing. Pencils are weatherproof." Friar: "Didn't you use a pen?" Tony: "Yes, I let Greg take my mechanical pencil." Friar: "And you used the pen, knowing it would give you trouble later?" Tony: "Yes." Friar: "Why did you do that?" Tony: "I knew I could make it work. If I gave it to the others, they would think it was out of ink and throw it away."

Friar: "Who did most of the talking, you or Leo?" Tony: "Leo divided the work and we both agreed." Friar: "He just got out of the service. He is accustomed to giving orders." Tony: "He didn't issue orders. It was more like participative management, the sort of leadership appropriate for managing volunteers." Friar: "That is just what Leo will need when he has his own parish. Leo was concerned he did not pull his own weight." Tony: "I thought he did, but I might've hogged more of the door knocking." Friar: "Why is that?" Tony: "I had better gloves. His fingers froze early on." When the Friar was finished, he smiled and said, "Enjoy the rest of your afternoon."

Ex Opere Operato

Javier stopped by Tony's on his way back from dinner. "What's new?" Tony: "In class we covered *ex opere operato*. The sacraments are valid even when the priest is a heretic, or is somehow unworthy." Javier: "What is "somehow unworthy" supposed to mean?" Tony: "I said "somehow unworthy" instead of saying blah-blah-blah. The instructor had a list of specifics. Basically, anyone who is ordained to the priesthood dispenses valid sacraments. All four of my homosexual classmates looked at me in class and grinned after the instructor explained this." Javier: "What's their problem?"

Tony: "Mr. Stevens has been wearing me out with that piece of business ever since. Before class, after class, in the lunchroom, after Evening Prayer, every chance he gets he reminds me." Javier: "Reminds you of what?" Tony: "He gets in my face with it. He can't tell me enough times. No matter how bogus he is, the sacraments he will dispense will still be valid." Javier: "Can you imagine that guy as a priest?" Tony: "Not in my worst nightmares." Javier: "Did he actually use the word bogus?" Tony: "No, but he clearly understands he is not priest material. He wore me out. He said I will work hard and do everything right, he will do as he pleases, and in the end there will be no difference. We will both be priests. The sacraments we dispense will be the same."

Javier: "What did the others have to say?" Tony: "David interjected his agreement every once in a while. Greg and Leo are usually quiet, but even they chimed in on this one. There is nothing in any of our classes that energized these guys as much as this one item. Basically, they bragged their dalliance and dearth of fidelity will be without consequence, and they are proud of it." Javier: "Didn't one of your courses tell you the influence a priest has on the sins of his flock?"

Tony: "Yes, the Friar covered that at the beginning of the semester in his course. We read the *Curé of Ars*, an example of what a holy priest can accomplish. I saw an example of this in my parish priest. A holy priest brings people to Mass and to the confessional. The Friar explained a priest who does not teach and inspire his flock causes them to stray. By failing to do his job, his congregation becomes more sinful." Javier: "What did your classmates think of this?" Tony: "They objected loudly and raucously." Javier: "What did you think?" Tony: "I can see how a lackadaisical or uninspiring priest would fail his congregation. A priest who does not apply himself will surely cause sin to multiply."

Logic Final

Leo knocked on Tony's door. He sheepishly said, "You know I've been having trouble in our logic class. You helped me study for the midterm. I was hoping you'd be willing to help me cram for the final." Tony: "I –well, –ok. We can study for an hour." Leo: "An hour?" Tony: "I want to get to sleep on time." Tony pulled out a chair for Leo. Tony had been studying. His notes and book covered his desk. The two sat down to study. Leo: "Before we get started, the other guys asked me to find out if you'd help them too. Will you?" Tony was surprised, "They want my help?" Leo: "They're not doing well in logic class either." Tony: "I guess." Leo cowered, "Even (Mr. Stevens)?" *What?* Tony: "Yeah, him too." Leo dashed into the hall, looked right, and announced, "It's ok! He said yes. Everybody! Yes, you too! Come on!"

The entire logic class assembled in Tony's room. Greg is an articulate man, proud, sharply dressed, slim, and well kempt. He is the natural leader of the gay transfer students. David dressed business casual, is portly, and well groomed if you appreciate hair mousse. Leo dressed jeans casual, struggles with his academic studies, and regularly prays the rosary. Mr. Stevens is phlegmatic, morbidly obese, and generally disheveled. Tony wears dark trousers and long sleeve shirts. Tony gained weight from eating too much bacon since he came to the seminary.

The four wanted Tony to start from the beginning and cover the entire course. After an hour, they covered less than half the material. Tony wanted to end the session so he could sleep. David suggested pulling an all-nighter. Tony: "Look, I'm ready for the test. All I need is a full night's sleep. Staying up all night for no reason will work against me. I need my beauty sleep." "Nobody needs beauty sleep more than you do," Mr. Stevens said half under his breath. Greg, Leo, and David instantly glared at him. Greg apologized for Mr. Stevens and asked Tony for another hour. Greg: "If you could at least cover all the material once–." The others nodded. Tony agreed to another hour.

Mr. Stevens was surprised, "Why would you help us? After all the things we have done to you, why would you help us? You have to be mad at us." Tony: "I came here to serve God. I didn't come here to fight with you guys." Greg, David, and Mr. Stevens were astounded! Greg: "You actually believe there is a God? Seriously?" David: "You used to be an engineer. As a scientist you know there's no such thing as God." Mr. Stevens: "You're joking. Everyone knows there is no such thing as God. Ha-ha, everyone except Leo. He believes the same as you do. He thinks there is a God." Leo blushed.

Tony was bewildered. "Why would you guys want to be a priest if you don't believe in God?" Greg intervened, "We can discuss this over dinner tomorrow after the test. Tonight we need to crib for the exam and you need your sleep." Tony agreed. The studies moved forward. At the two-hour mark, the material was not completely covered. The four begged Tony to continue. Another twenty minutes covered the remaining material. They thanked Tony and hastily gathered their things. Greg: "Let's go to my room and keep studying," and they were gone.

Why Join the Priesthood

After a long day, Tony shuffled into the refectory. He took his tray to a table and sank into a chair. People were calling his name, trying to get his attention. Tony turned around to see his classmates sitting across the room. Greg: "What are you doing over there? Come on over, sit with us." Tony stood up and looked. Their table was full. There was no place to sit. Tony shrugged his shoulders with arms out, palms up, signaling there was nothing to be done, and sat back down. Moments later, all four joined him at his table. They all thanked Tony for helping them study. David: "We wouldn't have passed that test if you didn't tutor us." Greg: "Thanks Tony."

Mr. Stevens: "I still can't believe you helped us! Even after all the awful things we've done to you. Things you don't even know about." Greg shot a look of death at Mr. Stevens to shut him up. Greg: "A deal's a deal. You had questions." Tony: "Why would you guys join the priesthood if you don't even believe in God?" Mr. Stevens: "Ha-ha, Leo believes. It's the three of us who don't believe."

David offered, "I graduated from business school. I worked in an office. Gays are discriminated against in business. By the time I was 30 I realized I did not have a future working in corporate America. Then I found out I could make a living as a priest. No matter what parish I'm assigned to, there's going to be a Catholic car dealership." David's face lit up and he smiled, "I'll never pay retail for a car again. As a priest, I will be able to get off speeding tickets if I am wearing my collar. I will be able to travel all over the country. No matter where I go, there will be a rectory. I'll have a free place to stay." David smiled and glanced at the others, "At most rectories I'll meet people like us. I will make a new friend. At the very least, I will have a free place to stay. In fact, I can travel the world, or at least to countries that have Catholic churches. I won't have to pay for a hotel room ever."

Mr. Stevens said that as a priest he would have the respect of the community, he enjoys singing, and he'd only have to work one day a week with no heavy lifting, hard work, or sweat. He said they would make better priests than straight priests. Mr. Stevens: "No one can be celibate, that's silly. Straight priests end up cheating with women. They always get caught. Everybody knows they are having sex with a woman, and they know who the woman is. With us," he glanced at the others with a knowing smile, "we can never get caught. With two of us living in the same rectory, who will ever know we are having sex?" David and Greg exchanged sly smiles with Mr. Stevens.

Mr. Stevens continued, "The only downside is dealing with the women of the parish. That's something I'm not looking forward to." They agreed Greg was likely to become a bishop. They asserted Greg would have career opportunities, more so than they would. Greg was in general agreement with the first two men. He did not tell stories on himself. Leo was concerned about salvation. As a priest, he would work on his own salvation full time and help his congregation with theirs. His cohorts snickered at him. Greg: "What about you Tony? Why are you here? You had property and savings. You were successful in your field. Why would you give that up to be a priest?"

Tony: "I wouldn't get carried away with the concept of success. I got sick of working for criminals and thieves. I got sick of the economy going down the toilet every time the Democrats control Capitol Hill. We have become a nation of moral imbeciles. I wanted to work for God and help turn the tide." All four laughed at Tony! They roared! Tears streamed down their faces. They were embarrassed for laughing in his face, especially for laughing so hard, but they could not stop laughing. When he could breathe again, David said, "You're saying you wanted to join the good guys and fight bad guys?" Tony: "Well, –pretty much, yes." All four roared! No embarrassment, no self-consciousness: they laughed hard!

Mr. Stevens asked Tony, "What makes you think you'll be able to be celibate?" Tony: "I've been unemployed for quite a while. I have been living like a hermit. I won't be giving up anything to be a priest." Mr. Stevens: "How come you're not married?" Tony: "When I was nineteen I dropped out of college and moved to a major city. I searched the bulletin board in a nice apartment complex for roommate wanted notices. I found a decent guy to share rent with. I asked him why a single man had such a nice place. He was married and his wife left him, so he needed a roommate to help pay the rent. His friends came over to drink one weekend. They were all in their 20s. They were all divorced. They all told me their story.

One man came home from work and could not find the light switch. It was winter. It got dark early. He got a flashlight from the car and went back inside. The light switch was gone. While he was at work, his wife moved out and took everything: all the furniture and all the chattels. She took all the food. She had a crew pull up the wall-to-wall carpeting and remove the light switches and light fixtures. The internal doors and door jams were gone. The house looked like it was under construction, with wires hanging out of the ceilings and walls where fixtures and receptacles used to be. He went to the bank, but she closed the accounts. He had to stay with his parents until payday. The other men's stories were not much better. They warned me to be careful. Maybe I was too careful, I don't know. So many people my age are divorced."

Mr. Stevens: "What do you think is the reason behind so much divorce?" Tony: "Expectations are too high and resolve is too low. I worked in Europe for a while. I met two or three Europeans who referred to the United States as God's country." Mr. Stevens: "God's country? Why did they say that?" Tony: "They focused mainly on the Pilgrims, but they mentioned the United States (eventually) did the right thing with the Nazis, unlike the pope." The four exchanged blank stares.

David: "We've never heard the United States called God's country before." Tony: "Neither did I." David: "What did you tell them?" Tony: "I said that was old news. They've been trying to kick God out of our country since the early 60s, and they've been making steady progress." David smiled mischievously, "When Christ returns, will he find anyone who still believes? What do you say to that Tony?" Tony: "If He wants to find believers He better hurry." The four classmates grinned. Everyone was finished eating. Greg and David politely excused themselves. Leo nodded a congenial departure.

Icon

Tony asked the Byzantine priest to bless his icon. The priest explained blessing an icon is different than blessing other objects. It has to participate in the Mass.

The Byzantine priest invited his class to attend Sunday Mass at his church before Christmas break. Students had to arrange their own transportation. Tony took his icon, Karl, and Javier to Mass. The three were surprised to see Tony's classmates in attendance. The Byzantine Mass had much more substance, texture, and color than the Roman equivalent. Most notable to Tony was the epiclesis. After Mass, the priest explained the icon was now a window into heaven. He gave Tony a pamphlet that detailed the proper handling and etiquette for icons. Tony thanked the priest for blessing his icon and for the invitation to participate in a Byzantine Mass.

On the return drive to campus, Karl voiced his surprise and trepidation at seeing Tony's classmates at Mass, "Why didn't you tell us they would be there?" Tony: "I had no idea. They never said a word." Karl: "Now they've seen us together!" Javier was also concerned. Tony: "Not to worry. I will tell them I talked to the Byzantine priest about blessing my icon. He said foreign students wanted to come but did not have a ride. I gave two foreign students a ride." Karl: "I'm not going to lie." Tony: "It's not a lie. I had that conversation with the priest, except I told him I was already taking Karl and Javier in my pickup. The priest was happy I was taking Karl." Karl: "I talked to him about needing a ride, that's true, but I'm not going to lie to those guys."

Tony: "There's no reason to lie. Just don't admit we know each other." Karl: "What are you asking me to do?" Tony: "You talked to the priest, which IS how you got invited to the Byzantine Mass?" Karl: "That's right." Tony: "And you needed a ride?" Karl: "I did." Tony: "And you found a ride. You rode with me, the lunchroom crazy." Karl: "I'm not going to call you that." Tony: "Do it. It's true, yet it gives the impression you don't know me." Karl: "It's still deceitful." Tony: "You don't have to lie. Just don't admit to knowing me. Ask them how they got there and thank them for not helping you. You had to ride with the lunchroom crazy, spank you very much, because they didn't share the wealth. That'll shut them up." Karl: "I don't know–." Javier: "He's right. They didn't help us and they knew we needed a ride. Make them feel guilty, since they are."

After lunch, a disquieted David approached Tony. David: "I was surprised to see you at the Byzantine church." Tony: "Why? You know I have a truck. I got the same invitation you did. I was surprised to see the four of you. How did you guys get there?" David: "Jack, the pub manager, and his assistant Art, took us in the pub's van. You could've ridden with us." Tony: "I could have if you guys said something." David: "Who were those two guys with you?" Tony: "I asked the Byzantine priest to bless my icon. He told me there were foreign students who wanted to attend but they needed a ride. I could only take two in my truck." David: "Those guys live on our floor. They live down by me." Tony: "And you didn't share your ride with the foreign students? No American hospitality? No Christmas spirit? Nice guy. Very nice guy."

A red-faced David said, "Never mind that. What did you think about the Byzantine church?" Tony: "I like their service much more than our own." David: "Not that, I mean the church itself, the artwork inside the church. I thought the painting of Jesus in the dome looked frightening–." David spoke of the paintings as art objects and critiqued them. Tony: "Why did you guys go if you don't believe in God? That's why I was surprised you were there." David: "We were curious. It was something different. I'm glad we went. We all are." David engaged Tony in a discussion of the artwork inside the church.

Javier and Karl stopped by Tony's room after dinner. Karl: "Did you talk to those guys yet? They haven't said a word to us." Tony: "Yeah. David asked who was with me. I told him the priest said foreign students needed a ride." Javier: "What did David say?" Tony: "He said you both live down by him." Javier: "We do." Tony: "The two guys who run the pub used the pub's van. They could have taken you too. I told David what a nice guy he was for not giving the foreign students a ride." Javier: "Good. Maybe that's why they haven't said anything to us." Karl: "What did David have to say about the Byzantine Mass?" Tony: "David critiqued the artwork, as if it was a field trip to an art museum. For the most part, it didn't suit his taste." Javier: "Can you believe those guys even want to be priests?"

Friends

Tony's friends met in his room before Christmas break. Brian asked Tony, "Did you go to the prayer vigil at the abortion clinic?" Tony: "No." Brian: "Why not?" The three friends simultaneously questioned, chastised, and expressed disbelief. Javier: "You're a good Catholic Tony, why didn't you go to the prayer vigil at the abortion clinic?" Brian's voice bristled with disdain, "Was it too cold that day for you Tony?" Tony: "No, I didn't go because I'm a Catholic, not a disciple of Mahatma Gandhi." Javier: "What does Gandhi have to do with a prayer vigil at an abortion clinic?"

Tony: "Civil disobedience, passive resistance: that's the philosophy of the Mahatma. I'm Catholic, not Hindu. In the Old Testament God instructs us to be obedient to civil authorities." Javier: "Catholics follow the New Testament. Jesus was a pacifist." Tony: "Passive, not passive aggressive. The Old and New Testaments speak to each other. Whatever is written about Jesus can be referenced in the Old Testament. You guys know that. On the subject of taxes, Jesus said to render to Caesar what is Caesar's, and to render to the Lord what is the Lord's. The Old Testament statement is clear: be obedient to civil authorities. Gathering at an abortion clinic is civil disobedience. Praying instead of carrying protest signs fools no one."

> Matthew 6:5 (DRA) [31] "And when ye pray, you shall not be as the hypocrites, that love to stand and pray in the synagogues and corners of the streets, that they may be seen by men: Amen I say to you, they have received their reward.

Karl: "Did you discuss this with the Vice Rector?" Tony: "No. I overheard the Vice Rector strategizing with the Rector about fundraisers and the prayer vigil at the abortion clinic when we worked on the pavers last fall. The purpose of the prayer vigil was to have an activity that would keep the Pontifical Jeroboam in the public eye. That would accomplish two things: it would look good to the Board of Directors and it would look good to patrons and potential donors. My take on that was; it would make it appear this place is still a seminary and is still doing its job. The PR generated by a public display of action was to be exploited to urge donors to give more money to the seminary and add to the $123 million the Jeroboam is already sitting on." Karl: "Seriously? The Jeroboam has $123 million?"

Tony: "They do." Karl: "How do you know?" Tony: "It came up in the conversation between the Rector and Vice Rector while we were laying pavers." Javier: "Did they know you were listening?" Tony: "No, they thought I was too far away to hear." Brian: "You said to make this place look like it's still a seminary. What do you call it if it's not a seminary?" Tony: "*La Casa del Puto.*" Javier was livid! Tony: "I'm sorry, that is inaccurate, *La Casa del Maricón.*" Javier was absolutely furious! Brian and Karl exchanged blank expressions. Tony: "The first was Spanish for house of male prostitutes. The second was house of queers." All three of Tony's friends were livid! Tony: "Homosexuals commandeered the Church's real estate assets at this location. They use the Church's good name, goodwill, and tax exemption to collect tax deductible donations and bequests, and they live here on the spoils, and the spoils are bountiful."

Brian emphatically objected, "That's ludicrous!" Tony: "Is it? The only place I ever saw food like what they serve in the refectory was on a cruise ship. All that is missing is the ice sculpture and capers. What do you guys think? Have you ever eaten, seen, or heard of cafeteria style food that compares to the fine cuisine we eat here every day?" Javier and Karl both shook their heads. Javier: "This is America. I thought this is how Americans normally eat." Karl nodded agreement and looked to Brian. Brian: "I never ate like this until I came here." Tony: "Don't you find it a bit odd humble seminarians eat such sumptuous cuisine at every meal?" Brian: "To tell you the truth, I never thought about it. Now that you mention it, it does seem a little extravagant." Tony: "Only a little? What about that toasting machine? I have never seen such a contraption before.

That monstrosity burns more electricity than any apartment I have ever lived in. They light it up before seven and run it until lunch." Karl: "Depending on what we have for lunch. Sometimes it runs until two in the afternoon." Javier: "Do you use the toaster Tony?" Tony: "Sure I do, and it's amazing: perfectly browned toast, bagel, or Danish every time. Such effusive opulence for humble seminarians. It's astounding! All that good food they fix for breakfast and no one gets up early enough to eat breakfast." Brian: "Yeah, what do they do with the leftovers?" None of the men knew. Javier: "What would we use if we didn't have that stainless steel toasting tower?" Tony: "Regular toasters. Two two-slice toasters would be much faster; no line, no waiting, and they would only burn electricity while actually making toast." Javier: "You can't toast Danish in a regular toaster, and if you adjust the toaster for bagels it will burn toast."

One possible motive for cooking breakfast for the seminary's entire population every day when only a handful of students eat a full breakfast is to look like a fully functioning seminary on paper. A forensic accountant examining the books would find it suspicious if breakfast food expenditures were a negligible fraction of those of lunch and dinner. If the seminarians prayed Morning Prayer, electrical power consumption would reflect higher use than if the majority of students slept in. The stainless steel toasting tower may help camouflage early morning seminarian indolence on the electric bill.

Brian: "Two toasters plus two toaster ovens would be faster and cheaper." Karl thought the chain-feed toaster was an excessive extravagance. Karl: "Why do you think they feed us so well and waste so much?" Tony: "This place is sitting on a mountain of cash. The administration's biggest challenge is how they can spend the money on themselves. I have to admit, homosexuals sure know how to eat well." Brian: "You make me angry! Not all seminarians are gay!" Brian was a big man, six feet two with broad shoulders. In his current state of anger, he was most foreboding. Tony: "I'm not smiling either. Ask Javier how much sleep he gets thanks to his noisy next-door neighbor and his late night study sessions.

The second day of class the Vice Rector made it clear that queers have the right-of-way at the Jeroboam. I understand systems were put in place eons ago to weed out homosexuals from the priesthood. Now that homosexuals run this facility, those same systems are being used to exclude straight men from the priesthood. You ARE painfully aware the queers outnumber us here, yes?" Brian: "For one thing, they prefer to be called gay. Why do you insist on using the word queer?" Tony: "They destroyed our language to promote the word gay and eliminate the word queer, which better enables their duplicity. I object. I refuse to comply."

Karl: "Tony, did you sign up for the bus trip to see the pope when he visited the United States?" Tony: "No." Karl: "Why not?" Tony: "Close your eyes and get a picture in your mind of me sitting on a bus full of homos for seven hours, spending the weekend with them in a hotel, sharing a room with one or more of them, and returning by spending another seven hours packed inside a tin can full of homos. Describe what you see." Karl: "I don't see anything. I can't picture it." Tony: "Exactly. Neither could I." Brian and Javier scoffed. Tony asked if they went to see the pope. Everyone had a polite (*though bogus*) excuse for why he did not go. Karl turned to Javier, "See? I told you."

Tony told the others the Vice Rector assigned the man in the mailroom to monitor mail traffic. Brian: "Do you have proof?" Tony: "I overheard their conversation on four separate occasions. I can assure you, that man's job is to monitor the mail. Do I have physical evidence to take to court? No, I don't. I'm telling you this so you are aware, so you can be careful and take countermeasures. One time when I checked my mail, the Vice Rector quizzed me about my bank and credit card statements, as if they were any of his business." Since tampering with the mail is a federal offense, Brian and Javier refused to believe the Vice Rector was directing a seminarian to monitor the mail, much less tamper with it.

Tony: "The telephones are even easier to play games with." Karl: "Every time we come into your room to have a real discussion, you unplug your phone. Can someone listen to our conversation when the phone is hung up?" Brian smirked. Javier laughed. Tony: "Yes, they can." Brian and Javier both laughed! Javier jeered, "You can listen to what goes on inside anyone's room?" Tony: "I can't. You need the right equipment. These old rotary phones are secure if no one has modified them. The Vice Rector can monitor conversations in this room if he's made a small modification." Brian: "That doesn't work when the phone is on hook." Tony: "Yes it does. Once someone who knows what they're doing has played with the phone." Javier: "Wait a minute Brian, Tony used to be an engineer. Tony, are you saying the Vice Rector can eavesdrop on us using our telephone?"

Tony: "The infrastructure set up here easily lends itself to eavesdropping. I have every confidence in the Vice Rector. I'm sure he has people and equipment in place to monitor the phones and phone calls of students he's interested in." Karl was concerned. Javier laughed at him, "You and Tony are both paranoid." Tony: "Javier, we know we are both targets. We know they really are after us. Are we paranoid for taking countermeasures against someone we know really is after us?" Javier laughed at Tony's concerns. Tony told Javier he read one too many psychology books. Karl told Javier it would not hurt to be a little careful. Karl asked Tony, "What do you do when you want to make a phone call?" Tony: "I use the phone in my room. I have a calling card, so I dial out myself. What do you do?"

Karl: "I have an account. I call into the switchboard. The junior year seminarian in charge of accounts places the call and I am billed at the end of the month. We get a really good discounted rate doing it this way." Tony: "That makes it too easy for the Vice Rector. That gives him a record of every call you make. I'm sure they have the equipment in place to listen to my calls and collect the dialing information. If I ever need to make a private call, I will go off campus and use a payphone. If you ever need to use my calling card, just say so. I'll take you off campus if you want privacy." Brian and Javier were not convinced security measures were needed for the phone or the mail. They thought it was a big hassle for no reason.

Brian challenged Tony, "Check your phone. Show us where it has been modified." Tony took the cover off his phone. Javier pointed, "What's that? Is that supposed to be there?" Tony: "It's a socket for a dual in-line chip. You spotted it immediately because of the sloppy soldering job." Javier objected, "But there's nothing plugged into it." Tony: "Look through here. See, there's a discrete component underneath." Javier: "What is it?" Tony: "It's a resistor." Javier: "Why didn't they plug it into the socket?" Tony: "You mean why hide it underneath?" Tony's friends shared an ah-ha moment. Brian: "You had your phone apart before. You knew it was there." Tony: "This is the first time I opened my phone." Brian: "How did you know without looking?" Tony: "I know the Vice Rector and I know his methods."

Brian wanted to discuss abortion. "Priests have been telling us to vote against the abortion rights law ever since I can remember." Tony: "When Roe versus Wade was decided, my parish priest gave a roaring, chastising sermon. He argued good Catholics needed to change the abortion law. He urged the congregation to vote to change the law." Brian and Javier asked, "What's wrong with priests urging their congregation to change the law?" Tony: "That should be their second priority, not their first." Brian, Javier, and Karl shared an emotional episode! "Are you crazy?" "What are they supposed to do?" Tony: "Their job! Nobody does their job anymore, that's the problem."

Brian: "What do you think the priests' job is?" Tony: "Their job is to instruct their congregation, remind them the Fifth Commandment is: "Thou shall not kill." Explain that only sinners have abortions. Good cannot fight evil if it does not know what is evil." Javier objected, "Priests have been told to stop preaching hellfire and brimstone. They were told to stop preaching out of the Old Testament." Tony: "The pope gave that order? Which pope?" No one knew. Tony: "I know priests were told to stop preaching from the Old Testament, but I don't remember when. I don't know if the pope gave the order or if renegade bishops used the confusion Vatican II provided to perpetrate that directive." All four men thought either scenario was plausible.

The Roman Catholic Church is invested in the Old Testament. Ecclesiasticus (Sirach) and 1 & 2 Machabees (Maccabees) are not in the Jewish canon, but are received as canonical and Divine by the Roman Catholic Church. The Liturgy of the Hours embraces both the Old and the New Testaments.

> Matthew 5:17-18 (DRA) [31] 17 "Do not think that I am come to destroy the law, or the prophets. I am not come to destroy, but to fulfill. 18 For amen I say unto you, till heaven and earth pass, one jot, or one tittle shall not pass of the law, till all be fulfilled.

Tony: "A priest's job is to teach about sin and morality. Everyone's job is to learn all they can about God. Even the homosexual priests here tell us that. If you are sucking air, God's air, then it is your duty to learn everything you can about God during your lifetime. We've all heard this since we arrived here at the Jeroboam." Everyone agreed. Tony: "Since I've been here, most of the priests I've dealt with have not read the Old Testament, even though it makes up three quarters of the Bible. If you are going to learn about God the Father, Abba, you have to read the Old Testament. The Jesuit and the Byzantine are the only priests I know who have read the entire Bible."

Javier added, "(The Old Testament Instructor) has read the Old Testament. How else can he teach the Old Testament?" Brian added a fourth priest (Karl's confessor) to that list. Tony: "You own a Bible, it sits on your shelf, and you only read the last one-fourth of it. You can't tell yourself you're learning all you can about God when you skip reading three quarters of the official book." Brian: "What do you think they should preach?" Tony: "Murdering your unborn baby is a sin against God, against your unborn child, against yourself, and against the child's father. Shedding innocent blood is especially heinous. What is more innocent than an unborn child, and what is bloodier than an abortion?"

> Proverbs 6:16-19 (DRA) [31] 16 Six things there are, which the Lord hateth, and the seventh his soul detesteth: 17 Haughty eyes, a lying tongue, hands that shed innocent blood, 18 A heart that deviseth wicked plots, feet that are swift to run into mischief, 19 A deceitful witness that uttereth lies, and him that soweth discord among brethren.

Karl asked Tony, "What do you think about legalized abortion, about the civil law?" Tony: "When civil law is the same as God's law, how do you know which law you follow? Do you follow civil law for fear of punishment, or do you love God and follow his commandments? Since Roe versus Wade, the difference itself sifts the wheat from the chaff. People can exercise free will and not be influenced by civil code. They can choose to obey God's law for the love of God, or they can choose to provoke God and sin egregiously. Legalized abortion gives atheists what they call "their civil rights" and it gives God-fearing souls the opportunity to exercise free will and prove themselves before God and man, to be tried in the furnace as purest gold.

The law would not affect God-fearing souls if the Church still taught from the entire Bible. For lack of instruction, churchgoing people do wickedly. A democratic nation of Christians has not voted the law out of existence. Shame on us!" Brian: "Then it is important to have the law overturned!" Tony: "The law would have been overturned soon after it was written if Christians were properly instructed. Our nation has failed to do that in more than two decades. We have proven ourselves to be an evil people and a wicked nation. We were once called God's country, but look at us now." Brian never heard the U.S. referred to as God's country. Javier and Karl explained to him why Europeans (*used to*) call the United States God's country.

> Jeremias 5:7-9 (DRA) [31] 7 How can I be merciful to thee? thy children have forsaken me, and swear by them that are not gods: I fed them to the full, and they committed adultery, and rioted in the harlot's house. 8 They are become as amorous horses and stallions: every one neighed after his neighbor's wife. 9 Shall I not visit for these things, sayeth the Lord? and shall not my soul take revenge on such a nation?

Tony: "I have met five women who had abortions. Years after the abortion, they were still messed up from it. "No one told me" is what four of them said. "I killed my baby. I had life inside me and I killed it! Everyone told me it's nothing, it's ok, it's no big deal, but it was a big deal! I murdered my own baby." I was surprised people need to be told something so obvious, but these women were in high school when they had their abortions. Where were their parents? What were the parents telling these girls? Where were the priests and clergy? As hard as I tried to have no compassion whatsoever for these women, I could not resist. Their souls were so tormented by what they did. They were profoundly pitiable."

Javier: "What about the fifth one?" Tony: "That was one bloodless, scary woman. I wonder if she was that way before she had her abortion." Javier: "Have you ever discussed this with a priest?" Tony: "Yes, I have. Storefronts for astrologers and psychics are common in California. I asked my parish priest why I have never heard a priest warn his congregation against using astrologers and psychics. He scoffed and said I sounded medieval."

> Deuteronomy 18:10-12 (DRA) [31] 10 Neither let there be found among you any one that shall expiate his son or daughter, making them to pass through the fire: or that consulteth soothsayers, or observeth dreams and omens, neither let there be any wizard, 11 Nor charmer, nor any one that consulteth pythonic spirits, or fortune tellers, or that seeketh the truth from the dead. 12 For the Lord abhoreth all these things, and for these abominations he will destroy them at thy coming.

> Isaias 47:13-14 (DRA) [31] 13 Thou hast failed in the multitude of thy

counsels: let now the astrologers stand and save thee, they that gazed at the stars, and counted the months, that from them they might tell the things that shall come to thee. 14 Behold they are as stubble, fire hath burnt them, they shall not deliver themselves from the power of the flames: there are no coals wherewith they may be warmed, nor fire, that they may sit thereat.

Javier chuckled, "You have to admit Tony; you do sound a bit medieval. What did you say?" Tony: "The priest chuckled and said he'd like to hear my view on legalized abortion. Since he was smirky, I told him I liked the abortion law. He was bewildered and asked why. I said, in the war between good and evil, abortion will guarantee victory for the forces of good. Abortion makes it a war of attrition. Evil people kill their own offspring and God-fearing people continue to multiply. Eventually God-fearing souls will vastly outnumber the wicked." Tony's friends were aghast and agog!

Javier: "What did he say to that?" Tony: "The priest complained he hears many confessions of Catholic women who have had abortions. I told him only sinners have abortions." Tony's friends remained startled! Brian: "Were you serious? Do you think that will actually work?" Tony: "I was messing with him and he knew it. Sadly, he did not have a response. The Church needs to properly teach from the entire Bible so priests know right from wrong. Only then can priests teach their congregation right from wrong. Having people think God is a bundle of unconditional love, a big teddy bear in the sky, is the real problem." Javier objected, "Jesus is loving and compassionate!" Tony: "Yes, and we are supposed to emulate Jesus, but in the end, each will be rewarded according to their works."

Ecclesiasticus 16:13 (DRA) [31] According as his mercy is, so his correction judgeth a man according to his works.

Sirach 16:12 (RSV-C) [40] As great as his mercy, so great is also his reproof; he judges a man according to his deeds.

Ecclesiasticus 5:6-7 (DRA) [31] 6 And say not: The mercy of the Lord is great, he will have mercy on the multitude of my sins. 7 For mercy and wrath quickly come from him, and his wrath looketh upon sinners.

Matthew 16:27 (DRA) [31] For the Son of man shall come in the glory of his Father with his angels: and then will he render to every man according to his works.

One of the men asked again if it would actually work. Would abortion cause evil to diminish by attrition? Tony: "No, it won't. I was messing with that priest because he was cheeky. I was ashamed I did it afterwards." Javier: "But it seems like it should work." Tony: "Abortion is evil. It can only multiply wickedness. Abortion sets the value of a human soul equal to zero. It makes human life worth less than the life of a house pet. Try publicly drowning a burlap bag of kittens and see what happens." Brian reiterated the urgency to have the abortion law overturned. Tony contended that will only happen after individuals are able to discern the difference between good and evil.

> Romans 3:8 (DRA) [31] And not rather (as we are slandered, and as some affirm that we say) let us do evil, that there may come good? whose damnation is just.

Brian expressed concern Tony was too critical of the overall job the Jeroboam was doing for priestly formation. Tony: "Ok, let's talk about confession. At the beginning of the semester, we were told we were expected to go to confession every week. Two priests would be on duty from eight to nine a.m. every Saturday. I adhered to the schedule; the priests did not. On the fourth Saturday, only one priest showed up. The next two Saturdays there was no priest." Javier offered, "Maybe they overslept and showed up late and you left before they got there." Tony: "I brought a book to read so that wouldn't happen. I sat there the full hour twice in a row. The priests take turns servicing the schedule, which means five separate priests were remiss in a three-week period.

These are the priests who are training us. One other seminarian showed up the first time both priests were a no show. I was the only seminarian that showed up the second time." Brian and Javier flushed. Karl proudly stated, "I found a priest I trust to be my confessor. I don't go Saturday morning anymore. I make an appointment in his office." Brian asked Tony, "Did you talk to anyone about it?" Tony: "I talked to my spiritual advisor." Brian: "What did he say?" Tony: "He admitted the obvious: no one gets up that early on Saturday. He said I should not act surprised since I'm the only one at breakfast on Saturday." Javier: "How does he know that?" Tony: "He must talk to the refectory staff."

The friends discussed their plans for Christmas break. Brian had plane tickets, Tony was making a long drive, and Javier was taking a bus. They all wished each other a safe trip. Tony asked Karl, "What are you doing for Christmas? Will you visit your family?" Karl: "No, it's too expensive to fly back to my country. I've made arrangements to stay with a local family over the holiday." Each wished the others a Merry Christmas.

9 WAGES OF A DOG

After Christmas

When Tony returned from Christmas break, he confronted the Vice Rector. Tony: "You sent my grades to my parent's house instead of sending them to me. What was that? You said you weren't going to bother my parents." Vice Rector: "You made dean's list Tony. Your parents must have been proud–." The Vice Rector's dialog could have been in earnest, but his facial expressions underscored his duplicity. He was smug and self-satisfied. Tony regretted capitulating to the Vice Rector's demand for his parent's address at the beginning of the school year.

Javier asked Tony what he told his family when he visited over Christmas break. Tony: "I told them most of the students are homosexuals and I'm going to quit." Javier: "Did your family believe you?" Tony: "Some did, some didn't. I told them the Vice Rector said the pope granted permission to ordain homosexuals as long as they are celibate. They didn't believe it and neither do I." Javier: "It's true Tony. The Vice Rector told you the truth. Why don't you believe him?" Tony: "I don't trust him. Besides, how can the pope say it's ok to ordain homosexuals? In the Old Testament God instructed the Israelites to kill homosexuals and the pope says to ordain them?"

> Leviticus 20:13 (DRA) [31] If any one lie with a man as with a woman, both have committed an abomination, let them be put to death: their blood be upon them.
>
> Leviticus 20:13 (KJV) [32] If a man also lie with mankind, as he lieth with a woman, both of them have committed an abomination: they shall surely be put to death; their blood shall be upon them.

Romans 1:24-32 (DRA)[31] 24 Wherefore God gave them up to the desires of their heart, unto uncleanness, to dishonour their own bodies among themselves. 25 Who changed the truth of God into a lie; and worshiped and served the creature rather than the Creator, who is blessed for ever. Amen. 26 For this cause God delivered them up to shameful affections. For their women have changed the natural use into that use which is against nature. 27 And, in like manner, the men also, leaving the natural use of the women, have burned in their lusts one towards another, men with men working that which is filthy, and receiving in themselves the recompense which was due to their error. 28 And as they liked not to have God in their knowledge, God delivered them up to a reprobate sense, to do those things which are not convenient; 29 Being filled with all iniquity, malice, fornication, avarice, wickedness, full of envy, murder, contention, deceit, malignity, whispers, 30 Detractors, hateful to God, contumelious, proud, haughty, inventors of evil things, disobedient to parents, 31 Foolish, dissolute, without affection, without fidelity, without mercy. 32 Who, having known the justice of God, did not understand that they who do such things, are worthy of death; and not only they that do them, but they also that consent to them that do them.

Tony: "The Church excommunicated homosexuals for nearly two thousand years, now the pope says ordain them if they pretend to be celibate their senior year? That makes no sense. Has the pope read the Old Testament? It's impossibly difficult for straight men to be celibate. What makes him think homosexuals can be celibate? What makes him think they will even try? They define the essence of their being by their sexual excesses and their deviant proclivities." Javier reiterated gays only have to be celibate for one year before ordination. *Who thinks that is credible? My classmates certainly don't.*

Ecclesiastes 1:15 (DRA)[31] The perverse are hard to be corrected, and the number of fools is infinite.

Ecclesiastes 1:15 (RSV)[20] What is crooked cannot be made straight, and what is lacking cannot be numbered.

Javier: "What questions did your family ask?" Tony: "One uncle asked if I thought it was possible for a homosexual to be celibate. A celibate pervert? Not possible. Another uncle asked about my classmates. I told him there are only five transfer students, me and four homosexuals. Only one homosexual is trying to be celibate. My uncle asked if that guy would make a good priest. I told him that guy's sense of right and wrong is why he's not having sex with the others. He is having trouble academically. He's going to have a tough time graduating, but at least he believes in God. The other three don't even believe there is a God. The uncle asked why they wanted to be priests if they don't believe in God.

I told him what they said: employment opportunity, respect of the community, use of Catholic rectories as a worldwide homosexual hostelry (*Free travel accommodations with gay benefits*), and buying new cars at dealers cost. My uncle asked how I was doing. "I live in a five story queer's nest, I hate my life. Academically? I made dean's list. I'm not going to be a priest. I'll be lucky to finish out the year." My uncle asked if I thought I had an actual calling. I said I thought so but I wasn't sure. The Jesuit is convinced I have a true calling. The Jesuit loved it and said so."

My uncle asked if I had already quit, or was I going to quit after Christmas break. "No." He asked what I was going to do. I told him I would buy a tape recorder when I get back. Uncle: "You have a plan." I told him I didn't have a plan, only an idea. I would surreptitiously tape conversations until I had enough to constitute credible witness to what was going on at the seminary. I would try to stay in the seminary until I had something tangible. He vociferously insisted such tape recordings cannot be used in court. "I don't intend to use them in court." Uncle: "How will you use them?" "One problem at a time. Tape is the only tangible thing I can reasonably gather intel with, so I am going to gather voice recordings." Uncle: "You won't be able to use illegal tapes!" "I'll worry about that problem later."

(I will have to be careful to keep my tape recording activities absolutely secret until they are complete.)

Javier: "Did you tell them about me?" Tony: "Yes, my uncle asked if I made any friends. I told him I met Javier, who started telling me his girlfriend problems. Over the summer, Javier dated a girl from the parish where he interned. My uncle asked what my reaction was. At first I thought, "What is that?" He asked what I did next. I said I thought for a few seconds, and then smiled and said, "Buddy!"" Javier was alarmed, "What did he say to that?" Tony: "We both chuckled and repeated, "Buddy!"" Javier: "You think it was wrong I dated a girl in the parish where I did my internship?" Tony: "It was wrong." Javier: "What did your uncle think?" Tony: "He thought it was wrong." Javier: "So, the only reason you and I are friends is because of the gays?" Tony: "Pretty much." Javier: "What did your uncle think?" Tony: "He thought the same thing I did; you and I needed a friend."

Javier: "The gays have been trying to get me kicked out after I told them I had a girlfriend." Tony: "If you could have been kicked out for that, you would already be gone. They would not have spent the last four months trying to invent a lie sufficient to get you expelled. I told you about the lies I heard them concocting." Javier: "Did I tell you what happened?" Tony: "No." Javier: "I had been fasting. I didn't eat food for two days. That evening (the gay seminarian from Minnesota) came to visit me. I thought he was my friend. He had a sweet tasting alcoholic drink. He invited me to drink with him. On an empty stomach I didn't have to drink much."

Tony: "What happened?" Javier: "I don't remember what happened. I passed out. I can't refute their allegations. I have no idea what happened." Tony: "Sure you do, you passed out. If something happened, they would not continue to make up different stories until the Rector tells them it's enough to get you expelled. I listened to them devise three separate lies. The Rector critiqued each one and found them insufficient to expel the seminarian. That seminarian is you. Truth is; you did nothing that would get you expelled, because if you did you would already be gone."

Javier: "Did you visit anyone in your diocese over the holiday?" Tony: "No." Javier: "Did you call your parish priest?" Tony: "No." Javier: "Why not?" Tony: "My parish priest was maneuvered into sponsoring me. He resented it. I didn't get a Christmas card from him either." Javier: "You must have had some friends. You lived there for three years." Tony: "I sent Christmas cards to several people. I didn't call any of them because I didn't want to say what I found here. They would draw conclusions about our current parish priest, and I don't want to go there. Besides, I'm not absolutely sure about him yet. I was tempted to call the neighbors. Their son rode with me to a vocations meeting last summer. I need to call them. I have to warn their son."

Javier objected, "You can't do that! You can't jeopardize his calling! That's wrong, don't do it!" Tony: "It would be negligent of me not to. It's not just the sin of omission. I'd feel responsible for allowing him to go in blind, knowing they'll do the same thing to him they're doing to us." Javier: "You're not supposed to interfere with a religious calling!" Tony: "I didn't call because I'm not ready to call. I don't have the full story yet. I will have to call eventually, not warning that innocent kid is criminal negligence. His parents will have questions. I want to have at least a few answers."

South Side 3

Christmas break was over. The Friar called the transfer students to his office. "You will go on retreat Monday. Since nothing is scheduled until then, I spoke with the south side priest. You will canvass tomorrow afternoon and Saturday." With a sharp edge in his voice the Friar said, "You now have experience canvassing. You know exactly what you need. I expect all of you will be properly prepared tomorrow. This means tonight you will lay out the clothes you intend to wear tomorrow. Dress to spend the entire afternoon outdoors. You need paper and something to write with. Last time, the priest was appalled at your complete lack of preparation. This demonstrates a lack of commitment and brings your formation into question.

The dismal results at the end of the day were no surprise to anyone. I have made arrangements with the refectory staff again specifically to serve the five of you. I expect them to be ready to serve at 11:30, just as I expect you to be there by 11:30. After all, they are there to accommodate you. The van leaves at twelve noon. Last time, I expected all of you to be inside the van before twelve, and the driver to drive away promptly at twelve. This time, I have instructed him to promptly drive off at twelve o'clock. If you are unable to meet these simple expectations, how can you possibly perform the duties of a priest?

I expect to see significantly improved results tomorrow and even better results Saturday, and so does the south side pastor. I reminded you last time you are ambassadors of the Pontifical Jeroboam. I said your actions directly reflect on all of us here. You embarrassed yourselves and you gave the Jeroboam a black eye, and you have cast a shadow on us all. Are there any questions?" Silence. Friar: "Ok, give us your best effort. Make us proud." The Friar motioned to Tony, so when the others left the office Tony stayed behind. Friar: "Those things I said don't pertain to you." Tony: "I know." Friar: "I had to say them for the benefit of the others." Tony: "I know. We needed to hear it as a group." Both men smiled.

Friday morning Tony got ready the same as before, but this time he added a second stocking hat, a heavy scarf, and lip balm. He did not miss the cheese sandwich last time, so he decided he did not need reserve food. Tony walked into the refectory at eleven twenty-five and set his cold weather gear on a table. One of the staff called to him, "We're ready to start serving." Tony was eating when three of his classmates arrived. All four were eating before Mr. Stevens showed up. There was quiet chatter. Tony's classmates were checking with each other to make sure that they all had supplies. They were all worried by the things the Friar said the day before. Mr. Stevens sniped, "No cheese sandwich today Tony? I don't blame you, it tasted terrible."

When Tony got up from the table, the others asked what he was doing. Tony: "It's five minutes to twelve, time to go." Tony started putting on his cold weather gear. Mr. Stevens: "My jacket is back in the room!" David moaned, "Not again." Tony had the third row seat to himself again. Leo, David, and Greg sat in the second row seat again. The driver started the motor and shifted into drive. David yelled, "There he is! Wait! He's almost here!" The other two chimed in. The van pulled away from the curb. Driver: "I was told to drive away promptly at twelve noon. I was instructed not to wait." David: "He's here, he's here! Stop! Let him get in!" The driver stepped on the breaks, and Mr. Stevens opened the front passenger door.

Whatever Mr. Stevens started to say was drowned out by David. "Shut up! You didn't make it, so just shut the hell up! He started the motor at twelve noon." That bought everyone a blessed ten minutes of silence. Eventually the men in the second row seat quietly discussed the Friar's briefing. They were worried. Last time, the group's results were dismal. It was imperative to perform well today. David was hopeful. Four out of five were in the refectory by eleven thirty and were seated in the van before twelve noon. Greg was realistic, "As a team, nothing has changed. The refectory staff will report one late arrival and the driver will report stopping for one late arrival." The van was filled with consternation.

David asked Tony for his input. Tony: "I've been doing the best I can. I don't know what else we can do but our best." That triggered several muttered comments. Greg: "If we can produce a good list of names by the end of the day all of the other problems will be overlooked." Everyone agreed they needed a good showing by the end of the day. The three men in the second row seat were upset with Mr. Stevens, which made for a peaceful ride.

The south side priest briefed the seminarians and dispatched them. The classmates rushed to the restroom. Tony was last in line. Today the teams were Leo and Mr. Stevens, Greg and Tony, with David working alone. There was no wind and a few patches of sunshine. It was Friday, a workday; many houses were empty.

When Greg and Tony reached their first house, Tony walked up to the door and knocked. There was no answer. At the second house, Tony knocked. A man answered the door. The man listened to Tony's pitch, but said he was not interested and closed the door. As the two men walked to the next house, Greg got in Tony's face, "Who do you think you are? We are supposed to be working together. You're not in charge!" Tony: "Fine. I'll follow your lead." Greg knocked on the next dozen doors. On two occasions, someone opened the door and then slammed it shut before Greg could finish one sentence. Greg complained his hands were cold and it hurt to knock on doors. He asked Tony to knock on doors for a while, but he wanted to greet the people. Tony: "Ok."

After knocking on a few dozen doors, Greg faced six or eight cantankerous and one quarrelsome homeowner. Each homeowner slammed the door in Greg's face! It was as disquieting as it was discouraging. Greg complained he was frozen. Tony: "Is it time to switch?" Greg agreed it was. Tony knocked on some doors, had a few opportunities to give his pitch, and was finally invited inside a house. The woman offered the two seminarians hot coffee. Tony reflexively said, "No thank you." The woman smiled, "It's no bother. I just made a fresh pot. Your partner looks like he needs some hot coffee. This will give you boys a chance to warm up." The nice lady went to the kitchen to get coffee. Tony turned to see Greg glaring at him.

Greg snarled, "You don't speak for me. Just because you don't want coffee doesn't mean I don't! I know you and Leo had coffee when you two worked together." Tony: "We told everyone no thank you until three in the afternoon. We can't count on having access to a toilet until the end of the day. It's too early to start drinking coffee." Greg: "I'm cold! I need hot coffee!" The nice lady served coffee. Tony gave his pitch. She was not interested in having someone give her a ride to church, but she was happy to chat and give the seminarians a chance to warm up. Tony finished his cup when Greg finished the last of his refills. Tony thanked the nice lady and the two men resumed their canvass.

Several houses later, a man answered Tony's knock on the door and invited the two seminarians inside. Tony started to give his pitch, but Greg asserted himself. Greg intervened and started delivering the pitch. The homeowner exploded in rage! He ordered Greg out of his house immediately! He glared at Tony and accusingly growled, "I invite you into my house, and you bring THIS in with you? Get out! You too, both of you, GET OUT!" The two seminarians left. *That was uncomfortable!*

Tony: "If you want to take the lead, just say so." Greg was absolutely silent for the next few houses. Finally, he asked Tony if it was like this when he and Leo worked together. *Only at first, when Leo greeted the homeowners. Leo solved that problem by having me deal with the people, and I agreed.* Tony: "No, people were nice. Women offered us coffee and cookies. We held out until three o'clock before we accepted coffee." Greg: "Why would you say no?" Tony: "We're not supposed to impose. They offer hospitality. We are supposed to politely refuse." Greg: "What do you do when they insist?" Tony: "The correct response is "no thank you," but extenuating circumstances are taken under advisement."

Greg: "Has anyone ever told you you're bossy?" Tony: "Yes, especially when I was a supervisor. Why?" Greg: "When you and Leo worked together you must've completely taken over the way you tried to do with me today." Tony: "If you have a better idea, tell me. It doesn't matter who knocks on the door. One of us greets the homeowner and is the primary speaker after that since he has already started to establish a rapport when the door opened. One guy takes the lead and the other one is the silent partner. We share the workload by taking turns." Greg: "You and Leo took turns I suppose?" Tony: "I thought we did." Greg: "Leo is a follower. He probably let you walk all over him." Tony: "Tell me what you want to do, and that's what we'll do."

It was a cold, overcast day. Greg was not able to knock on many doors because his hands were so cold. He was willing to delegate door knocking to Tony. The two did not gain entry to even one house when Greg greeted the homeowner at the door. Homeowners were incredibly surly toward Greg. When Greg was frozen and urgently needed to use a toilet, he reluctantly told Tony it was his turn to take the lead. There was another nice lady who insisted the two seminarians come inside to warm up. She made a fresh pot of coffee. Both men needed to impose and asked to use the toilet. She gave Tony her information so someone could give her a ride to church.

The five seminarians covered more territory than they did the first time since it was a workday and so many houses were empty. At the end of the day, they returned to the office frozen and exhausted. Greg and Tony entered the office last. They were punctual; it was five o'clock. The angry priest bellowed, "And how did you two do today?" Tony was embarrassed, "We only have one." Old Priest: "One? ONE! Five seminarians spend all afternoon in the neighborhood and you come back with only one address? You can't be serious! This is unacceptable!" The priest demanded ideas that would guarantee better results. Nobody had an idea. Old Priest: "No one leaves this office until I hear an idea that will guarantee vastly improved results tomorrow!"

Tony was inspired, "Seeing two men at the door is intimidating. If we work separately, it will be less imposing and we will be better received. Also, by working in pairs, we only have three teams. Working separately, we will knock on five doors at a time instead of three. We can canvass sixty percent more of the neighborhood by working alone." The priest was delighted, "Your first idea makes sense. Whether or not it is true, we can only guess at this point. By splitting up, you will definitely knock on more doors. It's decided. Tomorrow you work separately. Today was a workday. You knocked on the doors of a lot of empty houses. Tomorrow is Saturday. I expect spectacular results tomorrow." The seminarians were excused.

Seething anger filled the van on the return trip. After the first canvass, only Mr. Stevens muttered under his breath. This time David joined him. They complained about the treatment they received when homeowners answered the door. Eventually Leo murmured, "I know what you mean." When they reflected on the debriefing and Tony's good idea, they all turned and glared at Tony. They gave Tony the silent treatment for the rest of the ride. *Yeah! Thank you Lord.*

Saturday everyone was on time in the refectory and in the van. The priest was not in his office. His secretary handled the canvass briefing. All four classmates looked daggers at Tony. When the briefing was over, the classmates hurried to the restroom ahead of Tony.

It was a cold, sunny day with a light breeze. It was the nicest weather yet on this assignment. After a long day, Tony was the last one to reach the priest's office, which was locked. He heard the others exchanging war stories about how nasty the residents treated them. Tony heard the end of one, two full accounts, and part of another before they were aware of his presence and fell silent. Once the silence was uncomfortable, they complained about the priest being late.

Tony: "How rude. How disrespectful and insulting. How hard is it to be on time?" There was a hubbub of agreement and more grousing for two or three minutes before they saw the irony. Tony went to use the restroom. When he returned, the others commented on what a relief it is to have access to a restroom. Tony asked if they had access to a toilet during their canvass.

Greg: "I was never inside anyone's house. I didn't have access to a toilet." Tony: "What did you do?" Greg became surly, "The only thing I could do, go in back of an empty house, and find some bushes. One time the neighbor next door caught me and pounded on the window, swearing at me the whole time." David: "I had to do the same, we all did. We had no choice. One time no one answered the door. I thought the house was empty, so I went in the back yard. There were no bushes. A woman was inside the house and saw me. She screamed she had kids in the house. She come outside screaming and chased me."

The seminarians were left standing for forty minutes before the priest showed up. He asked each seminarian in turn for the names and phone numbers they collected. Leo had one. The next three seminarians were empty handed. Lastly, the priest glared at Tony. Tony handed him six. The old priest aimed his penetrating stare directly into the focal plane of Tony's eyes and asked, "How do you think you did today?" Tony: "Not so good Father." Old Priest: "Why not?"

Tony: "I must have knocked on a hundred doors and I only have six names and phone numbers." The priest toned down his gruffness. "Did someone answer the door at every house?" Tony: "No. I would guess eighty-four or eighty-six people answered the door." Old Priest: "Why not just tell me eighty-six? Why do you think it's important you knocked on a door if no one was home?" Tony: "There were times people were home but wouldn't answer the door. I'm not sure what that was about." The priest was no longer starchy. "Don't let that bother you. This is a poor neighborhood. There are a lot of reasons people don't answer the door."

The ride back to campus was blissfully silent. Peaceful, if you ignore the smoldering anger and contempt the other four had for Tony. They were forty minutes into the trip before Mr. Stevens said in a low voice, "How did you do today? Not so good Father, I only have six." David and Greg's bodies spontaneously quaked with rage! Leo cowered from the others, hoping to be ignored.

Leo engaged in conversation with Tony for the remainder of the ride. He discussed the anti-homosexual animus of the people in the neighborhood. Leo: "What did you think? Was it obvious to you when we worked together?" Tony: "It was obvious something was going on, I just wasn't sure what." *It was spelled out for me when I worked with Greg.*

It was nearly eight p.m. by the time the group entered the refectory. The door was still open, but there was only emergency lighting. The place was deserted. The staff left a note instructing the five seminarians which refrigerator held the leftovers reserved for them. Mr. Stevens was loath to eat leftovers and profusely vented his disdain. Tony fixed a plate and found a table with adequate lighting. The others tentatively scanned the refrigerator. Greg decided to rifle through all the refrigerators. Three more students joined Tony at the table. Mr. Stevens started to fix himself a plate, but never stopped complaining.

In the privacy of his room, Tony reviewed his tape of the day's conversations. The telling conversations in the rectory were muffled and faint. Keeping the small $35 recorder concealed in his clothing required more volume than the recorder was capable of. The jackpot conversation with Leo in the van was overwhelmed by road noise. Using a cheap tape recorder cost Tony dearly.

Sunday afternoon the Friar called Tony to his office. Friar: "How did you do this time?" Tony: "One with Greg on Friday and six by myself yesterday." Friar: "Why do you think you got more when you worked by yourself?" Tony: "Maybe people answered the door more often when they saw one man instead of two." Friar: "How did the people in the neighborhood react to you?" Tony: "About what I expected. People who did not open the door treated me like a salesman saying, "We don't want any." Most people would let me tell them why I was there, and then say they weren't interested. A few said they weren't Catholic." Friar: "What about the people who said they were interested?" Tony: "They invited me inside. Five of them felt guilty. They play bingo at least one night a week, but don't go to Mass on Sunday."

Friar: "Did they offer you refreshments?" Tony: "Four of them offered me cookies, coffee, or both." Friar: "What did you tell them?" Tony: "I told them I was working with four other seminarians. I'd feel guilty taking it easy while the others were slaving away going door to door." Friar: "You didn't offend them by refusing their hospitality did you?" Tony: "No. One woman offered me cookies and insisted I take one with me. I held out until mid-afternoon before accepting coffee. Late in the day, another woman absolutely would not take "no thank you" for an answer. I said what I really needed was to use her bathroom, and she was more than happy to oblige. My excuse of not slacking off while the other four were working was well received."

Friar: "Did you give out your phone number?" Tony: "Yes. When Leo and I worked together last December, the first woman asked for our phone number to guarantee she would have follow up. Leo instantly agreed. I gave her my number since I was taking her information. After we left her house, I told Leo we don't want people calling us. They need to call the parish office. At the end of the day I asked the priest to give us a business card so we would have the parish phone number with us." Friar: "Did she ever call you?" Tony: "She called twice before Christmas complaining no one gave her a follow up call. I suggested she call the parish office. She said she did. She left three messages and no one returned her call. I apologized. I told her the seminary is an hour away from the parish and I couldn't help her."

Friar: "Have you figured out the meaning of the priest's warning about people in the neighborhood being able to know what you're made of?" Tony: "On my own I would've never figured it out, but each day after we finished, the other guys would grumble about the way people treated them. I didn't know what they were talking about. Yesterday I overheard them while we were waiting for the priest. People got ugly with them and verbally accosted them with what the guys called "gay bashing."" The Friar was decidedly starchy when he dismissed Tony.

Looks like the Friar has his own sure-fire test to sort out straights from gays. The south side priest's interest was in testing, not evangelism or increasing church attendance, as evidenced by the parish's failure to return the phone calls of the lady asking for a ride to church. An increase in registered parishioners would cause an increase in the Vatican poll tax on the parish.

Leo joined Tony at dinner. Leo: "Why did you suggest we canvass individually?" Tony: "Just what I said, it would give us 60% more coverage, and I thought seeing two men at the door was imposing." Leo: "Did that work the way you thought it would?" Tony: "The increased coverage worked as advertised. I was wrong about the other part." Leo: "How so?" Tony: "The old priest told us those people would see what we were made of. Now I see he meant they can identify homosexuals on sight. Most people think they can accurately do that, but cannot. The people in that neighborhood can actually do it. That's what you guys were complaining about last night, how the people in the neighborhood got in your face. How bad was it?"

Leo: "People insulted me for being homosexual. It was worse for Greg and David. The people were absolutely brutal to (Mr. Stevens). We could not believe how awful they were to him. We didn't expect people to be so vicious. Working separately sure made you look good. Did you know it would turn out that way?" Tony: "(*Polite lie*) No I didn't. Besides, it would be my turn to work alone eventually. You did ok. You got an address. How did you manage to snag an address if you were being harassed?" Leo smiled, "When the woman opened the door, I saw a photograph of her son in a Navy uniform. I quickly told her I served in the Navy too. Since I had that in common with her son, she invited me in.

She offered me coffee and cookies. I needed hot coffee. She gave me her information so someone could take her to church on Sunday. That was the only place that was friendly to me, except for when you and I worked together. All the people were nice when we worked together. How was it when Greg worked with you?" Tony: "I could feel the difference. No one said anything specific, but his presence was a dark cloud and a hindrance. We did get one address." Leo smiled, "When I worked with you we got two." Tony: "And there was no negative static in the air when we worked together." Leo: "There was with Greg?" Tony: "Between Greg and me and between the people and Greg; yes, there was static."

Tony in Trouble

Tony's friends stopped by his room to visit after dinner. For security purposes, his was the best room to meet to minimize detection. Javier, Brian, and Karl told Tony they were jealous of his location. Brian: "You seem a little pensive today Tony, what happened?" Tony: "I got myself in trouble." Brian laughed, "You get in trouble? That's not possible." Tony: "I did, I got in trouble." Javier's face looked doubtful. Brian chuckled, "What did you do that was so bad? It's not possible for you to be bad."

Tony wagged his head. With a voice imitating a nasty second grader he said, "Tony doesn't play nice with the faggy boys." The others howled! They realized their raucous reaction just blew the clandestine nature of their meeting. They were out of control. They could not stop laughing. Karl swirled his index finger, indicating he wanted Tony to repeat what he said. Tony obliged. Everyone exploded with more laughter! When they were done laughing Brian said, "We blew our cover and should discreetly disperse." The three friends left the room one at a time.

Retreat

A retreat was scheduled after Christmas break and before the start of the second semester. A retreat is a time of prayer and contemplative thought. Pre-theology students and the five transfer theology students were sent to an off campus location. Each student had a tiny room with a bed, a chair, and a table with a lamp. There was no lock on the door. Tony chose the room next to the priest's room at the beginning of the hallway. If nothing else, it was a location with good egress and close to the meeting room. The other students were elated with Tony's choice of rooms. A retreat is for prayer and contemplation, but the noise and activity after dinner more closely resembled Mardi Gras.

Tony spent his free time in his room. He propped the chair beneath the doorknob as a security measure. Night three of the retreat, Tony was awakened shortly after nine p.m. by the thunderous roar of cheering. Cheers started at the far end of the hall, moved past his room, and into the meeting room. Students stampeded down the hall cheering! They were celebrating because "the holdout" had rejoined the group. One voice declared, "The lost sheep has returned to the fold." Another asked, "Who was it?" "Greg." A cheering crowd gathered in the meeting room. The lone holdout, Leo, had rejoined the fold!

The next day Leo sat next to Tony at lunch. Leo hung his head in shame, "Do you know what happened last night?" Tony: "Yes." Leo was surprised, "How do you know?" Tony: "How could I not? They woke me from a sound sleep. Everyone was cheering and celebrating. They said Greg brought you back into the fold." Leo's face turned red, "What do you think of me?" Tony: "Your cohorts made it obvious you were the only gay not having sex last semester. It is good you were trying to do the right thing. Too bad you were the only one who was." Leo: "Is that the reason you and I get along?" Tony: "Pretty much." Leo: "How long did it take you to figure it out?" Tony: "It took me a few weeks to figure it out because you weren't having sex with the others. You were trying to be an honest seminarian. That counts for something."

Leo: "Why do you have problems with the others?" Tony: "Problems with the others were not initiated by me. Mr. Stevens decided not to get along even before I met him." Leo: "What about Greg?" Tony: "Greg pretended to be straight by bitching about queers in an attempt to get me to say something he could use to tattletale to the Vice Rector. Basically, he challenged me to play a game: who can be the biggest jackass. I chose to play. I decided I was a contender. Not only did I beat him, I trounced him soundly." Leo: "You sure did. You didn't start it, he did?" Tony: "He forgot to mention he was being clever? Yeah, well, his face turned purple. His head looked like it was going to explode. His visceral reaction gave him away in case there was any doubt."

Leo: "What did the Vice Rector say to you because of that?" Tony: "Oh yes, the Vice Rector told me in no uncertain terms he does not want to hear me say homosexuals are "fuel for the fires of hell."" Leo: "What did you think of that?" Tony: "I loved it. It was much more eloquent than what I said to Greg. I was going to use it as my own, but that would be plagiarism. I have to credit the Vice Rector." Leo was disappointed Tony was not upset the Vice Rector chewed him out. Leo: "David admits you were oblivious until he and (Mr. Stevens) overreacted. The upperclassmen are angry with those two. What do you think about me now that I've fallen off the wagon?"

Tony: "What do you intend to do going forward?" Leo: "I failed. I'm one of them now." Tony: "You went an entire semester without having sex with those guys. Next time, go longer before falling off the wagon." Leo: "It's going to be harder to say no to them. They are all so happy they won me back." Tony: "You don't have to give in. When they test your resolve, redouble your effort. What matters is what you want, not what they want." A small, weak smile came to Leo's face. Leo: "Yes, I will try to go longer next time, but what happens if I fall off the wagon again?"

Tony: "You fall down, you get back up. You go farther each time you pick yourself up until you can go the distance. You can do it if you decide to. Good luck." Leo smiled. The vote of confidence appeared to bolster Leo. Tony remembered nothing else from the retreat after the Leo incident except eating pancakes and bacon for breakfast and holing-up in his room like a feral rabbit. It was not a proper retreat. It was not the prayerful, meditative, contemplative exercise, the spiritual journey it was supposed to be.

After Dinner Saturday

Javier, Karl, and Brian gathered in Tony's room. Brian and Karl felt bad and apologized for wanting a clandestine meeting. Tony offered, "I understand. Being seen with Javier and me will jeopardize your ordination. Javier is doomed and so am I. Neither of us will be allowed to finish. We all know this, and we all need to protect the two of you. The world needs to have some straight priests." The four discussed their observations. Each man in turn told who he had confirmed was gay and who he hoped was straight. As one man gave his observations, the other three critiqued his hopeful candidates. By the time all four reviewed their latest intel, the accounting was sad. There were 54 confirmed homosexuals, 14 confirmed straights, and a group of 10 unknowns.

Javier: "There is one seminarian you've never seen Tony. He is doing his internship." Tony: "Making the total 79?" Javier: "That's right." Tony: "The 10 unknowns are a cohesive group that defied study. They are like a bubble. I was unable to effectively interact with any of them. They have banded together for self-preservation. They are separate and insular from the homosexuals at least." Karl: "They isolate themselves from us too." Javier: "Even if they are straight, would you be friends with those guys?" Tony: "Not really. They seem pretty frazzled." Javier: "We are frazzled, those guys are weird. What do you say Brian?" Brian: "I have to agree with Javier, they are strange. I always steer clear of them." Karl: "You must have talked to some of them Tony, what did you find out?" Tony: "I learned nothing. They avoid everyone. I did notice the homos shun them." Javier: "The gays think those guys are weird too."

Brian, Javier, and Karl encouraged Tony. They said he should transfer to another seminary. All he had to do was finish the year without having the gays slander him, and he could transfer to a safer school. Each man told what he knew of seminaries that might be suitable for Tony, seminaries that were honest: straight friendly if you will. As each man put forth his recommendations, the others shot down most of them.

Karl offered a seminary in Connecticut, "This seminary is safe for straights to go to, but no diocese sends their candidates there because they are afraid it will close. With an enrollment of only 23 seminarians this year, there are too few students to keep the place going." Tony: "My uncle has contacts with clergy and religious across the country. I asked him for a list of recommendations. He came up with seven. My insurance agent here in town has a sister who is a nun. He gave me three recommendations, but my uncle shot down all three." Karl and Javier shot down six of the uncle's seven. Karl and Javier did an impressive amount of investigation before choosing to attend the Pontifical Jeroboam. One or the other had personally visited each of the seven seminaries on Tony's uncle's list.

The one left standing was in Philadelphia. Karl laughed, "You won't like it Tony. The showers are in one big room with fixtures along the walls, just like in high school." Javier laughed, "And there are no doors on the bedrooms." Tony: "Why did they remove the bedroom doors?" Javier: "So the faculty and staff can make sure there is no homosexual activity." Tony: "What percentage of the population is homosexual?" Javier: "Thirty percent." Karl nodded agreement. Tony: "You guys are right, I won't like it." All three laughed at Tony.

Tony: "I came to the Pontifical seminary because it's the pope's own school. I came here thinking it was safe. My mentor graduated from here two years before I started." Brian: "Have you talked to him since you've been here?" Tony: "Yes I have. I asked him to estimate what percentage was homosexual when he was here, and he estimated it was only 30%. Later I learned a man from my hometown went here years ago. He quit and has since married. I called him. He estimated at that time the population here was 30% homosexual. Everyone estimates the homosexual population is 30%. The reason their estimates are so low is because they are not actively testing."

Brian blurted, "Nobody else antagonizes his fellow seminarians by telling them gays should go back to hell where they came from. I can't believe you actually did that." Tony: "You should've seen how purple his face turned." Brian: "You can't wonder why you're going to be their next victim after Javier." Tony: "No, I did this the old fashioned way, I earned it." Brian: "The Vice Rector must've had something to say to you about that." Tony: "Oh yes, he said he didn't want to hear me ever again say homosexuals are "fuel for the fires of hell."" Brian: "You said that?" Tony: "No, that was much more eloquent than what I said. Fuel for the fires of hell. I was going to use it as my own, but I have to credit the Vice Rector." Brian warned Tony not to be so glib. Tony: "There's no amount I can be careful that's going to change anything. I will leave after Javier goes, one way or the other."

Brian: "What about transferring to another seminary?" Tony: "That's not going to happen. I did not realize the pope knowingly ordains homosexuals. The concept of a celibate homosexual is an unconscionable joke." Brian: "What do you think about celibacy for heterosexuals?" Tony: "That is a mistake the Roman Church made hundreds of years ago. A celibate homosexual is an exponentially worse mistake. I wish I knew more about the Byzantine Church." Brian: "Have you looked into it since you've been here?"

Tony: "Yes I have. I am too old for them to consider my candidacy.

Unfortunately, even the Byzantine Church has been tainted. In one of my classes, I learned the patriarch of the Byzantine Church cut a deal to come under the pope of Rome. It was a raw deal." Brian: "What makes you say it was a raw deal?" Tony: "Look at what the pope has done. He allows homos to be ordained and he brought psychology into the Church." Javier interrupted, "What is wrong with psychology?" Tony: "Psychology is irreligion. Irreligion has no place in the Church. The pope opened the floodgates for annulments. Part of the annulment process now includes a laundry list of [number withheld] psychological excuses for why I need an annulment.

> Titus 2:11-12 (DRV) [19] 11 For the grace of God our Saviour hath appeared to all men, 12 Instructing us, that, denying ungodliness and worldly desires, we should live soberly, and justly, and godly in this world.
>
> Titus 2:11-12 (RSVwA) [43] 11 For the grace of God has appeared for the salvation of all men, 12 training us to renounce irreligion and worldly passions, and to live sober, upright, and godly lives in this world,

With a list that long, anyone who wants an annulment can qualify. The Byzantine Orthodox Church has signed on with the pagan Roman Church that allows homosexuals to be priests and gives easy annulments. The most convoluted part of the deal is that European Orthodox priests can still get married as they traditionally have, but in the United States, Orthodox seminarians must be celibate and cannot get married. Orthodox priests ordained and married in Europe can come to America. The Orthodox Church will not be able to properly compete head-to-head with the pagan Roman Church in the United States."

Javier: "What makes you think there would be competition between the two Churches?" Tony: "If people understood the overwhelming percentage of homosexual priests in the Roman Church, and they had the ability to go to a Byzantine church with a family man for a priest, the Roman churches would empty out. Javier and Karl disagreed. They told how the Europeans have had the problem with homosexual priests longer than the United States and Europe has Orthodox churches. The Roman churches have not emptied into the Orthodox churches in Europe, so they did not expect that to happen in the United States either. *The nature of the deal the pope cut indicates he thought Americans would defect in order to avoid homosexual priests.*

Brian objected, "You insult the Roman Catholic Church by calling it pagan." Tony asserted, "Well? The Roman Empire did not fall to a foreign invader. It rotted from within. It was overwhelmed by its own sexual depravity. It looks to me like the Roman Church is returning to its pagan roots. In one of my classes, we were told Christ was not born on December 25th. That date was chosen as a way to usurp the Roman sun celebration. The "Christmas" tree, wreath, and lights are all pagan symbols the Roman Church appropriated in an effort to displace the pagan sun celebration as well as the solstice festival (Dec. 21st)." Karl agreed, "The Eastern Orthodox Church celebrates Christmas in January."

Deuteronomy 23:17-18 (DRA) [31] 17 There shall be no whore among the daughters of Israel, nor whoremonger among the sons of Israel. 18 Thou shalt not offer the hire of a strumpet, nor the price of a dog, in the house of the Lord thy God, whatsoever it be that thou hast vowed: because both these are an abomination to the Lord thy God.

Deuteronomy 23:17-18 (KJV) [32] 17 There shall be no whore of the daughters of Israel, nor a sodomite of the sons of Israel. 18 Thou shalt not bring the hire of a whore, nor the price of a dog, into the house of the Lord thy God for any vow: for even both these are abomination unto the Lord thy God.

Deuteronomy 23:17-18 (RSV) [20] 17 "There shall be no cult prostitute of the daughters of Israel, neither shall there be a cult prostitute of the sons of Israel. 18 You shall not bring the hire of a harlot, or **the wages of a dog** [t], into the house of the Lord your God in payment for any vow; for both of these are an abomination to the Lord your God.
[t] Or *sodomite*
(Bold type added by author.)

1 Kings 14:24 (DRA) [31] [Same as 3 Kings 14:24 (DRV) [19] below but without the footnote.]

3 Kings 14:24 (DRV) [19] There were also the effeminate in the land, and they did according to all the abominations of the people whom the Lord had destroyed before the face of the children of Israel.
Ver. 24. *The effeminate*. Catamites, or men addicted to unnatural lust.

Tony: "The pagans are using PC to take back their holiday." Javier: "How's that?" Tony: "It's not PC to say Merry Christmas. It is almost illegal to say Merry Christmas if you work for the Post Office. The Post Office issues fewer and fewer religious stamps for Christmas every year. Is it still possible to buy a nativity stamp during the Christmas season?"

The discussion moved to the dwindling number of priests and nuns. Tony: "I went to a Catholic grade school in the 1960s. Back then, the nuns were talking about declining vocations and the lack of priests. I was in the third grade when the Second Vatican Council convened. The Church deteriorated subsequent to Vatican II." Javier and Karl agreed Vatican II allowed a flood of homosexuals to infiltrate the Church in Europe. Javier: "What was it like in the United States at that time?" Tony: "Even as a child, I understood there were a few pedophile priests in the late 1950s. Homosexuals were infiltrating the Church before Vatican II." Brian: "This pope says gays can be ordained." Tony: "Sure. They infiltrated the church and worked their way up the ranks for decades. They have to get a lock on the top spot eventually." Javier: "How do you know the current pope is not gay?"

Tony: "David and Greg explained in detail to Mr. Stevens last semester that, "This pope is not one of us, but he is the best friend we've ever had for a pope. He is the only pope who has ever been a friend to gays."" Brian: "Why would they discuss that in front of you?" Tony: "They didn't do it on purpose. Once Greg saw I was listening they lowered their voices and became secretive. I wasn't privy to the rest of the conversation." Javier asked Tony, "Do you remember Pope Paul VI?" Tony: "Sure. John Paul I succeeded Paul VI. He died three months later." Javier: "Do you remember the conclave that followed?" Tony: "When they elected the next pope? With the color of smoke coming out of the chimney telling how the voting was progressing?" Javier: "Yes. Do you remember how long it took?" Tony: "It took forever. The voting was deadlocked."

Javier: "Do you remember why?" Tony: "Yes, there were two factions equally divided." Javier: "Did you know what the two factions were that could not reach an agreement?" Tony: "Not at the time." Javier: "From what you know now, can you guess what the two factions were and the age of the men in each group?" Tony: "The young cardinals coming in were homosexuals who infiltrated the Church. The straight cardinals who had been there all along were old." Javier: "Correct. Do you remember what happened next?" Tony: "The two groups finally agreed on a compromise candidate, one that was the least objectionable to each faction." Javier: "Do you remember why he got the nod from both sides?" Tony: "I didn't know at the time. Now I do. He is the best friend gays ever had for a pope."

Javier: "That's right. The straights voted for him because he was straight and the gays voted for him because he was soft on gays." Tony: "Look at what he has done. Ordaining homosexuals is wrong." Brian: "What makes you think it's wrong? The pope said it's ok." Tony: "And we think the pope freely decided this? We think his decision was not made under duress?" Brian: "What duress?" Tony: "Threatening his life for example." Brian laughed, "That's ridiculous! That's absolutely ludicrous!" Javier: "It makes perfect sense. Remember the assassination attempt against this pope? The popemobile was built because of it." Brian retorted, "That was just some crazy." Tony: "High profile shooters are always crazies. The real question is: was he self motivated or was he a patsy?" Brian scoffed.

Karl shared the European perspective of the incident with his friends. Brian paled and his eyes widened.

Karl asked Tony, "What do you think about ordaining women?" Tony: "The Old Testament tells us God is displeased when his sanctuary is defiled. Corrupting the Lord's sanctuary provokes God to profound anger. The reason women are not allowed in the sanctuary is because of human blood: menstruation and child birth." Javier: "Women are allowed in the sanctuary Tony."

Leviticus 12:4 (DRA) [31] But she shall remain three and thirty days in the blood of her purification. She shall touch no holy thing, neither shall she enter into the sanctuary, until the days of her purification be fulfilled.

Leviticus 21:23 (DRA) [31] Yet so that he enter not within the veil, nor approach to the altar, because he hath a blemish, and he must not defile my sanctuary. I am the Lord who sanctify them.

4 Kings 23:7 (DRA) [31] He destroyed also the pavilions of the effeminate, which were in the house of the Lord, for which the women wove as it were little dwellings for the grove.

Tony: "Yes, since Vatican II, but for nearly 2,000 years: no." Brian and Javier chuckled. Brian: "Get with the times Tony." Javier: "These are the 1990s, not the Middle Ages." Tony: "I see. –God has changed?" Brian, Javier, and Karl were silent and uncomfortable.

Malachias 3:6 (DRA) [31] For I am the Lord, and I change not: and you the sons of Jacob are not consumed.

Tony: "I was discussing something from the Old Testament with the Vice Rector. He chuckled and said Christians are subject to the New Testament, not the Old Testament. He dismissed the point I raised as irrelevant, so I asked him, "God has changed?" His reaction was similar to yours only more so. What does "modern times" really mean? We now have science; we no longer need God? Unless God has changed, the Old Testament is relevant and instructive. That's why women are not ordained to be priests." Javier: "What about altar girls, how do you feel about altar girls Tony?"

Deuteronomy 22:5 (DRA) [31] A woman shall not be clothed with man's apparel, neither shall a man use woman's apparel: for he that doeth these things is abominable before God.

Tony: "Altar girls look angelic. I like it. The argument priests have against altar girls is they displace altar boys. Callings to the priesthood are dramatically influenced by having been an altar boy. Priests argue having altar girls decreases callings to the priesthood. That is a fair consideration. I say pedophile and homosexual priests are a much greater deterrent to callings to the priesthood."

Javier: "Altar girls will aspire to be priests. The pope will eventually ok the ordination of women as priests as a solution to the priest shortage."

Tony: "Female priests are contrary to the Old Testament. Once the Church is completely taken over by homosexuals there is even less chance of women becoming priests, think about it." Javier agreed, "The pope we have now is the last straight pope. Like Tony said, the straight cardinals were old 18 years ago. Can any of those cardinals still be alive? How many of their replacements are going to be straight? Gay cardinals already have a clear majority. When this pope dies, they will elect a gay pope. The Church in North America and Europe is rife with gays. The only hope we have for a straight pontiff is one who comes from South America or Africa." Brian's reaction was tentative. He could not argue with the logic, but he hoped Javier was wrong.

Tony asked Javier what it was like when he was in the Vatican. Javier laughed, "You could never stand it Tony." Javier grinned as he told how inundated Vatican City was with gays. Tony was aghast! Javier: "What do you know about the Vatican Tony?" Tony: "I was doing research for a paper when I was an undergrad. I read, *The Oldest Profession: A History of Prostitution* [06]. It said during the mid-1400s Rome had 10 times the number of prostitutes per capita than most modern capitals (p 92)." [06] Javier laughed, "And celibate men require a large number of hookers. Well, that's old news. Prostitutes won't find many customers in Vatican City today." Javier told what he saw during his stay in the Vatican. Tony was mortified!

Brian was wide-eyed and silent. Tony turned to Karl, who solemnly nodded agreement. Javier chuckled, "You think you are uncomfortable here Tony? You seriously do not want to go to school in the Vatican." Brian took exception, "What makes you guys so sure homosexuals here are sexually active?" "Please," Tony deadpanned, "be serious. You've never heard two men in the room next to you in the middle of the night, or the middle of the afternoon for that matter?" Brian: "Yes, but it didn't sound like they were having sex." Tony: "Ok, what does having sex sound like?" Brian: "Ah-ah-ah-ah." Tony: "Is that a man's voice or a woman's voice making those sounds?"

Brian: "Oh, I never thought about it before. I guess its women that sound that way during sex." Tony: "What does the male half of that sound like?" Blank stares all around. Tony: "The Vice Rector tried to tell me two men were studying until three a.m. after the first day of class." Javier: "Those two don't waste their time studying." Brian: "What noises have you heard in the room next to yours Tony?" Tony: "I've heard sounds like a cow grunting during a pregnancy check." Karl: "I've never been on a farm. How do you pregnancy check a cow?" Tony explained how a (veterinarian does that). Many contorted facial expressions in reaction to that one. Javier: "You don't think the gays you heard actually (veterinarian does that)?"

Tony: "Cows are much larger than humans, and no, I specifically did not think about it. I did not want that image inside my head. I'm just saying; the sound was the same. Another signature sound was like pigeons cooing." Karl: "What do you think they were doing when they were cooing like pigeons?" Tony: "They cooed like pigeons after they finished what they were doing." Karl: "What were they doing?" Tony: "I have no way of knowing what they were doing, they were quiet, but I know for certain what they were not doing." Again, blank stares all around. Javier: "What was it they were not doing?" Tony: "They sure as hell were not studying." Everyone laughed.

Karl: "When I got back from Christmas break I wanted to pay my phone bill. I could not find the student in charge of accounts. I had to go to his room to pay my bill. While I was there, I looked at all the telephone equipment in his room." Brian: "What do you mean equipment? Doesn't he have a phone like the rest of us?" Karl: "There was all of this other equipment. I think Tony is right, I think he does listen to our calls when he's in his room." Tony: "Did you see any recording equipment?" Karl: "I couldn't tell. I didn't want to be obvious by staring." Javier and Brian shrugged it off.

10 RADIO FREE AMERICA

Library

Day one of spring semester the Vice Rector approached Tony. Vice Rector: "Everyone is expected to pull their weight. You were not given a job assignment your first semester so you could get acclimated to seminary life. Going forward you will be assigned regular duties, the same as everyone else." Tony: "Like work-study in college?" Vice Rector: "Yes, exactly like work-study." The Vice Rector led Tony to the library and introduced him to Mark, the student on duty. Vice Rector: "On the back wall next to the filing cabinet is the work schedule. Everyone's hours are posted. You are responsible for your hours. You are welcome to trade hours with your coworkers if you need to, but you are still responsible for your hours. If the person you trade with does not fulfill your duties, you are at fault. Any questions?" Tony: "No." Vice Rector: "Good."

Turning to Mark, the Vice Rector said, "I want you to explain things to Tony. Show him what you do here and what his duties are. I want the two of you to review the schedule together to make sure he knows how to read the schedule and that there are no conflicts with his class schedule. If there are, work them out. Tony, I want the two of you to work together today until Mark's shift is over. If you need more training, spend more time with Mark on his next shift. Be certain you know all of your duties before you start working your scheduled hours. If you need me, I'll be in my office." The Vice Rector turned and briskly walked away. Mark was an upperclassman, six feet four, quiet, and shy.

Mark: "We get very busy the first and last weeks of the semester. The rest of the time there is little or nothing to do, so bring your homework and work on it here. Accuracy in records keeping is essential." After Mark covered every detail he said, "You have the worst hours since you are a first year student. Don't forget to lock up when you leave Friday. Remember, you have to open Saturday morning. During the week, you relieve me of duty Tuesday and Wednesday. I can't go to lunch until you are here to take over, so please be on time. It's ok if you show up early, but I won't leave until the end of my shift. If you have to leave for any reason, such as to use the bathroom, make sure no one is inside and lock up before you leave. Never leave the room unattended."

Tony: "I thought the school's library would have more books than this." Mark: "This is the theology dorm library. The main library is on the other side of the administration building. The books needed for classes during the semester are kept here for the student's convenience. The stock is changed every semester to match the needs of the classes currently being held." Once Tony had no more questions Mark said, "There's no reason for you to stay until the end of my shift. Show up early tomorrow in case you have more questions." Tony thanked Mark and left.

The Enemy

Mark seemed congenial but aloof. One Tuesday when Tony showed up for library duty fifteen minutes early, he heard Rush Limbaugh on the radio. Tony: "You listen to Limbaugh?" Mark was excited, "You listen to Rush too!" Tony: "I don't listen to the radio, but I used to watch him on TV." Mark was thrilled! He found a kindred spirit! *I thought this guy was homosexual, but homosexuals don't listen to Rush Limbaugh.* While Tony was thinking this, Mark was talking non-stop. Mark: "Gays like us are smart; we're Republicans! We believe in fiscal responsibility and stable government, not crazy like Bill Clinton and gay Democrats. They want to destroy this country. –."

All the air went out of Tony's lungs. He assumed Mark must be Republican and therefore straight. Mark assumed Tony was gay. *I hate my life.* Mark was surprised Tony was a Republican "like himself." Tony was amazed a homosexual was telling him gays want to destroy this country. *Tony recalled Julie's conversations in 1973. She was frightened by discussions she overheard between doctors and other professionals. "Homosexuals, men of power and means, public figures with families who want to destroy society out of hatred of straights–." She said what they planned to do was massive and they had the means to make it happen. She said they would cause anarchy.*

Once Tony could breathe again, he wanted to keep Mark talking. Mark saw the shock on Tony's face and asked what was so surprising. Tony: "I didn't know there was such a thing as homosexual Republicans." Mark smiled, "We are log cabin Republicans." Tony: "What is a log cabin Republican?" Mark explained, "We are called log cabin Republicans because Abraham Lincoln was homosexual. That's where the name Log Cabin Republican comes from."

Mark railed at length against gay Democrats. He concluded with, "I look at it this way. We fought for gay rights, and we've gotten everything we wanted. I say let's enjoy what we have. Gay Democrats are crazy like Bill Clinton. They want to destroy society because they hate straights. They are angry with straights for picking on them and bullying them when they were kids, so they want to destroy society to punish them. How stupid is that? Sure, straights will lose everything, but so will we! It will hurt us too! I say, let's enjoy what we have. When they destroy straight society, we lose what we have too."

Mark wanted to leave for lunch, but Tony had more questions. Tony knew he would not be able to learn any more once Mark talked to the others. Tony asked a question, and then another. Finally, Mark said apologetically, "I have to leave now. I have a class immediately after lunch. We can talk more tomorrow. Come in early so we can talk. You and I have so much to talk about!"

The next day Tony got to the library ten minutes early. Mark was in the chair in the corner, curled up in the fetal position. Tony: "What's the matter? You look like something's wrong?" Mark moaned, "Why didn't you tell me?" Tony: "Tell you what?" Mark: "That you're not gay. Why didn't you tell me?" Tony: "I was so interested to hear what you had to say I didn't want to interrupt. How did you figure out I'm not gay?" Mark: "When I went to lunch I was bragging to the others I found another Log Cabin Republican, someone smart like me. They asked who it was. I told them it was you and they said, "Don't talk to him! He's the enemy! He's not one of us! Why are you talking to him?"

Mark became self-conscious after telling Tony he was the enemy, and tried to apologize. Tony: "I understand. There's no need for apology." Mark reverted to his former quiet self. He offered no more information about gay Democrats or Bill Clinton. Tony pointed to the radio, "Isn't Rush Limbaugh on?" Mark was not sure Tony wanted to listen. Tony: "Sure, I like Rush. So do you. You don't need my permission to listen to your radio." Mark considered this. He turned the radio on.

Shrink Lady February

The Shrink Lady looked serene in a sharp, tomato red, wool business dress with a Scottish pattern: very professional. Shrink Lady: "How was your Christmas Tony? Did you visit your diocese?" Tony: "Fine, thank you. No, I went back east to visit family. How was your Christmas?" Shrink Lady: "I spent Christmas with friends I have here. It was much more relaxing than traveling over the holiday. How was your retreat?" Tony: "There's not much to report." Shrink Lady: "Have you been on retreat before?" Tony: "No, this was my first retreat." Shrink Lady: "Did you learn new prayer techniques?" Tony: "No." Shrink Lady: "What did you learn?" Tony: "Nothing." Shrink Lady: "You don't expect me to believe you spent a week on retreat and came away with nothing. What did you do while you were there?"

Tony: "I ate pancakes and bacon for breakfast every day." Shrink Lady: "What did you do the rest of the time?" Tony: "I spent most of my time in my room so I wouldn't disrupt everyone else's good time." Shrink Lady: "What good time? Everyone was sent on retreat for prayer and reflection." Tony: "Let's just say it didn't happen as advertised." Shrink Lady: "What did happen?" Tony: "During the day we had a few scheduled lectures and prayer sessions. Very few. The rest of the time, it was bedlam." Shrink Lady: "What do you mean bedlam?" Tony: "It was like Mardi Gras all week long." Shrink Lady: "How was it like Mardi Gras?"

Tony: "Everyone behaved themselves while the priest was there. The atmosphere was fairly raucous otherwise. After dinner it sounded like Hades."

Shrink Lady: "Where was the priest?" Tony: "I don't know. I was in my room." Shrink Lady: "Why did you stay in your room if everyone else was partying?" Tony: "I was being careful not to disrupt the nocturnal behavior of the indigenous wildlife." Shrink Lady: "Are you saying there was gay activity?" Tony: "No." Shrink Lady: "It sounds to me like you are." Tony: "No, I'm being very careful to specifically not say that." The Shrink Lady looked genuinely upset, "Where was the priest while all this was going on?" Tony: "As far as I know, he made himself scarce." Shrink Lady: "Why would he do that?" Tony: "I don't know. Maybe he wanted to establish plausible deniability." Shrink Lady: "You need to report this to the administration."

Tony: "Not my job. Anyway, I was in my room. I saw nothing." Shrink Lady: "You were busy establishing your own plausible deniability, is that it?" Tony: "Could be." Shrink Lady: "You should tell the Vice Rector." Tony: "Tell him I saw nothing? I don't think that's necessary." Shrink Lady: "Tell the Vice Rector the priest conducting the retreat wasn't doing his job." Tony: "I've never been on retreat before, so I don't know what is expected of the priest who conducts it. I have nothing to report." Shrink Lady: "I think you should tell this to the Vice Rector." Tony: "Ok, I'll take your recommendation under advisement." Shrink Lady: "You're not going to go to the Vice Rector are you?" Tony: "No, I'm not."

Shrink Lady: "Do you have any questions for me?" Tony: "No." Shrink Lady: "What about class? Do you have any questions related to the course I am teaching?" Tony: "No, I'm up on the material." Shrink Lady: "What about the discussions before class?" Tony: "You mean when Mr. Stevens was talking about how unhappy his life was until he came here?" Shrink Lady: "Did you find that interesting?" Tony: "I found it interesting that he felt comfortable telling you in front of me how he's made so many friends here by lying across his bed." Shrink Lady: "Why do you find that interesting?" Tony: "You didn't see any sexual content in that discussion?" Shrink Lady: "Did you?" Tony: "How about when you raised the discussion of phobias?" Shrink Lady: "You said you don't like snakes. You identify with Indiana Jones when it comes to snakes."

Tony: "And Greg butted in. He leered at me and said if I went up to his room he would show me a snake that would really scare me." Shrink Lady: "You believe there was sexual content in that?" Tony: "You would not have grinned the way you did if you didn't think so." Shrink Lady: "What makes you think I grinned?" Tony: "I was studying your reaction, not his. You grinned." Shrink Lady: "What do you feel this means?" Tony: "Greg and Mr. Stevens feel comfortable baiting me in front of you. It means they know for certain that you are with the program." Shrink Lady: "What do you mean? What program?" Tony: "What I mentioned in an earlier session, that your job is to ship political dissidents off to Siberia. Their cheek and their chutzpah confirm what I've known all along."

Shrink Lady: "Even if a student is gay, that doesn't mean he is not supposed to be here. As long as a student is celibate, they have every right to be here, same as you. You keep saying they're not supposed to be here, even after the Vice Rector told you the pope said it's ok to ordain gay seminarians as long as they are celibate." Tony: "You say this after ignoring all the friends Mr. Stevens has made here by lying across his bed. Ok, explain to me how I am able to sort out who is straight and who is homosexual in an all-male community if everyone is celibate?" The Shrink Lady stood with her mouth open.

Tony: "I don't even have to believe you. Lie, that's ok. String together sentences that are intelligible and construct an excuse or explanation for how I could possibly learn who is homosexual if all the students are celibate." The Shrink Lady had a bewildered look on her face. Her mouth was still open. Tony: "Invent any excuse. I don't have to believe it. It doesn't even have to be plausible. If you can deliver it in intelligible sentences, I will sign *ze* papers." Shrink Lady: "What papers?" Tony: "Whatever papers you need signed to ship me off to Siberia. *Da? Nyet?*" The Shrink Lady composed herself, "The administration takes formation very seriously! There is no homosexual activity here!" Tony: "Please. If the administration was serious, there would be surveillance cameras monitoring the halls in the dorm."

The Shrink Lady babbled about privacy and student's rights. Tony: "Baloney!" *The administration monitors the phones and the mail despite federal laws to the contrary! Privacy was the rallying cry for homosexuals with AIDS who did not want to be placed in quarantine.* Shrink Lady: "Besides, the school doesn't have the money to invest in so much surveillance equipment." Tony: "The school has $123 million in its coffers." That was news to her. Tony: "Two cameras per floor times five floors? Doesn't sound cost prohibitive to me. The administration takes formation seriously? Sure. There is only one way I can know who is homosexual and who is straight: actively fagging queers live in the dorm.

Explain to me why I can't walk down the hall to use the toilet during the night if the administration is so serious about formation. Explain why the Friar told me to piss in the sink so I don't get in trouble. Explain why the Vice Rector thinks two students are studying together until three in the morning after only one day of class. This place was built in the 1930s. The walls are paper-thin. There is no privacy in the dorms. Not only can you hear the conversation next door, you are able to identify whose voices they are." The Shrink Lady took several moments to gather her thoughts. Shrink Lady: "I think that's enough for today. You don't mind if we quit early?" Tony: "Works for me." She scheduled Tony's next appointment.

We're Here

Mr. Stevens smiled broadly, "We're here, we're queer, so get used to it." He said this for Tony's benefit throughout the day: before class if the instructor was not in the room, between classes, and in the refectory. "We're here, we're queer, so get used to it!" Mr. Stevens gleefully said this to Tony at every opportunity for three or four days before Javier heard him say it.

Javier stopped to see Tony after dinner. Javier: "What was that all about?"

Tony: "Mr. Stevens finally woke up to the fact the administration runs this place for the benefit of homos." Javier: "What convinced him?" Tony: "It was "homos gone wild" when we were on retreat and there was zero fallout."

Javier: "Did you report what you saw to anyone?" Tony: "There was no one to report to. The priest that was on-site made himself scarce." Javier: "What about the Rector?" Tony: "I'm not ready to meet with him yet. Besides, I have no proof, no physical evidence." Javier: "What is the significance of that chant (Mr. Stevens) keeps peppering you with?" Tony: "I said homosexuals don't belong here in private conversations with the Vice Rector and the Shrink Lady. That chant is Mr. Steven's comeback. More like his come-uppance."

I don't want to meet with the Rector until the Vice Rector goes on vacation. Why? Divide and conquer. In my case, divide and lower my downside risk. The Vice Rector is the brains of this operation. The Rector will be easier to deal with if he is by himself.

Gelatin

Students heckled both Ugandan seminarians for refusing to eat Jell-O ®. During the fall semester, Americans noticed the Ugandans' aversion to gelatin, and their curiosity grew. A group of seminarians became obsessed with the Ugandans' refusal to eat gelatin dessert and made themselves an incipient nuisance. The Ugandans' explanation was, "Gelatin is for sick people. Only women and small children eat gelatin." Hearing this answer, the American students commented, "Sick people, sure, it's hospital food, but what's the big deal? You're not sick. Eating gelatin isn't going to make you sick." The mystery increased the American's fascination.

One of the aggravating students made a wager on the Super Bowl with Thomas, one of the Ugandans. The loser had to eat gelatin. The day after the Super Bowl, a small mob stood around to watch Thomas pay off his wager in the refectory. The young man's face dramatically changed colors as he choked down the gelatin. The Chinese and Ugandans often shared a table with Tony. This day, both Ugandans and Javier were eating lunch with Tony when the insufferable crowd gathered. After the cacophony of hecklers left, Javier asked, "What's the big deal about eating gelatin?" The Ugandans said nothing.

Tony: "It's a food taboo, isn't it?" Javier: "What taboo?" Tony: "They said only sick people eat gelatin." Javier agreed, "It's hospital food." Tony: "You miss the point. Look at the second part: only women and children eat gelatin." Javier was stymied. Tony: "It's a food taboo. Gelatin will make you limp wristed. If you eat gelatin, you'll get gelatin wrist." Tony demonstrated by raising his forearm and dangling his hand. Javier: "Where do you get that?" Tony restated the Ugandans' response, "Only women and children eat gelatin. Sick people eat gelatin. It's a food taboo. They're not talking about nutrition." Javier chuckled, "That doesn't make sense."

Tony: "Here we say, "Real men don't eat quiche." Apparently, in Uganda they don't just say, "Real men don't eat gelatin," they absolutely mean it." Thomas, the man who lost the sports bet asked, "How do you know this?" Tony: "Was I right?" Thomas: "Yes. How did you know?" Tony: "Your limbic reactions gave it away, but I didn't know for sure. You were embarrassed beyond the extreme." Thomas: "Why did no one else figure it out?" Tony: "Americans don't have food taboos. They don't understand the concept." Thomas: "You are American. Why do you understand?" Tony: "I travel and read a lot. I speculated based on your limbic response." Javier still didn't get it. He thought it was silly.

Yabba Dabba Doo

Tony was getting ready to call it a day. He returned from the lavatory and was unlocking his door when he heard, "Yabba dabba doo," echo down the long corridor. He turned to see David at the far end of the hall grinning.

Music

The five transfer students were taking a music class with a total of fourteen students. On the first day of class, the instructor and the other students were shaken by Tony's profound ignorance of music. Tony did not know the scales or how to read music. When asked a simple question about his voice, he had no clue. The instructor had the class sing a familiar song. While everyone sang, the instructor walked around the room from student to student. When the exercise was over, Tony learned he was a low tenor. When the class practiced singing, everyone cringed at Tony.

During the break, Mr. Stevens took the opportunity to heckle Tony. David stood next to Mr. Stevens. David smiled and enjoyed the show. When David grew bored, he turned to Mr. Stevens and suggested, "Maybe Tony is tone deaf, in which case there's nothing he can do about it. How about it Tony? Are you tone deaf?" Tony: "Could be, I don't know." David: "Oh, come on, you must have some idea." Tony: "When troubleshooting problems people tend to go for the complex, technical aspects and overlook the simple and obvious. To be thorough, you have to take everything into consideration." David: "What are we overlooking?" Tony: "Maybe I'm just stupid." Mr. Stevens and David left in a huff.

Art, from the pub, was also taking this class. He overheard the conversation and approached Tony. Art said consoling things starting with, "Don't say that about yourself–," and ended with, "–why would you say that anyway?" Tony: "Because it's a likely cause. I used to be able to sing when I was in grade school and now I can't." Art: "What did you do to sing then?" Tony: "I mimicked what everyone else was doing, and it worked fine. I can't do that now." Art: "Since then, your voice changed. After the break, I'll sit next to you. I am a high tenor. My voice is slightly higher than yours, so you don't want to imitate it exactly, but it's a reference point, and it might help."

Art offered more happy talk and reassurance. He asked, "Why were those guys so miffed when you called yourself stupid?" Tony: "I made dean's list last semester." Art: "That's right, only two guys made dean's list. Who was the other one?" Tony: "The guy from Minnesota." Art: "Those two just giving you a hard time, where did they place?" Tony: "How should I know?" Art: "When the grades are posted, all students are shown in rank order. How could you not see that when you checked your grades?" Tony: "I never looked. Another student checked his grades and told me at lunch I made dean's list." Art: "Weren't you curious how your classmates did?" Tony: "Not even a little. I didn't bother to check my own grades."

When class resumed, Art sat next to Tony and coached him during the singing exercises. The instructor was pleased to see this. Everyone noticed Tony's constant dissonance became intermittent, but it was still insufferable. The moment class ended there was a mad rush for the door, leaving the instructor, Art, and Tony in the room. The instructor conferred with Art, then had the two sing the last exercise again. He coached Tony and gave Art some pointers to help Tony. Tony thanked the instructor and Art for their time and effort.

Yabba Dabba Doo Again

Tony was getting ready to go to sleep. He unlocked his door when he heard, "Yabba dabba doo." He turned and saw David grinning at the far end of the hall.

And Again

Returning from the lavatory, Tony unlocked his door, tired and ready for bed. "Yabba dabba doo," echoed down the corridor. Tony turned to see David flitting, prancing, smiling, and then disappear into his room.

Flute

One of the theology instructors invited his class to his parish for Sunday Mass. Walking into the church was like walking into a theater in the round. It was not obvious what to reverence, or where. Tony genuflected to reverence the holy relics in the altar. The tabernacle was obscurely placed somewhere in an alcove off to one side. There was a side room with comfortable, informal, plush seating that faced a wall of glass, giving the sensation of being in an atrium or an air conditioned outdoors. It was art gallery posh. The architecture was not traditional single purpose construction built for the worship of God.

The choir was talented and accomplished. Their singing was beautiful. Different instruments were used throughout the Mass. The choir sang the communion hymn to the light and lively tones of flutes. After the hymn ended, six flutists continued their instrumental. The delicate, haunting, and flickering breath of the flutes was like a sparkling, babbling brook. It was incredibly inspiring Divine praise!

> 2 Kings 6:5 (DRA) [31] But David and all Israel played before the Lord on all manner of instruments made of wood, on harps and lutes and timbrels and cornets and cymbals.
>
> 2 Samuel 6:5 (RSV) [20] And David and all the house of Israel were making merry before the Lord with all their might, with songs and lyres and harps and tambourines and castanets and cymbals.
>
> Ecclesiasticus 40:21 (DRA) [31] The flute and the psaltery make a sweet melody, but a pleasant tongue is above them both.
>
> Sirach 40:21 (RSVwA) [43] The flute and the harp make pleasant melody, but a pleasant voice is better than both.

And Again Again

Tony returned from the lavatory. He was ready to turn in. He heard, "Yabba dabba doo," echo down the corridor.

The next day while going between classes, Leo asked Tony if he heard David say "Yabba dabba doo?" Tony: "Sure." Leo: "Did that make you mad?" Tony: "No." Leo: "What did you think?" Tony: "I thought it was curious." Leo: "It didn't make you mad?" Tony: "After a few times it got to be annoying." Leo: "He's doing it to mess with you." Tony: "I get that." Leo: "Do you know what it means?" Tony: "He thinks he's Fred Flintstone?" Leo's shoulders slumped, his head tipped forward in dejection. Leo: "No, he's messing with you. Did you ever watch the Flintstones?" Tony: "Sure."

Leo: "Do you remember the song at the end of the show? Can you sing it now?" Tony: "I don't think so. Let's see, –if I can get started– one day, maybe Fred will win the fight, then that cat will stay out for the night. When you're with the Flintstones, you'll have a doo time, a dabba doo time, you'll have a gay old time." Leo smiled like the Grinch who stole Christmas. Tony was horrified and his face clearly showed it! Leo smiled malevolently, "Yabba dabba doo." This was the first time Tony saw evil on Leo's face. *Looks like Leo really has rejoined the herd.*

Leo: "Does that bother you now, Tony?" Tony: "Yes it does." Leo was elated! "Why does it bother you Tony?" Tony: "You guys pervert a children's cartoon? What is THAT?" Leo was animated, "It's only a song Tony. Why does it bother you?" Tony: "Pervert a children's cartoon, I don't know–." Leo: "Is that logical Tony? There's no reason it should bother you." Tony: "The effort invested, the evil intent, the perverse nature of despoiling something that belongs to small children: I don't know where to begin." Leo beamed! He took a few steps to improve his line of sight, and then gave a thumbs-up to a group of men far down the corridor. Leo's motion was answered with audible approval from his friends.

After Class

Leo paced Tony as they returned to the dorm after class. Leo: "Have you had a problem with (Mr. Stevens) recently?" Tony: "Mr. Stevens is his own problem all by himself. I'm surprised the upperclassmen put up with him. Doesn't he cause you guys' grief?" Leo: "Yeah, the upperclassmen aren't happy with him." Tony: "Why do they put up with him?" Leo: "What do you mean put up with him?" Tony: "I would've thought two or three upperclassmen would sit him down and explain things to him." With a vicious edge in his voice Leo demanded, "What are you suggesting?" Tony: "This is not a metaphor. I'm saying sit him down and explain the way things are. He is not making life easy for you guys. Sometimes peer pressure is a good thing."

Leo: "Oh, you mean tough love." Tony: "No, I mean discipline." Leo: "We call it tough love." Tony: "If that's what you call it. I expected you guys would do something to get him acclimated, but nothing happened." Leo rolled his eyes, "The Vice Rector said (Mr. Stevens) has had a hard time in life. He wants the whole community to make an extra effort to support (Mr. Stevens) and make him feel welcome." Tony chuckled, "The Vice Rector told everyone to stand behind Mr. Stevens?" Anger flashed across Leo's face, "What's that supposed to mean?" Tony: "Mr. Stevens bragged to the psychology instructor before class how he's made so many friends since he's been here by lying across his bed."

Leo was genuinely surprised, "He said that in front of you? Did he know you were there?" Tony: "I was seated before he entered the classroom. He stood next to me while talking to the instructor." Leo: "How do you know he wasn't joking?" Tony: "That's some joke to tell your psychology instructor." Leo: "Maybe he was messing with you." Tony: "I'm sure he was." Leo: "So what do you think he was trying to say?" Tony: "He was bragging about his sex life and bragging how happy he is that he has made so many new friends." Leo said menacingly, "What makes you so sure he's having sex?"

Tony: "Mr. Stevens spent the weekend before Halloween with the guy next door to me (*and has returned several times since*). You know the walls are paper thin." Leo: "What did you hear?" Tony described grunts similar to a cow's grunts during a pregnancy check. Leo snapped, "Are you saying one of them (veterinarian does that)?" Tony: "No, I'm saying the sound was the same." Now Leo was curious, "What other noises did you hear?" Tony described the cooing of pigeons. Leo blushed. Leo: "Did one man make that sound or did both?" Tony: "Let's see, —first one guy made that sound, —later, the other guy made the same sound. By the end of the weekend they both made the same sound at the same time." Leo blushed a deep beet red.

Father Gary's Visit

Father Gary called Tony. "I'm on vacation next week. I will be visiting friends at the seminary. While I'm there, I want to stop by to visit. After I get there and see what my schedule is, I'll call so we can arrange to get together." Several times the following week Tony saw Father Gary on campus with one of the priests who teaches undergrads in the liberal arts college. Thursday evening Father Gary called Tony to say he would visit Saturday afternoon. The priest came to Tony's dorm room. "I brought you a gift," he said, and handed Tony a bottle of single malt scotch. Tony: "Wow! Thank you! We should have a drink." Tony set up two glasses and poured a double jigger in each. Father Gary was much more friendly and conversant than Tony remembered.

When they finished their drinks, Tony suggested having another. Father Gary: "No, I thought we could take a ride. I want to show you some of my favorite haunts when I was a student here. Do you get off campus much?" Tony: "No Father; hardly ever." Priest: "You should spend more time off campus. Do you know your way around the city yet?" Tony: "No Father, I don't really know the campus." Priest: "That's not good. You should get out more. Let's go for a drive. This city has a lot to offer."

Father Gary drove past a park he enjoyed when he was in the seminary, "–and it's close to campus. I found it relaxing. I spent a lot of time there. It's so close to campus and so convenient, there's no excuse not to go there."

Father Gary drove into a neighborhood and explained it was a homosexual neighborhood. Tony: "How can you tell?" The priest pointed to a rainbow flag, "Two lesbians live in this house." He pointed across the street, "Two men live in this house." Tony: "How can you tell Father?" Priest: "By the way the flag is displayed and the order of the colors." Tony saw no difference from one flag to the next. Father Gary continued to read information about the occupants of houses based on what looked like identical flags to Tony. They passed a small bookstore. Father Gary: "This is my all-time favorite bookstore." In the same neighborhood, the priest stopped at a small restaurant. Father Gary: "I know it's not mealtime, but I would like to stop here. Is that all right with you?"

Tony: "We can have afternoon tea." Father Gary: "Is that something you do?" Tony: "No, but it's the right time for it." The place was overly cute. Tony decided it was nouveau granola. The priest said this was a favorite haunt of his when he was in school. Tony ordered a cup of tea and a cookie. Since Americans do not do high tea, the place was deserted. As they drove back to the seminary, Father Gary said that restaurant was popular with the homosexual community. *Wait a minute.* Tony realized he was hearing without listening. Back on campus, the priest wished Tony good luck with his studies. Tony thanked him for the scotch and the tea and wished Father Gary well. Tony: "Enjoy your vacation Father." *What just happened?*

Tony's Friends Commiserate

Tony: "Last fall my classmates talked incessantly about prostate cancer. They're at it again." Javier named an elderly priest on campus, "He's dying from prostate cancer, that's why they can't stop talking about it." Tony: "Mr. Stevens found it especially humorous. He was delighted to point out priests who actually practice celibacy get an enlarged prostate and die from cancer." Javier: "He's right. There was a piece on the news about prostate cancer." Tony: "Yes, and Mr. Stevens was too happy to tell me about it. He says that is another reason gays make better priests, they will never die from prostate cancer. He was quite inventive with the number of ways he explained how I am guaranteed to die of prostate cancer. He told me again and again and again only a serious traffic accident will thwart his prediction."

Karl: "Tony, you always refer to that guy as mister. He is the only one you call mister. Why do you refer to him as mister?" Tony: "He made a point of not introducing himself for weeks. The Vice Rector tried to put me on the spot in core board for not knowing his name. The next day my classmates joined me at dinner so they could odiously say his name several dozen times. Mr. Stevens (not his actual name) parsed his last name to create an Italian word and an English reference to pernicious sex. It was as clever as it was foul. He carefully linked my heritage to his perversion in a creative manner. He got in my face. He tied me and "my people" to his filthy predilection."

Javier: "That must have made you angry." Tony: "He tried hard to provoke me. He doesn't understand. My ancestry is from a city-state south of Rome. My grandfather regarded Romans as foreigners. Mr. Stevens thinks Italian is synonymous with Roman." Brian did not understand. Karl explained it to him. Karl: "Tony, you honor his insult by calling him Mr. Stevens, why?" Tony: "To give him the recognition he requested." Brian: "He isn't very PC. Neither are you Tony."

Tony: "Can you imagine that guy being ordained?" Brian: "If the pope says it's ok, then it IS ok." In a conciliatory voice Javier said, "The pope said it's ok as long as they are celibate." Tony: "Then the pope has not read the Old Testament and he has not observed human behavior." Karl: "What does the Old Testament say on the subject?" Tony: "In Leviticus it says if a man lie with a man as with a woman, both shall be put to death. In Ecclesiastes, it says the perverse are hard to be corrected. That doesn't sound like a candidate for ordination to me." *(Leviticus 20:13 and Ecclesiastes 1:15).*

> 1 Corinthians 6:9-10 (DRA) [31] 9 Know you not that the unjust shall not possess the kingdom of God? Do not err: neither fornicators, nor idolaters, nor adulterers, 10 Nor the effeminate, nor liers with mankind, nor thieves, nor covetous, nor drunkards, nor railers, nor extortioners, shall possess the kingdom of God.

> 1 Corinthians 6:9-10 (RSV-C) [40] 9 Do you not know that the unrighteous will not inherit the kingdom of God? Do not be deceived; neither the immoral [v], nor idolaters, nor adulterers, nor homosexuals,[j, w] 10 nor thieves, nor the greedy, nor drunkards, nor revilers, nor robbers will inherit the kingdom of God.
> [j] Two Greek words are rendered by this expression.
> [v] 6:9 *the immoral*: literally, "fornicators."
> [w] 6:9 *homosexuals*: Greek has "effeminate nor sodomites." The apostle condemns, not the inherent tendencies of such, but the indulgence of them.

Brian: "Tony, it's ok because the pope said it is. You know where that comes from. (Matthew 16:19 "I will give you the keys to the kingdom of heaven, and whatever you bind on earth shall be bound in heaven, and whatever you loose on earth shall be loosed in heaven.")." Tony: "The Bible warns against excess burdens they cannot carry, like the mistake of requiring priests to be celibate, a mistake the Roman Catholic Church made centuries ago. The remaining Orthodox Churches did not make that mistake."

> Matthew 23:4 (DRA) [31] For they bind heavy and insupportable burdens, and they lay them on men's shoulders; but with a finger of their own they will not move them.

> Matthew 19:11-12 (DRA) [31] 11 Who said to them: All men take not this word, but they to whom it is given. 12 For there are eunuchs, who were born so from their mother's womb: and there are eunuchs, who were made so by men: and there are eunuchs, who have made themselves eunuchs for the kingdom of heaven. He that can take, let him take it.

Brian and Javier argued celibacy was not a mistake. They reiterated the Church's position. Tony: "One instructor said priests used to marry and have families. After the priest died, the congregation supported his widow and children. He said celibacy was a way to save the Church money. He told us there were periods of corruption in the Church over its long history." Brian: "He said that? Did you believe him?" Tony: "How can I sort the truth from the lies? That's why I need to discuss these things with you guys. The same instructor told us the once sterling academic program at the Pontifical Jeroboam deteriorated precipitously. He said that by the early 70s the academic program here was an embarrassment. He said he knows because he was a seminarian here in the early 70s."

Javier: "He's teaching at the same school he graduated from?" Brian shook his head in dejection, "This is a Pontifical college. If this college was a joke, think how bad other seminaries must have been. Think how bad they must still be!" Tony: "The instructor told us a concerted effort is underway to restore the Pontifical Jeroboam to its former level of academic excellence." "That implies we're not there yet," objected Javier. Tony: "We're not. I am taking a philosophy class. One of the books we are reading is *The Plague*, by Camus." Brian: "So?" Javier: "What's wrong with that?" Tony: "How is a story of a rat infested medieval city dying of disease a philosophy?" The three friends exchanged confused looks. Sounding a bit testy, Brian challenged, "What would you suggest instead?"

Tony: "Oh, I don't know: Voltaire, Locke, Hobbes, Descartes, Spinoza, —." Javier objected, "Renée Descartes was a mathematician." Tony: "Yes, and a philosopher. We could read Karl Marx, and examine the fallacies of an atheistic paradise, or existentialism, and have a good laugh. We can take a quick look at Nietzsche: "God is dead," Nietzsche; "Nietzsche is dead," God." Javier: "There it is again, "God is dead." Why did you just say that?" Brian: "Nietzsche was a German philosopher in the mid-to-late 1800s. He was the first philosopher to posit God is dead. Tony has a point; maybe we should cover Nietzsche in class." Javier: "Why should we do that?" Tony: "Know thy enemy." Javier did not think it was necessary. Brian made an effort to convince Javier it was a good idea.

Tony: "My point is: that priest admitted he was taught here when the academic program was a joke. What is the integrity of his knowledge base?" Brian: "What are you saying?" Tony: "All priests: good and bad, holy and not, have had substandard educations since the early 70s. That makes most of my teachers suspect. Of course, the homosexual ones have no credibility at all with me." Brian objected, "Are you saying the priests here are homosexual?" Tony: "Many are, yes." Brian emitted a loud, base sounding blast of air, indicating anger and exasperation! Javier assured Brian, "One of Tony's instructors is more than a little swishy. Even the gays snicker at him."

Tony: "I take the instructor at his word. The academic excellence of the Jeroboam was seriously compromised by the early 70s. Do you guys agree the damage was done by homosexuals who infiltrated?" Brian was leery, but Karl and Javier eagerly agreed. Javier: "What you're seeing with gays in the Church in America today happened years earlier in Europe. The problem first appeared in Europe. Not just in the Catholic Church, but clergy of all religions. Celibacy in the Roman Church made them an easy target." Brian: "What do the gays in your class have to say about what the instructor said?"

Tony: "They loved it. It's their success story. Their conversations for the next three or four days were about having leverage on the pope. They claimed the cash flow from America is too big for the pope to jeopardize. They bragged he looks the other way rather than confront problems in order to protect Vatican revenues." Karl and Javier were loath to agree but admitted the United States is the most generous nation on earth. Javier: "The missionaries and the funding from the United States in the 1960s built the strength and membership the Church has today in Africa and South America. The Church is dying in Europe and North America. The southern hemisphere is the future of the Church."

Brian objected to the idea the pope could be bought off like some corrupt politician. Javier wavered, "There has been talk in Italy for years about corruption in the papal bank." Tony: "While we laid pavers last fall, I listened to the Rector and Vice Rector talk about fundraisers and finances. The Jeroboam has 123 million dollars in its coffers, and they were discussing patrons, fundraisers, and bequests." Karl changed the subject, "We were talking about celibacy and got sidetracked on money. What do the gays in your classes say about celibacy?"

Tony: "I helped them study for their logic final. In exchange, they answered my questions on why they came to the seminary." Brian: "How do you know they were telling the truth?" Tony: "I'll tell you what they said. See what you think. Three of the four came for employment for life. They described the Church as a homosexual hostelry. They can travel the world, stay in rectories instead of hotels, and expect to make a new friend like themselves at most stops. These three scoff at the idea of celibacy. They laugh at priests who die of prostate cancer, which proves they did not have sex often enough, a problem three of my classmates brag they will never have. These three don't even believe in God."

Karl: "What about the fourth one?" Tony: "He believes in God. The others laugh at him for that. He wants to be a priest to focus on working on his salvation. He went the entire first semester without fraternizing. The third day of our retreat everyone went crazy celebrating the fact they won him back. "The lost sheep has returned," is what they were shouting. He talked to me the next day. He sounded like that was the end of his attempt to be celibate." Karl: "How about you Tony? Do you think you can be celibate?" Tony: "I lived like a hermit the last couple of years." Karl: "Is that a yes?" Tony: "It's a yes, but I don't recommend it. I agree with the Bible and the Orthodox Church."

Brian: "I want to hear more about corruption in the papal bank that Javier mentioned. What was that about?" Javier: "In the early 1980s a huge scandal broke concerning the papal bank's involvement in money laundering and its ties to criminal organizations which were thought to include the Italian Mafia." Brian: "Why have I never heard anything about this?" Karl and Javier laughed. Karl: "This story appeared every day in Italian newspapers for months on end." Javier agreed, "All other countries laugh at what passes for news in the United States. What your TV calls news is a joke. The reason you never heard about it is because none of your news outlets ever covered the story."

Brian looked to Tony. Tony: "I appreciate your patriotism Brian, but Javier and Karl are correct. When I lived up north, I was able to get Canadian TV. In the early 1990s, they had a documentary on chemical pollution in the food supply. One of many examples was plastic milk jugs. Milk chemically reacts with NON, which is present in some plastic jugs. (NON, a chemical anomaly that sometimes occurs in the manufacturing process of plastic jugs.) The reaction creates a chemical structure similar to a human hormone. Milk and certain other foods packaged in plastic containers cause precocious puberty. When will American TV's self-proclaimed "investigative reporters" report on something substantial like that?

The things they do report have less credibility than the supermarket tabloids. Our media is a sad joke. During the Cold War, we funded Voice of America and Radio Free Europe to bring capitalism, free enterprise, and democracy to Eastern Europe. What we need now is Radio Free America." Brian: "I don't believe that. We have professional journalism in this country." Tony: "We used to. I'm sorry Brian, but the last professional TV news journalist was Walter Cronkite. He was an intelligent journalist of the highest professional standard, a trustworthy reporter with integrity and honor. TV no longer has journalists. They replaced Cronkite with a shill, a copyreader, a talking head. What we have today is propaganda and tabloid trash masquerading as news."

Brian: "What about Rush Limbaugh?" Tony: "I like Rush, he tries to show the public what a joke the so called news outlets are. Too bad he doesn't own his own news service." Javier asked Tony, "Was there any mention of the papal bank scandal in the United States?" Tony: "The movie, *Godfather III*, was fiction based on the death of Pope John Paul I and the bank scandal that erupted a few years later. A foreign made film, *The Pope Must Die*, showed on late night TV. It had a storyline with similar elements." Javier objected, "But that's not news." Tony: "That's right. It's brilliant counterintelligence." Brian: "How is that counterintelligence?"

Tony: "If someone knowledgeable of actual events discusses the subject, any fool can say, "Yeah, I saw that one," and the truth becomes irrelevant." Javier: "I didn't know they made a movie." Tony: "And Americans didn't know about the two scandals in the Vatican." Brian: "Two scandals?" Tony: "The poisoning of the pope in 1978 and the papal bank scandal of the early 1980s. The movie I watched got it right. The pope's assistant poisoned his bedtime cup of tea." Javier: "How did you know about that? How did you know the pope's tea was poisoned?" Tony: "That IS what happened, right?" Javier: "Yes, but how did you know?"

Tony: "My uncle is a ham radio operator. Instead of trusting TV, the electronic narcotic, he stays in touch with the rest of the world directly. Like I said, what we need in this country is Radio Free America." Javier asked dryly, "You don't think Radio Free Europe was American propaganda?" Tony: "Of course it was. Now we need to play our own propaganda back to Americans. It was propaganda that espoused capitalism, free enterprise, the concepts of Adam Smith, and democracy. The unblinking hypnotic eye (TV) has brainwashed Americans into thinking the government should supply them with everything they want and need, and somehow this is not socialism, communism, or Marxism." Brian objected, "It's not that bad."

Tony: "I think it is. Communism and Marxism are atheistic. Consider this: when you went Christmas shopping this year, how many store clerks wished you a Merry Christmas?" Brian: "None. Their managers instruct them not to say Merry Christmas." Tony: "They advertise on TV like crazy for you to go Christmas shopping, but when you go to the store the clerks are told not to wish shoppers a Merry Christmas. Does this make sense to you?" Brian: "Well, it's not PC to say Merry Christmas." Tony: "What is PC and what makes PC an important imperative?"

Brian offered an unfocused, fairness, niceness, warm puppy palaver as his answer. Tony: "Brian, PC grants feel good to the godless." Brian looked to Karl and Javier. PC made no sense to them. They did not suffer from long-term exposure to American television. Brian did not see a problem.

Apparently, this is a trick question. Tony has yet to have someone give any explanation of what PC is, where it comes from, what makes it important, or why it is imperative. Was the propaganda called PC fed into everyone's mind directly through the optic nerve by TV without being logically and consciously processed?

Tony: "Brian, when you're a priest you'll teach people to love one another based on the teachings of Christ. Your reference book will be a fourteen hundred page Bible. Being good in the eyes of the Lord is hard work. The crib sheet is the Ten Commandments. PC is a vapid placebo. PC asks so little: stop using certain words and feel good about yourself." Brian: "What's wrong with that?" Tony: "PC is bubble gum for the soul, an inert miniature substitute for religion, sorely lacking in substance. I think PC is being used to wean the public off religion. The Bible addresses insults. It teaches us to guard our mouth, that words once released cannot be called back." Javier chuckled, "Have you considered finding those passages and giving them another look Tony?"

> Leviticus 19:14 (DRA) [31] Thou shalt not speak evil of the deaf, nor put a stumbling block before the blind: but thou shalt fear the Lord thy God, because I am the Lord.

> Matthew 5:22 (DRA) [31] But I say to you, that whosoever is angry with his brother, shall be in danger of the judgment. And whosoever shall say to his brother, Raca, shall be in danger of the council. And whosoever shall say, Thou fool, shall be in danger of hell fire.

> Matthew 5:22 (RSV) [20] But I say to you that every one who is angry with his brother[i] shall be liable to judgment; whoever insults[j] his brother shall be liable to the council, and whoever says, "You fool!" shall be liable to the hell[k] of fire.
> [i] Other ancient authorities insert *without cause*
> [j] Greek *says Raca to* (an obscure term for abuse)
> [k] Greek *Gehenna*

> Ephesians 4:29-32 (DRA) [31] 29 Let no evil speech proceed from your mouth; but that which is good, to the edification of faith, that it may

administer grace to the hearers. 30 And grieve not the holy Spirit of God: whereby you are sealed unto the day of redemption. 31 Let all bitterness, and anger, and indignation, and clamour, and blasphemy, be put away from you, with all malice. 32 And be ye kind one to another; merciful, forgiving one another, even as God hath forgiven you in Christ.

Ephesians 4:29-32 (*Liturgy of the Hours* [42]: Ordinary Time, Week I, Friday, Morning Prayer, Reading) Never let evil talk pass your lips; say only the good things men need to hear, things that will really help them. Do nothing that will sadden the Holy Spirit with whom you were sealed against the day of redemption. Get rid of all bitterness, all passion and anger, harsh words, slander, and malice of every kind. In place of these, be kind to one another, compassionate, and mutually forgiving, just as God has forgiven you in Christ.

Tony: "Yeah, I'm sure I could use more than just a quick look, that's true." Brian and Karl smirked. Tony: "PC has people feel good about themselves with little or no effort. Just be oblivious while our language, our religion, and our society are being corrupted and destroyed, and be happy. Let me quote Edmund Burke: "The only thing needed for the triumph of evil is for good men to do nothing."" Brian: "Why do you see PC as evil when no one else does?" Tony: "I didn't own a TV until 1991. The mass hypnosis that force-fed PC to the public happened without me. Everyone takes PC seriously and no one can explain why." Javier: "Is that why you insist on using the word queer? It's because you hate PC?" Tony: "You know it."

For a succinct and erudite second opinion, see *A Theory of Civilization,* [05] from *Decline Of Ideas*, part of *A Study Of Our Decline* by P. Atkinson.
Go to: <www.ourcivilisation.com/pc.htm>. [05]

Brian: "Tony, don't you feel funny that you're the only one who thinks PC is a bad thing?" Tony: "No. I feel like a lone lemming watching the rest of my kind throwing themselves off a cliff, headlong into the sea. *(This metaphor is based on the erroneous misconception of lemming behavior popularized in the 1950s, as seen in the 1958 Disney film, "White Wilderness.").* [24]

Homosexuals hide in plain sight. Many get married and hide behind a wife, especially in the eastern states. Their lexicon used to betray them. With everyone speaking PC, it's tougher than ever to identify them." Karl smiled, "Everyone but you Tony." Javier: "Why is it so important to be able to identify them?" Tony: "Last fall you said so yourself, they decided it's them against us. How can you know your enemy if you can't see them or identify them? Good cannot fight evil if it does not know what is evil."

Brian was incredulous! "You think gays are inherently evil?" Tony: "Yes." *(Romans 1:24-32)* Brian: "Yes! You say yes as if it's a fact!" Tony: "My classmates pride themselves on being the bad guys. When I asked them why they came to the seminary, they told me. Then they asked me." Karl: "What did you tell them?" Tony: "I said evil abounds, I wanted to work for God and help turn the tide." Javier: "What did they say to that?" Tony: "For clarification they asked, "You wanted to join the good guys to fight bad guys?" I confirmed I did." Brian: "What did they say?" Tony: "They laughed harder than I've ever seen anyone laugh." Karl flushed: "Javier and I laughed at you once, remember?" Tony: "I remember." Karl: "Did they laugh harder than that?" Tony: "Yeah they did."

Annulment 1996

Fall semester a holy priest told his class of a pending high profile annulment. Joseph P. Kennedy II filed for an annulment from his first wife, Sheila Rauch Kennedy, after the couple's 1991 civil divorce. The wife was fighting the annulment her husband was seeking.

The priest was compelled to follow up with his former class on the results of the February proceedings. The priest was furious! He located Tony. Priest: "Two hours ago they granted the annulment without including the wife in the proceedings!" Tony asked if the wife was at least notified. Priest: "No, she was not notified, and they don't intend to notify her for months! They won't notify her until sometime around Halloween, maybe even after Halloween, but definitely before Thanksgiving."

Football Game

Tony was sitting by himself eating dinner when his four gay classmates breezed up to the table with their trays to join him. *Now what?* Greg smiled. David grinned, "May we join you?" Tony: "Sure." The four sat on the opposite side of the table. David and Greg started a conversation about their romantic interests on campus and gave details. This passed as dinner patter. It reminded Tony of conversations among young women at work when he was a supervisor. The four leered at Tony, searching for a reaction. *I wish to deny them the satisfaction.* Tony: "Did you guys see the football game on campus the first day of orientation?"

Greg's expression was quizzical, "I played, why?" David watched the game. Leo was embarrassed by the bad behavior on the field. Mr. Stevens made a sour face. Tony: "I was surprised you guys play football." Greg was stunned. The others gasped in disbelief. Greg: "You think gays don't play football?" Tony: "No, I didn't think so." All four roared with laughter! David tried to comment, but the only intelligible word was "stereotype." Tony: "What about professional football?" All four became hysterical!

Laughing, Greg said, "Anyone involved in professional football has fame, a huge paycheck, and shares the locker room with all these healthy, perfect bodies. Being on TV, it's everything gays like. What makes you think gays don't play football?" David was still wheezing "stereotype" and laughing with the others.

Tony: “How many gay players are in the league, a handful maybe?” The table exploded with laughter!!! The onslaught of laughter was unbearable. Tony shoveled the last of his meal into his face and swallowed it like a pelican so he could leave. Tony’s leaving the table triggered the laughter to increase in force and volume. Tears were streaming down David’s face. He was holding his stomach and wincing in pain from laughing so hard.

11 HE IS ONE OF US

Chicken Wings

On his way back from class, Tony saw the Vice Rector and Jack talking outside the refectory. The acoustics in the corridor connecting the refectory to the academic building are excellent for eavesdropping. The Vice Rector asked a question and Jack said he knew a place that served chicken wings. Jack assured the priest he could get the others to agree. Vice Rector: "The other thing is important too. Make sure as many people as possible know you are all from the Pontifical Jeroboam." When Tony's approach was in close proximity, the Vice Rector glanced at him. There was a pause in the conversation. Tony nodded and smiled as he passed by. The priest resumed, "It's important you don't do anything to arouse suspicion."

Friday Tony carried his lunch tray into the crowded refectory. Several voices called him to join them at their table. Javier, Karl, Art, and Jack sat together. *This is curious.* Art was discussing single malt scotch. He never had any and was curious to try it. After Tony was seated, Art declared the group should go out for chicken wings. Art: "It will be great to get off campus. I get sick of eating here all the time." Javier and Karl nodded with enthusiastic agreement! Tony: "The refectory serves excellent food. Chicken wings are drunk food." Art: "What is drunk food?" Tony: "It's cheap food you feed to drunks." Karl sounded angry, "I have to eat here. I don't have any money."

Art was surprised, "You said you like wings Tony. I got the idea from you. I've been talking to Javier about it. We both want to try hot chicken wings. You're the one who knows about hot wings, you have to come with us." Tony: "I do like wings. I'm just saying, refectory food is high quality and costs us nothing." Karl repeated, "I have to eat here. I don't have any money." Jack smiled, "We all need to get off campus and let our hair down. We need to get away from here for a couple of hours." Javier and Karl agreed! Jack continued, "I'll submit a requisition to the Vice Rector. If he says yes, I can put it on the pub's credit card." Tony: "Why would the Vice Rector agree to use pub money to pay for our beer and wings?"

Javier deadpanned, "Don't be so negative Tony." Jack: "The Vice Rector authorizes requisitions all the time for indigent students. He believes it is important to provide excellent food to maintain student morale. He told you this himself at the beginning of the year Tony." *Yes, he did. And you know this how?* Tony: "Yes, I marveled at the cuisine served in the refectory and that was the Vice Rector's response, but using pub money to pay for my beer and wings seems unlikely." Javier: "Tony, the Church issues small grants to needy people all the time. We are needy people, and this is good for student morale." *Spoken like a true Democrat. Let me guess: "And Jack cares!" "And the Vice Rector cares!" Please.*

Karl challenged, "What are we supposed to use for a car?" Jack smiled, "That's one of the perks of running the pub. We have use of the pub's van." Javier: "This is great!" Art agreed, "Getting off campus and hot chicken wings, you can't beat that. You have to come with us Tony. Tell us about hot chicken wings." Tony: "I've always heard them called Buffalo wings." Art: "Buffalo? Why Buffalo?" Tony: "Buffalo, New York style chicken wings. A bar in Buffalo made hot spicy chicken wings. During the 1970s, bars set out baskets of popcorn like you do in the pub, or peanuts in the shell. Copycats started offering hot chicken wings, which sold a lot more beer than popcorn or peanuts."

Art: "Wings are a lot more expensive than popcorn or peanuts." Tony: "Back then wings were dirt cheap. The popularity of Buffalo style chicken wings drove the wholesale price through the roof." Jack excused himself to get the ok from the Vice Rector, who was just leaving the refectory. Jack returned with good news. Jack: "Let's all meet outside the refectory at six o'clock and I'll show you where the van is parked." Jack left. Art stayed until Javier and Karl were ready to leave.

Art and Jack were waiting when Tony showed up at the rendezvous point that evening. Javier and Karl arrived shortly. Jack led the group to the van. Jack broke the silence of the ride by asking everyone's favorite Bible quote. Silence. Jack went first, "Oh, that you may suck fully of the milk of her comfort, that you may nurse with delight at her abundant breasts!" Jack and Art smiled. Javier: "Is that really a quote from the Bible?" Jack: "Isaiah 66:11." Tony protested, "It doesn't appear like that in my Bible [18] (© 1950). What translation is that supposed to be?" Jack: "That's exactly how it appears in *The Liturgy of the Hours* [42] (© 1975). You know, the book we use every day for Evening Prayer." (Ordinary Time, Week IV, Thursday, Morning Prayer).

Javier was impressed. He liked it. Jack put Tony on the spot, "You're next Tony. Tell us your favorite Bible quote." Tony: "Drink strong drink when the heart is filled with sorrow, drink wine to fill the heart with joy." Javier: "Is that an accurate quote?" Tony: "It's close. I paraphrased a verse from the last chapter of Proverbs." Javier said under his breath, "You told me before your favorite Bible passage was Psalm 149, what happened?" Tony confided, "I decided to use my favorite misquote. It seemed more appropriate for the occasion."

After a twenty-minute drive, Jack parked the van and everyone followed him into the bar. Jack chose a centrally located booth. The waitress brought a chair for Jack, and stood ready to take orders. Art was curious to try scotch. Javier and Karl agreed. Tony insisted, "No, you don't drink scotch with chicken wings. Let's order a pitcher of beer." Javier and Karl wanted scotch, especially since it was *gratis*. Art and Jack were supportive, "Let them order what they want. We're all here to have a good time." Tony insisted beer was the only drink to have with Buffalo wings. Art said he wanted to try scotch too. Jack and Art were disappointed when Tony garnered agreement on beer. Tony told the waitress, "We'll have a pitcher of beer and a plate of wings."

Art thundered, "No! We're ordering by the glass!" The intensity of his objection was startling. Tony stated, "It's cheaper by the pitcher. We should get a pitcher." Art: "No! Serve our drinks by the glass!" Jack took control by handing the waitress a credit card. Jack: "Serve our drinks by the glass and bring us our first platter of hot chicken wings." Waitress: "Regular hot wings or extra hot?" Jack looked at the others–, "Extra hot." Tony ordered a beer that was on tap and everyone else ordered the same. When the waitress brought the first platter of wings, Jack ordered another platter. When she returned with the second platter, the first was empty. Jack left the table before Javier and Karl ordered their third beer.

Art said, "I'm good," before he disappeared to the men's room. Tony: "No more for me, thank you." Javier and Karl encouraged Tony. "Yours is almost empty. Go ahead, get another." Tony: "No thank you, no more drinks for me." The waitress disappeared. Javier: "What's the matter with you Tony? What is your problem?" Tony: "I haven't seen you guys alone to tell you. I overheard Jack talking to the Vice Rector a few days ago. Jack confirmed chicken wings, the Vice Rector said to be careful not to raise suspicion. The Vice Rector had a secondary agenda associated with chicken wings." Javier laughed, "You don't trust anyone. Relax. Besides, why would the Vice Rector let you listen to his conversation?"

Tony: "I was walking from the academic building to the refectory. You know what the acoustics are like in that corridor." Karl: "Yes, you can hear everything, the sound travels forever." Tony: "It seems the Vice Rector doesn't realize this. People catch him as he leaves the refectory and talk to him in the corridor with total disregard for passers-by." Karl: "It's true. I've seen it more than once myself." Tony: "Let me tell you before Art comes back. Art ordered separate drinks so they have proof of how many drinks we have. Notice they have not ordered a third drink. You saw the menu, you saw how much cheaper it is to buy beer by the pitcher. Why buy beer by the glass when we're all drinking the same beer that's on tap?"

Javier objected, "Art encouraged us to order scotch. He wanted one himself." Karl became suspicious, "But he never ordered one, and he got a little crazy when Tony ordered a pitcher of beer. I believe Tony. These guys are up to something." Javier spotted Jack talking to a young woman. Javier was inspired, "Come on, let's meet some women." Tony: "Be serious. We're here with the two pub snitches." Karl: "Why do you call them the pub snitches?" Tony: "Their job is to report to the Vice Rector anyone ordering more than two beers." Javier: "How do you know that?" Tony: "The first time I went to the pub Art confided this to me." Karl laughed, "That was before they knew you were straight. Did you think he was straight?"

Tony: "Yes, I did. After I figured out he wasn't, I pretended I still thought he was." Javier: "Jack is straight." Tony: "No he's not!" Javier: "He certainly is! Look at him! Now he's talking to two women, and they cannot get enough of this guy. Look at the expressions on their faces! And what about his favorite Bible quote? What do you think about that?" Tony: "With your background in psychology and you don't recognize a sociopath when you see one? The Vice Rector sent Art and Jack to get dirt on us tonight. At lunch, you said the Church hands out small grants to the indigent. The Church, not the pub. Using the pub's van and money to buy three students chicken wings and beer is malfeasance and embezzlement: using business assets and revenue for personal gain. It's a criminal offence."

Karl turned pale. "Tony's making sense. These two are up to no good. You know what this means?" Tony: "They know the three of us went out for scotch." Javier challenged, "What makes you think so?" Karl: "Art wanted scotch as bad as we did Javier, then he never ordered one. I don't think it's a coincidence they invited the three of us to go drinking, and why would the Vice Rector authorize using pub money to pay for it? How else do you explain ordering beer by the glass?" Javier objected, "What about meeting girls? Look at Jack. He's talking to three women at once. There are plenty of good-looking women here. I say we mingle instead of sitting here staring at a plate of chicken bones."

In a menacing voice Karl said, "I thought you were so much in love with your girlfriend. Why would you want to meet someone here?" Javier flushed. Karl: "Javier, listen to Tony. I believe him. The Vice Rector sent those guys to get dirt on the three of us–." Tony interrupted, "Art is coming back." Tony finished his beer. Tony: "Look at these guys Art. The wings were too hot for them. They had to order a third beer. We should've ordered the regular wings for these rookies." Everyone enjoyed the wings. Everyone agreed the wings were hot. Art commented on Jack's success with women. Art: "Why aren't you guys putting the moves on some of these fine ladies?" Tony: "That's a good idea. You are the upperclassman. Show us how it's done." Karl was stunned. Art sat on the outside edge of the booth next to Javier.

Tony's remark animated Javier, "Tony's right! Let's show these underclassmen how to meet women!" Art's jaw dropped. He made a litany of excuses, "–but you guys go ahead. Don't let me ruin your fun." Tony looked directly into Javier's eyes and finally saw them flash with understanding. Javier calmed down. He and Karl still had a third of a glass of beer. Tony encouraged them, "Drink up before it gets warm." Jack returned to the table and encouraged everyone to order another round. Art ordered another beer. Jack: "I can't believe it. Once women know I'm a seminarian, they start confessing their sins to me. I tell them I'm not a priest, I'm only a student, but they continue telling me their darkest secrets."

Jack's soliloquy continued for several minutes. His accounts of how easily women trust seminarians and how quickly they tell intimate details of their lives were like catnip to Javier. Javier looked at Tony. Tony raised one eyebrow. Javier looked at Karl and then calmed down. Jack saw he had no takers, and went back to chatting up the ladies. Jack was smooth, a real social butterfly. Javier carped, "How do you explain Jack's success with women?" Tony: "He's pretty amazing, that's a fact. No shortage of animal magnetism with that one." Art: "Are you going to let Jack show you up Tony?" Tony: "Yes, I am. I made that decision before coming to the seminary." When Jack returned he looked at Art. Art shook his head. Both men's faces evidenced defeat. Jack called it a night and everyone agreed.

When they got back to campus, the three amigos went directly to Tony's room. Javier snidely asked, "Karl, what happened to being careful about being seen with Tony?" Karl: "It's too late for that now, they're on to us. Tony, at the bar you said they know the three of us went out for scotch. What makes you think so?" Tony: "They made an effort to get the three of us together to go drinking." Javier: "That's easily explained." Javier gave his explanation, but it was not convincing. Karl: "I didn't tell anyone about the time we went out." Tony: "You know I didn't talk about it." Javier: "You don't trust anyone. You don't know anyone here except me, Karl, and Brian, and Brian said you didn't say anything to him about it."

Karl's eyes narrowed, "You told Brian? Who else did you tell?" Javier paused, "I told Brian." Karl: "Who else?" Javier: "No one." Karl: "You told Brian. Who else did you tell?" Javier hemmed and hawed before remembering another person he told. Karl: "You know he is homosexual! Why did you tell him?" Javier: "He's ok, I trust him." Karl: "You trust him! Now they target me the same as they target you and Tony! No wonder Tony doesn't tell you everything. He knows you can't be trusted to keep quiet!"

> Ecclesiasticus 37:18 (DRA) [31] The soul of a holy man discovereth sometimes true things, more than seven watchmen that sit in a high place to watch.
>
> Sirach 37:14 (RSVwA) [43] For a man's soul sometimes keeps him better informed than seven watchmen sitting high on a watchtower.

Javier: "Is Karl right? Are there things you don't tell me because you don't trust me to keep it quiet?" Tony: "Yes, yes, and yes. What he said." Javier was crushed. "How does Karl know this?" Tony: "Karl is most intelligent, highly observant, and a brilliant judge of character. If any man can see into the soul of another human being, my money is on Karl." Javier: "Are there things you tell Karl you don't tell me?" Tony: "No." Javier: "I don't believe you." Tony: "There's no need, Karl knows without asking. How many times have I started to explain something and Karl finished the explanation? He doesn't need to be told things he already knows." *Although he did ask me for intel once.* Javier considered this and saw it was true.

Karl: "How many times did Tony say we have to protect Karl, and still you had to talk?" Javier flushed, "I'm sorry." Karl: "You're sorry? Too late for sorry! Now

I'm a target, the same as you and Tony. At the bar, Tony told us we were being set up. He told us to be careful, and still you wanted to pick up girls! You make it too easy for them to get rid of you. Tony, you said the Vice Rector had a secondary goal. Can you tell us what it was?" Tony: "I didn't know ahead of time. After watching Jack talk to every woman in the bar, the Vice Rector's instructions to make sure as many people as possible know we are all seminarians became evident. The Vice Rector wanted to generate gossip about seminarians fraternizing with the ladies in a bar."

Javier: "Why would he do that?" Tony: "To counteract stories of queers at the Jeroboam. You think Jack is straight, how much more convinced are those young women he was talking to?" Javier argued, "That doesn't make sense. Gossip about seminarians picking up women in bars isn't good PR." Tony: "It's better than knowing the seminary is full of queers. The Vice Rector is managing the public perception of this institution. He does not want the public to know queers have commandeered the Jeroboam. He doesn't want donor money to dry up." It made sense to Karl. Tony: "If you tried to pick up women, you'd have given the Vice Rector everything he wanted: rumors of seminarians chasing girls and a solid reason to give you the boot." Karl agreed. Javier was ashamed.

The Vice Rector plans to expel Javier, Tony, and now Karl too, simply for being straight, for not being "one of us." Had any of these three men ("The Enemy") tried to pick up women in the bar, with patrons of the bar knowing they were seminarians, how could the Vice Rector exploit the situation (of his own making) to his advantage? Such an incident would justify the expulsion of above said seminarians and make the Vice Rector a hero, a dauntless defender of righteousness, morality, probity, and the Church! And the Vice Rector had two staunch seminarians in good standing (the two pub snitches) for eyewitnesses.

Limbaugh

Limbaugh's half hour TV show was popular. It was moved to another time slot. That did not dilute his following. His show was moved to three a.m. His audience taped the show and watched it during breakfast. The network could not foil his following, so they canceled the show. Their excuse was they needed the airtime for the Olympics. Right. Only one network carries Olympic coverage, the others could have signed the show. The show had strong "numbers." Other networks should have been clamoring for it, but Rush was no longer on TV. Rush left quietly. He denied rumors he was forced out. *Uh-huh.* When Limbaugh's show was pulled, the gay seminarians were elated! "Now Clinton will get reelected!"

From the first class of the day until he fell asleep at night, Tony had to endure the gays raucously congratulating each other and carrying on. Not just Tony's classmates: all of them, all day long. Tony's classmates got in his face, especially David. The overall frenzy of joy and victory was just short of riotous. Three days of this was insufferable. The Log Cabin Republican who worked in the library was incredibly morose. He looked even gloomier than Tony felt, but he did not discuss it with Tony. David reminded his cohorts time and again they heard it from him first. David: "I told you it was a reliable source! I told you he was an insider! They made this happen in time! This will change the election!" *Liberal media my eye: the gay Democrat media.*

Tunes

Tony's classmates joined him for dinner and were conversant. They noted the effort Tony put into singing and the progress he made in a short period of time. David chided, "Going to teach an old dog new tricks, is that right Tony?" David said he was impressed by Tony's progress. The four were talking music. They asked Tony what his favorite music was. Tony: "I like jazz." David: "Who are your favorite artists?" Tony: "I don't pay enough attention. If I hear a song I like, I'm lucky to remember the title." The discussion continued without Tony until he took exception to something David said. Tony interjected, "What about the Black contribution to American music? You make it sound like American music is a white boy thing."

There was a long pause. Greg: "I thought you said you don't know anything about music Tony." Tony: "I don't, but even I know if it's American music, and it is good, then it was originally Black music." David: "Nothing is more American than rock 'n roll Tony. Rock 'n roll started with Elvis Presley, the King of rock 'n roll, and the last time I checked he was white." Tony: "Rock 'n roll was performed in the Black community by artists like the Ink Spots and Fats Domino. The Ink Spots made their first recording around the time Elvis was born." David and Mr. Stevens snickered at the artists names. David: "Then why do they call Elvis the King?" Tony: "Because he brought rock 'n roll mainstream?" The group was not swayed.

Tony: "Rock 'n roll is rooted in the blues. The blues are definitely Black music. You've heard of rhythm and blues: Little Richard and Chuck Berry?" David: "You like jazz so much Tony, what about jazz?" To make his point, David named three white jazz musicians. Tony: "Be serious. New Orleans, the birthplace of jazz? Even you guys have heard of Louie Armstrong." David: "Satchmo." The way he said it was cloying. David made a big deal out of record sales. David: "How do you explain that?" Tony: "You've got a point. The Black community creates a genre of music. They perform the music in small clubs and barely make a living doing it. Some white guy starts performing the same music, and the money flows." David: "What about rap? It's American and it's Black, does that mean it's good music?"

Tony: "You guys took the same logic class I did. If it's American and it's good, then it's Black music. You can't scramble the terms and maintain the logic. To answer your question: no, I don't like rap." David: "What about country music Tony? It's American and it's certainly white music. That disproves your logic formula. What about that?" Tony: "Hello. Country music does not meet the qualifier. You guys didn't do so well in logic class did you?" All four laughed.

"You don't like country music either." Leo: "Is there any other music you like Tony?". Tony: "I like River music. It's a combination of Dixieland jazz and Bluegrass." David: "What is Bluegrass?" Tony: "I don't know what to tell you. It was popular in the 1970s. I can't think of any examples either."

Two weeks later in class, the teacher was discussing the Black contribution to American music. The four classmates glanced at Tony in acknowledgment of their earlier discussion.

Single Malt

Shortly after eight p.m., there was a knock on the door. It was the Vice Rector. Tony: "Yes?" Vice Rector: "I understand you have a bottle of scotch in your room Tony, is that correct?" Tony: "Yes, that's right." Vice Rector: "Give it to me." Tony: "Excuse me?" Vice Rector: "This is a seminary Tony. You can't have alcohol in your room." Tony: "I live here. Where am I supposed to keep it?" Vice Rector: "I will hold it for you in my quarters." Tony: "I don't think so." Vice Rector: "You can be expelled for having alcohol in your room Tony. Why do you have it to begin with?" Tony: "My parish priest gave me that scotch. He was on campus three weeks ago. While he was here, he visited me. The scotch was a gift. I opened the bottle and we had a drink. Since then it has been in my closet."

Vice Rector: "I take it you and your parish priest are close." Tony: "No, not really." Vice Rector: "You must be close friends. Otherwise, why would he give you a bottle of scotch?" Tony: "It was a shocker to me too. It's a single malt." Vice Rector: "Is this priest your sponsor?" Tony: "Not by choice. Father Nick is my mentor, he recruited me." Vice Rector: "I remember Father Nick. This is his alma mater." Tony: "When Father Nick was sent to the Vatican for Canon Law, this priest replaced him. When he came to our parish, I was an extra project foisted on him. He fit me into his schedule by going to dinner together after the 5:15 Mass every Saturday. We took turns picking up the tab. We always had scotch after our meal."

Vice Rector: "That doesn't seem reason enough to buy you a bottle as a gift." Tony: "I was surprised he gave me a gift, especially a bottle of scotch. I have no idea why he did. Now you are telling me I'm in trouble because I have this scotch. Mystery solved. You suggest my parish priest wants to sabotage my candidacy. People in my parish are going to ask why I was expelled. What are they going to think when I tell them I was expelled because our parish priest gave me a bottle of scotch at the seminary? (*Socratic irony).*" The Vice Rector's mouth was agape. For several moments, he said nothing. He was perplexed. Vice Rector: "You haven't told me the name of your parish priest."

Tony: "Father Gary. He graduated from here two years ago with Father Nick." Vice Rector: "I remember Father Gary. Why didn't you mention his name?" Tony: "(*It is part of my interrogation technique.*) He was on campus for a week visiting friends three weeks ago. I thought you knew." Vice Rector: "No, I didn't see him. I didn't know he was here." *That explains why Mr. Stevens and company did not wear me out about my parish priest's visit.* Vice Rector: "Tony, I'm simply saying you can't keep alcohol in your room. You won't be in trouble if you hand over the bottle." Tony: "The bottle has been opened. I'm not giving you an open bottle of my scotch." Vice Rector: "I'm not going to drink your scotch. I'm only going to hold it in my quarters." Tony: "I'm sorry, that's not going to happen."

Vice Rector: "I don't want to drink your scotch Tony. You simply cannot keep it in your room. I will hold on to it for you." Tony: "No thank you. I am not keeping my scotch in your quarters." Vice Rector: "The bottle of scotch is not a problem. Refusing to hand it over is a serious problem. You cannot have that bottle in your room." Tony: "Wait a minute. I have a storage unit eight miles from here. I can put the bottle in storage. It would be to my convenience if I can do that tomorrow in the daylight." Vice Rector: "You would put your scotch in storage?" Tony: "Sure, if I can't keep it here. It's alcohol, it won't spoil." The Vice Rector expressed suspicion (at great length) the bottle would not be sufficiently out of reach.

The Vice Rector remembered in core board Tony said he owned a shotgun. Vice Rector: "Is your shotgun in storage too?" Tony: "No, I gave all my guns to my brother to sell. He sold all but one, so I still own a shotgun." Vice Rector: "Where is the gun now?" Tony: "It's at my brother's house. He lives in another state." Vice Rector: "I'm leaving here with that bottle Tony, or you have a big problem." Tony: "If you have a problem with that bottle being in my room, I'll put it in storage. I prefer to do that tomorrow in the daylight." The Vice Rector was uncomfortable with the storage unit. He voiced concern again (at protracted length) that it would not actually be out of reach.

Tony: "That's ridiculous. Anyone can go down the street to a liquor store, buy whatever, and come back here. The reasons you've mentioned might be valid if I were an alcoholic. I'm not. With your permission, I'll take care of this tomorrow." Vice Rector: "I want that bottle out of your room right now!" Tony: "Fine. I'll take it to storage right now." Vice Rector: "I thought you said the bottle has been opened." Tony: "That's right." Vice Rector: "It's illegal to transport an open bottle of alcohol in this state. It would be safer for you if I keep it in my quarters." Tony: "My scotch will be safer in storage. I'll worry about getting it there." The Vice Rector turned and walked away. Tony put his jacket on, stuck the bottle in his gym bag, and headed to his truck.

Scotch

The next day Tony's classmates vacillated between being sullen and aloof. *Finally, peace!* Of course, Leo joined Tony at dinner. Leo: "Everyone saw the Vice Rector outside your room last night. He was talking to you for a long time. What was that all about?" Tony: "My parish priest was in town three weeks ago. He visited me on Saturday and gave me a bottle of scotch. We had a drink. Last night the Vice Rector decided to put the grab on my scotch." Leo: "Grab? Oh, you mean confiscate. He confiscated the bottle?" Tony: "Not." Leo looked disoriented. He shook his head, "You can't keep alcohol in your room Tony. You have to give him the bottle. He's the Vice Rector. You really didn't give him the bottle?"

Tony: "He walked away empty handed." Leo: "You still have the scotch in your room?" Tony: "No. He wanted it gone, so I took it to my storage unit." Leo: "Was he ok with that?" Tony: "Not so much." Leo: "Oh Tony, that's not good. You should try to get on his good side." Tony: "That man wasted nearly two hours of my life last night. It was raining, so in addition to being inconvenienced, I got soaking wet. I don't see us being first buddies anytime soon." Leo considered, "Still, he's the Vice Rector. Why do you think he came to your room like that?" Tony: "He came at the request of Mr. Stevens." Leo turned red, "How do you know that?" Tony: "The way the Vice Rector behaved, the way Mr. Stevens and friends acted today, and you confirmed it just now." Leo turned an even deeper red.

After dinner, Javier knocked on Tony's door. Javier: "Everybody saw the Vice Rector in front of your room last night. He was there for a long time. What did he want?" Tony: "He wanted to confiscate my scotch." Javier: "I told you! I warned you we aren't supposed to have alcohol in our room. Now he has your scotch." Tony: "No he doesn't. I took it to my storage unit." Javier: "You had to go out in the rain?" Tony: "I got soaked, plus the flashlight in my truck is dead." Javier: "I told you to keep it quiet. You asked people to have a drink with you, I know you did. Who did you ask?" Tony: "Besides you, Karl, and Brian, I asked the Friar and the two pub snitches on three separate occasions. Remember the pub snitches wanted to try scotch when we went out for wings?"

Javier: "Yes." Tony: "Well, they don't. They weren't the least bit interested." Javier: "Who do you think turned you in?" Tony: "Your next door neighbor." Javier: "I really can't stand that guy. Can you confirm it was him?" Tony: "Yes. Leo ate dinner with me tonight. He always eats with me when he wants to get information for those other jokers. Leo asked me the same question you just did. I gave him the same answer and he turned brick red. That's on top of watching Mr. Stevens and company throughout the day. If someone responsible reported my scotch to the Vice Rector, he would have talked to me during normal business hours, so the Friar and the pub snitches were not suspect."

Javier: "The Vice Rector stood in the hall a long time talking to you. I take it he was not happy you refused to hand over the scotch. What happened?" Tony: "I told him I'd put it in storage." Javier: "What did he say to that?" Tony: "He blathered at length, as if I'm an alcoholic. Then he asked if my shotgun was in storage too." Javier: "I didn't know you had a storage locker. You could've put it in storage to begin with and avoided all this." Tony: "I could have made the trip in the daylight when it wasn't raining, that's true." *And miss an opportunity to confirm the Vice Rector's duplicity? The Minnesota gay had alcohol to poison Javier, and that was ok.* Javier: "I told you to keep it quiet. You didn't believe me, did you?" Tony: "I knew your concern was genuine." Javier: "Why didn't you take my advice?"

Tony: "(*Cover story*) Your advice was to adopt the behavior of an alcoholic. That would backfire on me later." Javier: "You could have put the scotch in storage, why didn't you?" Tony: "I didn't think of it until the Vice Rector got in my face." Javier: "Why not?" Tony: "(*I wanted to provoke an adversarial interaction with the Vice Rector where I controlled the outcome.*). The bottle had been opened. If I got pulled over on my way to storage it would have been expensive and unpleasant." Javier: "Ha-ha-ha! You don't trust the Vice Rector! It's not like he was going to drink it." Tony: "Ok, close your eyes and picture me drinking that scotch after it sat in the Vice Rector's quarters for three or four months." Javier: "Ha-ha-ha! You don't like him at all, do you?" Tony: "Not so much, no."

The next day Mr. Stevens exasperated Tony by obsessing over his storage unit. Mr. Stevens: "I know you own a gun. I know you keep it in your storage unit." David believed as much and made his righteous indignation known to Tony. Tony answered their questions with the truth, which should have allayed their baseless fears, but did not. Mr. Stevens: "I know you lie Tony. I know you have a gun in storage." *Please.*

Supply Run

The next time Tony went to the pub, Art was miffed. Tony quietly sat for several minutes before Art set a half basket of stale popcorn on the bar. Tony sat munching the rubbery, day old popcorn. When he finished, he set the empty basket to the back of the bar. Tony quietly waited for a refill. At long last, Art glared at Tony, "How long did you know?" Tony: "Know what?" Art: "Come on, how long did you know I'm gay?" Tony: "It took me a couple of weeks to figure it out." Art: "Why didn't you tell me?" Tony: "I figured you already knew you were gay." Art: "Very funny, you know what I mean." Tony: "There was nothing to say. The Vice Rector told you and Jack to run a sting operation on scotch drinkers. You didn't tell me because there was nothing to say."

Art considered this–, "Oh, what the hell." He started popping a fresh batch of popcorn. Art: "Why do you spend so much time in the pub?" Tony: "I already told you, I come here for the popcorn. It's the most insidious kind. It's popped in coconut oil. It smells like movie theater popcorn." Art: "You come here twice as often as Karl. Karl has to come here because he has no money at all. He can't go anywhere else. Why do you come here so often?" Tony: "My room is directly across from the stairwell. Minutes after you pop a batch, my room fills with the smell of freshly popped movie theater popcorn. If popcorn were liquid, I would have an I.V. drip in my room. Since it's not, I come down to the pub."

Art and Jack found it curious that Tony continued to come to the pub. As always, Tony came down when he smelled fresh popcorn or was completely bored and hungry. Since this happens early, when the pub first opens, the only person in the pub is Art, and on rare occasions Jack. During one of Tony's subsequent visits to the pub, Art and Jack asked Tony if he had any questions about gays. Tony asked why they wanted to join the priesthood. They didn't answer that, but they were willing to answer Tony's general curiosity about gays. Tony: "Gays complain they are born that way and don't like it, is that true?" They both agreed many are born gay and not all of them like it.

Tony: "Gays try to recruit straights, is that right?" They both agreed that was true. Tony: "How does that work? I don't understand how you can convert someone." Jack chuckled, "To the dark side? Adults can't be turned; they have already established themselves. Young people, teens and early 20s, who have not yet established themselves or are confused or unsuccessful can still be turned." There wasn't much else Jack and Art were willing to discuss, so Tony decided to return to his studies. Before he left, they invited Tony to go to Sam's Club with them the next time they bought supplies for the pub. Tony: "No thanks, I hate shopping." They both insisted, "It's a good excuse to get off campus. Who needs an excuse to get off campus anyway? Just say yes." Tony: "Fine."

A few days later, Art called Tony from the pub after class. "We're going to go to Sam's Club today. Can you knock on Jack's door and tell him it's time? He's probably taking a nap. I can't get him on the phone. He'll fall back asleep if you don't wait for him. Once he's ready, the two of you meet me here in the pub." Tony: "I don't know his room number." Art gave Tony Jack's room number. Art: "He's on your floor, on the same side about halfway down."

Tony quickly prepared for the ride to Sam' Club with Jack and Art. He put on the long sleeve shirt with his new directional mic (Cost: $65) sewn into the cuff. He put on the trousers with the hole cut on the inside, on the top of the left front pocket, to accommodate the wires to his micro recorder.

The $250 micro recorder was the size of a Zippo ® lighter. This replaced the cheap recorder Tony first purchased. Concealing this recorder in his pocket required close proximity to the speaker, which limited its utility. The tapes Tony made with the cheap recorder in the school's van were flooded with road noise. Tony hoped the directional mic together with the quality recorder would remedy that. Today he would test their combined performance.

Tony knocked on Jack's door. Tony: "Art says it's time to go to Sam's Club." No answer. After a few more tries, Jack threw a shoe at the door and shouted, "Go away!" Tony insisted, "Art says we have to do this now." It was unintelligible, but Jack cursed between his teeth. Eventually Jack opened the door. He finished buttoning his shirt and slipped on his shoes. He grabbed his keys off the desk, and headed to the door. Another voice deep inside the room asked Jack a question. Jack replied, "I'm going to be gone for a couple of hours, don't wait." There was a hint of embarrassment on Jack's face as he pulled the door shut. In the pub, Art was peeved, "I have too many things to do to sit around waiting for you."

Jack drove the van, Art rode in front, and Tony sat in the back seat. Once they were on the road, Art turned to Tony, "He was in bed wasn't he?" Tony: "It took him awhile to answer the door." Art: "He wasn't alone was he?" Tony: "I didn't see anybody." Art: "Don't lie. He had someone in his room, didn't he?" Tony: "I didn't see anyone." Art thought for a moment, "Did you hear someone else's voice?" Tony: "Yes." That precipitated an exchange of angry looks between Art and Jack and a few words were spoken between the teeth. After the air cleared, Jack made conversation with Tony. Eventually Jack invited Tony to join him and Art.

Jack: "We are all friends Tony. Art and I would like to help you out. What a man does by himself in the shower; we are willing to do that for you." Tony was horrified! Jack: "It's not homosexual Tony. Think of it as friends helping a friend." "Good friends, giving you a helping hand," Art said. Jack reiterated, "There's nothing homosexual about it Tony. It's something you already do yourself, we all do." Art insisted, "It would make it easier for you. Better too!" Tony burst out laughing, "Nothing homosexual about that!" Tony continued laughing. Art and Jack exchanged disappointed glances. When they got to the store, Tony stayed in the van.

Evolution

Tony was approaching the checkout desk in the main library when the phone rang. The seminarian manning the desk answered it. Eventually he said, "Evolution has been proven to be a fact. –That's right. –That's right. The Church now supports evolution as scientific fact. –Well, the Church has been proven wrong in the past and had to change its position before on other things–." After the seminarian hung up the phone, Tony asked, "When did the Church change its position on evolution?" The man at the desk tightened his jaw and ignored Tony.

One of Us

Tony left the main library and headed to the dorm. "Hi, Father," he said as he passed the Vice Rector. Vice Rector: "Tony." Tony continued down the long corridor. Greg ran past Tony toward the Vice Rector. Greg: "I just heard about Cardinal [name withheld]! They tell me he's the one most likely to replace the pope after he dies!" Vice Rector: "What's going on?" Greg: "They call him God's Rottweiler!" Vice Rector: "Calm down, what's the problem?" Greg: "They call Cardinal [name withheld] God's Rottweiler!" Vice Rector: "Forget that, it's just public relations, don't worry about it." Greg: "But they call him God's Rottweiler, and they tell me he works closely with the pope! He's the most likely to succeed the pope!" Greg was in a tizzy!

The priest calmly assured Greg, "There's no reason to worry. He is one of us." Greg: "But they call him God's Rottweiler!" Vice Rector: "Ignore that." Greg: "Why do they call Cardinal [name withheld] God's Rottweiler?" Vice Rector: "It's only public relations, it means nothing. He is one of us. There is nothing to worry about." Tony slowed his pace to listen, but when he was almost out of earshot, he stopped and looked back. The Vice Rector saw Tony trying to listen. He put his hand on Greg's shoulder to start him walking in the opposite direction. "He is one of us–" the Vice Rector said, lowering his voice and looking over his shoulder at Tony. Greg looked back and saw Tony stopped in the corridor. *Bad move Tony. You are slipping. You just calibrated the eavesdropping range for the Vice Rector.* Tony continued on his way. He could only hear the priest's hushed tones of reassurance to Greg.

> Deuteronomy 23:18 (DRA) [31] Thou shalt not offer the hire of a strumpet, nor the price of a dog, in the house of the Lord thy God, –.
>
> Deuteronomy 23:18 (RSV) [20] You shall not bring the hire of a harlot, or **the wages of a dog,** [t] into the house of the Lord your God–.
> [t] **Or *sodomite***
> (Bold type added by author.)

Evolution Discussed

The next time Tony's friends stopped to visit, he told them what he overheard in the library. Brian was incensed, "He actually said that to someone on the phone? Who was he talking to?" Tony: "I have no idea." Javier: "Someone called the Pontifical seminary library to do facts checking and that's what they got for an answer? Who was it? Who was the seminarian talking on the phone?" Tony described a medium height upperclassman. Javier: "I don't hate gays, but I never did like that guy. That is an outright lie! You're the scientist, Tony, what is the scientific community's current position?"

Tony: "Recently I read an article that discredited the notion that all life evolved from a single cell organism while it acknowledged short range evolution within species." Javier: "Was it definitive?" Tony: "I wouldn't call it definitive. It confirmed what I already thought, so I liked it. I don't see the scientific community can put this to rest any time soon, so I can't imagine the Church has a reason to change its position. What do you guys know? Has the Vatican published something on this?" Javier: "The pope recently made a speech to the Pontifical Academy of Sciences, known as *Truth Cannot Contradict Truth.* "–new knowledge has led to the recognition of the theory of evolution as more than a hypothesis."

I can see how that can be construed as a softening of his position on evolution, but in no way is that a reversal. That guy working in the library lied, pure and simple. Someone calls the Pontifical seminary library to facts check and they are lied to. That's messed up. How is someone supposed to know the truth?" Tony: "I have that same problem when I sit in class. Professors that I know are not trustworthy are feeding me tons of information. It can't all be lies, and yet I know I cannot trust all of it is true. When we graduate this place, how much incorrect information will we take with us without knowing it?" This thought was alarming to all four men.

Tony: "The Vice Rector is highly intuitive. He assigns work to students to best serve his long range plans." Brian: "What do you mean by that?" Tony: "He assigned a sociopath to manage the pub. His two pub snitches are affable, sociable, and well suited for the task." Brian: "Pub snitches?" Javier flushed. "I'll explain later," he told Brian. Tony: "The Vice Rector has his most trusted homosexuals in key communication positions such as the main library desk, the mailroom, student long distance accounts, and the pub." Brian laughed, "What is that supposed to accomplish?" Tony: "This gives the Vice Rector full control over monitoring the straight students and controlling the Jeroboam's public image." Brian scoffed.

Karl: "The three of us together saw the pub snitches in action–." Karl related the chicken wing outing to Brian. Brian: "The Vice Rector authorized the pub van and credit card to be used to entertain five students?" Tony: "To run a sting operation on the three of us, yes. My work assignment is in the theology dorm library where I have no strategic value and no public access." Karl: "What about the guy you work with?" Tony: "Mark is gay, but he's a Republican, so the Vice Rector has him in quarantine the same as me." Tony explained "Log Cabin Republican" and "The Enemy" to his friends and what he learned from Mark. Brian: "Lincoln was not gay. What makes you think he was?" Tony: "The homosexuals think he was. That's not something I worry about. I'm busy dealing with the homosexuals we've got here."

Brian: "The Jesuit asked me to sit at your table at the beginning of the year. Does that mean the administration knows I'm straight?" Tony: "The Jesuit assigned you, not the Vice Rector. No, it means the administration thought I would think so. The second upperclassman, Juan, appeared to be straight too." Javier: "But he's not. He had you fooled for a long time Tony." Each man reviewed his job assignment with the group. No one held a position of strategic value or trust that could compromise gay seminarians.

Brian looked dejected, "I was thinking about our last conversation. How did this happen? How did gays infiltrate the Church to begin with, much less take control?" Tony: "Looking at past events plus what I've seen here, I theorize pedophiles infiltrated first, at least in the U.S. They would have been impossible to detect in an all-adult environment. They could have snuck in and held the door open for the "adult" homosexuals. That scenario is the most efficient. Such a long-term infiltration requires coordination. It's less likely each group infiltrated independently, given that pedophiles appeared first. As always, evil colludes with evil." Brian: "How could they move up the ranks?" Tony: "Once they controlled low level chokepoints they were guaranteed victory through attrition. Such a plan requires a long time horizon."

Modern behavioral testing techniques can effectively screen out both pedophiles and homosexuals before admission to the seminary. Since the Church embraced psychology sometime before the mid-1990s, why isn't this being done? Third party (or Board) oversight is necessary to prevent perverts from running the tests and screening out straights.

Javier: "What are low level chokepoints?" Tony: "The vocation director of the diocese is a chokepoint. All seminary candidates in the diocese pass under that one man's purview. I don't imagine it's a prized position, but the power it offers infiltrators is tremendous." Brian: "What does that accomplish?" Tony: "That man turns away true callings and allows homosexuals to enter the seminary. He steers his incoming confederates to targeted seminaries and overwhelms them over time." Brian: "How do students take over a seminary?" Tony: "Flood one level, infiltrate the next level up, and repeat the process to move further up. With a long enough time horizon, you can climb all the way to the top. One of my instructors was a student here in the early 70s."

Brian was glum, "Wasn't there any way to stop them?" Tony: "During the 1960s, women confessing they used birth control were refused forgiveness unless they stopped. Some women told their girlfriends when they found a priest that forgave using birth control. There were priests who told women inside the confessional, "The pill is good for your nerves." Those priests were probably homosexual infiltrators. Certainly, they were infidels. Those women supported bad priests and shunned good ones. If the reprobate priests had been reported to the bishop, they would have been defrocked, and infidels would not be in control of the Church today. Evil colludes with evil. If bishops took proper action in full measure, infidels could not have climbed higher up the ladder."

> *"Who is going to save our Church? Not our bishops, not our priests and religious. It is up to the people. You have the minds, the eyes, the ears to save the Church. Your mission is to see that your priests act like priests, your bishops like bishops and your religious act like religious."* [36]
> *Archbishop Fulton J. Sheen (1895-1979).* [36]

Karl: "If the bishops defrocked pedophile priests instead of sweeping them under the rug, they could've put a stop to this. Things never would have gone this far." Tony: "So much for psychology in the Church. Psychology recognizes there is no chance of rehabilitating pedophiles, but bishops send pedophile priests to rehab anyway." *Yet behavioral testing methods are not applied to screen out pedophile and homosexual candidates.* Javier: "The Bible says don't talk about my priests. That's why people don't make trouble for priests." Tony: "It also says to bear witness, and that the Lord loves justice and truth. The Bible tells us to talk and not to talk. We need to discern which one to do at what time." Brian: "Do you think the Church will die out?" Tony: "I think it is dying."

Javier laughed, "You Americans think the United States is the whole world. It's not! Get over yourselves. The Church is stronger today than it has ever been. Tony, what did the Church in the U.S. do during the 1960s?" Tony: "We sent missionaries to Africa and South America. The diocese where I grew up sponsored missionaries to Kenya." Javier: "And what happened?" Tony: "I don't know. We were told they were successful." Javier: "They were wildly successful. The Church has grown so fast in both Africa and South America there is no way to minister to all the faithful. Their explosive growth is happening while the Church in the United States and Europe is dying. Overall, the Church is growing at an accelerating rate." Karl nodded agreement.

Tony: "What about the Vatican?" Javier: "That problem won't go away until South America and Africa can start sending cardinals to Rome. This pope is our last straight pope. Don't expect a future pope to be straight until we get one from Africa or South America." Brian objected, "The United States still has some good bishops." Javier explained the process of selecting cardinals, and who gets sent to Rome. Now that infidels are in control of the process, it is unlikely a holy man would be allowed to move up the ranks. Tony: "Once homosexuals take control of the top position it's game over." Javier passionately disagreed, "God said He will stay with His Church until the end of time!" *(But the Roman Church split from Orthodoxy, the one true Holy Apostolic Church, nearly a thousand years ago.)*

Tony: "Then the end of time is going to happen on our watch. He destroyed His temple in Jerusalem after the effeminate polluted His sanctuary." Karl: "Twice. He destroyed His temple twice, both times to cleanse it." Tony: "Maybe God will just chastise us like in the time of Noah. (Genesis 6:11, "Now the earth was corrupt in God's sight, and the earth was filled with violence.")." Javier: "Chastise! There were only eight people on the Ark!" Brian and Javier thought God would protect His Church, and they were confused by the current situation.

Tony: "God destroyed Solomon's temple when the temple was polluted with homosexuals." Karl: "The Byzantine Church prays to the Holy Spirit during Mass to protect the Church. The Roman Church used to pray to Saint Michael the Archangel to protect the Church, but they stopped using that prayer after Vatican II. Stewardship of the Church is the responsibility of everyone who has received Confirmation, but what can we do against an overwhelming infiltration of homosexuals that goes up to the highest levels?" Everyone was silent.

Tony: "Mentioning Noah got me thinking about the rainbow, God's covenant with mankind after the deluge. Homosexuals have desecrated the rainbow by using it as their symbol." Tony told his friends how his classmates have been giving him the business. He told them about "yabba dabba doo," how his classmates despoiled a children's cartoon. Tony: "Their latest business is to tell me they are all the same and I'm the freak. I am the one that does not belong here. I am the one that's not normal, I am not like them." Brian: "What makes them think they're normal and you're not?" Karl: "They are the freaks Tony, we are normal."

Tony: "They have a point. On this campus, they outnumber us by more than three to one. They took the "I don't belong here" line from something I said in core board last semester. I was not like Californians. I didn't belong in California, so I left. The queers are telling mc to leave, just like I left California." Karl: "You aren't going to are you?" Tony: "I will leave, just not the way they want me to." Brian: "When did they tell you this?" Tony: "Every chance they get; before class, after class, during meals, in transit between classes. This semester they have started a new strategy. They don't just heckle; they wear me out with the same piece of business." Brian: "Why would they do that?"

Tony: "To get my blood pressure up. It's working, and they know it." Javier agreed Tony was starting to look the worse for wear. Javier told Tony it was not too late for him to transfer to another seminary. Tony: "I don't want to transfer. I don't see myself taking a vow of obedience to a homosexual bishop." Javier chuckled, "People might think you've got issues with authority Tony." Tony: "People would be absolutely correct if they stipulate corrupt authority, and this bunch here adds a whole new dimension to the concept of corrupt." Everyone was sad to be reminded.

Pope's Address

Javier stopped by Tony's after lunch Saturday. Tony asked for his help, "I want to write to the pope and tell him what goes on here. How can I find the pope's mailing address?" Javier: "Do not use my name! You can never mention my name! You see how these queers are. I know you. You have to do the right thing. You can't help yourself. You won't be able to let it go. You won't rest until you do the right thing. Are you crazy? Why don't you take on something you can handle, like the mob? Why don't you just go after the mob? At least the mob will only kill you. Do not go after these queers! There's no winning with them. They will all tell the same lie and you are only one person. Who is going to believe you when two priests and four seminarians are telling the same lies about you?"

Tony promised he would not include Javier in his letter to the pope. After repeating his promise five or six times, Javier calmed down. Javier: "It won't do any good to write to the pope. The pope is an important man. He doesn't open his own mail. When the guy who opens his mail sees the letter is about a Pontifical college, he will forward the letter to the cardinal in charge of colleges. The pope will never see your letter." Tony: "Do you know who is in charge of the Pontifical colleges?" He did. Tony wanted the mailing address of both the pope and the cardinal in charge of the colleges. Javier: "What will that accomplish? If the man who opens the pope's mail is gay, he will see your letter is about gay misconduct and throw the letter away. The pope will never see your letter."

Tony: "If I send the pope a letter and carbon copy the cardinal, both guys will know the other one has a copy of the letter. If there is any chance of the pope seeing my letter, this is my best shot." Javier: "It's still a long shot, but there is a slim chance it could work. Even if the pope never sees your letter, the cardinal will know you are determined to see corrective action. For internal politics alone, this plan could accomplish something. It won't be anything meaningful, but some sort of action will be taken simply to make you lose interest." Javier agreed to help.

The two men went to the library. Javier found the book he was looking for. It had addresses for all the various offices of the Vatican written in Italian. Tony: "I can't read Italian." Javier was surprised, "You're Italian. Can you speak Italian?" Tony: "No. When my grandfather came to this country he learned English." Javier smiled, "I learned Italian before I went to the Vatican my junior year." Javier got both names and addresses for Tony.

The two men left the library. Javier was grave, "Do not use my name." Tony: "I won't. You went to the Vatican for your junior year?" Javier: "That's right." Tony: "And you were still a junior last fall? What happened?" Javier: "My mother got sick my second semester. It was a chronic illness. I had to leave school to take care of her. I was still a junior last fall. I am a senior now. I have one more semester after this."

Amazing Grace

The seminarian in charge of managing logistics for the campus church was a quiet man. His face evidenced former employment in a steel mill. "Tony, everyone takes a turn selecting the music for Sunday service. Next Sunday is your turn to choose the music for Mass. Here is the book to draw your selections from."

The next day Tony turned in his selections, including Amazing Grace and the Battle Hymn of the Republic. "We can't use these Tony. These songs are appropriate for a different time of the year if we could use them, but we cannot. Amazing Grace is about slavery. It is insulting to Blacks. The Battle Hymn of the Republic is insulting to Southerners."

Tony disagreed, "Black choirs sing Amazing Grace. What makes you think Battle Hymn of the Republic is insulting to Southerners?" "I'm a Southerner, and I find Battle Hymn of the Republic to be offensive." Tony: "I don't see how." "Trampling out the vintage where the grapes of wrath are stored. The grapes of wrath are Confederates, Southerners. Trampling out the vintage is the Northern army defeating the Confederacy. I am not the only Southerner here at the Pontifical. The other Southerners are as insulted by it as I am. Here, take the book and try again. Make appropriate selections for next Sunday."

Irish Priest

Sunday Mass was held in the church for the entire campus. The church was also used for holy days, Lent, and special occasions. Tony's turn to serve on the altar of the church came due on a weekday during Lent. Tony performed his duties. After Mass, Tony was returning the cassock to its hanger when the priest made friendly conversation. The silver haired priest flew in from Ireland. With his sparkling accent, he told Tony how he first came to know the Pontifical Jeroboam, how he likes to come to visit for a week every year around the same time, schedule permitting.

The priest told Tony what his interest in the Jeroboam is, and the things he enjoys during his visits. Tony listened to the priest's friendly voice and colorful accent. Tony noted the twinkling in the priest's eyes as he told of his early association with the Jeroboam. As the timeline of his story moved toward the present, Tony saw the twinkling diminish, dim, and then extinguish. The priest asked Tony, "What is it currently like being a theology student at the Jeroboam?"

He knows what happened to his beloved seminary. He is afraid it is true, but hopes it is not. He is looking for confirmation of his suspicions. Like the nun, I want to help him but I don't dare. This is crazy, being afraid to tell a priest the truth about this place.

Tony answered the priest in a halting, uneasy manner. While his words said: "I like it here, everything is fine," his halting, wavering voice, and his body language told of unspoken horror. The priest was startled! Tony saw understanding in the priest's eyes. The priest's fears and suspicions were confirmed. The priest attempted to make more small talk, but was too rattled, and excused himself. His parting well wishes were beautifully and distinctly Irish.

After dinner that evening, Javier and Karl stopped by Tony's room to say hi. Tony told them of the visiting priest from Ireland and his conversation. Javier blurted, "I hope you didn't tell him! You don't know who he is. You can't trust him!" Tony explained how he tersely quoted the company line, but made it obvious it was not true. Javier: "How can you be sure he got the message?" Karl assured Javier, "Tony did the right thing. He did the only thing he could." Tony: "When the priest was young, the Jeroboam was a great place, and he loved it. He indicated there were changes in the early 70s and he has had concerns ever since. He was looking to me to confirm his suspicions."

Javier: "You don't know who this guy knows!" Tony: "By saying everything is fine while looking and sounding tense, I confirmed his concerns are well founded. If he were unable to do anything about this for over two decades, my giving him specific information would prove useless. I felt bad I couldn't give him full disclosure." Karl and Javier agreed. You feel guilty no matter what you do. Talk, don't talk, you crashed into our culture's strongest taboos in every direction. Action or inaction, you feel dreadfully guilty no matter what you do. On a lighter note, Tony shared the parting well wishes of the priest. They loved it too.

12 PSYCHOLOGICAL WARFARE

Javier

There was an excited knock on Tony's door. Javier: "Have you heard the latest? The Rector contacted my bishop to get me thrown out. He wanted to expel me immediately. I begged the Rector to wait until after Monday. When he asked why, I told him I cannot get my green card until Monday. I am here on a student visa. If I am expelled before Monday, I will no longer be a student and will not be eligible for a green card. It will be a death sentence for me. I will have to leave the United States and return to my country. All of the men in my family were killed by political enemies. I am still alive because I was in the United States when the men in my family were killed. If I return to my country, they will kill me too. When I told the Rector, he smiled this evil smirk. I can't describe it and I know it sounds funny, but it sent chills down my spine."

Tony reassured him, "I know exactly what you mean. I've seen that same smirk myself." Javier: "The Rector was happy to hear this and was determined to have me expelled by the end of the day! I called my bishop and begged him to allow me to get my green card so I could stay in the United States. I explained to him why I would be killed if I returned to my country. He told me to make sure I get my paperwork done on Monday because I will be expelled on Tuesday no matter what. I thanked him again and again. I was still thanking him when he hung up. He called the Rector and told him I had until Tuesday.

The Rector was angry my bishop allowed me the chance to get my green card. The Rector actually wanted me to be killed! I couldn't believe it! Do you believe this guy? He was disappointed I was not going to be killed!" Tony: "I have seen enough of the Rector to know what you're saying is true." Javier: "But he's a priest! More than that, he's the Rector! How can he want me to be murdered? Why would he want me to be murdered?"

Osee 6:9 (DRA) [31] And like the jaws of highway robbers, they conspire with the priests who murder in the way those that pass out of Sichem: for they have wrought wickedness.

Hosea 6:9 (RSV) [20] As robbers lie in wait for a man, so the priests are banded together; they murder on the way to Shechem, yea, they commit villainy.

Hosea 6:9 (KJV) [32] And as troops of robbers wait for a man, so the company of priests murder in the way of consent: for they commit lewdness.

Osee 5:1 (DRA) [31] Hear ye this, O priests, and hearken, O ye house of Israel, and give ear, O house of the king: for there is a judgment against you, because you have been a snare to them whom you should have watched over, and a net spread upon Thabor.

Tony: "When the queers call us "The Enemy," that's exactly what they mean." Javier: "What am I going to do? I bought a used car from that tall guy who works with you in the library. I didn't realize the car has a stick shift. I don't know how to drive a stick. Can you teach me how to drive a stick shift?" Tony: "Sure, no problem."

Javier: "There's something else. The nearest immigration office is a six-hour drive from here. Can you drive me there Monday? I'm afraid I'll get lost and not make it there on time. My life actually depends on it! Can you? Will you?" Tony: "I'll have to skip all of my classes Monday." Javier: "Monday is the only day I can go to get my green card. I cannot go earlier. I am not eligible until Monday. My bishop told me I have to get it Monday!" Tony was loath to cut his classes. Javier pointed out, "You'll leave or they'll chase you out before the end of the semester, so what does it matter?" Tony: "Yeah, you're right. Ok, I'll blow off classes Monday. We'll have to leave right after breakfast."

Javier: "Thank you! Thank you so much! You don't know what this means to me!" Tony: "Sure I do. It means you get to live." Javier: "Yes! Yes it does! That's exactly what it means!" Javier thought for a moment and smiled, "You realize once I'm gone they're coming after you?" Tony: "I know." Javier: "So, what are you going to do?" Tony: "I watched what they did to you. I watched four guys trying to concoct a lie sufficient to get you thrown out. They worked on their lies for months. Lies, slander, and psychological warfare: they did all of these things to you. I'm not going to allow them the satisfaction of grinding me up the same way. I'll leave shortly after you."

Javier: "They did the same thing to Jake. Remember Jake? He is from your diocese. This past year he has been staying with his sister. All he does is drink. He was not a drinker when he came here, but he has a real drinking problem now.

Don't let them get to you the way they got to Jake." Tony: "That's good advice for me and you both." Javier nodded agreement with a sad look on his face. The next two days Tony went to his classes but spent time teaching Javier how to drive a stick shift. They practiced Saturday and Sunday too. Tony forgot his library duties for Saturday morning.

Bye Javier

Brian, Karl, and Javier gathered in Tony's room after dinner Sunday. Tony offered to take everyone out for drinks, but Brian and Karl had studying to do. Javier did not feel like going out. Everyone felt bad for Javier. They chuckled at Tony, saying he was next. Brian: "What are you going to do?" Tony: "I don't intend to give them the satisfaction. I'll leave before they can slander me the way they did Javier." Brian: "When people ask you why you left the seminary, what are you going to tell them?" Tony: "I'm going to tell them the truth." Javier, Brian, and Karl turned white. Javier: "You can't do that! You know what people will think!"

Tony: "Yes, they're going to think I'm a queer. When I tell them the place was full of queers, something stupid inside their head will say, "He said queer! Must be he's a queer!"" Everyone was silent. Brian: "Tony, don't do it. If you tell people about gays in the seminary, and you left because of it, they won't believe you." Karl added, "They will think you are one." Javier agreed, "That's a mistake. Don't tell anyone. Why would you?" Tony: "In the Old Testament we are told to bear witness. God loves honesty. If I don't tell people about the queers, how will they ever know? The Jesuit is on my core board and is my formation director. During my first core board he gushed that I was the first genuine calling from the Old Testament he has seen in many years."

Brian started to speak but Tony cut him off, "I know, he wasn't supposed to tell me he thought my calling was genuine, but he did, and he thought it was from Jeremiah. It doesn't bother me that I'm not going to be able to be a priest. For me to leave here and not tell people what I saw would be so wrong. If I was called here to bear witness, I must do it. If I fail to bear witness, I have not fulfilled my calling." Javier: "But you can't tell anyone! They won't believe you! They will think you're gay!" Tony: "If I don't bear witness against the queers, they win." Javier: "If you do, you lose and they win anyway."

Tony: "I know you're right. That still doesn't talk me out of it. What you've said tells me there is no downside. Whether I bear witness or not people will think I was kicked out. They won't believe I quit. If I do not bear witness, I have failed my calling; I have failed God. I lose. No matter what, the queers win the day. I hate it when the bad guy wins. I'm going to tell everyone the truth, not just my family, everyone. When they ask what happened, I'm going to tell them." Brian, Karl, and Javier were aghast! Tony: "Do you guys intend to tell people what you saw here?" The three men shook their heads no and admitted as much in low, small voices.

Tony: "You guys have no intention of bearing witness against these criminals because you're afraid to say the word queer?" Brian: "What criminals?" Tony: "Slander, bearing false witness; these are criminal offenses. I thought the Eighth

Commandment was "Thou shall not bear false witness." Look at what these malefactor infidels did to Jake. Several witnesses lied on numerous occasions to and about Jake. More than one priest and a counselor colluded with lying seminarians to drive Jake over the edge. It's tough to gather physical evidence for a crime like that, but it's a crime. Look at what shape Jake is in today. We can't bear witness on Jake's behalf because we are too afraid to say the word queer in court?"

Javier: "Look at what they've been doing to me!" Karl snarled, "You brought some of that on yourself." Javier flushed. Tony: "Jake was squeaky clean, yes?" Brian shrugged, "I didn't really know him." Karl and Javier both nodded yes. Tony: "The administration, a counselor, and homosexual seminarians colluded to do serious and irreparable harm to Jake. They colluded to use psychological warfare and a series of lies and false testimony. That is criminal. That is patently illegal. They did serious harm to Jake. We will not go to court on Jake's behalf because we will not stand up in open court against a bunch of queer clergy and queer seminarians."

> Job 36:13-14 (DRA) [31] 13 Dissemblers and crafty men prove the wrath of God, neither shall they cry when they are bound. 14 Their soul shall die in a storm, and their life among the effeminate.
>
> Job 36:13-14 (RSV) [20] 13 "The godless in heart cherish anger; they do not cry for help when he binds them. 14 They die in youth, and their life ends in shame. [b]
> [b] Heb *among the cult prostitutes*

Brian demurred, "A bunch of priests and seminarians. What is the testimony of one witness against that of several priests and seminarians?" Tony: "That's right. That's why they isolate their victim, so there is no second witness to the truth. I witnessed four reprobate students conspiring against Javier: Mr. Stevens, David, Greg, and the guy from Minnesota. I witnessed several of their mealtime meetings starting early in the fall semester. As they ate, they discussed their most recent lie, why the Rector rejected it, and plotted their next move. I told Javier about this skullduggery, but what could he do about it? I can't prosecute those four men on Javier's behalf because there is no second witness." There was a long silence.

Karl: "What can we do?" Tony: "We need hard evidence we can take to court." Javier: "Like what?" Tony: "I don't know, but they can't be allowed to keep ordaining atheists and destroying honest applicants who answer the call." Brian objected, "How many of your classmates don't believe in God?" Tony: "Three of the four." Brian: "You don't know they will make it through core board. They may never be ordained." Tony: "The one guy that believes in God can't handle the academics." Brian: "You don't know who will get dropped because of core board." Tony: "I told Javier, I don't think I told you. I went to my first core board on Tuesday night. The Vice Rector is one of the five people on my core board. The next day my four classmates ate with me so they could rehash my core board interview."

Brian and Karl were shocked! Tony: "The next month it happened again, my classmates rehashed my core board from the night before." Karl: "Did you report it?" Tony: "Report it to whom, the Vice Rector? Isn't this exactly what they did to Jake? I report this to the Rector, and the Vice Rector and my four classmates all deny it. Somehow, I don't expect that will work real smooth." There was a long silence. Javier: "I didn't meet you until Halloween. How did you know to not report it?" Tony: "The few holy priests I found here warned me reporting homosexual activity brings reprisals. Even the holy priests fear the jaundiced attention of the administration. From their dread and their warnings I induced straight seminarians are personally destroyed, not simply vilified or expelled."

Several moments of silence. Brian said softly, "You think the Vice Rector is telling your classmates the dialogue from your core board, don't you?" Tony: "Yes. The Vice Rector is a criminal genius. He has turned a Pontifical seminary into a queers club, but it still looks like a seminary. How did you spend four years here without seeing this?" Brian: "Well, I guess I've known all along something was wrong. Remember you dropped off some papers on my desk when I left my door open?" Karl and Javier wanted to know what that was about. Tony: "I was in a hurry, and Brian's door was open. I took the liberty of going in and placing the papers on Brian's desk." Brian turned deep red. Javier: "Why is that embarrassing?" Tony: "The room smelled like Brian."

Javier: "Big deal, I'm sure my room smells like me." Tony: "No, this was different. It smelled like Brian died and his rotting corpse was under the mountain of dirty clothes on the floor." Javier and Karl exchanged blank stares. Brian was still red-faced, "It was the dirty clothes." Javier objected, "Dirty clothes don't smell that bad." Brian: "My clothes do. I wear them for more than one day. I do it on purpose to make sure they smell. People keep their distance. I was never slovenly until I came here. I did this in self-defense. After four years, I forgot I was doing it. I'm glad Tony reminded me. I guess this place messed me up a lot more than I realized." Tony: "I wondered how you survived four years without knowing what was going on."

Brian: "I guess I knew all along, I just didn't want to admit it." Javier: "It's called denial." Karl: "He's probably more careful than Tony about using the word queer." Everyone laughed. Javier: "They're doing a number on Tony. The other night I wanted to talk to him. I called on the phone so he'd be expecting me. He left his door unlocked so I wouldn't have to knock. When I got there, he was staring at the wall. The look on his face scared me. His body was in the room, but his mind was somewhere else. You're not going to make it Tony. It's good you plan on leaving before they screw with your head. From what I saw, they have already screwed you up. I hope you've set a date you plan to leave."

Tony: "I really want to hold out until Easter." Javier: "I don't think you're going to make it. You have a good idea; leave before they do serious damage. I mean no disrespect Tony, but it's already too late. What I saw the other night wasn't good. You should consider packing your things." Javier persisted in trying to convince Tony to set a departure date. Karl intervened, "Tony's already making arrangements." Tony: "What makes you think so?" Karl: "Three times in the past two weeks I saw you go out to the parking lot early in the afternoon. You never leave campus. Suddenly you're leaving during business hours. I expect you went to an insurance agent." Tony: "That was the first thing I did." Javier's jaw dropped. Brian blanched.

Karl: "I saw you smuggle packing boxes in Wednesday night. Your timing was perfect. No one was around to see you." Tony was surprised, "I didn't see you. I thought I pulled it off, that I went undetected." Karl smiled. Javier: "So when do you plan on leaving?" Tony: "You're leaving Tuesday. It will be after that. I'll see how it goes, but I expect the worst." Everyone was glum and silent. Tony wished Javier the best and asked him to stay in touch. Tony wrote his contact information on a 3.5" x 5" index card and gave it to Javier. Javier: "If you're leaving, how can I mail you a letter?" Tony: "I'll leave a forwarding address with the U.S. Post Office, not with the school. I'll get your letters." The three wished Javier well and asked him to stay in touch. Everyone was sad.

Immigration

After breakfast Monday, Tony and Javier made the long drive to the immigration office. Shortly before three p.m., the two stood in a dingy, dimly lit hallway in front of a counter. Javier handed his paperwork to the young woman on duty. She picked up a rubber stamp, hit an inkpad, and then hit his paperwork. She picked up a second stamp and repeated the motions. She handed Javier some crisp looking papers. After a long pause Tony asked, "Is that it?" The woman looked confused, "What did you expect?" Tony turned to Javier and shook his hand, "Welcome to America!" Javier smiled. The woman's confusion turned into a smile, "Yes, welcome." The two men returned to the truck and started the long drive back to campus. Javier had his green card.

Tuesday morning Tony cut a class to give Javier one more practice session. Tony: "How can you drive without a license?" Javier: "I still have my international license. It will be valid long enough for me to get a regular license. The Rector told me breakfast is my last meal here. I have to be gone before lunch." Javier's mood was understandably dark. Javier: "I have a lot to do between now and noon. I have to get going and you have library duty today don't forget." Tony: "Thanks. I did forget. Let me give you some traveling money before you go." Javier: "I sold all my books and some other things to raise cash. I have money. I don't want to take your money." Tony wished Javier well and asked him to stay in touch. Javier was unresponsive.

Appointment

Last fall the Rector took a trip: first to China, then to the Vatican, and was gone for a month. Now, the Vice Rector was on vacation. It was finally time for Tony to meet with the Rector. Tony wanted to meet before the Vice Rector returned from vacation. Tony wished to discuss a couple of inconsequential items with the Rector. He called the Rector's office to make an appointment. The Rector's schedule had an opening the following week. Tony sat in his room at his desk, staring at the wall. He intended to study. His book was open, but he was staring at the wall. When Tony snapped out of it, he realized he missed another afternoon class. If he ran directly to class, he would be disruptive and only catch the last twenty minutes. He decided against it.

After dinner, Brian and Karl stopped by Tony's room. They said Javier showed no intention of keeping in touch. Karl: "He's been through a lot. I would be surprised if any of us hear from him again. Did he tell you guys how they finally got him expelled?" Brian: "No, he didn't say anything to me." Tony: "Yeah, he told me on the drive back from the immigration office." Karl: "He told me too. Why would anyone believe something so ridiculous?" The bizarre lies four gay seminarians concocted got Javier expelled. Javier's bishop was able to confirm the Rector's report that Javier dated a woman in the parish where he interned. That truth gave credibility to the outrageous and convoluted lies four gay seminarians told about Javier. The Minnesota gay's alcohol was the foundation those lies were built on.

Missed Appointment

Shortly after Tony sat down to lunch Wednesday, the Shrink Lady asked if she could join him. Tony: "Sure." Shrink Lady: "How is everything going Tony?" "Fine," he said reflexively. Shrink Lady: "Where were you Monday? You missed our appointment. You didn't call or leave a message. I didn't know what happened to you. I was worried." Tony: "Oh– I forgot all about it." Shrink Lady: "Are you sure there are no problems?" Tony: "I'm sorry." Shrink Lady: "I understand you missed all of your classes Monday. How did that happen?" Tony: "I drove my friend to the immigration office. We left after breakfast and got back late. I cut a class Tuesday morning to help him before he left." Shrink Lady: "That's commendable Tony, but you should have told someone where you were going. You had everyone worried."

Tony: "It never occurred to me. I was running an errand." Shrink Lady: "An errand that made you body absent all day. People were worried about you Tony. I didn't know what to think when you didn't show up for our appointment. You are always so prompt." Tony: "I'm sorry. I did not intend to be rude." Shrink Lady: "You took your friend to immigration to renew his visa?" Tony: "No, to get his green card. The woman stamped some papers and that was it. I shook his hand and said, "Welcome to America."" Shrink Lady: "That must have made him feel good." Tony: "It did. He needed something to cheer him up. He was expelled. He had to leave yesterday."

Shrink Lady: "Maybe that's why you've been so uncharacteristically irresponsible this week. You must be depressed your friend had to leave. You also missed a class yesterday afternoon, why was that?" Tony: "I was tired from putting in a long day Monday." Shrink Lady: "Sometimes when people are depressed they sleep. You don't have to wait until next month to make another appointment. When you are ready to talk, call my office and make an appointment. We have to schedule your next appointment anyway." Tony: "Thank you. I appreciate your pointing these things out to me." The Shrink Lady excused herself. She said she promised to have lunch with a faculty member. She took her partially eaten lunch to the faculty table.

Formation Director March

Tony went to his evening meeting with his formation director. The Jesuit was especially cheeky. Jesuit: "I understand you think there is homosexual activity going on here at the seminary," he chuckled. Tony: "Yes Father, there is." The priest's voice flashed with anger, "I suppose you have proof of this?" Tony: "Physical evidence? No Father, I only have my own eyewitness." Jesuit: "There is no homosexual activity here at the Pontifical Jeroboam Tony! You are paranoid and delusional. The next time you see homosexual activity photograph it so you have proof." He chuckled some more. Tony did not share the priest's sense of humor. The Jesuit moved on to the business of the meeting.

Photographs

The next day Tony's classmates joined him at lunch. Mr. Stevens smiled, "I understand you think there is homosexual activity here Tony." Tony: "That's the same thing the Jesuit said. He was cross when he asked me if I had proof. Then he laughed and said to take photographs the next time I see homosexual activity so I have proof." Tony's classmates laughed. Tony: "He's an old man. He does not understand technology. I can rent a professional camera and tripod and use infrared film. I'll get more pictures than he can stomach looking at." The four classmate's mouths dropped open. They stared at Tony. Greg: "What would you photograph?"

Tony: "I can walk down the hall after ten p.m., set the camera and tripod in front of each dorm room door, and take a picture. With the proper lens, a 35 mm camera will take excellent pictures through the closed door." They demanded to know what Tony knew of such equipment. Tony described the professional camera equipment he owned until his house was robbed. Greg objected, "The only thing you'll have on film are red shadows, you won't be able to make a positive identification."

Tony: "Not when I rent professional equipment. The detail will scare you. Besides, the room number on the door already identifies one occupant or the lack thereof. I'm guessing half the rooms will be empty. The rest will have two men inside. Odds are good some photographs will show men in compromised positions or interesting poses. When the Vice Rector gets on my case for taking such pictures, I simply explain my formation director told me to." Hearing this paralyzed all four of Tony's classmates. They exchanged glances and their faces turned white. Everyone finished their meal in total silence. *Miracles still happen!*

Shrink Lady March

The Shrink Lady saw Tony at lunch Friday. "Hi Tony, you never rescheduled the meeting you missed. I have an opening after lunch if you're available." Tony: "Sure. One o'clock?" "One o'clock," she smiled.

After lunch, Tony went to the Shrink Lady's office. She stood behind her desk fidgeting. Shrink Lady: "Welcome Tony, it's good to see you. I understand you've been busy." Tony: "No more than usual." Shrink Lady: "I understand you've recently taken up photography as a hobby." Tony: "Your understanding is misinformed unless you consider twenty years ago is recent." The Shrink Lady was caught off stride. She comported herself, "Did you talk about photography to your classmates recently?" Tony: "Yes."

Shrink Lady: "What did your formation director have to do with that conversation?" Tony: "At our last meeting he was especially cheeky, taunting me to get photographic evidence the next time I witness homosexual activity." Shrink Lady: "How did this make you feel?" Tony: "I laugheth not." She considered this–, "So, you've been taking photographs?" Tony: "No." Shrink Lady: "No? I thought you said your formation director told you to." Tony: "He did." Shrink Lady: "I don't understand." Tony: "He was taunting me. His idea of photography is taking happy snaps with an Instamatic ®. I used to own a real camera." Shrink Lady: "Used to?" Tony: "Yes, until a burglar stole it six or eight years ago. I never replaced it." Shrink Lady: "What did you tell your classmates?"

Tony: "I told them I had such equipment until it was stolen. I described the capabilities that camera had. Renting similar equipment is cheap, and I can blame it on my formation director." The Shrink Lady sat down, "Why did you tell them that? Why would you warn them you would be taking pictures?" Tony: "I don't want a bunch of pictures that amount to homosexual porn, and I certainly don't care to take them. That would be a formation problem, having a stack of photos of seminarians in congress." Shrink Lady: "I should say so! You did say your PFD told you to get photographic evidence." Tony: "If I do that, he will deny ever saying it, and he said it twice. He messed with me with that same piece of business at the beginning of the school year. He didn't give me an imperative, he was messing with me."

Shrink Lady: "So you messed with him by telling your classmates." Tony: "How very trite of me." Shrink Lady: "How did your classmates react?" Tony: "Since they are homosexually active, they were scared out of their minds." Shrink Lady: "The administration is vigilant to ensure there is no homosexual activity on campus!" Tony: "The absence of surveillance cameras in the dorm hallways proves that is a boldfaced lie." Shrink Lady: "What are you feeling right now?" Tony: "My recent spate of ill humor tells the story. You have a PhD in shrinkology and you have to ask?" The Shrink Lady flushed, "I don't have my doctorate. I'm still taking classes. That's why I took this job, to finish putting myself through school." Tony: "That explains why you were so self-conscious about my choosing you for a counselor."

Shrink Lady: "You really didn't know?" Tony: "No, I didn't. Like I said before, you won by default." Shrink Lady: "Earlier you said you think the FBI and the military effectively use psychology, but you don't respect counseling, human resources, or the court's use of psychology. What's the difference?" Tony: "Quantum mechanics works because it uses statistics. Try to locate one electron at a precise moment and it doesn't work. Apparently, the same goes for psychology. It works if you properly apply statistics and numerical methods to a sufficiently large population. The FBI uses sophisticated mathematical analysis and statistics. It does a job for them." Shrink Lady: "You don't seem to respect counseling. You refer to it as shrinkology."

Tony: "When straight doctors ran psychology, they diagnosed homosexuals as mentally ill. The cure was to reprogram their brain, like in the book, *A Clockwork Orange*. What is the ontology of the subject after being treated? No moral problems there, right?" Shrink Lady: "Homosexuality was removed from the DSM in 1973. Homosexuality is no longer a mental illness." Tony: "Now, people who shun homosexuals have a mental problem, they are homophobic. Who do I think runs psychology now?" Shrink Lady: "That is a dramatic oversimplification." Tony: "I like to think of it as clarity." After a long pause the Shrink Lady asked, "What did you expect to accomplish by embarrassing your formation director?" Tony: "I didn't have any expectations."

Shrink Lady: "Your discussion of photography with your classmates was meant to scare them?" Tony: "They did seem overly concerned." She paused, –then asked, "Are you planning to leave the seminary?" Tony: "No, I am not making plans of any sort." Shrink Lady: "It seems you are. Antagonizing your classmates and embarrassing your formation director are not the actions of someone who plans on living and working with these people for the next three years." Tony: "Four years. I'm a transfer student. I'm in a five-year program." *There was more conversation. It was and remains a blur.* The Shrink Lady decided Tony was uncooperative and unproductive. She ended the session early.

After Tony left the Shrink Lady's office, he realized he had given up actionable intel. She got Tony to divulge that 10 of the 11 foreign students were straight. Tony was so ashamed! He compromised the foreign seminarians! *SHIT! –Merde! Merde! Merde! Pardon my French.* Tony stayed too long. *They broke me! They broke me and I'm still not finished.* Tony returned to his room. He stared at the wall for a long time and then took a nap. When he awoke, he was late for music class. He grabbed his books and ran to class. When he got there, the room was empty. Tony's head was swimming. This was the second time he missed music class. He understood he could not hang on until Easter break.

The Jesuit's Counsel

Saturday evening the Jesuit phoned Tony and said to come to his office at once. When Tony arrived, the Jesuit was furious! His ranting indicated he believed Tony had taken photos of homosexual activity. The Jesuit handed Tony a handwritten memo (Appendix 1) signed and dated, asking for the photographic evidence Tony offered to show him at their last meeting. *What?* Tony: "What photos Father? You told me to take pictures, but I don't own a camera." Jesuit: "I am not a homosexual Tony! I am obedient to my superiors! I am not homosexual." Tony: "Evil colludes with evil Father. The military is required to disobey illegal orders. Certainly priests must disobey immoral orders."

The Jesuit was livid! He glared at Tony long and hard. The veins in his forehead and neck distended. When he could speak again, the old priest said, "When I was eight years old, both of my parents died in an automobile crash. My younger sister and I were placed in a Catholic orphanage. I was raised by the Catholic Church almost my entire life. I was an altar boy in grade school. I attended a Jesuit high school. I went on to be ordained a priest. My sister became a nun. I owe everything to the Church. I am and always will be loyal to the Catholic Church. I will protect the Church every way I can."

Tony was disappointed. The Jesuit's life story did not mention God or his religious beliefs. The old priest's story was that of a company man. He owed his allegiance to the organization, not to the Lord. The Jesuit asked Tony if he understood why he took the actions he did. Tony repeated, "Evil colludes with evil Father." The Jesuit was furious! More glaring! After a long silence, Tony told the Jesuit, "I no longer want you to be my PFD." That torched the Jesuit's rage! It took some time for the Jesuit to comport himself.

Jesuit: "Tony, you should leave the seminary. The other students are not able to find good employment, but you are. You should leave the seminary and continue to pursue your calling. You won't have any trouble finding gainful employment." Tony: "Once you follow a calling to the seminary Father, you have to see it through. You can't quit." Jesuit: "Tony, it is ok for you to leave. Follow the calling you had before you came here. I suggest you do this, it is best for everyone." The Jesuit gave Tony an imperative to bring him the photographs he requested in the memo the following day. Tony: "There are no photographs Father, and you know it." Tony rose to his feet and left.

Tony went back to his room and stared at the wall for a long time before praying and going to sleep. The next day, on his way to Mass, Tony slipped a letter under the door to the Jesuit's office recounting the first time the priest said to take pictures so Tony would have evidence. In the letter, Tony stated he performed all due diligence in this matter and was sorry the Jesuit failed his own responsibility to do so.

Leo made a point to talk to Tony after Sunday Mass. Leo: "I saw you going down the corridor to your formation director's office last night. You met with him two nights earlier. Why did he have you go to his office again last night?" Tony: "He told me his life story. It was both inspirational and melancholy." Leo: "Why would he do that?" Tony: "He and I share a deep understanding, we have a special rapport." Leo looked confused. He began to object, but stopped in midsentence.

Karl

After dinner, Karl stopped by Tony's room to say hi. Tony: "Good! I'm glad to see you. Have you heard anything from Javier?" Karl: "No, have you?" Tony: "Nothing. I want to tell you what happened. My PFD got cheeky. He told me to photograph homosexual activity so I would have proof. The next day when the queers regurgitated my meeting with him, I told them what the Jesuit said." Karl: "Why did you do that?" Tony: "I had a real attitude problem with the Jesuit's sense of humor. I decided to share my ill humor with him. I told the queers he is an old man and doesn't understand technology. I can rent a camera with infrared film and give him all the photographs he wants." Karl: "No! They must have gone nuts! What happened next?"

Tony: "The Jesuit signed and dated a memo in his own handwriting telling me to deliver the photos I offered to show him." Karl: "Do you have any photos?" Tony: "No, I don't even have a camera." Karl: "What did the Jesuit say?" Tony: "He said it would be better for everyone if I left the seminary." Karl: "You can't quit!" Tony: "My formation director asked me to. He gave me an out." Karl: "What are you going to do?" Tony: "Before I make any decisions, I want to meet with the Rector. I wanted to tell you now before things get crazy." Karl: "Things are already crazy! You shouldn't have talked about photography to your classmates!" Tony: "You and Brian stay clear of me to protect yourselves." Karl: "I'm so sorry Tony."

Tony: "I know. Tell Brian for me, tell him to protect himself and avoid me for a while." Karl: "You're not going to be like Javier are you? You will keep in touch after you leave, won't you?" Tony: "Yes, I will. Give me your mailing address the next time you see me." Karl: "I thought you said they go through the mail?" Tony: "They do." Karl: "Give me your address and phone number." Tony: "I don't have my next address yet." Karl: "I'll give you my phone number." Tony: "The phone is worse than the mail. Trust me. I have an idea how to sneak a letter past them. Forget the telephone, there's no way we can get around their telephone surveillance."

13 TAPED CONVERSATION

Rector's Office

It was time for Tony's meeting with the Rector. Tony prepared for the meeting by dressing in his micro recorder enhanced shirt and trousers. When Tony got to the Rector's office, the door was open. The Rector invited him in and indicated with his open hand to have a seat. The chair faced the Rector's desk, but was eight feet from it. The Jesuit sat in a chair eighteen feet to the right of Tony's chair. *Now what? What is the Jesuit doing here?*

Rector: "Ok. I'll be right with you Tony. The Jesuit mentioned that you, you were going to come in, so I asked him to be with us at this meeting, if that's ok with you."

Tony: "Makes sense." *No it doesn't. I made this appointment with the Rector.*

Rector: "You asked to meet, so I'll let you proceed."

Tony: "Ok. I'd like to give you that." *Tony handed copies of the Jesuit's memo and Tony's response to the Rector.*

Rector: "Good."

Tony: "The Jesuit's letter is underneath; maybe you should read that one first."

Rector: "Ok. *Reading aloud:* Thank you for the long conversation we had last night, which was March 17, will you please let me see the photographic evidence you have offered. Ok. Let's see. *Long pause–.* Fine. Do you have the photographic evidence that you referred to?"

Tony: "No, see, that's the whole point. He refers to something that was; I have never used the word photographic and, and, or evidence in a sentence. So here he is telling me: bring this in, and you said you were going to give it to me, but I didn't. I am seriously confused folks. This does not make sense."

Rector: "Ok, ok. Father?"

The Jesuit: "I, I really, really, I understood him to say that. What did you say to the Father? If I misunderstood, what was it that you said?"

Tony: "I told you the chain of events–."

The Jesuit: "Yes."

Tony: "And your reaction to that was, well Tony, I think you're paranoid, and you were discarding the, the entire thing out of hand as a reality. At that point I had nothing to say."

The Jesuit: "Before that though, you had said to me, I have, you were looking for evidence, I have photographic evidence, and at that point I said, Tony, you don't have to show that to me, because I am only interested in my, uh directing you, and to show that to the Vice Rector or the Rector. Then after, after our meeting, uh, in that letter I said, I wrote down, I wrote that memo to you I said maybe I should see this photographic evidence that you said you had."

Tony: "Let's, let's take it from, from what you read there, I mean, in his handwriting, you've got: I made an offer of evidence and he refused it. Now that doesn't make sense, does it?"

Rector: "Ok, what is the evidence?"

Tony: "He suggested that I get photographic evidence at the first time that I told him this back last fall."

The Jesuit: "I never did that. I never did that."

Rector: "Did you? Let's start, let's back it up even further, what is the charge you're making?"

Tony: "Alright. Initially, there was a rumor, because, over a two-hour period half of the theologate uh, formed some sort of extremely negative opinion where people would gawk at me, with, I don't know, part outrage and part anger."

Rector: "How, how, how, what, can you give me a timeline for when that was?"

Tony: "Oh, that was in the afternoon of parent's weekend."

Rector: "Ok. Ok, and they had formed an opinion about you, concerning?"

Tony: "People, people had an extreme expression on their face when they would look at me. It's similar to the expression when, when people gather around an automobile accident, there is a, a horrific look on their face."

Rector: "Uh-huh."

Tony: "Alright, they would look at me with such an expression on their face."

Rector: "And this is half the student body, at least half the student body?"

Tony: "I estimated thirty-nine students, yes."

Rector: "Thirty-nine students; and you came to that determination of thirty-nine that same weekend?"

Tony: "That's an estimation."

Rector: "That same weekend? And, so, that means within a month's time of being here that feeling developed?"

Tony: "Yeah."

Rector: "And uh, so, then you, you feel as though about half the community had an opinion about you. What was that opinion?"

Tony: "I don't know. It was very negative, that's for sure."

Rector: "And what was it related to? Why, why, –do you have any explanation for it?"

Tony: *Heavy sigh, pause–.* "When that happened I tried to backtrack, and the only thing that happened unusual before that event was the two weeks preceding that, two students, uh, had a fear, panic, of me, and the expressions on their face indicated extreme panic."

Rector: "Ok, and who were they?"

Tony: "That would have been David and Mr. Stevens."

Rector: "Ok. And uh, did you talk to them about it?"

Tony: "No, I talked to the Vice Rector, because–."

Rector: “No, ah, did you talk to these students about it? And ask them about it?”

Tony: “No.”

Rector: “Ok.”

Tony: “At that point, what would be solved?”

Rector: “No, I mean, I was just curious that you saw that. Did you, did you in any way approach and say what’s the problem here, because it’s unexplainable, isn’t it?”

Tony: “I don’t know. It’s very unexplainable.”

Rector: “So, why those two and nobody else?”

Tony: “I don’t know.”

Rector: “Ok, so, they didn’t do anything to you, for instance, to you that would have precipitated this?”

Tony: “Not during that two-week period. However, when, when I re-looked at that, then I realized that what had preceded that was, one night I got up in the middle of the night to use the bathroom and I saw David in the hall. He came out of a room, and I waived to him, because I could see his silhouette, and I knew if I waived sideways he would see my silhouette, and I waived, because I recognized him, that it was him. And he stopped and then, he went into his room, and it was a positive that he went into his room because it is right next to the window, so there is no mistake. He went into that room. And, but I could not have made a positive identification of which room he came out of.”

Rector: “Ok, you did not know which room he came out of?”

Tony: “No, and I could not have known because it was too dark.”

Rector: “Ok. And, how, about what time of the night was this?”

Tony: “It, after that, when I finished walking to the hallway where the lavatory is, I looked at the clock, it was exactly three in the morning.”

Rector: “Three a.m. And uh, how, how was David dressed?”

Tony: “Street clothes.”

Rector: “Ok. Did it look like he had just come in from the outside? Did he have a jacket on?”

Tony: “No jacket.”

Rector: “Ok. It was warm. It was still September.”

Tony: “Err, right, it would’ve been. That was the second week of school, whatever, whatever that was. Yeah, it would have been the first or second week of September.”

Rector: “Was it a weekend or a week night?”

Tony: “Oh, I don’t remember that now. Uhm, the next day was a school day, because I saw them in classes.”

Rector: “Ok. So it could have been a Sunday night?”

Tony: “It could have been, yes.”

Rector: “Ok. Alright. And so, he came out of a room that was not his own, and went into his own room, and he was dressed in street clothes, and not in pajamas or anything?”

Tony: “No.”

Rector: “Ok, fine. And uh, then afterwards it was that you, you recalled that incident perhaps as an explanation that might have provoked his uh, negative reaction towards you, uhm, two weeks later, or in that same period, and uh, then that mushroomed into thirty-nine people participating. But you had mentioned that David and Mr. Stevens particularly started this ball rolling. What, why Mr. Stevens do you think? Did you see him in the hallway?”

Tony: “No. Ah, this, this was after the fact. Uhm, it, it seems to me that Mr. Stevens is the one that precipitated whatever negative uh, story was circulated, uhm, because our classmates David and Leo uh, were embarrassed.”

Rector: “David and Leo.”

Tony: “Were embarrassed.”

Rector: “Embarrassed about?”

Tony: “After this had happened, they were embarrassed for me. So now if David–.”

Rector: “After what happened?”

Tony: "The rumor, that, where the thirty-nine people are all looking at me with this extreme emotion."

Rector: "So, you said Mr. Stevens participated, precipitated this story about you?"

Tony: "I have to surmise that, yes."

Rector: "Because your classmates were embarrassed, I don't understand."

Tony: "Towards me, for me. In other words, when I would face these guys in class,"

Rector: "Yeah."

Tony: "Mr. Stevens would have a seething anger toward me. The other two guys would be embarrassed for me. In my presence, they would be embarrassed."

Rector: "And how would they either, how would Mr. Stevens communicate this seething toward you. Did he say anything? Uh, did he uh, make any gesture?"

Tony: "No."

Rector: "Ok."

Tony: "When you are in a small class, and you have eye contact with the other people, either it's congenial, or it's something else."

Rector: "And, uh, you said that Leo and David were embarrassed. How did they express that?"

Tony: "Facial expressions."

Rector: "They never said a word to you?"

Tony: "No."

Rector: "So, this is your perception of their facial expressions."

Tony: "Yes."

Rector: "Ok."

Tony: "When I questioned Leo, if he knew anything, uh, he said that it was some little thing, nothing, to forget it. Uhm, I don't know, a couple of months later, I asked him again, and he made that he didn't remember anything about it. So, I have no way of finding out."

Rector: "Ok, so, I still don't understand. So, the charge that you are making is that half of the theologate has a negative opinion of you, which you say was precipitated by Mr. Stevens. Uh, and it's unrelated or is it related to seeing David in the hall?"

Tony: "I have to believe that it is. Because, why would, would Mr. Stevens have a reaction to me when he and I have never interacted with each other for me to give him the ability to form a negative? Uhm, the approximate area were David came out from could very well have been Mr. Stevens' room."

Rector: "But you're not sure?"

Tony: "I could not make a positive determination at the time, no."

Rector: "So your, your, uh, your, uh, uh, I guess uh, your uh, guess here about why Mr. Stevens had a negative reaction to you is based for the most part on a guess that it was out of his room that David came, ok, but you're, you don't know for sure?"

Tony: "I could not make a positive determination at that time."

Rector: "And so, what you think, uh, why would, let's say, let's grant that it in fact, that David did come out of his room. Why would that have made Mr. Stevens upset?"

Tony: "See, that is what I don't understand. And why would, would thirty-seven other people join, band together with them?"

Rector: "Do you think that they have some kind of common difficulty like they are all drinking? Are, are, are, are we talking about a drug ring, or what are we talking about here? What, what, what is the, what is the thing that you feel is taking place that would lead such a sizable group of people to converge their negative feelings towards you? What's happening here?"

Tony: "It would occur to me that there's homosexual activity."

Rector: "Ok, and what, what would you lead that to you as opposed to that they are either peddling drugs or that they're uh, or uh, drinking, or that uh, they're uh, uh, studying Carl Reiner? Or, what, why, why, that?"

Tony: "Because after that, uh, one night in the pub, uh, where there was David and I and no one else was within earshot, made some comments to the effect that he only had three hours sleep and he felt great. And he carried on how, how good he was feeling, and it was spoken in clichés where the punch line to that is, "It must be love," which I was not going to put that forth. A week or so after that, another time in the pub David again was, to me, and privately just the two of us, was saying about how nice it was being in love, and, and the, the goodness of being in love. He was happy."

Rector: "Ok. And did uh, did you, did in fact, did his being in love uh, it, was it, was there a possibility that it was heterosexual love, homosexual love?"

Tony: "He seemed to think I would understand."

Rector: "Why would he think you would understand homosexual love?"

Tony: "Ah, he knew that I saw him in the hall that night"

Rector: "Oh."

Tony: "He made, he made the presupposition that I would understand–."

Rector: "How do you know he did?" *Pause–.* "Did you talk to him about it?"

Tony: "He didn't give me an explanation."

Rector: "Yeah, but how can you talk about his perception? How can you read his mind is what I'm asking? How do you know that? If he didn't say that."

Tony: "When he, when he makes these statements to me–."

Rector: "Yes."

Tony: "Without some former explanation–."

Rector: "Yes."

Tony: "He's making those statements with, as if there's an understanding, and–"

Rector: "I mean, that's, that's, that's a stretch."

Tony: "Ok, alright, well, it's a stretch. Fine, it's a stretch."

Rector: "It's a stretch. I guess my, my concern here Tony is that David, Mr. Stevens and thirty-nine other people here, they all have a right, they have a right to their reputation."

Tony: "So do I."

Rector: "Ok, but I, I guess what I'm saying is, you are coming forward and saying something about people in terms of what your conjecturing is a homosexual ring that's going on in this house. Is that the charge you're making, that these thirty-nine people–."

Tony: "I think that."

Rector: "Yeah, you think that. And that this institution and these individuals have a right to their reputation, and what you're giving me is all conjecture in your own mind, because somebody looked at you funny?"

Tony: "Thirty-nine people? All at once?"

Rector: "Yeah, that you are, you are, in some way accusing thirty-nine people. And so you are, let me ask you this, are you willing to allow yourself to be confronted, I'll call all thirty-nine people in here. And to have them sit down and have you accuse them of partaking in a homosexual ring, because if you do, and you make that charge against them, I will have the obligation to ask our lawyer to visit with them to let you know, let them know their rights, because they have a right to their reputation, and if you liable them in front of their superior who makes a recommendation about their future, they have to be informed by me of their rights. And I wouldn't be surprised if one of them uh, takes action. So I want to be very clear with you, I'm going to call them in here, I will also inform them of their, of their legal rights. I'll have our lawyer come in, and you can make the charge against them, of, of forming a homosexual ring. So, I need the names. Thirty-nine names."

Tony: "Before we start on that, because obviously it's not an easy thing to produce physical evidence for that."

Rector: "Oh, no, no! I, I'm saying that if you want to give me the thirty-nine names of people that you, you consider are in fact, you, you don't, you are not saying you have hard evidence. I'm willing, in fact, to go with what you feel is, is their uh, their conspiracy against you as a group, uh, and to uh, to say in effect, this is the way you feel, and to allow you to have your say in front of them uh, and to make the charges, I'm going to ask them. I do not want any conspiracy in this house. I do not want any homosexual ring. I do not want people to act out inappropriately. This institution has a right. I'll throw all thirty-nine of them out, if I find, in fact, that they are in some sort of illicit activity, and that it is to the detriment of the Church, and I am going to do that, and I will do that. But I'm going to have to call them in here and talk to them about it. At the same time, I will inform them of their legal rights."

Tony: "Well, certainly. Certainly."

Rector: "Ok. So give me the names. You gave me two already, David and uh, Mr. Stevens."

Tony: "What I'm, what I have to consider is, when I went to the Vice Rector, and I asked him if he was able to check on this. Alright, how come he's not able to check on this?"

Rector: "Well, I, I don't know. All I know is that if he, if he told you that he would check on it, I trust that he would. He has always been very forthright and deliberate."

Tony: "No, he said he would not."

Rector: "Well, ah, I don't know, I could ask him about it, so I'll call the Vice Rector in too. So, do you think, is he part of the ring?"

Tony: "I would like you to talk with the Vice Rector, and not talk with the students, because I don't have–."

Rector: "No, no, no. I'm already going to call David and Mr. Stevens. I've already going to call them in. You have made a charge to me against them. I have to call them in. They have a right to know this. Alright, I will call them in. I will call the Vice Rector in. And you said he has been neglectful in his responsibilities and not follow through. I have responsibility to make him accountable and call him in to do that."

Tony: "Thank you."

Rector: "And I think that I am going to ask, I will advise him of his rights as well with regard to this because you're making a charge against him. At the same time, I want to know whether or not it is your feeling, is the Vice Rector a part of this ring, either with David or with Mr. Stevens? Is he covering up because he's involved?"

Tony: "No. There was no indication at all. *Only now did Tony consider that possibility. Tony's mind flashed to the night the Vice Rector came to his room at 8:02 p.m. to confiscate his scotch–.*

Rector: "No. Ok, fine. Ah, you feel that David and Mr. Stevens are involved with each other. Who else is involved? *Long pause–.* Do you need a student list?"

Tony: "No, I don't need a student list. Now, once, once you start questioning these people, it's, it's very obvious that I will need to pack and leave, because–."

Rector: "No."

Tony: "Yes."

Rector: "Why?"

Tony: "Because it has been uncomfortable for me all year long so far. Something like this uh, is going to be beyond uncomfortable."

Rector: "Well, uh, wait a minute. This, you're talking about people's future here. And you're also talking about the future of the Church. We have 39 people who are acting irresponsible. The Church has an obligation to all to deal with it, even if it means dismissing half of the student body, which I am prepared to do. And I will do. So I, you have made a charge. You feel as though there's a conspiracy in the house of a homosexual ring, and I want to follow through on it. If, however, you are not willing to cooperate with that, now, then, I will have to tell you that you are not to talk about this again outside of here, because in fact, we will have to take legal action against you as an institution, because, because you will be saying things that will be, that you are, that you have been unwilling for us to follow through on. So uh, either, you're going to come through with the names here, or we're going to drop this."

Tony: "Ah, we'll probably drop it. What uh, what's my liability in this is what I'm saying?"

Rector: "Well uh, your liability is that if you're going to make an accusation about somebody, uh, that they have a right to defend themselves totally. They have a right to their reputation. And if you're going only on circumstantial evidence, your liability is pretty high."

Tony: "That's what I'd figure, ok."

Rector: "Yeah, so, you're either going to–"

Tony: "I'm going to drop the charges."

Rector: "You're either going to, you're going to not only drop them, you're going to retract them."

Tony: "I will retract them."

Rector: 'You will retract them. You will retract them in writing."

Tony: "I will retract them in writing."

Rector: "Ok. I, I want a letter in by the end of this day, which in fact, you fully retract any charges that you have made about any students uh, uh, involved in any kind of uh, uh, immoral or illicit behavior. And also you will retract any charges that you've made against faculty members, the administration, or staff with regard to any kind of cover-up."

Tony: *Writing down the Rector's instructions:* "Ok, alright, illicit–"

Rector: "Any charges that you have made against students of illicit or immoral activity, "

Tony: "Illicit and immoral–"

Rector: "And any charges that you have made against faculty, staff, or administration concerning a, a cover-up or a lack of follow-through with information that was brought to their attention. *To the Jesuit:* Father, is there anything else that we need to do here?"

Jesuit: "No, I think that that is adequate."

Rector: "I, I, I want to, I have to protect all the students, this is my responsibility."

Tony: "That's true."

The Jesuit: "I am glad Father, –that you are taking this step that you have taken; I think that what Mr. Stevens has felt all along is that no one was willing to take any action."

Rector: "Oh, I will."

The Jesuit: "I think that you are, –have expressed yourself absolutely, that you would throw out half the student body and I have always felt that way."

Tony: "Mr. Stevens or Tony?"

The Jesuit: "Pardon?"

Tony: "Mr. Stevens or Tony? You said Mr. Stevens."

Rector: "Tony he meant, yes."

The Jesuit: "Pardon. I'm sorry, uh, Tony then. Tony, that is, wanted to see that uh, what he perceived as a problem that somebody would take vigorous action, and I think that you could, have really shown that. I believe that the Vice Rector was in somewhat the position that I was in, that is, not seeing enough evidence to act on, because if you call people in, you know, it's, it's, very, very damaging."

Rector: "Yes, it is. But, but, it is, I would rather do the damage than to have something fester."

The Jesuit: "Yes, Father. That's admirable Father, I think that."

Rector: "I would rather do that than have something fester. I do think, however, uh

Tony, on this whole business that, if in fact there is conflict, that you feel people have with you, that you need to talk to them. We all have to do this in life. Maybe, in fact, people are giving you, uh, a look that's uncomfortable."

Tony: "See, that's why I was hoping that the Vice Rector would actually sit me down with some of these people and he said well, why don't you go directly to them. I said, at this point, it's volatile, I don't understand there's anything to be solved or gained."

Rector: "Ok. Would you like me to convene a meeting Tony: with Mr. Stevens, and you, and David?"

Tony: "That was, that was last October. At this point, conversation–"

Rector: "Ok, I'm at your disposal, and I'm at your service."

Tony: "I appreciate the offer, I really think it's five months too late."

Rector: "And it's not, it's not the uh, it's not the first time that, in fact, I've had students in here who have had a need for conflict resolution. Things like this happens all the time, they certainly do. So, you give me that document by the end of the day and that would be important. Is there any other point you need to bring up?"

Tony: "Do I need to name names or just–"

Rector: "You could say, all, any and all students, you do not have to name names."

Tony: "Alright, that will work. Thank you very much Father."

Rector: "Thank you very much Tony."

Tony: "Now, uh, there's a second thing; I fired my PFD."

Rector: "Who is that?"

Tony: "The Jesuit."

Rector: "You have to work with the Dean of Formation on that. You cannot unilaterally do that. You have to talk with the Dean of Formation about changing any formation process. You are responsible to the Dean of Formation."

Tony: "Are you willing to still be the PFD?"

The Jesuit: "Ah, Tony, I am willing to do whatever you and the Dean of Formation work out."

Tony: “Fine.”

Rector: *The Jesuit has a sidebar with the Rector before the Rector dismisses Tony.* “Thank you very much.”

Tony: “Thank you Father.”

Rector: “Ok, bye-bye.”

14 THE ENEMY

Retraction

Tony left the Rector's office. His head was swimming. Tony tried hard to walk at a normal pace as he returned to his room. Once inside, Tony reached into his left pocket to turn off and disconnect the directional mic. He had sewn the mic to the inside of the left cuff of his shirt and strung the wire to the power and volume controls in the left pocket of his trousers. Tony could not breathe as he undid his belt to lower his trousers. He removed the Ace ® bandages that secured the micro recorder to the inside of his left leg and switched it to stop, and then rewind.

Tony had to force himself to breathe. It took forever for the tape to rewind. He dialed down the volume and pressed play. Tony thought his chest would explode as he listened to the tape through the earpiece until he heard the Jesuit's voice. It was intelligible! "YES! –YES!" Tony's voice reverberated off the walls of his room, "THANK YOU LORD!"

When Tony saw the soft-spoken Jesuit sitting across the room and his own chair eight feet from the Rector's desk, it confirmed his classmates knew he had a recorder and they shared that knowledge with the administration. Fortunately, they saw the cheap one, the useless one. When Tony saw how far he was from each priest, he reached into his pocket to turn up the gain on the mic. With no sound test, he was dying the entire meeting. What if he did not have enough volume? Too much gain on the directional mic would overdrive the recorder. The Jesuit's voice is barely audible to begin with. How good does his equipment have to be to pick up the Jesuit's voice from 18 feet away? It worked! "Thank you Lord!"

Tony reflected on the ride he took to Sam's Club with the pub snitches. The memory of that skeevy experience caused involuntary shivers. *Gathering good tape is nasty business!* Any doubts Tony had about the timing of when to leave the seminary were gone. It was time. This was the decision the Rector wanted Tony to reach. Tony begrudged giving the Rector what he wanted, but there was nothing else to do. It really was time. Tony put off quitting the seminary until he spoke with the Rector. Well, now Tony had spoken with him. As uncomfortable as his meeting with the Rector was, dealing with the Vice Rector would have been worse. The Vice Rector is the brains, the one with the operations savvy. The Vice Rector would return from vacation in a few days.

Tony typed a retraction letter (Appendix 2) to the Rector's specifications and a terse letter of resignation on his desktop computer and printed duplicate copies. He signed them and returned to the Rector's office. Tony walked up to the Rector and handed the letters to him. The Rector read both letters and smiled that evil smirk Javier described. Smiling, the Rector looked Tony in the face and said, "Tony, you don't have to leave. You have excellent grades and you have been doing well here." The Rector blathered on. His facial expressions and body language in no way matched his rhetoric. The Rector asked what time Tony planned to leave. Tony decided he would like to take the next day to pack and leave after lunch the day after that.

The Rector's flowery palaver ended. His voice turned vicious, "If you are leaving, you should leave quickly. I want you gone before lunch tomorrow." Again, Tony lobbied for an extension, "I can leave after dinner tomorrow night." The Rector declared lunch would be Tony's last meal. Tony agreed, but said he would not have his things loaded into his truck until late in the afternoon. He would leave the premises before dinner. The Rector said he would get students to help Tony pack and to carry boxes to his truck to expedite his departure.

Tony was resolute: having other people pack his things was unacceptable. Having other people carry his things to his truck was not necessary. Tony agreed to leave campus by five p.m. Tony asked the Rector to expunge his parent's contact information from the seminary's records. Again, with the Rector's evil smirk, "Once you join the community of the Pontifical Jeroboam Tony, you are always a member of the Jeroboam–."

Tony had things to submit to the office. When he exited the office, he saw the Rector sharing his good news with the Shrink Lady in the hallway. The Rector's broad smile and beaming countenance displayed his pride of accomplishment in running Tony off. The Shrink Lady showed no emotion. Tony continued down the hall.

Bye Tony

Tony was busy packing. While the seminarians gathered in the chapel for Evening Prayer, Tony went to the refectory for dinner. Not everything was ready, but Tony made a meal of what was available. He was back in his room before Evening Prayer ended. Everything he would need for the next few days went into his suitcases. Everything else went into cardboard boxes. Tony had already packed rarely used items in boxes in anticipation of this day. Tony worked feverishly. He had more stuff now than the day he moved in, and he would leave nothing behind. He could not give anything to Karl or Brian without putting his stink on them, and he certainly was not leaving spoils for the infidels.

Tony stopped packing. He was exhausted. Just as he stopped, he thought he heard a faint tapping on the door. He checked the door and found Karl, who instantly slipped inside to avoid being seen. Karl: "Everyone was going crazy in the refectory tonight! They said you are out. They said that by this time tomorrow you will be gone. What happened?" Tony: "I finally talked to the Rector. Last week I made an appointment with him for something inconsequential. I don't remember what my excuse was." Karl: "But then you made the queers crazy. You told them the Jesuit said to take pictures. You made them afraid by talking about infrared photography. You scared them too much! So what happened?"

Tony: "Saturday night the Jesuit called me to his office. He gave me a copy of a memo he wrote, recounting our conversation concerning the photographic evidence that I offered to him." Karl: "But you don't have any photographs, do you?" Tony: "No, I don't even have a camera." Karl: "So what was he talking about?" Tony: "He lied. It was a craven attempt to protect himself from the Rector." Karl: "You got him in trouble when you told the queers he told you to take pictures. You shouldn't have done that." Tony: "Things got more exciting than I expected, that's true. The Rector invited the Jesuit to my meeting. The Rector interrogated me. I said the Jesuit told me to take pictures so I would have photographic evidence." Karl: "Did he really?"

Tony: "Yes, but he was taunting me. The man is a regular Henny Youngman. He said it as a condescending joke." Karl: "What did he say when you told the Rector he said to take pictures?" Tony: "He lied. He said he never did that. He did it last fall, and he did it again at my last formation meeting." Karl: "Did the Rector believe him?" Tony: "The Jesuit groveled, lied, and sucked up, so it doesn't matter." Karl: "Did you say anything about the Vice Rector?" Tony: "Yes, I said I asked the Vice Rector to check into the three a.m. incident and he refused." Karl: "Is that true? You asked and he refused?" Tony: "No. He is guilty, but not the way I said. The Vice Rector got in my face because I was awake at three a.m. and saw David in the hall."

Karl: "Why didn't you tell the Rector what actually happened?" Tony: "I didn't want the Rector to get crazy too. I told him innocuous things that he could easily shrug off and feel comfortable about it." Karl: "What will you say to the Vice Rector when he says you are lying, that you asked him no such thing?" Tony: "I will apologize profusely and say, oh that's right, you explained to me David was so angry because he had expectations of dating me, and you explained David was having a study session until three a.m. with a friend after the first day of class." Karl: "You should've told the Rector that if it's true." Tony: "It's true, and there was no reason to tell the Rector. He was not searching for the truth."

Karl: "Did David really want to date you?" Tony: "David acted like a nut-job during orientation weekend, and I didn't know why. I felt contaminated when the Vice Rector explained David wanted to date me. The fact that the Vice Rector explained it to me was the one nice thing that man has done for me." Karl: "I didn't know David tried to pick up on you. Did you tell Javier?" Tony: "No, I didn't tell anyone." Karl: "I can see why. The Vice Rector really explained it to you?" Tony: "Yes, he did, and he was disgusted that I had absolutely no clue. That, and my condescending, –well, –overall attitude with the situation."

Karl: "So, what did the Rector do to you?" Tony: "He said he would call the thirty-nine students (*as of parent's weekend*) into his office and have me accuse them of being homosexual, and then he would get the school's lawyer for them. That's his version of an investigation." Karl: "That's not how you do an investigation!" Tony: "That's how the Rector investigates. He said if I don't cooperate, I have to write a letter of retraction." Karl: "What does he want you to retract?" Tony: "Any and all allegations I have made against any and all students, faculty, staff, and administration." Karl: "Don't do it! If you do, you won't be able to tell anybody what goes on here!" Tony: "That's what he thinks too. That's why I soft pedaled and gave him testimony with little or no traction."

Karl smiled, "You have something planned." Tony: "I wouldn't call it a plan. So far it's only an idea." Karl: "Can you tell me? No, maybe it's better if you don't." Tony: "I don't want to say it out loud on campus. We can go off campus if you really want to know." Karl stopped smiling, "No disrespect Tony, but it's not safe to be seen with you right now." Tony: "That's right. You're right. Ok, say goodbye to Brian for me and God bless him." Karl: "He asked me to say goodbye to you for him too. He's afraid to be seen with you right now." Tony: "That's smart." Karl: "Here's my address and phone number like you asked. I want you to stay in touch. Don't be like Javier, I still haven't heard from him."

Tony always ate breakfast early, so he was able to avoid seeing other seminarians at breakfast. Two or three of the refectory staff were annoyingly smirky this morning. Midmorning Tony made his way to the Byzantine priest's office as inconspicuously as possible. Tony said goodbye to the priest, who was shocked and asked why Tony was leaving. Tony gave him a quick rundown. The priest most emphatically offered his help. Tony thanked him, but assured him there was nothing to be done. Tony: "Please don't jeopardize yourself Father. At this point, I want to leave. I appreciate your offer, but I don't want you to get hurt on my behalf, especially for no reason."

The priest shamefacedly acknowledged he needed his job, but truly wished to help. Tony: "I really must leave Father." It was a short goodbye. The priest had a class to teach. He thanked Tony for coming to his office to say goodbye. Byzantine Priest: "I'm sure you've got plenty of others to see before you leave." Tony: "No Father, only you and one student. He will say goodbye for me to a second student in order to protect the second one from being seen with me." The priest understood the need for such measures and it made him sad.

Tony ate lunch while the seminarians were at Mass in the theology dorm chapel. The refectory was filled with pre-theology students while Tony ate lunch. They were unnervingly giggly and smirky.

Tony finished packing around the time the theology students finished Evening

Prayer. Tony waited until they went to dinner before he loaded his truck in order to avoid hecklers. It was well after five p.m. before the campus was in Tony's rearview mirrors. He drove to his storage unit and finished shortly after dark.

Tally

December	%	March	%
54 homosexual	68%	54 homosexual	71%
14 straight	18%	12 straight	16%
10 unknown	13%	9 unknown	12%
1 off site	1%	1 off site	1%
79 Total		76 Total	
14 straight	3 U.S.	12 straight	2 U.S.
	11 foreign		10 foreign

Analysis of School of Theology Population
by Brian, Javier, Karl, and Tony.

The 12% figure, the 9 unknowns in March: Tony was convinced they are pedophiles, but there was no way to verify that in an all-adult environment. Tony's three friends vehemently disagreed. They said Tony had no proof. Tony was the only one of the friends who tried to engage the unknowns in conversation on several occasions. True, his findings were inconclusive.

Two years later, a man who worked in the same machine shop where Tony worked was described by coworkers as weird. Harmless, but weird. One day the man did not show up for work. In Thursday's newspaper, an article told of that man's arrest for pedophilia. Everyone in the shop exclaimed that explained the weirdness they could not name earlier. Having worked with this man renewed Tony's conviction that the 9 unknowns at the seminary were pedophiles.

Karl Called

Weeks later Tony wrote to Karl. Karl wrote back. Karl heard from Javier, who did not sound very good when they talked on the phone. Karl asked Tony to send him his phone number the next time he wrote. Karl said he would call Tony from a pay phone. Tony also wanted to use a pay phone. Tony wrote back with the number of a pay phone and instructions to call at nine p.m. on Friday. If Karl is unable to reach Tony, try again the following Friday. When Tony went to the pay phone, it was windy and raining. At 9:01 p.m., the phone rang. Tony was so happy to hear from Karl! Karl: "How are you doing? Do you still have a problem staring into space?"

Tony: "I'm not in good enough shape to look for a job, so I'm buying property. Developing a property will keep me busy and productive. It's just what I need. It's going to take a while for that staring thing to go away. I shouldn't be around other people until it does." Karl: "Javier was concerned about that. I saw you staring at the wall one time. Javier was right; the expression on your face was frightening. What is going through your mind when you're like that?" Tony: "When I think too much about the situation at the seminary my body shuts down and my mind takes off." Karl: "That's what Javier described. He said your mind goes to another place, is that right?" Tony: "Pretty much."

Karl: "Where does it go?" Tony: "You know how people say, "My life flashed before my eyes?" Well, when you see my body parked and my mind is somewhere else–." Karl: "Yes! That's exactly what it looks like! What's going on?" Tony: "It's not my life that flashes before my eyes. It's the evil that I have witnessed, especially the evil at the Jeroboam. What does the expression on my face look like when I'm in that trance-like state?" Karl: "It's very disturbing. Javier was right to be concerned." Tony: "Yeah, well, it's going to take a while for that to go away. Meantime, I'll be working mostly alone doing plenty of physical labor. I hope to be fit to be in public again after a few weeks." Karl: "Or months?" Tony: "Or months."

Karl: "You said mostly alone, who else will be working with you?" Tony: "I'll need to bring in contractors, people I know." Karl: "That's good. Sounds good. So, you haven't started drinking like Jake did?" Tony: "No. Drinking sparks those fits of staring, so I don't feel like drinking." Karl: "Good! No drinking, that's good to hear! I got your letters. How did you mail letters from two different states when you don't live in either one?" Tony: "The letters I mailed were inside another envelope mailed to the postmaster of the city I chose. The postmaster opens the envelope, finds a stamped, addressed letter inside, and mails it. That gives me a postmark from that city. I chose cities where queer seminarians are from so the mailroom spy would ignore them." Karl loved it!

Karl: "It worked! They never opened your letters, I am certain of it. They do open our mail here. You were right about that. I got a letter from my mother. The next day at lunch, the queers all discussed the contents of my letter and laughed about it. They made fun of my family and where I come from. How did they do that? How did they open the letter and reseal it without damaging the envelope? It looked like it had not been opened."

Tony: "Simple: steam it open, read the contents, replace them, and reseal the letter. The glue on the envelope works like it's brand new, the steam doesn't damage anything." Karl was ashamed, "I didn't believe you when you were here. You tried to tell us, but we didn't believe you. I didn't know you were right until the queers were laughing at me over what they read in the letter my mother sent." Tony: "How do you know they didn't read the letters I sent?" Karl: "If they did, they would've bragged about it." Tony: "How about you? How is Karl doing?"

Karl: "I have great news! Over Easter, I was in contact with a bishop in California. His diocese is wealthy. He is anxious to sponsor me. His diocese is desperate for good priests. He will reimburse the diocese that sponsored me this year. He won't officially be my bishop until after the end of this school year. Once it's official, his diocese will pay for school, books, and living expenses, plus a stipend! The stipend is so I can get off campus. I will be able to buy things at the store or have a beer. They will also pay for plane tickets to fly me home to my country so I can visit my family at Christmas. They will take good care of me. My new diocese is desperate for good priests. I told the bishop about the situation here, about the queers. I told him what happened to you. I hope you don't mind I told him."

Tony: "It's good you told him. Now he knows what you're up against." Karl: "He already knew. I did not have to tell him. I hope you're not mad." Tony: "Not at all. Give him my name and contact information in case he wants to talk to me." Karl: "That's not necessary, he already knows. He said he will support me no matter what the queers do. If they kick me out of here, he will move me somewhere else. He is serious about getting good priests for his diocese." Tony: "Did you tell him about Javier?" Karl: "No, I didn't. What did you think about Javier dating during his internship?" Tony: "It was wrong." Karl: "I thought so too. I'm worried about Javier. He didn't sound good when I talked to him. Did you call him yet?"

Tony: "I tried, but the number you gave me was disconnected. You said you were going to call me from a pay phone, but it doesn't sound like you did." Karl: "No, I'm calling from my room." Tony: "No! That's a mistake! I told you guys, the Vice Rector monitors the mail and the telephones too!" Karl: "Do you think that short guy who takes care of the long distance account is listening?" Tony: "Yes!" Karl: "Now?" Tony: "Yes." Karl: "Don't call me again! My new sponsor is great, and you're going to be ok. Please don't call or write to me again! No disrespect Tony, you know the danger better than I do." Tony: "Congratulations on your new bishop. God bless you Karl." Karl: "God bless you Tony."

Neighbors

Tony called the neighbors he had when he lived up north. Their son was in high school when he carpooled with Tony to the vocations meeting. That was a year ago. Tony felt remiss. He should have called sooner. The boy's mother answered the phone. Tony told her what he found at the seminary. Tony: "I don't want to talk your son out of entering the priesthood. I want to warn him what he's going to find when he gets there so he can be prepared." "Thank you. I knew something was wrong." Tony: "How did you know?" "It was in the parish bulletin that you quit before Easter. I suspected what the problem might be, but I could not be sure.

Thank you for thinking of our son and calling us." Their son was doing fine. He had a summer job and a girlfriend. His long-range plans included the girlfriend and not the priesthood.

Why Leave the Seminary

People Tony knew asked why he left the seminary. He told them. Four or five people hung their heads and said they already heard about the things Tony described. They had hoped these things were not true. They were sad Tony confirmed the worst. A few people listened to Tony's testimony and shook their heads. They agreed it was sad. Most people vigorously denied Tony's eyewitness accounts. They told Tony to his face this was not possible. *Brian, Javier, and Karl knew it would be like this.*

Tony's Grandmother asked, "Do you know what people around town are saying?" Tony: "No, I don't." Grandmother: "What do you think they're saying?" Tony: "It can't be good. I've been bug-eyed and manic, telling people about the queers. No one wants to hear it. They're probably saying, "He said queers, must be he's a queer."" Tony's Grandmother's jaw dropped. She considered this. She comported herself and said, "That's right, that's exactly what they are saying." *I really didn't need to have that confirmed Grandma. Brian, Javier, and Karl told me what all of us knew: they won't believe you Tony.*

Grandmother: "Well, what are you going to do about it?" Tony: "I can't argue a negative Grandma, no one can. There's nothing to be done." Grandmother: "Nothing?" Tony: "I have excellent eyesight. This is what I saw. If that's too complicated for them, there's nothing I can do about it. I can't change someone's mind if they refuse to see the truth." Tony's Grandmother was confounded. Tony: "Grandma, if they want to know the truth, they'll ask me. Most people would rather make up their own story than learn the truth." Grandmother: "Doesn't that bother you?" Tony: "Sure it bothers me, but there's nothing to be done. There's nothing I can do."

Tony and his Mom had a similar conversation. Mom: "They don't doubt your eyesight, they think you're lying." Tony's brother chuckled, "Everybody lies. Of course they think you're lying, everyone lies." Tony: "Ok, so I tell the truth and everyone else lies. The differential should be conspicuous." The brother laughed, "How's that working for you?" Tony: "Yeah. They see the difference and think I must be an even bigger, fatter liar."

People who challenged Tony's account asked, "How can you know for sure?" Tony: "The dorms were built in the 1930s. The walls are paper-thin. You can hear what goes on in the next room." Tony's Mom was the only one who asked, "What does it sound like when two men are having sex?" Tony described the sound of cooing pigeons and the grunting sounds a cow makes during a pregnancy check. Tony's brother agreed, "Yeah, that's what it sounds like." Tony: "How do you know?" Brother: "When I was in basic training in the Army, two hundred men slept in the same barracks. Every night I heard those noises."

Rage

Now that it was too late, Tony's uncle loaned him a paperback, *Ungodly Rage: The Hidden Face of Catholic Feminism* [39] (© 1991). The author tells of large defections of clergy and religious from 1966 to 1976 (p20) and its relation to a "general theological dissent, broader political feminism and neo-gnosticism," and witchcraft (p21). "Adult Catholics, empowered by the sacrament of Confirmation are obliged [36] by faith and honor to defend her (the Church) (p25)." [39] "–the ideas that led to their collapse originated among masculine dissenters, who have been numerous, influential and rarely disciplined. Ultimately it is those who hold but fail properly to exercise hierarchical authority who bear the heaviest responsibility (p26)." "And while their disintegration reached crisis proportions only after the Second Vatican Council, the original infection was contracted in the late 1940s and early 1950s, —(p255)." "Pope Pius X condemned modernism in 1907, calling it, "The synthesis of all heresies." In 1910, – (*Pascendi Gregis*) (p257)." [39]

When Tony returned the book his uncle asked, "What did you think?" Tony: "The author was thorough. She noted this onslaught against the Church started in the late 1940s." Uncle: "Why is that significant?" Tony: "The Vice Rector was not simply using military tactics; he was using Soviet Cold War tactics. It bothered me the whole time I was there. How did homosexual clergy receive Cold War training?" Uncle: "Maybe one of them was ex-military." Tony: "No, I don't think so. The personal discipline from being in the military was distinctly lacking. It was appalling to see the Vice Rector pitting himself against unsuspecting civilians." Uncle: "No one expects being attacked by a priest." Tony: "No one expects a lot of the things they were doing at the seminary."

Uncle: "How did you fare?" Tony: "They broke me. I fell on my face about a week before I quit." Uncle: "Why didn't you leave before that happened?" Tony: "I couldn't." Uncle: "Why not?" Tony: "I didn't want to leave until after Javier left." Uncle: "You wanted to protect him. You wanted to cover his six." Tony: "More than that, I wanted to witness his departure. There was another student, someone I didn't know, who left. Supposedly he left of his own volition, and yet he left under duress." Uncle: "Was he straight?" Tony: "I had no way of knowing. He was one of the 10 unknowns." Uncle: "How long after Javier's departure did you leave?"

Tony: "I left the following week. I had unfinished business. I wanted to meet with the Rector before I left." Uncle: "You said you fell on your face." Tony: "I did." Uncle: "After Javier's departure and before meeting with the Rector?" Tony: "Yes." Uncle: "Was it worth it?" Tony: "I hope so." Uncle: "Did you get everything you needed?" Tony: "Maybe, I don't know yet." Uncle: "When will you know?" Tony: "I need to go to the federal building before I'll know where things stand." The uncle chuckled, "What makes you think the Feds will be interested in what goes on in a seminary?" Tony: "Somebody has to." Uncle: "What do you think they can do about what you saw in the seminary?" Tony: "I won't know until I talk to them."

When Tony visited his parents, he saw a letter from the Pontifical Jeroboam. Tony did not smile. The letter contained his failing grades for the second semester, and calculated his cumulative grade point average for both semesters. Tony asked his mother if the seminary bothered her with mail. She did not want to talk about it, but Tony would not let it go. Tony's mother eventually admitted the seminary periodically sends her letters asking for donations. Such chutzpah!

Not on TV

Tony went to visit his brother. Tony's visit coincided with a visit by other guests, devout Catholics active in the Church. They wanted to hear Tony's account. They were sad. "We've heard rumors of these things, but it was always second or third hand. We wanted to hear firsthand an eyewitness account." They had many questions for Tony. They were knowledgeable of how things are supposed to work, and they wanted to know in detail how specific safeguards were thwarted. These were intelligent, informed people with concise questions and concerns. When the discussion ended, one woman wistfully asked, "Why haven't we ever seen this on TV? Why haven't we ever heard about this on the news?"

After the other guests left, Tony's brother chuckled, "Knowing how bogus you think TV news is, I thought you'd have a stroke when she said that. You had no reaction at all. I couldn't believe it. How did you manage that?" Tony: "Information overload. They had enough bad news for one night." Brother: "You had no comment on the liberal media? That's not you." Tony: "Since they are now referred to as the liberal media, thanks to Rush, they are obviously something much worse. At the seminary, the queers went crazy when one of "their people" said Clinton would not get reelected as long as Limbaugh was on TV. They were worried sick. Several weeks later, Limbaugh's three a.m. TV show was canceled.

The public was given the lame excuse the airtime was needed for the Olympics. At three a.m.? Only one broadcast network carries Olympic coverage. None of the other networks picked him up. Did this alert the public to how bogus American television news is? No. I listened to gay Democrat seminarians discuss the urgent need to remove Limbaugh from TV so Clinton could get reelected. Weeks later, Rush's show got the boot. That's when I coined the phrase "gay Democrat media."" After a long pause Tony's brother said, "Thank you for not sharing that with my guests. You're right, that would have been information overload."

Federal Building

It was more than a year after Tony drove away from the seminary before he was ready to go to the FBI. Tony was a walk-in; he did not make an appointment. Upon arrival, he was sent to the cafeteria to drink coffee. Tony grew old waiting. He had a second cup. Finally, an agent was ready to see him. Tony was directed to a tiny room. He spotted the camera pointed at him. It was in the corner of two walls and the ceiling. The agent asked Tony (pointless) questions. Tony: "You've read my file. You're familiar with my work." Agent: "What makes you think we have a file on you?"

Tony: "I've delivered intel to the FBI before. You know the quality of my work. I grew old drinking coffee while you read my file. You are one slow reader." The agent dispensed with the small talk, "Why did you come to our office today?" Tony told the agent homosexuals have commandeered the Pontifical seminary in Columbus, Ohio. Agent: "Are you serious? How does that concern the FBI?" Tony: "Democracy cannot function without a solid moral foundation. The fact that homosexuals have infiltrated the Catholic Church undermines our society and jeopardizes the American way of life."

For a concise examination of this subject [17] go to: <abcnews.go.com/blogs/politics/2012/11/ron-paul-departs-with-our-constitution-has-failed/>. [17]

The agent agreed with Tony's civics observation but repeated his question, "Why did you come to us?" Tony: "I am here to report sedition by a foreign entity: Vatican City." The agent stated the obvious legal concerns. Tony: "I agree. Everything you said is true for all the seminaries in this country except this one. The Pontifical College Jeroboam is under the direct auspices of the pope. This is the only seminary on American soil that is under the direct control of a foreign entity: Vatican City. The charge is sedition." The agent was nonplussed. Tony told him the seminary had $123 million in their coffers, there were five Red Chinese students at the seminary, and Tony asked, "What business does the Rector of an American seminary have in Red China for two weeks?" Agent: "The Cold War is over. We are trying to establish relations with China."

Tony: "Our country has stopped being vigilant, I know. I listen to the news too. Tell me Russia and China have stopped being vigilant the same as we have." No response. Tony raised a couple of salient points before repeating, "What business does an American priest have in Communist China for two weeks?" Agent: "How much money did you say the seminary has?" Tony: "One hundred and twenty-three million dollars." Tony started to open his briefcase, but the agent told him not to. Agent: "If you had something to take to court, you would not have come to us. Am I right?" Tony: "No, you are not right. What I have in here I collected specifically for you guys. I went to a lot of trouble to get this. I would appreciate it if you would at least take a look at what I have." The agent was emphatic, "Do not open the briefcase."

The agent questioned Tony about his concerns. Tony: "The last pope was poisoned by insiders. There was an assassination attempt on this pope. I believe the pope is under extreme duress and needs outside help. I came to you." Agent: "Why did you come to us?" Tony: "I've dealt with you guys before. If you're not the right outfit, you know which one is. This pope needs help." Agent: "We can't get involved in religion. We cannot go after the Catholic Church. The political problems are obvious. What do you expect us to do?" Tony: "Open an investigation. Based on the tapes I have in here–." Agent: "Don't open that. Can you use those tapes in court?" Tony: "No." Agent: "Why did you make them if you can't use them in court?" Tony: "I made them specifically for the FBI. I have enough here for you to open an investigation."

The agent was concerned Tony taped by bugging the room. Tony assured him the recorder was concealed on his person. Agent: "What will an investigation accomplish?" Tony outlined what he hoped to accomplish by rendering assistance to the pope. This included protecting innocent seminarians from criminal treatment by homosexual clergy. The agent was not interested. Agent: "Our hands are tied. Ever since the Jack Kennedy fiasco, this organization has been paralyzed with inaction–." Tony blurted, "What were you guys thinking? Even the mob has more class than that. The mob would never drop a man's brains in his wife's lap! That man was the President of the United States! He deserved a uniformed firing squad." Agent: "You don't understand. We can't use the military." Tony: "You can't use a military firing squad to enforce the national security laws?"

Agent: "Not without the public realizing our government is no longer a democracy and hasn't been for years." Tony: "So instead of solving the quandary of enforcing secret laws, your organization has sat on its hands for over three decades." The agent was highly agitated, "What do you expect to accomplish here today?" Tony: "I want you to listen to what I collected for you. The charge is sedition. We both understand you are enjoined to investigate charges of sedition under penalty of treason. Do your job." The agent squirmed in his chair. Agent: "We are not going after homosexuals, especially as long as Bill Clinton is in the White House." Tony: "You guys know the President is homosexual?" No response. Tony: "Of course you do. How did you allow this to happen? How did you allow a homosexual to get a security clearance that high?"

The agent flushed with embarrassment, "When Clinton first threw his hat in the ring, he was such a joke we ignored him. Two weeks later, he was riding a wave of popularity. By then it was too late." Tony lost it, "Why is that man still sucking air? How many hundreds of counts of treason does he have to commit before you guys do your job?" Agent: "The Secret Service protects the president. We can't go up against the Secret Service. They are good at their job." Tony: "So you stop doing yours? I am supposed to report government fraud, waste, and abuse to the FBI. I'm reporting to you now that every man, woman, and child on the FBI payroll is guilty of fraud, waste, and abuse every time they cash their paycheck on the fifteenth and thirtieth of the month ever since Bill Clinton took office, and continues to be as long as that man is still sucking air. By your own admission, that has been the case for the last three and a half decades."

The angry agent took exception, "No children work for the FBI!" Tony: "I'm sorry, I apologize. I was trying to be polite. I said children instead of saying lazy bastards or treasonous incompetents." The agent's facial expression was too unique to name. It was a combination of shock, shame, guilt, and the sudden realization of a newly discovered ugly truth. Tony: "Allow me to remain polite. Let's stick with children." The white-faced agent slightly nodded, and then objected, "I suppose you can do better! It's harder than you think, reaching over the top of the Secret Service." Tony: "Do better than nothing? You know I can!" The agent's face filled with a sly, evil sneer, "Do you want to kill the President?"

Tony: "(*I get it, wise guy.*) Why should I do your job for you for free? You draw a paycheck, earn your money." Agent: "You won't be able to do it." Tony: "Put me on the payroll and we'll find out." Agent: "That's not going to happen." Tony: "Do your job today and look at what I have in here." The agent again ordered Tony to keep the briefcase closed. Tony: "Ok, call Rumor Control. Tell them what I have." In a condescending voice the agent asked, "What is Rumor Control?" Tony: "Rumor Control, in Columbia, Maryland." The agent feigned ignorance, "I don't know what you're talking about." *Wise guy, trying to trick me into saying the organization's name, the one word in the English language that is illegal for me to use under penalty of treason.*

Tony: "Call Fort Meade, see what they have to say." The agent looked fearful and flatly refused. Tony: "Call and let me talk." The agent maliciously smirked, "Drive down there yourself and show them what you have." Tony: "If you can't be bothered to make a phone call, why should I drive seven hours?" The agent was amused by his vision of Tony showing up at the front gate of Rumor Control with his tapes. Tony had a bad feeling about that. *Who cuts the FBI's orders? Who is at the top of the food chain?* The agent again ordered Tony to keep his briefcase closed. He told Tony to take what he had and deal with it himself. Agent: "You've handled situations yourself before." *Wise guy. I thought you didn't read my file. That won't work this time pal.* Silent pause.

Agent: "Obviously you have a plan." Tony: "I don't have a plan. The best I can do is to write to the pope, but that won't accomplish anything." Agent: "See if the Church can handle the problem internally. If not, form a grassroots movement. Our hands are tied. Do what you can. I have every confidence in you." *Yeah you do.*

Tony: "Homosexuals take over a key pillar of our society, turn it into a global deviant sex club, and you guys can't be bothered? They appropriated the assets of the Catholic Church! That's bad enough. What's worse, it's all tax free." Agent: "That's it! Report them to the IRS and let them handle it." Tony: "That's your solution? Turn the dogs loose?" The agent's biggest concern was that Tony not open his briefcase. The meeting ended with the agent refusing to investigate and continuing to insist Tony not open his briefcase. The agent was resolutely useless.

Tony's mood was exceedingly dark. He could barely contain his outrage until he was inside his vehicle and driving away from the Federal Building. *I lived in a five-story queer's nest for seven months to collect intel and he wouldn't even look at it!* Foul epithets thundered from Tony's face in a fierce torrent of vile rage and indignation! Tony: "That's the trouble with the world today, nobody does their job!" Suffice it to say, Tony had a gigantic emotional episode. Other cars on the highway gave Tony a wide berth.

Tony: "And what about all those FBI files the Clintons and a gaggle of college kids destroyed when Clinton was first in the White House? What was that? Why destroy those files? Which files were destroyed? People in this country under the age of thirty are desensitized to homosexual taboos. I'm thinking mystery solved. Am I the only one that finds it disturbing the Clintons pillaged the FBI with impunity without consequence? What happened to national security? The sentinels who are supposed to be safeguarding our nation aren't sleeping on the job, they're comatose!" Tony continued giving a loud voice to his rage for several more miles in the presumed privacy of his vehicle. *Tony did not consider that the sentinels themselves had been infiltrated and co-opted.*

Vatican

In June, more than a month after the massively disappointing visit to the Federal Building, Tony was ready to write to the Vatican. He asked the Holy Father to please clean up the Pontifical College Jeroboam. Tony mailed a copy to the Pope (Appendix 3) and carbon copied the Cardinal in charge of Pontifical colleges. Tony wrote a letter to the Cardinal (Appendix 4, 5) and carbon copied the Pope. Tony sent each a copy of the tape he made of his meeting with the Rector. In mid-November, Tony received an envelope from the Nuncio's office (Appendix 6) in Washington DC. Inside the envelope was a letter from the Cardinal (Appendix 7) in Vatican City acknowledging receipt of Tony's letter. The Nuncio's job includes the oversight of the Pontifical Jeroboam.

Four years later, word came to Tony the Vatican cleaned house at the Pontifical Jeroboam. It happened the school year subsequent to Tony's receipt of the envelope from the Nuncio. Source: "Everyone was thrown out: the administration, instructors, staff, secretaries, all of the students, kitchen staff, janitors, and even the groundskeepers. They emptied the place right to the walls! All the people were gone. They used a wide broom and made a clean sweep." Tony was disappointed. *They used a wide broom and cleanly swept everything under the carpet.* Source: "Why the disappointment?" Tony: "They did no investigation." Source: "What makes you think so?"

Tony: "They never questioned me or asked me for more information. They swept out the good with the bad. They didn't bother to sort it out. They swept it all under the rug. Showboating is all that was. They made everybody relocate, big deal." The source seemed to think something was actually accomplished. Source: "You think the pope swept this under the rug?" Tony: "It's doubtful the pope ever saw my letter." Tony wanted a second opinion. He told his Catholic friend at work. Coworker: "That changes nothing." Tony: "It will set nefarious operations at that seminary back ten years." Coworker: "How do you figure?" Tony: "No one will trust each other at first. It will take years to rebuild their criminal network." Coworker: "Big deal. Like I said, it changes nothing."

Proverbs 20:26 (DRA) [31] A wise king scattereth the wicked, and bringeth over them the wheel.

Library Research 1997

Tony continued to wonder how the Vice Rector of the Pontifical College Jeroboam received training in Soviet Cold War techniques. This nagging question haunted Tony all the more since having read *Ungodly Rage: The Hidden Face of Catholic Feminism,* [39] and learning the subversion of the Church started in the late 1940s. Tony went to the Rundel Library in Rochester, NY. His search efforts were futile. He searched in vain for two days. Late in the afternoon of the second day, the research librarian asked what he was looking for and offered to help. Twenty minutes later, she handed Tony three yellowed microfiche that held the information Tony sought.

The periodicals that published the following information in 1946 were two staid business publications and one newspaper. The readership for the business publications would be the upper management of large corporations, not the general public.

The Soviet Union planned to send KGB Officers to the United States to train dissident groups of American citizens in infiltration, subterfuge, and subversion. To qualify for Soviet investment of resources, a dissident group must have sufficient membership to assure long-term sustainability. The member's hatred of American society must be sufficiently virulent to survive favorable social change. A specified amount of organizational structure was requisite for a group to be considered viable. The KGB located nine such groups.

In 1946, the Kremlin deployed one KGB Officer to each of the 9 groups for training and one year of mentoring. Each group was given $5,000 in seed money. The ACLU was given $600. They did not need it, the money was given as an honorarium in recognition of the good work they were doing on their own. (In 1946, $5,000 would buy five new cars or one "salt box" house.) The groups were instructed to infiltrate the pillars of society (Family, religion, business, arts & entertainment, education, media, and government.) and destroy them from within. The groups were told their effort would not succeed if they failed to infiltrate the Roman Catholic Church in America. Homosexual men were one of the nine groups. Tony believes they were the most successful group at infiltration and subversion.

Today we might describe the KGB's actions in 1946 as weaponizing American dissident groups. What the KGB did was weaponize evil.

Before the reader develops a sanctimonious outrage at Russia, please refer to the 16-page synopsis, *Bankrolling the Bolshevik Revolution* [45] online at:

<http://www.modernhistoryproject.org/mhp?Article=NoneDare&C=4>. [45] It tells of American financiers starting and bankrolling both sides of World Wars I and II, and American and British financiers financing the Bolshevik Revolution.

Collection

Acquaintances were surprised Tony continued to go to church. Many told Tony his experience was more than reason enough to stop going. Tony: "God is still the same. The Church has been infiltrated by homosexuals and is being destroyed from within. That does not change God." Tony admitted he sought an Orthodox church to go to instead. There was a Roman Catholic church twelve minutes from his house, and there was an Orthodox church an hour and twenty minutes away. Tony decided going to an Orthodox church was the best idea, but a short drive, especially during the winter months, seemed prudent. Tony opted for the short drive. Besides, Tony was not ready to acclimate to a new set of Church traditions. *I am not taking on any new problems this week.*

Unfortunately, the local parish priest was like the men at the seminary. The parishioners didn't seem to mind either. Celebrating Mass with this priest was unconscionably distracting for Tony. He felt he wasted his time going to church on Sunday. Yet, out of sloth, Tony continued to go to his local church instead of looking into the Orthodox Church. Tony continued going to church on Sunday, but he did not put money in the collection. After a year or so, Tony's nagging conscience enjoined him to contribute to the overhead of his parish. In Canada, there is a tradition of paying for your seat before the service starts. During the service, you place your alms in the collection plate.

For the next couple of years Tony put a small amount in the collection basket on Sunday, enough to pay for his seat. God expects alms giving, and Tony could not think of an organization he trusted. So many organizations the public once thought were charities now spend the preponderance of their funding on administration and advertising, leaving precious little for actual charitable works. Tony decided to go back to putting his alms in the collection basket. If money contributed to God for his work is misappropriated, let those people answer to God for their misdeeds. Tony did not think this was the best solution, it was the only one he had.

The young parish priest died. The new priest that replaced him was a holy man from Kenya. The holy priest introduced himself to the parish by explaining, "In the 1960s, Bishop Fulton J. Sheen, Bishop of the Rochester, NY Diocese, sent missionaries to Kenya. Those missionaries brought the good news to Kenya." The new priest expressed his and Kenya's gratitude by volunteering to serve in the diocese that brought the good news to Kenya. Now that Kenya produces more priests than are needed within its own boarders, the Church in Kenya wishes to repay its debt of gratitude to Bishop Sheen and the Rochester Diocese by sending priests from their surplus to backfill the priest shortage in the Rochester Diocese.

VHS recordings of Bishop Fulton J. Sheen's nationally syndicated TV series, "Life is Worth Living," [35] *(1951-1957) and other works on DVD are available at the link below. His message is timeless. Bishop Sheen is a renowned theologian, a gifted orator, and author of over 50 written works.* <http://www.bishopsheen.com/>. [35]

Sadly, the redneck parishioners of the parish were ingrates. Did they not recognize or appreciate that the new priest from Kenya was a holy man? They murmured complaints that the new priest's English was difficult to understand. This parish was in a fruit-growing region, with a history of using seasonal migrant farm labor. It seemed the negative attitudes toward (racial/ethnic) migrants were enduring and fluidly transferable.

I Thought of You

Eventually Tony found professional employment in another state and moved. The priest in his new parish was gifted at giving sermons. Tony forgot about finding an Orthodox church. Tony told friends in his new parish about his experience at the seminary. They listened and nodded.

One day Tony's new friends started telling him, "I saw on TV the thing about pedophile priests in Boston. I thought of you." Tony hated it! Tony: "Why would that make you think of me?" "You were right, what you said about what went on in the seminary."

The next time Tony called his mother he told her, "After people see the trouble in Boston on TV they tell me I was right, as if I needed to be told I actually saw the things I saw. What would I know? I am only an eyewitness. I don't understand people's inane trust of TV." Mom: "It was like that with radio before there was television. Franklin Roosevelt recognized this. He said, "If you didn't hear it on the radio, it didn't happen." That's how it is today with TV."

You are two hundred times more open to suggestion while watching TV than normal. [Proprietary research. Source withheld].

For related information see: "Weapons of Mass Induction." [38] Go to: <http://www.kindredmedia.org/2007/09/weapons-of-mass-induction/>. [38] (An excerpt from Dr. Aric Sigman's book, *Remotely Controlled*.)

At Work

Tony worked with a man who had a degree in theology, Coworker One. They discussed abortion. Tony asserted, "If our Supreme Court justices were atheists, that still doesn't explain Roe versus Wade. The Declaration of Independence states our nation aspires for the "inalienable rights of life, liberty, and the pursuit of happiness." Abortion denies life to the most innocent and most vulnerable. Our social institutions are supposed to protect the weakest. Their bogus argument was that the fetus is not human. What do they think it is, a puppy?" Tony related the experience of women he met who had abortions, and the curiously high incidence of infertility subsequent to their abortion.

Coworker One: "The doctors who performed the abortions sterilized those women. A sterilization procedure adds less than a minute to the abortion procedure." Tony: "Why would a doctor do that?" Coworker One: "His own personal agenda or just plain evil. The people who started Planned Parenthood intended to limit population growth of targeted ethnic groups: initially Blacks. Over time, other interests with evil intent have supported Planned Parenthood. It is the easiest way to kill the people you hate. Get their mothers to do it for you." Tony: "These women were middle-class, attractive, intelligent, and white. Who painted a target on them?" Coworker One: "Homosexuals are big supporters of Planned Parenthood, and they don't like what they call "breeders.""

Coworker One asked Tony if he ever discussed evolution. Tony: "Yes, I've met a few people who had very convincing arguments that they descended from apes." Coworker One: "You believe in evolution?" Tony: "Please." Coworker One: "You just said their arguments were convincing." Tony: "They were. They explained how THEY descended from apes. I know I didn't descend from apes, but these people convinced me they did, and I trust their judgment. Who would know better than they?" Tony discussed his misadventures at the Jeroboam.

Coworker Two said he was quitting work to join a monastery. Tony warned, "I also considered going to a monastery rather than transfer to another seminary. Javier and Karl laughed at that. They explained homosexuals infested monasteries before they infiltrated the seminaries because monasteries were easier to gain entry to." Coworker Two was repulsed by Tony's fat-mouthed remarks. "This is a working monastery. They work in the community." He discussed the monastery and was looking forward to starting in the fall.

Coworker Two quit the monastery three months after he joined. When he came back to visit, he refused to discuss the monastery with Tony. He only told Tony, "I went there to work and pray. No one else worked. I could not believe how lazy they were. Their only interest was smoking cigars and drinking brandy." There are simply too many taboos involved. No one is willing to bear witness.

Tony's health deteriorated. His doctors could not diagnose the problem. Their prescriptions produced outsized side effects without relieving symptoms. Tony finally had to quit his job. Word came to Tony concerning seminarians attending the Jeroboam. Source: "I asked him what it was like at the Pontifical Jeroboam. He was evasive–. When I asked another one, his voice wavered–." The embarrassment and fear on the faces of three different seminarians, their wavering voices, and their dearth of verbal response reminded Tony of his own conversation with the Irish priest. Tony felt bad. Honest young men going to the seminary need to be warned the facility has been hijacked by the forces of evil, by infidels, by homosexuals. Tony had no ideas. Tony had no energy.

The Enemy Two

Last fall President Obama referred to Republicans in Congress as "The Enemy." The inflection in the President's voice sounded exactly like that of the Log Cabin Republican at the seminary when he repeated what the gay Democrats said, "Why are you talking to him? He is "The Enemy!" Don't talk to him! He's not one of us! He's "The Enemy!"" Hearing President Obama say "The Enemy" gave Tony flashbacks of the pontifical seminary. Tony remembered telling his core board about "the catch and the fix."

The [unique sequence] he described to his core board was precisely what had been ailing Tony for years, but he did not associate it with "the catch and the fix" until now. In the past year or so, Tony learned seminarians going to the Pontifical Jeroboam were afraid to discuss what goes on there. The supposed housecleaning of the Jeroboam had obviously worn off. Tony washed his hands of the situation after writing to the Vatican. Tony had more to do. He never finished the job. *That's the trouble with the world today. Nobody does their job.* Tony was ashamed. He remembered one of his lamentations when he was in the seminary: "*Lord, you must have at least one standup guy you can count on.*" Sadly, no.

> Ezekiel 22:30 (DRA) [31] And I sought among them for a man that might set up a hedge, and stand in the gap before me in favour of the land, that I might not destroy it: and I found none.

"The catch and the fix" symptoms [unique sequence] eroded Tony's health until his situation was grave. During core board, the Jesuit explained to Tony, "This is how God works. This is how the hand of God guides us." In the Bible, God tells us: do not talk about my priests. Tony's friends at the seminary had that reason, the importance of not interfering with potential callings to the priesthood, and more for Tony not to talk about the Pontifical Jeroboam. Tony thought it was necessary to warn innocent seminarians of the treachery that awaits them in a facility appropriated by homosexuals. *Preparedness: forewarned is forearmed.*

But Tony only warned one potential seminarian. When President Obama referred to the Republicans as "The Enemy," Tony's memory was jogged. He saw that he was remiss. The Bible also says God loves the truth. Tony started writing about the things he witnessed at the Jeroboam. After many weeks of writing, his health slowly garnered tiny increments of improvement. Obama's clarion call, "The Enemy," focused Tony's attention and set him back on the path, which initiated a miniscule trend of improving health. It was not enough to bring relief, but it was an affirmative indicator. *Obama saved my life.* Still, Tony wanted be sure he was doing the right thing.

> Jeremias 4:19 (DRA) [31] My bowels, my bowels are in pain, the senses of my heart are troubled within me, I will not hold my peace, for my soul hath heard the sound of the trumpet, the cry of battle.
>
> Jeremiah 4:19 (RSV) [20] My anguish, my anguish! I writhe in pain! Oh, the walls of my heart! My heart is beating wildly; I cannot keep silent; for I hear the sound of the trumpet, the alarm of war.

> Isaias 50:5 (DRA) [31] The Lord God hath opened my ear, and I do not resist: I have not gone back.
>
> Isaiah 50:5 (RSV) [20] The Lord God has opened my ear, and I was not rebellious, I turned not backward.

15 SHOULD I BEAR WITNESS?

Do Not Write

Proverbs 20:25 (DRA) [31] It is ruin to a man to devour holy ones, and after vows to retract.

Proverbs 20:25 (RSV) [20] It is a snare for a man to say rashly, "It is holy," and to reflect only after making his vows.

Amos 5:13 (DRA) [31] Therefore the prudent shall keep silence at that time, for it is an evil time.

Osee 4:4 (DRA) [31] But yet let not any man judge: and let not a man be rebuked: for thy people are as they that contradict the priest.

Hosea 4:4 (RSV) [20] Yet let no one contend, and let none accuse, for with you is my contention, O priest.

Ecclesiasticus 7:31-33 (DRA) [31] 31 With all thy soul fear the Lord, and reverence his priests. 32 With all thy strength love him that made thee: and forsake not his ministers. 33 Honour God with all thy soul, and give honour to the priests, and purify thyself with thy arms.

Ecclesiasticus 21:31 (DRA) [31] The talebearer shall defile his own soul, and shall be hated by all: and he that shall abide with him shall be hateful: the silent and wise man shall be honoured.

Sirach 21:28 (RSVwA) [43] A whisperer defiles his own soul and is hated in his neighborhood.

Ecclesiasticus 42:1 (DRA) [31] Repeat not the word which thou hast heard, and disclose not the thing that is secret; so shalt thou be truly without confusion, and shalt find favor before all men: be not ashamed of any of these things, and accept no person to sin thereby:

Jeremias 6:10 (DRA) [31] To whom shall I speak? and to whom shall I testify, that he may hear? behold, their ears are uncircumcised, and they cannot hear: behold the word of the Lord is become unto them a reproach: and they will not receive it.

Jeremiah 6:10 (RSV) [20] To whom shall I speak and give warning, that they may hear? Behold, their ears are closed, they cannot listen; behold, the word of the Lord is to them an object of scorn, they take no pleasure in it.

Ecclesiastes 3:7 (DRA) [31] A time to rend, and a time to sew. A time to keep silence, and a time to speak.

You Must Write

Ezechiel 33:6 (DRA) [31] And if the watchman see the sword coming, and sound not the trumpet: and the people look not to themselves, and the sword come, and cut off a soul from among them: he indeed is taken away in his iniquity, but I will require his blood at the hand of the watchman.

Ezechiel 33:9 (DRA) [31] But if thou tell the wicked man, that he may be converted from his ways, and he be not converted from his way: he shall die in his iniquity: but thou hast delivered thy soul.

Ezechiel 3:19-21 (DRA) [31] 19 But if thou give warning to the wicked, and he be not converted from his wickedness, and from his evil way: he indeed shall die in his iniquity, but thou hast delivered thy soul. 20 Moreover if the just man shall turn away from his justice, and shall commit iniquity: I will lay a stumbling block before him, he shall die, because thou hast not given him warning: he shall die in his sin, and his justices which he hath done, shall not be remembered: but I will require his blood at thy hand. 21 But if thou warn the just man, that the just may not sin, and he doth not sin: living he shall live, because thou hast warned him, and thou hast delivered thy soul.

Isaias 62:6 (DRA) [31] Upon thy walls, O Jerusalem, I have appointed watchmen all the day, and all the night, they shall never hold their peace. You that are mindful of the Lord, hold not your peace,

Proverbs 24:11-12 (DRA) [31] 11 Deliver them that are lead to death: and those that are drawn to death forbear not to deliver. 12 If thou say: I have not strength enough: he that seeth into the heart, he understandeth, and nothing deceiveth the keeper of thy soul, and he shall render to a man according to his works.

Proverbs 24:11-12 (RSV) [20] 11 Rescue those who are being taken away to death; hold back those who are stumbling to the slaughter. 12 If you say, "Behold, we did not know this," does not he who weighs the heart perceive it? Does not he who keeps watch over your soul know it, and will he not requite man according to his work?

Ecclesiasticus 4:28 (DRA) [31] And refrain not to speak in the time of salvation. Hide not thy wisdom in her beauty.

Ecclesiasticus 4:33 (DRA) [31] Strive for justice for thy soul, and even unto death fight for justice, and God will overthrow thy enemies for thee.

Sirach 4:28 (RSVwA) [41] Strive even to death for the truth and the Lord God will fight for you.

Ecclesiasticus 4:24-25 (DRA) [31] 24 For thy soul be not ashamed to say the truth. 25 For there is a shame that bringeth sin, and there is a shame that bringeth glory and grace.

Isaias 51:7 (DRA) [31] Hearken to me, you that know what is just, my people who have my law in your heart: fear ye not the reproach of men, and be not afraid of their blasphemies.

Proverbs 16:3 (DRA) [31] Lay open thy works to the Lord: and thy thoughts shall be directed.

Jeremias 23:11 (DRA) [31] For the prophet and the priest are defiled: and in my house I have found their wickedness, saith the Lord.

Sophonias 3:4 (DRA) [31] Her prophets are senseless men without faith: her priests have polluted the sanctuary, they have acted unjustly against the law.

Ezechiel 22:26 (DRA) [31] Her priests have despised my law, and have defiled my sanctuaries: they have put no difference between holy and profane: nor have distinguished between the polluted and the clean: and they have turned away their eyes from my sabbaths, and I was profaned in the midst of them.

Acts 20:28 (DRA) [31] Take heed to yourselves, and to the whole flock, wherein the Holy Ghost hath placed you bishops, to rule the church of God, which he hath purchased with his own blood.

It is the watchman's duty to sound the trumpet: to serve the Lord, and for the salvation of his soul.

TAKE HEED United States of America

Isaias 3:4-5 (DRA) [31] 4 And I will give children to be their princes, and the effeminate shall rule over them. 5 And the people shall rush one upon another, and every man against his neighbour: the child shall make a tumult against the ancient, and the base against the honorable.

Ezechiel 22:27 (DRA) [31] Her princes in the midst of her, are like wolves ravening the prey to shed blood, and to destroy souls, and to run after gains through covetousness.

Jeremias 6:11-19 (DRA) [31] 11 Therefore am I full of the fury of the Lord, I am weary with holding in: pour it out upon the child abroad, and upon the counsel of the young men together: for man and woman shall be taken, the ancient and he that is full of days. 12 And their houses shall be turned over to others, with their lands and their wives together: for I will stretch forth my hand upon the inhabitants of the land, saith the Lord. 13 For from the least of them even to the greatest, all are given to covetousness: and from the prophet even to the priest, all are guilty of deceit. 14 And they healed the breach of the daughter of my people disgracefully, saying: Peace, peace: and there was no peace. 15 They were confounded, because they committed abomination: yea, rather they were not confounded with confusion, and they knew not how to blush: wherefore they shall fall among them that fall: in the time of their visitation they shall fall down, saith the Lord. 16 Thus saith the Lord: Stand ye on the ways, and see, and ask for the old paths, which is the good way, and walk ye in it: and you shall find refreshment for your souls. And they said: we will not walk. 17 And I appointed watchman over you, saying: Hearken ye to the sound of the trumpet. And they said: We will not hearken. 18 Therefore hear, ye nations, and know, O congregation, what great things I will do to them. 19 Hear, O earth: Behold I will bring evils upon this people, the fruits of their own thoughts: because they have not heard my words, and they have cast away my law.

Also: Jeremias 5:7-9

Wisdom 14:22-26 (DRA) [31] 22 And it was not enough for them to err about the knowledge of God, but whereas they lived in a great war of ignorance, they call so many and so great evils peace. 23 For either they sacrifice their own children, or use hidden sacrifices, or keep watches full of madness, 24 So that now they neither keep life, nor marriage undefiled, but one killeth

another through envy, or grieveth him by adultery: 25 And all things are mingled together, blood, murder, theft and dissimulation, corruption and unfaithfulness, tumults and perjury, disquieting of the good, 26 Forgetfulness of God, defiling of souls, changing of nature ***(GMOs)***, disorder in marriage, and the irregularity of adultery and uncleanness.
(Bold type comment added by author.)

Leviticus 19:19 (DRA) [31] Keep ye my laws. Thou shalt not make thy cattle to gender with beasts of any other kind. Thou shalt not sow thy field with different seeds. Thou shalt not wear a garment that is woven of two sorts.
(GMOs forbidden)
(Bold type comment added by author.)

Leviticus 19:19 (RSV) [20] "You shall keep my statutes. You shall not let your cattle breed with a different kind; you shall not sow your field with two kinds of seed; nor shall there come upon you a garment of cloth made of two kinds of stuff.

Ecclesiasticus 17:30 (DRA) [31] What is brighter than the sun; yet it shall be eclipsed. Or what is more wicked than that which flesh and blood hath invented? and this shall be reproved.
(GMOs)
(Bold type comment added by author.)

Sirach 17:31 (RSVwA) [43] What is brighter than the sun? Yet its light fails. [a] So flesh and blood devise evil.
[a] Or *suffers eclipse*

Daniel 2:43 (DRA) [31] And whereas thou sawest the iron mixed with miry clay, they shall be mingled indeed together with the seed of man, but they shall not stick fast one to another, as iron cannot be mixed with clay.

Ecclesiastes 1:9-10 (DRA) [31] 9 What is it that hath been? the same thing that shall be. What is it that hath been done? the same that shall be done. 10 Nothing under the sun is new, neither is any man able to say: Behold this is new: for it hath already gone before in the ages that were before us.

Genetic engineering is not something new under the sun. The *Ancient Book of Enoch*[22] tells of the Holy Watchers, Angels in heaven who deserted their post to consort with human women. These Fallen Angels performed genetic tampering, creating horrendous abominations that were incongruous with God's creation (nature). The Almighty was set to destroy everything in order to completely remove the genetic blights from existence, but Enoch asked God to spare his progeny. God granted his request. Enoch's descendent Noah, Noah's wife, and Noah's three sons and their wives were spared from the flood.

The children of the unions of the Fallen Angels and human women were giants. When the giants died in the flood, their spirits remained on earth. Those spirits are demons.[22]

Ecclesiasticus 16:7 (DRA)[31] In the congregation of sinners a fire shall be kindled, and in an unbelieving nation wrath shall flame out.

Ecclesiasticus 16:12-13 (DRA)[31] 12 For mercy and wrath are with him. He is mighty to forgive, and to pour out indignation: 13 According as his mercy is, so his correction judgeth a man according to his works.

Ezechiel 14:13 (DRA)[31] Son of man, when a land shall sin against me, so as to transgress grievously, I will stretch forth my hand upon it, and will break the staff of the bread thereof: and I will send famine upon it, and will destroy man and beast out of it.

Ezechiel 22:30-31 (DRA)[31] 30 And I sought among them for a man that might set up a hedge, and stand in the gap before me in favor of the land, that I might not destroy it: and I found none. 31 And I poured out my indignation upon them, in the fire of my wrath I consumed them: I have rendered their way upon their own head, saith the Lord God.

Nahum 3:16 (DRA)[31] Thou hast multiplied thy merchandises above the stars of heaven: the bruchus hath spread himself and flown away.

Nahum 3:16 (RSV-C)[40] You increased your merchants more than the stars of the heavens. The locust spreads its wings and flies away.

Malachias 2:17 (DRA)[31] You have wearied the Lord with your words, and you said: Wherein have we wearied him? In that you say: Every one that doth evil, is good in the sight of the Lord, and such please him: or surely where is the God of judgment?

Micheas 5:14 (DRA) [31] And I will execute vengeance in wrath and in indignation among all the nations that have not given ear.

1 Machabees 3:59 (DRA) [31] For it is better for us to die in battle, than to see the evils of our nation, and of the holies:

29 January 2012

Tony's parish had two priests, but when the assistant priest deserted his post, there was no replacement. Priests from surrounding parishes were recruited to fill a rotating schedule to make up the shortfall. Today the parish had a visiting Byzantine priest celebrate half of the scheduled Sunday Masses. This is the Sunday following the "health insurance companies owe me free birth control" flap. Tony appreciated the priest's sermon.

> "I'm not sure I should talk about politics, but I feel I must. We must be true to our conscience. There is a decree that our health insurance must include birth control and abortion starting next year. This is against our good conscience. This is against our religious beliefs. I say decree, because it is not legal legislation passed by Congress or law passed by the courts, but a decree from the White House. I have a question. Where is it I am living? How is it we must compromise our conscience and our religious beliefs by order of executive fiat? The woman behind this is the head of Health and Human Services. She is an unhappy lapsed Catholic. The President is acting on her recommendation. We will be given one year to abandon our conscience, or be punished in some manner: fines, imprisonment, jail, something.
>
> I must apologize to you. Priests have not spoken very much about birth control, little of abortion. Some forms of birth control are actually abortion. The pill for example: it does not prevent an egg from being fertilized. The pill prevents a fertilized egg from being implanted in the wall of the uterus. The pill is really a form of abortion, preventing a fertilized egg, a living being, from being implanted into the uterine wall and receiving nourishment.
>
> We must do something to stop this decree before it goes into effect next year. If this decree goes into effect, we will be fined or imprisoned for our good conscience and our religious beliefs. We have been given one year to abandon our conscience and our religious beliefs. –."

The visiting Byzantine apologized to the congregation for priests not having sufficiently discussed birth control. He personally apologized for not fully teaching the faithful about birth control or abortion for so long.

The following week, the visiting priest was Roman Catholic. His sermon started, "We have supported this administration until this–." *We? WE?* In his youth, Tony wondered how clergy could support the Democrats, but now he has a better understanding. Tony was disappointed the Byzantine priest felt he had to apologize for discussing politics. Clergy who support the Democrats' policies are exercising their freedom of speech. Clergy who speak against the Democrats' policies are violating the separation of church and state and are told they endanger the Church's tax-exempt status. *Yeah, right.*

TV Morality

If Americans no longer believe in God, what moral values guide their decision-making? Tony discerns what he calls, "TV Morality." "TV Morality" has no moral criterion as such. "TV Morality" is a vapid, atheistic placebo, a pseudo-morality "the media" (books, movies, TV) substitutes for religion and traditional time-honored values. It grants "feel-good" to the godless. Don't say queers, don't use insults (except against Republicans, "the rich," or God-fearing souls), don't smoke cigarettes, register Democrat, and you're a nice person. AND YOU CARE! The only evil act that merits public censure is smoking. Thou shalt not smoke.

The Bible extols virtue. The books of Proverbs, Wisdom, and Ecclesiasticus (Sirach) teach us to pursue virtue through prayer, fasting, knowledge, and wisdom. We are told in 4 Maccabees (Greek [41]) the highest virtue is rational judgment (4 Maccabees 1:2), that reason is the guide of the virtues (4 Maccabees 1:30). Without self-control, our passions lead us to sin. "TV Morality," on the other hand, is bereft of virtue. It esteems the emotions and "feelings" and subordinates logic and reason. (Psychology likewise is insufferable, focusing on "feel" and not on "think.") "TV Morality" substitutes a nebulous and undefined "fairness" for justice. PC pretends to replace the virtue of compassion as well as civility.

fair (fer) adj. 13) apparently favorable but really false; **specious** [01]
(Bold type added by author.)

"TV Morality" supersedes the ability to seek God's blessings with charitable acts and alms giving. It does not recognize virtue in charity: you "give back." Your good deeds are something you owe the community. You are "giving back to the community," as though it is a debt you owe the general public. In addition, there is "pay it forward:" feel good about giving, with the unlikely expectation karma, nature, or the universe will pay you back with someone else's "pay it forward." Advertisers have product promotions tied to charitable causes. If you want to give to that charity, buy their product and the company promises some of the proceeds will go to said charity. Of course, the company takes the tax deduction.

Tobias 4:11-12 (DRA) [31] 11 For alms deliver from all sin, and from death, and will not suffer the soul to go into darkness. 12 Alms shall be a great confidence before the most high God, to all them that give it.

Tobit 4:10-11 (RSVwA) [43] 10 For charity delivers from death and keeps you from entering the darkness; 11 and for all who practice it charity is an excellent offering in the presence of the Most High.

Nostalgia

When Tony was a child, TV was black and white and so was morality. Bad guys wore black hats; good guys wore white. Since then, hats went out of style. So did morality.

YouTube 2013

In 2013, Tony found YouTube clips of Yuri Bezmenov, a former KGB agent who defected to Canada and changed his name to Tomas Schuman. Below are notes Tony took based on the lecture given by Yuri in L.A. in 1983. Yuri's lecture is engaging, informative, and a real eye-opener.

<https://www.youtube.com/watch?v=8fQoGMtE0EY>. [44]

9 June 13 @ 1:38 pm EDT
Video is one hour 3 minutes long.
Tomas Schuman (Yuri Bezmenov) L.A. 1983 [44]
Uploaded on Jan 11, 2011

Russia's plan to defeat America was to subvert its social institutions and reduce the nation to an immoral wasteland. Crucial to the success of their plan was the infiltration and subversion of the Roman Catholic Church in America. As Tony witnessed, the Soviet plans and actions taken in 1946 have come to fruition.

TONY'S NOTES – taken from Tomas Schuman (Yuri Bezmenov): L.A. 1983 [44]

15% of time, money, and manpower KGB spends: Steal blueprints, espionage as such.

85% Subversion: (Soviet definition) Distractive, aggressive activity aimed to destroy the nation of your enemy.

Subverter: exchange student, diplomat, artist, journalist, etc.
Sun-Tzu: 2,500 years ago. Fighting on the battlefield is most foolish. Subversion is most effective.
Sun-Tzu is forced reading in Russia. Is the full translation available in U.S. or Canada?

DEMORALIZATION:

SUBVERSION: 6 areas of
Religion – destroy it, ridicule it, replace it with sex cults. Substitute with fake.
Education – teach them useless things.
Social Life – replace established groups with fake groups.
Power Structure – established power substituted by fake. THE MEDIA-effete snobs. Mediocre not excellent journalist to survive. Neither qualification nor the will of people and yet have power.
Law and Order – dumb, abusive. Moral relativity. Bad guys presented as nice.
Labor Relations (unions) Trade Unions – 100 years ago (from 1983), unions worked. No longer works for workers, only for leaders of trade union. Is for promoting ideology by use of violence; not for workers.

No mention of equality in Bible, or any religion. President Kennedy: people, we will make America to believe people are born equal. NYET. By your deeds, God will judge you. What you do is important. Merit of your personality!
Yet we build our society on the principle of equality. We say people are equal. We know it is false, it is a lie.
If we put the principle of equality in the basis of our social political structure, it is the same thing as building a house on sand.

DESTABILIZATION:
Economy –radicalization.
Law and Order – minutiae taken to court.
Media – opposition to society at large.

CRISIS:
Civil war
Invasion

NORMALIZATION: (term borrowed from 1968 Czechoslovakian takeover)
Radicalism no longer needed. The self-appointed rulers of the society do not need revolution or radicalism anymore. Stabilization. All the sleepers, the activists, social workers, liberals, homosexuals, professors, and Marxists, and Leninists are no longer needed and are eliminated.

CRISIS: reverse it by
Enormous effort needed to reverse the process. Military force needed.

DESTABILIZATION: reverse it by

Restrict sleepers, the activists, social workers, liberals, homosexuals, professors, and Marxists, and Leninists from being elected. Media restrained from (hypnotism). Deny unsavory companies and persons a few liberties. Self-restraint.

DEMORALIZATION: reverse it by

Stop importation of propaganda, foreign ideology.

Bring back religion.

He names 4 cultures that collapsed and disappeared the moment they lost religion.

To thwart ideological subversion, you need faith. Do not use force. Strike with the power of your spirit and moral superiority.

16 ANSWER THE CALL

Honest, God-fearing men answering the call to the priesthood must be prepared to battle evil inside the seminary. Ideally, candidates go to the seminary using the buddy system. Candidates need to plan for and establish proper support and backup. Choose a seminary that has surveillance cameras monitoring the dorm hallways and a security tip-line to the Board of Directors. The seminary's Board of Directors is not doing their job if there is no comprehensive surveillance system monitored by someone (the Board?) independent of the seminary's administration. Does this seminary pray (chant) Morning and Evening Prayer daily? Praise God, pray for your calling, and pray to the Holy Spirit to defend the Church.

When There Are No Priests

There are still a few good priests and bishops in the United States. God-fearing men and women recognize holy clergy. Holy priests currently find themselves in a very bad predicament. They desperately need our prayers. The number of priests continues to dwindle. When there are no priests available to celebrate Mass, (Liturgy of the Eucharist) keep holy the Sabbath by praying the *Liturgy of the Hours* [42] (Vatican II version of the Divine Office). The four volume set (the breviary) contains the Office of Readings and the prayers for the canonical hours of the day. Volume I contains the General Instruction of the Liturgy of the Hours.

Christian Prayer is an abbreviated version in a single volume containing Morning and Evening Prayer, a "starter edition" for the laity. Praying Morning and Evening Prayer on a daily basis is a solid foundation for offering praise to God. (Exodus 29:38-39). Using these books is neither simple nor straightforward. While you still have priests available, ask your priest to instruct you or your parish prayer group on how to use *Christian Prayer* to pray Morning and Evening Prayer.

If you need to learn on your own, refer to: "Congregation for Divine Worship General Instruction of the Liturgy of the Hours." [15,16] This 33-page document provides detailed information and instruction on how to use the tome(s) to pray the Liturgy of the Hours. It can be found online at:

<www.ewtn.com/library/curia/cdwgilh.htm>. [15]
or
<www.catholicliturgy.com/index.cfm/fuseaction/documentcontents/index/2/subindex/39/documentindex/2>. [16]

For more information about the Liturgy of the Hours [26], go to:
<www.ewtn.com/expert/answers/breviary.htm>. [26]

Ecclesiasticus 18:23 (DRA) [31] Before prayer prepare thy soul: and be not as a man that tempteth God.

Sirach 18:23 (RSVwA) [43] Before making a vow, [d] prepare yourself; and do not be like a man who tempts the Lord.
[d] Or *offering a prayer*

Ecclesiasticus 7:10 (DRA) [31] Neglect not to pray, and to give alms.

Sirach 7:10 (RSV-C) [40] Do not be fainthearted in your prayer, nor neglect to give alms.

Hebrews 3:13 (DRA) [31] But exhort one another every day, whilst it is called to day, that none of you be hardened through the deceitfulness of sin.

Hebrews 3:13 (*Liturgy of the Hours,* [42] Invitatory, Psalm 95 antiphon) Encourage each other daily while it is still today.

Joel 2:12-13 (*Liturgy of the Hours,* [42] Lent, Week I, Tuesday, Morning Prayer, Reading) Return to me with your whole heart, with fasting, and weeping, and mourning; Rend your hearts, not your garments, and return to the Lord, your God. For gracious and merciful is He, slow to anger, rich in kindness, and relenting in punishment.

APPENDIX 1

The Jesuit's Memo

March 17, 199[redacted]

Dear [redacted]

Thank you for the long conversation we had. last night and for taking me into your confidence. Would you please let me see the photographic evidence you offered to show me? I would be grateful

God be with you.

Fr [redacted] SJ

APPENDIX 2

Tony's Retraction

March 19, 199

Father

I retract any and all claims either made or implied of unseemly, illicit and or immoral activity by any and all students of the J

Also, I retract any and all claims I have either made or implied of the faculty, staff, and or administration of the J concerning cover-up or lack of follow-through when information was brought to their attention.

May God Bless you,

APPENDIX 3

Tony's Letter to the Pope

June 28, 199█

Dear Holy Father,

Please clean up the Pontifical College J█████ so that honest, God fearing seminary candidates who go there will be safe and will find a holy environment.

I attended the J█████ as a seminarian and was appalled and repulsed by the invasive state of moral degradation that exists there.

I called a meeting with rector Fr.█████ on March 19, 199█. For some reason, Fr.█████ attended the meeting. I recorded that meeting. The enclosed tape is advanced to the interesting part of the meeting; where Fr.█████ threatens me with the resources of the J█████ and coerces me into writing a retraction letter and signing it.

May you be blessed by the Holy Spirit,

Enc. (1) letter to Cardinal█████ (2) pages
(3) letters
(1) miniature audio tape

APPENDIX 4

Tony's Letter to the Cardinal, page 1 of 2

June 28, 199█

Dear Cardinal █████

I attended THE PONTIFICAL COLLEGE J█████ from August 199█ to March 20, 199█. It was the most frightfully evil place I have ever been.

In September and October of 199█, I reported immoral and unsavory activity to several Priests in the administration. Their only interest was, "What tangible evidence do you have?" Their advice was for me to stop reporting homosexual activities before it became a formation issue. █████ told me, "Piss in the sink in your room, then you won't get into trouble." The indication was that I would be in trouble for disturbing the nocturnal traffic patterns of the homosexuals if I used the toilet during the night.

Each Priest, in turn, was upset that I brought the problem to him. I asked where was the proper office to report these occurrences. There was no such office or administrator.

Reports, rumors and lies against heterosexual Seminarians were acted on by the staff and the psychologist's office until that Seminarian was either chased or kicked out. I witnessed one such occurrence and am well versed with a second.

The seminarians themselves claim that the Nuncio has not visited the College in 5 years. Those estimates were made in the Fall of 199█. The seminarians' answer to my objections to knowingly and willfully ordaining homosexuals was that "... it's the Pope's fault. He has not come right out and made a statement forbidding it." And besides, they would continue, he [the Pope] doesn't want to loose the money that comes into the Church from the United States.

At least one Priest had an excuse for ordaining homosexuals; "This is what the Bishops send us. What can we do?"

APPENDIX 5

Tony's Letter to the Cardinal, page 2 of 2

Sage economic council? No. And it does nothing to explain why the J█████ administration uses psychology in precisely the same fashion as the old Soviet government in order to discredit and dispose of political opponents. At the J█████, heterosexuals, specifically those who object to homosexual ordination, were subjected to the malevolent use of psychology.

I purchased a micro-miniature tape recorder in order to capture some incriminating conversation by the heretics. Father █████ laughed at me in the Fall of 199█ saying, "Take pictures the next time you see something going on."

It is only fitting that the enclosed copy of one taped conversation includes my voice, Fr. █████ and that of the rector, Fr. █████ The documents should be self explanatory.

The originals are in my lawyers' safe-keeping with specific instructions concerning same.

The Church is Christ's bride. I am doing my duty; to bear witness to the truth, on behalf of the Church herself; and on behalf of other unsuspecting Seminary hopefuls.

I have decided not to contact the Nuncio. If he is curious, let him travel to █████

I called a meeting with the rector, Fr. █████ on March 19, 199█. For some reason, Fr. █████ attended also. I recorded that meeting. The enclosed tape is advanced to the most interesting part of the meeting; where Fr. █████ threatens me with the resources of the J█████ and coerces me into writing a retraction letter and signing it.

May God bless you,

█████

Enc. (3) letters
(1) miniature audio tape

cc. Pope █████

APPENDIX 6

The Nuncio's Envelope

APPENDIX 7

The Cardinal's Letter, Sent to Tony inside the Nuncio's Envelope

Rome, 29 October 199█

CONGREGATIO
DE INSTITUTIONE CATHOLICA
(DE SEMINARIIS ATQUE STUDIORUM INSTITUTIS)

PROT. N 828/97
(Hic numerus in responsione referatur)

Dear Mr █████

With this letter we wish to acknowledge receipt of your communication of 28 June last concerning the Pontifical College J█████

Please be assured that it has been forwarded to the appropriate authorities.

With best wishes, we remain

Sincerely yours in Christ,

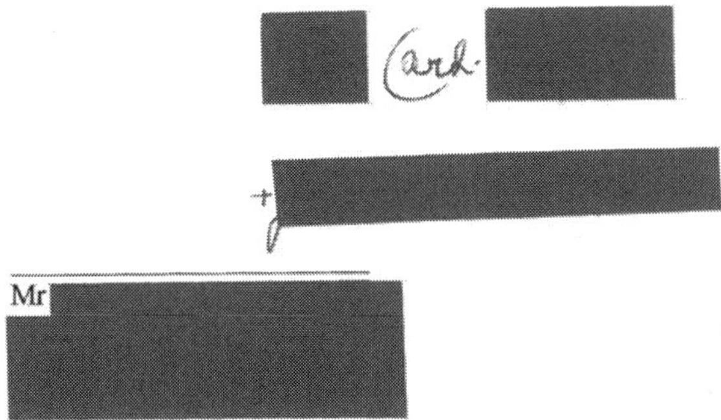

Mr █████

BIBLIOGRAPHY

01. Agnes, M. (1999). *Webster's New World College Dictionary*. (4th Ed.). New York: Macmillan USA. Print.

02. "April 18, 1970: Nixon on Apollo 13." *ABC News Video*. abcnews.go.com. 9 Feb 2010. Web. 17 Sept 2012. <abcnews.go.com/Archives/video/april-18-1970-nixon-apollo-13- 9788024>.

03. As recorded by the New York Times. "Text of President's Welcome and Lovell's Response at Honolulu." *New York Times*. 19 April 1970: 54. Print.

04. Associated Press. "Special Rights Set for a Day of Gratitude." *New York Times*. 19 April 1970: 53. Print.

05. Atkinson, Philip. "Political Correctness." *A Theory of Civilization*. ourcivilisation.com, Oct 2011. Web. 24 Oct. 2012. <ourcivilisation.com/pc.htm>.

06. Bassermann, Lujo. *The Oldest Profession: a History of Prostitution*. New York: Dorset Press, 1993. © 1967 by Arthur Baker Limited for this translation. Print.

07. "Bible Search RSV-Catholic (RSV-C)." *EWTN Global Catholic Network*. EWTN.com, 26 Oct 2004. Web. 20 July 2012. <http://www.ewtn.com/devotionals/biblesearch/asp>.

08. Chakravarty, Subrata N. with Weisman, Katherine. "Consuming Our Children?" *Forbes*. 14 Nov 1988: 222-232. Print.

09. Cogley, John. "God Is Dead Debate Widens." *New York Times*. 9 Jan 1966: E7. Print.

10. Dannemeyer, William E. "Militant Wolves in Sheepish Drag, No Longer!" *HeinOnline* 133 Cong. Rec. E 3081 1987. Web. 24 Sept. 2012.

11. Dannemeyer, William E. "Militant Wolves in Sheepish Drag, No Longer!" *Westlaw*, 2012 Thomson Reuters. 133 Cong. Rec. E3081-02, 1987 WL 950611. Web. 17 Aug. 2012.

12. Elson, John T. “Is God Dead?” *Time.* 8 April 1966: 82– 87. Print.

13. “Executive Order 12968 of August 2, 1995; Access to Classified Information.” *Federal Register* Vol. 60, No.151. Presidential Documents. 7 Aug 1995. Web. 01 Jan. 2013. <www.gpo.gov/fdsys/pkg/FR-1995-08-07/pdf/95-19654.pdf>.

14. Fisk, Edward B. ““God is Dead” Doctrine Losing Ground to “Theology of Hope.”” *New York Times.* 24 March1968: 1, 75. Print.

15. “General Instruction of the Liturgy of the Hours.” *EWTN Global Catholic Network*. EWTN.com. 2 Feb 1971. Web. 28 Nov 2012. <ewtn.com/library/curia/cdwgilh.htm>.

16. “General Instruction of the Liturgy of the Hours.” *The Catholic Liturgical Library*. catholicliturgy.com. 2012. Web. 28 Nov 2012. <catholicliturgy.com/index.cfm/fuseaction/documentcontents/index/2/subindex/39/documentindex/2>.

17. Good, Chris. “Ron Paul Departs With “Our Constitution Has Failed.”” *ABC News*. ABCNews.go.com. 14 Nov 2012. Web. 17 Nov 2012. <abcnews.go.com/blogs/politics/2012/11/ron-paul-departs-with-our-constitution-has-failed/>.

18. *Holy Bible*, (D-C) Douay-Confraternity ed. New York: P.J.Kenedy & Sons, 1950. Print.

19. *Holy Bible* (DRV), Douay-Rheims Version. Charlotte, North Carolina: Saint Benedict Press, 2009. Print.

20. *Holy Bible* (RSV), Revised Standard Version. New York: Thomas Nelson & Sons, 1952. Print.

21. Honolulu, April 18 (UPI) “Joyous Families Fly with Nixon to Three Astronauts.” *New York Times.* 19 April 1970: 54. Print.

22. Johnson Th.D., Ken. *Ancient Book of Enoch.* San Bernardino, CA: Biblefacts.org. 2014. Print.

23. “Joseph McCarthy–American Patriot.” *SenatorMcCarthy.com.* senatormccarthy.com. 2006. Web. 12 Jan 2015. <http://www.senatormccarthy.com/>.

24. “Lemming.” *Wikipedia Foundation, Inc*. en.wikipedia.org. 24 June 2015. Web. 2 July 2015. <http://en.wikipedia.org/wiki/Lemming>.

25. “Lewinsky Scandal.” *Wikipedia Foundation, Inc*. en.wikipedia.org. 24 June

2015. Web. 2 July 2015. <http://en.wikipedia.org/wiki/Lewinsky_scandal>.

26. "Liturgy of the Hours/Divine Office/Breviary." *EWTN Global Catholic Network*. EWTN.com. 26 Oct 2004. Web. 28 Nov 2012. <ewtn.com/expert/answers/breviary.htm>.

27. Machiavelli, Niccolò. *The Prince and The Discourses*. New York: The Modern Library. 1950. Random House. Print.

28. Nietzsche, Friedrich. "God is Dead." *Wikipedia Foundation, Inc.* en.wikipedia.org. 21 June 2015. Web. 2 July 2015. <en.wikipedia.org/wiki/God_is_dead>.

29. Noble, Terence P. "Wycliffe Bible (WYC) 2001." *The Zondervan Corporation*. biblegateway.com. 2010. Web. 20 July 2012. <www.biblegateway.com>.

30. Parker, Star. "Back on Uncle Sam's Plantation." *Townhall.com*. townhall.com. 9 Feb 2009. Web. 01 Jan. 2013. <http://townhall.com/columnists/starparker/2009/02/09/back_on_uncle_sams_plantation/page/full/>.

31. Public Domain. "Douay-Rheims 1899 American Edition Bible (DRA)." *The Zondervan Corporation*. biblegateway.com. 2010. Web. 20 July 2012. <www.biblegateway.com>.

32. Public Domain. "King James Version Bible (KJV)." *The Zondervan Corporation*. biblegateway.com. 2010. Web. 04 Feb 2015. <www.biblegateway.com>.

33. Rome, Jan. 6, Pope Paul VI. ""God is Dead" Theme Assailed by the Pope." *New York Times.* 7 Jan.1970: 3. Print.

34. Semple, Robert B. Jr. "Nixon, In Hawaii, Joins Astronauts and Honors Them." *New York Times.* 19 April 1970: 1, A54. Print.

35. Sheen, Fulton J. "Life is Worth Living." *Fulton J. Sheen Company Inc.* bishopsheen.com. 2015. Web. 08 Feb 2015. <http://www.bishopsheen.com/>.

36. Sheen, Fulton J. "Quote From the Late Archbishop Fulton J. Sheen." *Doug Lawrence*. douglawrence.wordpress.com. 21 Nov 2008. Web. 08 Feb 2015. <https://douglawrence.wordpress.com/2008/11/21/quote-from-the-late-archbishop-fulton-j-sheen/>.

37. Shilts, Randy. *And the Band Played On: Politics, People, and the AIDS Epidemic*. New York: St. Martin's Press, 1987. Print.

38. Sigman, Dr.Aric. "Weapons of Mass Induction." *Kindred*. kindredcommunity.com. 20 Sept 2007. Web. 31 Jan 2015. <http://www.kindredmedia.org/2007/09/weapons-of-mass-induction/>.

39. Steichen, Donna. *Ungodly Rage: The Hidden Face of Catholic Feminism*. San Francisco: Ignatius Press, 1991. Print.

40. *The Holy Bible* (RSV-C). Revised Standard Version. 2nd Catholic ed. San Francisco: Ignatius Press, 2006. Print.

41. *The Holy Bible with the Apocrypha* (RSVwA). Revised Standard Version. New York: Oxford University Press, 2002. Print.

42. *The Liturgy of the Hours*. New York: Catholic Book Publishing Company, 1976. Print.

43. *The New Oxford Annotated Bible with the Apocrypha* (RSVwA). Revised Standard Version. New York: Oxford University Press, 1977. Print.

44. "Tomas Schuman (Yuri Bezmenov) L.A. 1983." *YouTube.com*. youtube.com. 11 Jan 2011. Web. 09 June 2013. <https://www.youtube.com/watch?v=8fQoGMtE0EY>.

ADDENDUM

45. Allen, Gary, "Bankrolling the Bolshevik Revolution." Modern History Project. modernhistoryproject.org. 2015. Web. 26 June 2015. <http://www.modernhistoryproject.org/mhp?Article=NoneDare&C=4>.

ABOUT THE AUTHOR

Tony Ghepardo experienced a rude awakening in the pontifical seminary in Ohio. It was a defining moment for him. His further study of the affairs of the Catholic Church was spurred by an interest in making sense out of the scandals he experienced. Ghepardo was so moved by his discoveries that he wrote the book God-Fearing Souls to alert the faithful.

His worst fears were confirmed after a friend sent him another book illuminating the very issues described in his writings—but this time the setting was the Vatican. The horrific events that Fr. Martin Malachi witnessed included satanic rituals.

Ghepardo later discovered that other authors have exposed this seedy underbelly. This propelled him to market his book to a wider audience in order to pull down the velvet curtains and enlighten everyone to the war happening right under their noses.

Made in the USA
San Bernardino, CA
21 September 2018